Nova Scotia, New Brunswick & Prince Edward Island For Dummies, 3rd Edition

Nova Scotia, New Brunswick, and Prince Edward Island

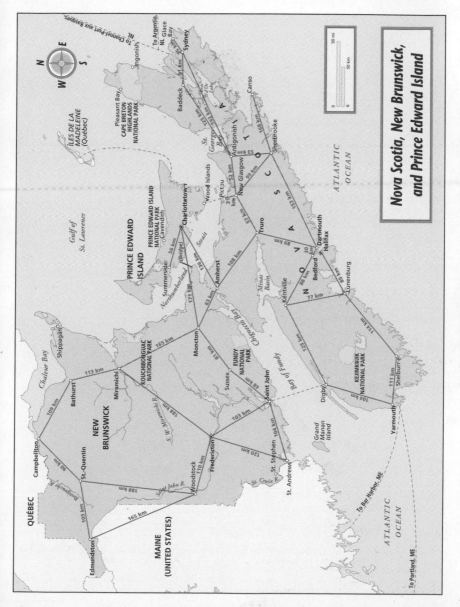

Prince Edward Island Ferry Schedules

Departing from Wood Islands, Prince Edward Island, to Caribou, Nova Scotia

Date	Time								
May 1–June 21	06:30	09:30	13:00	16:30	19:30				
June 22–Sept 3	(06:30)	08:00	09:30	11:15	13:00	14:45	16:30	18:00	19:30
Sept 4–Oct 15	06:30	09:30	11:15	13:00	14:45	16:30	19:30		
Oct 16–Nov 12	06:30	09:30	13:00	16:30	19:30				
Nov 13–Nov 30	06:30	11:30	14:30	17:30					
Dec 1–Dec 20	08:00	11:00	16:00						

Departing from Caribou, Nova Scotia, to Wood Islands, Prince Edward Island

Date	Time								
May 1–June 21	08:00	11:15	14:45	18:00	21:00				
June 22–Sept 3	(08:00)	09:30	11:15	13:00	14:45	16:30	18:00	19:30	
Sept 4–Oct 15	06:30	09:30	11:15	13:00	14:45	16:30	19:30		
Oct 16–Nov 12	08:00	11:15	14:45	18:00	21:00				
Nov 13–Nov 30	08:00	11:15	14:45	16:00	19:00				
Dec 1–Dec 20	09:30	12:30	17:30						

( ) Brackets indicate no Sunday departures
* All departures in Atlantic Time

Confederation Bridge Fares

All Vehicles	$40.75
Motorcycle	$16.25

FOR DUMMIES

The fun and easy way™ to travel!

Nova Scotia, New Brunswick & Prince Edward Island

FOR

DUMMIES®

3RD EDITION

Maps

Nova Scotia pg. 94-95

Cape Breton pg. 159
Island

New Brunswick pg. 180-181

Prince Edward pg. 245
Island

PEI NP pg. 261

Nova Scotia, New Brunswick & Prince Edward Island

FOR

DUMMIES®

3RD EDITION

by Andrew Hempstead

WILEY

John Wiley & Sons Canada, Ltd.

Nova Scotia, New Brunswick & Prince Edward Island For Dummies® 3rd Edition
Published by
John Wiley & Sons Canada, Ltd
6045 Freemont Boulevard
Mississauga, Ontario, L5R 4J3

www.wiley.ca

Library and Archives Canada Cataloguing in Publication Data

Hempstead, Andrew

Nova Scotia, New Brunswick & Prince Edward Island for dummies / by Andrew Hempstead. — 3rd ed.
Includes index.

ISBN 978-0-470-15334-5

1. Maritime Provinces—Guidebooks.
I. Title. II. Title: Nova Scotia, New Brunswick and Prince Edward Island for dummies.
FC2024.H44 2008   917.1504'5   C2008-900606-2

Printed in Canada

1 2 3 4 5 TRI 12 11 10 09 08

Distributed in Canada by John Wiley & Sons Canada, Ltd.

For general information on John Wiley & Sons Canada, Ltd, including all books published by Wiley Publishing, Inc., please call our warehouse, Tel 1-800-567-4797. For reseller information, including discounts and premium sales, please call our sales department, Tel 416-646-7992. For press review copies, author interviews, or other publicity information, please contact our marketing department, Tel 416-646-4584, Fax 416-236-4448.

For authorization to photocopy items for corporate, personal, or educational use, please contact in writing The Canadian Copyright Licensing Agency (Access Copyright). For an Access Copyright license, visit www.accesscopyright.ca or call toll free, 1-800-893-5777.

WILEY

About the Author

Andrew Hempstead is a travel writer and photographer who has traveled widely throughout Canada from his home in Banff, Alberta. His research trip for the third edition of this book took him to every corner of the Maritimes, and along the way he found himself searching for fossils along the Bay of Fundy, wine-tasting in Nova Scotia, and golfing the fairways of Prince Edward Island.

In addition to this book, Hempstead has authored guidebooks to Alberta, British Columbia, the Canadian Rockies, and Vancouver, and has co-authored guidebooks to Atlantic Canada, Australia, and New Zealand. His writing and photography have also appeared in many national and international publications.

Author's Acknowledgments

Thanks to the following people for helping out with information and planning at various stages of my research trip: Judy Dougan, Tourism Moncton; Carol Horne and Tracy Stretch, Tourism PEI; Susan Jeffries, Nova Scotia Department of Tourism and Culture; Sally Cummings and Candace MacCullum, Tourism Saint John; and Angela Watson, Fredericton Tourism. Thanks also to staff at information centers, innkeepers, and others on my travels who guided me in the right direction, all of whom contributed to making this book as useful and comprehensive as it could possibly be.

Publisher's Acknowledgments

We're proud of this book; please send us your comments at canadapt@wiley. com. Some of the people who helped bring this book to market include the following:

Acquisitions, Editorial, and Media Development

Executive Editor: Robert Hickey

Associate Editor: Gene Shannon

Copy Editor: Heather Ball

Front cover photo: © Janet Foster/ Masterfile

Back cover photo: ©Darwin Wiggett/ All Canada Photos/Getty Images

Cartoons: Rich Tennant (www.the5thwave.com)

Production

Vice-President Publishing Services: Karen Bryan

Publishing Services Manager: Ian Koo

Project Manager: Elizabeth McCurdy

Project Coordinator: Lindsay Humphreys

Layout and Graphics: Wiley Indianapolis Composition Services

Proofreaders: Jessica Kramer, Glenn McMullen

Indexer: Becky Hornyack

John Wiley & Sons Canada, Ltd

Bill Zerter, Chief Operating Officer

Jennifer Smith, Vice-President and Publisher, Professional and Trade Division

Publishing and Editorial for Consumer Dummies

Diane Graves Steele, Vice President and Publisher, Consumer Dummies

Joyce Pepple, Acquisitions Director, Consumer Dummies

Kristin A. Cocks, Product Development Director, Consumer Dummies

Michael Spring, Vice President and Publisher, Travel

Kelly Regan, Editorial Director, Travel

Publishing for Technology Dummies

Andy Cummings, Vice President and Publisher, Dummies Technology/General User

Composition Services

Gerry Fahey, Vice President of Production Services

Debbie Stailey, Director of Composition Services

Contents at a Glance

Maps at a Glance

Table of Contents

· ·

Introduction

● ●

*T*he most common term used to describe the Maritimes as a tourist destination is "underrated." After spending your vacation traveling through Nova Scotia, New Brunswick, and Prince Edward Island, I'm sure you'll agree. This area of Canada possesses a subtle magnetism that is impossible to define — you just have to experience it to understand — and offers spectacular scenery to rival that of many other top destinations. Each of the three provinces has its own distinct character, and yet they come together to create a single destination like no other place on earth.

How do you distill the essence of the Maritimes into one book? I faced that challenge as I sorted through my experiences to bring you only the best and most unique accommodations, restaurants, and attractions. And they're just the tip of the iceberg; you can't go wrong at any of the places this book describes, but you'll return home from your Maritime adventure with your own favorites.

About This Book

Nova Scotia, New Brunswick & Prince Edward Island For Dummies is a reference guide. It's not designed to be a comprehensive, tell-all guidebook that weighs you down. Each of the three provinces is discussed separately in individual parts, laid out in a logical sequence so you can refer quickly to a particular region, or skip a chapter completely if it's off your route (although you may want to reconsider after reading up on it). History is a big part of the Maritimes and travel, but I only dwell on the past when necessary.

Please be advised that travel information is subject to change at any time — and this is especially true of prices. I therefore suggest that you write or call ahead for confirmation when making your travel plans. The authors, editors, and publisher cannot be held responsible for the experiences of readers while traveling. Your safety is important to us; however, so we encourage you to stay alert and be aware of your surroundings. Keep a close eye on cameras, purses, and wallets, all favorite targets of thieves and pickpockets.

Conventions Used in This Book

To help you get the information you need easily and quickly, I take the liberty of using a few conventions throughout this book.

- I use the accepted term "Maritimes" to collectively refer to the provinces of Nova Scotia, New Brunswick, and Prince Edward Island.

- All prices in this book are given in Canadian dollars.

- Dollar sign ($) symbols preceding each listing are designed to give you an approximate price for a night's stay in a hotel or a meal in a restaurant. In the hotel section, the rates I quote are the rack rates (the hotel's official rates) for one night for a double room, although after you read Chapter 8, I hope you never pay this full amount. When recommending restaurants, I give the range of main course prices: appetizers, desserts, drinks, and tips are not included in this amount unless explicitly stated. If a restaurant doesn't serve dinner, the price range refers to the lunch menu. Lobster causes a small problem (not to eat, that's for sure!) — in almost every restaurant it's sold at "Market Price," so my price ranges do not include this Maritime delicacy.

The dollar signs represent the following amounts:

Dollar Signs	Hotel	Restaurant
$	$75 or less	$10 or less
$$	$75–$150	$10–$17.50
$$$	$150–$225	$17.50–$25
$$$$	$225 or more	$25 and up

In this book I often include abbreviations for commonly accepted credit cards. I only include the major ones, so if your particular card is not listed here, it may or may not be accepted. Call ahead to make sure. The credit cards and their corresponding abbreviations are as follows:

AE	American Express
DC	Diners Club
DISC	Discover
MC	MasterCard
V	Visa

Foolish Assumptions

In this book, I make some assumptions about you and what your needs may be as a traveler. Here's what I assume about you:

✔ You may be an experienced traveler who hasn't had much time to explore the Maritimes and wants expert advice when you finally do get a chance to enjoy that particular locale.

✔ You may be an inexperienced traveler looking for guidance when deciding whether to take a trip to the Maritimes and how to plan for it.

✔ You're not looking for a book that provides all the information available about the Maritimes or that lists every hotel, restaurant, or attraction available to you. Instead, you want a book that focuses on the places that will give you the best or most unique experience in the Maritimes.

If you fit any of these criteria, then *Nova Scotia, New Brunswick, and Prince Edward Island For Dummies* gives you the information you're looking for!

How This Book Is Organized

Nova Scotia, New Brunswick, and Prince Edward Island For Dummies is divided into six parts. The chapters within each part cover specific topics or regions in detail. You can read each chapter or part without reading the others — after all, there's no need to read about Prince Edward Island if you're heading for Cape Breton Island.

Part I: Introducing Nova Scotia, New Brunswick, and Prince Edward Island

This part introduces you to the three provinces, and highlights — well, the highlights. I tell you about the best times of year to visit, and describe the top festivals and events. I also propose four itineraries (a one-week trip, a two-week trip, a special trip for families, and another for seafood-lovers). I also offer tips for travelers with special needs, such as seniors and those with disabilities, as well as budget-planning advice that all travelers can use.

Part II: Planning Your Trip to the Maritimes

Call it Trip-Planning 101. Here, I lay out the basics and delve into details to help you get started on the right path. By the end of Part II, you will know

✔ The reasons you may or may not use a travel agent to help plan your trip

✔ The pros and cons of taking an escorted or package tour

✔ The ways to get to the Maritimes, and how to get around after you arrive

> ✔ The different lodging types available to you, and how you can save money when booking a room

> ✔ The useful details, such as the best way to carry your money and what type of travel insurance will meet your particular needs

Parts III, IV, V: The Provinces

These three parts form the bulk of the book, with each one devoted to a separate province. I break the parts down further into chapters that focus on specific regions. Each chapter has all the information you need to make the most of your visit, including:

> ✔ How to get there

> ✔ Where to stay

> ✔ Where to eat

> ✔ What to see and do

Part VI: The Part of Tens

Skip ahead to this part for the best of the Maritimes condensed into a few pages: ten classic Maritime experiences and my ten favorite seafood restaurants — with ten people you probably didn't know were from the Maritimes thrown in as a bonus.

In the back of this book I include an *Appendix* — your Quick Concierge — containing lots of handy information you may need when traveling in the Maritimes, like phone numbers and addresses of emergency personnel or area hospitals and pharmacies, lists of local newspapers and magazines, protocol for sending mail or finding taxis, and more. Check out the Appendix when searching for answers to lots of little questions that may come up as you travel. You can find Quick Concierge easily because it's printed on yellow paper.

Icons Used in This Book

I use five icons throughout this book to call your attention to different types of information. Here's what they mean:

Find out useful advice on things to do and ways to schedule your time when you see the Tip icon.

Watch for the Heads Up icon to identify annoying or potentially dangerous situations such as tourist traps, unsafe neighborhoods, budgetary rip-offs, and other things to beware.

Next to a hotel recommendation, this icon means that the establishment welcomes children. Next to a restaurant, it indicates that kids are offered their own menu. In front of an attraction, it emphasizes somewhere your kids will (hopefully) enjoy.

 If you see this icon, you're about to save some money. It doesn't necessarily mean that something is cheap — just that it's a particularly good value.

 This is my favorite icon. When you spot it, you're in for a special Maritime welcome.

Where to Go from Here

As you plan your Maritimes vacation, consider my recommendations while keeping your own interests in mind. Pore over maps and plot out an itinerary — the idea is to plan ahead, book your transportation and lodgings, and leave the rest until you get there.

This book is designed to help you juggle the practicalities of advance planning (like the security of knowing you have a comfortable room to retire to) with spontancity (like a spur-of-the-moment restaurant stop or an exhilarating whale-watching excursion). That way, you don't have to worry about the nitpicky details; you can just relax and enjoy the magnificent Maritimes.

Part I
Introducing Nova Scotia, New Brunswick, and Prince Edward Island

The 5th Wave   By Rich Tennant

In this part . . .

Okay, I know you're excited about traveling to the Maritimes! This part breaks it down, nice and easy, by listing the best places to go and sights to see in each of the three provinces. It also highlights the pros and cons of traveling to the region at different times of year, provides four itineraries to help you make the most of your time, and suggests tips for travelers with special needs and for those on a budget.

Chapter 1

Discovering the Best of Nova Scotia, New Brunswick, and Prince Edward Island

· ·

In This Chapter

▶ Focusing in on the best lodgings
▶ Checking out the greatest restaurants
▶ Exploring the top historic sites
▶ Driving the most scenic highways

· ·

*M*aritimes tourist literature is filled with pictures of lighthouses and seafood, and you'll see lots of the former and eat lots of the latter. But in addition, each of the three provinces that this book covers — Nova Scotia, New Brunswick, and Prince Edward Island — offers things that go beyond the ordinary, which is where this chapter comes in. I highlight the best and most unique accommodations, restaurants, attractions, and scenic drives.

 This chapter offers a quick rundown of what I consider to be the best that Canada's Maritime provinces have to offer. In the destination chapters in Parts III, IV, and V, I go into more detail about these experiences and destinations; just look for the "Best of the Best" icon you see here.

The Best Places to Stay

Finding comfortable accommodations with the facilities you require in the price range that fits your budget will go a long way to making your travels enjoyable. With that in mind, here are the best the Maritimes has to offer.

Best splurges

Cities across the Maritimes have a choice of top-end hotels. The only real surprise is the cost, which is generally a lot lower than elsewhere in North America.

✔ In Halifax, the **Lord Nelson Hotel & Suites** is an excellent choice for upscale lodging within walking distance of downtown. See Chapter 11.

✔ **Glenghorm Beach Resort** makes the grade for its Deluxe Suites. These contemporary, casual units are among my favorite rooms in all the Maritimes. See Chapter 14.

✔ For top-notch Saint John accommodations, it's hard to go past the old-world charm of **Homeport Historic Bed & Breakfast.** See Chapter 16.

✔ In St. Andrews, a resort town filled with elegant lodgings, none are more lavish than the **Kingsbrae Arms.** See Chapter 16.

✔ On the rural eastern portion of Prince Edward Island, **Inn at Bay Fortune** is a once-grand summer estate converted to luxurious lodging. See Chapter 21.

Best historic getaways

The Maritimes is saturated with historic lodgings — some have been taking in guests for a century or more, while others are converted residences.

✔ The **Lunenburg Arms Hotel** has undergone serious renovations, converting an old inn into a gracious lodging with character-filled rooms, some with water views. See Chapter 12.

✔ In Annapolis Royal, the gracious **Queen Anne Inn** is soaked in Victorian charm. See Chapter 12.

✔ Well-priced rooms and a harborside location are the main draws at the 1810 **Consulate Inn,** once home to a United States consulate. See Chapter 13.

✔ Along the Acadian Coast, the **Governor's Mansion Inn** offers up plenty of history at a reasonable price. See Chapter 15.

✔ In the heart of Charlottetown, the **Inns on Great George** oozes the charm of a bygone era. See Chapter 18.

Best ocean outlooks

Sure, a comfortable bed and clean surroundings are important to an enjoyable stay. But waking up to water views is especially memorable, which is what makes the following choices shine.

✔ Prospect Bed & Breakfast has a beautiful ocean setting in a small fishing village, and yet is within an hour's drive of Halifax. See Chapter 11.

✔ Yes, you really can hear the waves whispering at **Whispering Waves Cottages.** A lobster dinner delivered to your door is a bonus. See Chapter 12.

✔ The name says it all — **Water's Edge Inn** combines location with comfortable rooms to be the best choice in Baddeck. See Chapter 14.

✔ If you prefer location to luxury, make **Seaside Beach Resort** your base while exploring St. Andrews. See Chapter 16.

✔ Staying in a lighthouse guarantees sweeping ocean views, and so it is at **West Point Lighthouse**. One lucky party gets to stay in the actual light tower while other guests make themselves comfortable in converted living quarters. See Chapter 20.

Best for active travelers

Keeping in mind that not all travelers are drawn to urban hot spots, I present you with the best lodgings for those who like to wake up in the middle of the outdoor action.

✔ Whales and birds are the main attractions out on Brier Island, and the place to mingle with fellow wildlife enthusiasts is **Brier Island Lodge.** See Chapter 12.

✔ **Seaboard Bed and Breakfast** is the ideal hangout for surfers drawn to the waves of Lawrencetown Beach. No waves? No problem. Guests have use of canoes and bikes. See Chapter 13.

✔ **Glenghorm Beach Resort** has a beachy feel, and activities to match — think sea kayaking, ocean swimming, and sunbathing. See Chapter 14.

✔ For resort-style activities such as golf, tennis, and swimming, **Rodd Crowbush Golf & Beach Resort** will not disappoint. See Chapter 21.

The Best Places to Eat

Unless you plan on staying in accommodations with cooking facilities, you'll be eating out a lot on your Maritimes vacation. But restaurant pricing throughout the three provinces is reasonable and the choices — in cities and resort areas at least — are varied.

Best seafood

As you'd expect in a region dominated by the ocean, seafood is found on most menus. I dedicate a full chapter to the subject (see Chapter 23), but here is a quick glance at the best of the best.

- ✔ For the plumpest scallops you can ever imagine, go right to the source at **O'Neil's Royal Fundy Market** and order them cooked to go. See Chapter 12.

- ✔ Truro is in the rural heart of Nova Scotia. So **Murphy's,** with its perfectly battered fish and chips, is a welcome surprise. See Chapter 13.

- ✔ The **Chowder House** is a simple pine-paneled room. But what it lacks in ambience it more than makes up for with fresh, inexpensive seafood. See Chapter 14.

- ✔ Order crab and mussels, boiled to order on outdoor gas burners, at the **Muddy Rudder.** Just don't expect table service. See Chapter 14.

- ✔ At the back of Saint John City Market, **Billy's Seafood Company** is part seafood market, part restaurant, so you can be assured the blackboard menu features the freshest of fresh seafood. See Chapter 16.

- ✔ Steamed mussels are a common appetizer throughout the Maritimes, but at **Flex Mussels** they are the star of the show, with choices like mussels boiled with roast corn, scallions, kumquats, and bourbon. See Chapter 18.

- ✔ Plan on giving the touristy restaurants in Cavendish a miss and head to the nearby **Blue Mussel Café,** which dishes up fresh, innovative seafood. See Chapter 19.

- ✔ You should plan on taking in at least one lobster supper while in the Maritimes. My pick is **Fisherman's Wharf Lobster Supper,** which is halfway between touristy and traditional. See Chapter 19.

Best Views

Restaurants with views are notorious for high prices and bad food, but not in the Maritimes, as you'll find out at the following eateries.

- ✔ **Murphy's on the Water** is true to its name. This Halifax restaurant, at the end of a wharf extending well into the harbor, offers panoramic views from most tables. See Chapter 11.

- ✔ Restaurants are few and far between along the Eastern Shore, which makes the **Lobster Shack** even more popular. To make the most of the location, request an outdoor table, order lobster chowder, and watch the Salmon River flow by. See Chapter 13.

- ✔ You can see the ocean from many Cape Breton Island dining rooms, but none have the intimate atmosphere and creative cooking found at **Seascapes Restaurant.** See Chapter 14.

- ✔ In the tony town of St. Andrews, **The Gables** is a refreshingly casual seafood restaurant with a deck that extends to just above the high-tide mark. See Chapter 16.

✔ Yes, the **Blue Mussel Café** makes the cut when it comes to the Maritimes' best seafood restaurants. But every table has views across delightful Rustico Bay, so I include it here also. See Chapter 19.

Best pub dining

Forget about nachos and chicken wings. In the Maritimes, pub grub usually includes traditional British cooking or local seafood, and here are the best of the best.

✔ The hordes of university students living in Moncton gravitate to Main Street bars such as the **Pump House Brewery** for inexpensive dining (and drinking). See Chapter 15.

✔ **Captain Dan's** attracts a young, hip crowd of New Brunswickers with its prime waterfront location, well-priced seafood, and live music. See Chapter 15.

✔ In Fredericton, veer off the main street to **Rye's Deli & Bar,** a fancy pub known as much for its creative food as its beer. See Chapter 17.

✔ In downtown Charlottetown the **Merchantman Pub** serves a mix of classic pub fare and fresh seafood in a lively atmosphere. See Chapter 18.

Best Acadian

Forget about the waistline and dine on down-home, hearty Acadian cooking at one of the following establishments.

✔ Rappie pie, an Acadian staple, is the specialty at **Rapure Acadienne.** But arrive on an empty stomach — the servings are huge. See Chapter 12.

✔ At **Restaurant Acadian** in Chéticamp, traditionally hearty Acadian cuisine is served by waitstaff in traditional dress. See Chapter 14.

Best inexpensive dining

Everyone loves a bargain, but that doesn't mean eating poorly. So in this section I include dining establishments where the prices are as attractive as the food.

✔ Inhabiting a prime downtown Halifax locale is **Harbourside Market,** where food outlets like **Captain John's** serve up well-priced food in a casual setting. See Chapter 11.

✔ The décor is bright and cheery, but the prices will catch your eye at **Chez Cora.** See Chapter 17.

✔ At **Café Diem,** you can check your e-mail while munching away on healthy, inexpensive lunches. See Chapter 18.

✔ The **Bluefin Restaurant** in Souris is notable for its homey atmosphere and inexpensive seafood. See Chapter 21.

The Best Historic Attractions

Sure, the Maritimes has the usual array of museums filled with predictable collections of pioneer artifacts, but wait! The three provinces also offer an abundance of remarkable sites that delve into the region's long and colorful history.

I don't delve into too much history in this book. But if I mention a museum or historic site, you know it's good (or very important), like the following.

✔ **Halifax Citadel National Historic Site,** a 19th-century fort that holds the title of Canada's most visited National Historic Site, is worth visiting for the sweeping harbor views alone. See Chapter 11.

✔ Halifax played an important role in the aftermath of the *Titanic* tragedy. As a result, you can explore plenty of related history, from the mainstream **(Maritime Museum of the Atlantic)** to the offbeat **(Fairview Cemetery,** the final resting place of third-class seaman J. Dawson, who was immortalized by a fictional character of the same name, played by Leonardo DiCaprio in the movie version of the tragedy). See Chapter 11.

✔ South of Halifax, the entire waterfront core of attractive **Lunenburg,** home port for the famous schooner *Bluenose II,* has been declared a UNESCO World Heritage Site for its unaltered state. See Chapter 12.

✔ The British and French struggled for control of **Annapolis Royal** for almost a century, and many buildings from this era remain along the main street, including Canada's oldest wooden building. Just outside of town is **Port-Royal,** a replica of Canada's first permanent European settlement. See Chapter 12.

✔ The **Alexander Graham Bell National Historic Site** is a first-rate museum commemorating one of the world's best-known inventors. The basement is devoted to learning games for children. See Chapter 14.

✔ The **Fortress of Louisbourg,** Canada's largest historical reconstruction, is also one of its most remote, situated as it is on the northeastern tip of Cape Breton Island. See Chapter 14.

✔ History along the Acadian Coast revolves (not surprisingly) around the Acadians, a Francophone population who settled the region as early as the 1730s. To fully immerse yourself in the vibrant culture of these resilient people, plan on spending time at **Village Historique Acadien.** See Chapter 15.

✔ After fire destroyed much of **Saint John** in 1877, the city was rebuilt in brick and stone, and today these elaborate buildings form the nucleus of a historic downtown precinct. See Chapter 16.

✔ **Kings Landing Historical Settlement** is an outdoor museum that re-creates life as experienced by the Loyalists, who were driven out of America for their devotion to England after the American Revolution. See Chapter 17.

✔ The country's Fathers of Confederation gathered in **Charlottetown** in 1864 to discuss uniting the British North American colonies to establish the Dominion of Canada. **Province House,** where the meeting took place, is still home to the PEI legislature and open to the public. Charlottetown's top attraction is **Founders' Hall,** which tells the story of Canada from Confederation to modern times. See Chapter 18.

The Best Scenic Drives

In addition to scheduled stops at official attractions, be sure to allow extra time for taking in the scenery along the following routes.

✔ **Best in Nova Scotia:** For rugged scenery coupled with history and Francophone culture, the **Cabot Trail** will not disappoint. Baddeck is the ideal starting point for this 300km (187-mile) circuit that hits all the hot spots of Cape Breton Island. From this history-filled village, the road cuts across the Margaree Valley to the Gulf of St. Lawrence and Chéticamp, where Acadians go about the business of fishing, making arts and crafts, and filling travelers with hearty cooking. The Cabot Trail then hugs ocean cliffs and cuts through the rugged interior of Cape Breton Highlands National Park to the white-sand beaches of Ingonish. See Chapter 14.

✔ **Best in New Brunswick:** The drive along the Fundy Coast is geologically interesting rather than outrageously scenic. It's divided roughly in half by the city of Saint John. Head west from here along **Route 1** and pass by tranquil lakes and catch occasional glimpses of the Bay of Fundy before you reach the resort town of St. Andrews. Northeast of Saint John, **Route 114** passes through Fundy National Park and the fishing village of Alma before reaching Hopewell Rocks and heading up the Petitcodiac River to Moncton. See Chapter 16.

✔ **Best on Prince Edward Island:** Fill the gas tank and strike out in any direction from Charlottetown. Within minutes, you're surrounded by the bucolic landscape so vividly described by Lucy Maud Montgomery in *Anne of Green Gables.* Need a little more direction? Take **Route 1** west from the capital to Summerside, and then continue along the coastal Région Évangéline via **Route 11,** where Acadian culture thrives. As the Northumberland Strait opens to the Gulf of St. Lawrence, rolling green fields along **routes 11** and **14** come to a stark end at red cliffs that drop precipitously into the ocean. Stop for a slice of Seaweed Pie at Miminegash before returning to the capital via **Route 2.** See Chapter 20.

Chapter 2

Digging Deeper into the Maritimes

●   ●

In This Chapter

▶ Stepping back into the past

▶ Feasting on local cuisine

▶ Getting a taste for the Maritimes through books and movies

●   ●

*Y*ou can spend hours poring over maps and guidebooks while planning your trip to the Maritimes, but knowing a little background helps you appreciate the region's finer points. In this chapter, I do my best to condense four centuries of history into a few pages, introduce you to local cuisine, and then round out the chapter with a discussion of books and movies that give you the chance to get even better acquainted with the Maritimes.

History 101: The Main Events

Many centuries before the first Europeans arrived, the Maritimes provided a home for the Mi'Kmaq, coastal dwellers who fished with spears and hook and line, and also collected shellfish from the shoreline. For food, hunting was less important than fishing, but a successful hunter still held a high status among members of the group. Canoes with sails were used for summer travel, while in winter toboggans (the word toboggan originates from the Mi'Kmaq word *topaghan*) and snowshoes were essential.

Legend has it that a large boulder near Yarmouth (Nova Scotia) was inscribed by the fearsome Viking Leif Eriksson around 1,000 years ago. But the region's first documented European visitor was explorer John Cabot, who spotted Cape Breton Island in 1497. A century later, Frenchman Samuel de Champlain sailed into the Bay of Fundy and established a fur trading post on a small island in the St. Croix River.

Conditions were harsh, so the party relocated to what is now Nova Scotia and built Port-Royal, which is now protected as a National Historic Site, complete with a re-creation of the original fort. The settlement prospered and expanded into what became known as Acadia, or "Peaceful Land."

But French settlement didn't sit well with England, which had colonial aspirations along North America's east coast. The first major conflict between the two occurred in 1613, when the English attacked Port-Royal. This didn't stop Acadian settlements from springing up around the Bay of Fundy, including Grand Pré, which grew into the Acadian capital. The 1713 Treaty of Utrecht, which settled the Queen Anne's War in Europe, gave Acadia to England, which they promptly renamed Nova Scotia (New Scotland), designating Annapolis Royal as the capital. Having been granted Cape Breton Island and Prince Edward Island in the treaty, the French built the Fortress of Louisbourg, envisioning a major trading center and military base. The French also developed Port-la-Joye (now Charlottetown, the capital of Prince Edward Island), with the aim of farming the island's rich soils to provide food for Louisbourg. But hostilities between England and France continued, often mirroring events in Europe, such as the Seven Years' War between 1756 and 1763.

In 1755, England began enforcing an oath of allegiance from the Acadians. Those who were noncompliant — around 8,000 — were deported. They were loaded onto ships bound for the English colonies on the eastern seaboard or any place that would accept them. Some ships docked in England, others in France, and others in France's colonies in the Caribbean. In one of the period's few favorable events, the Spanish government offered the refugees free land in Louisiana, and many settled there, where they became known as Cajuns. The poet Henry Wadsworth Longfellow distilled the deportation tragedy in *Evangeline*, a fictional story of two lovers divided by the events.

After the British swept the Acadians from their land, they used free land grants to lure prosperous *planters* (gentlemen-farmers from New England) to the region. Merchants settled in Yarmouth in the 1760s, and other Anglo settlers went to Prince Edward Island. Even the inglorious defeat in the American Revolution benefited the British by helping settlement of the Maritimes. *Loyalists* (Americans loyal to England) by the thousands poured into Nova Scotia and New Brunswick. Around 14,000 Loyalists settled in Saint John, leading to its incorporation as a city (the first in Canada) in 1785.

One of the more remarkable aspects of Maritimes history was privateering. *Privateers* were government-sanctioned pirates who had permission to capture enemy vessels. They were required by law to take captured vessels to Halifax's Privateers Wharf, where the cargo was auctioned off, a portion of which was handed back to the privateer and his crew.

Maritimes timeline

1497 John Cabot sights Cape Breton Island and claims it for England.

1604 French explorer Samuel de Champlain establishes a winter camp on an island in the St. Croix River.

1605 Champlain's party moves across the Bay of Fundy and builds Port-Royal, a fortified settlement overlooking the Annapolis Basin.

1635 Port-Royal is declared the capital of French-speaking Acadia.

1713 After a century of conflict, the Treaty of Utrecht awards French Acadia to Great Britain while France falls heir to Cape Breton Island and Prince Edward Island.

1749 The British establish a fortified military base at Halifax Harbour.

1755 Around 8,000 Acadians are deported.

1758 The English capture and destroy the Fortress of Louisbourg.

1776 Even after the signing of the Declaration of Independence, many Americans remained loyal to England. Finding life intolerable, they flee north to the Maritimes, where they are known as Loyalists.

1785 Saint John, New Brunswick, becomes Canada's first incorporated city.

1800 A frozen pond on the outskirts of Windsor, Nova Scotia, hosts the first-ever game of hockey.

1864 The Fathers of Confederation meet in Charlottetown, signing the *British North America Act* and in effect creating the nation of Canada.

1885 The transcontinental railway, extending from Halifax to Vancouver, is completed.

1917 Two ships collide in Halifax Harbour. The ensuing explosion is, for its time, the world's biggest man-made explosion.

1997 The Confederation Bridge opens, providing a road link between Prince Edward Island and the rest of Canada.

In the early 1860s, with the American Civil War raging, England decided it needed to do something to reform its political influence in the New World. This was the impetus for the Fathers of the Confederation coming together at Province House in Charlottetown to discuss a union of colonies. The gathering formed the groundwork for the 1867 *British North American Act*, which established the Dominion of Canada as a confederation of Nova Scotia, New Brunswick, Quebec, and Ontario. Prince Edward Island joined in 1873. The final piece to the jigsaw puzzle was Newfoundland, which became Canada's tenth province by joining the dominion in 1949.

Taste of the Maritimes: Local Cuisine

To have a true Maritimes experience, eat plenty of seafood and be sure to experience Acadian cooking.

Swimming in seafood

If you love seafood, you'll love the Maritimes, where it is a staple for locals and dominates restaurant menus. Lobsters, crabs, scallops, mussels, clams, halibut, and salmon are all harvested locally. One of the true joys of local seafood is that you don't need to spend a fortune to indulge. For example, fresh boiled lobster is fresh boiled lobster, whether you pick it up at a market and cook it yourself, or you order it at the finest restaurant in Halifax. The same goes for other types of seafood. If you have cooking facilities at your accommodations (many cottage complexes do), stock up on mussels to steam in white wine, scallops to sauté with butter and garlic, and crab to boil in salted water.

But maybe you want someone else to do the cooking. Not a problem. Seafood finds its way onto menus at even the most unassuming restaurant. I purposely avoid recommending chain restaurants in this book, but McDonald's does warrant a mention for its local McLobster burger, which it offers throughout the summer. Moving up one step in style is the down-home atmosphere of a lobster supper in one of the community halls on Prince Edward Island. Other regional highlights include pickled Solomon Gundy herring sold from a roadside cart in New Brunswick and planked Atlantic salmon cooked over an open fire at a resort in Nova Scotia.

Eating Acadian

Not surprisingly, Acadian fare is based on seafood. Two common dishes include chicken *fricot,* a hearty stewlike soup chock-full of chicken, onions, and potatoes; and *poutine râpé,* boiled or deep-fried pork and grated raw potatoes, rolled into a ball and dipped in corn or maple syrup or molasses. Desserts such as sugar pie, apple dumplings, and cinnamon buns appear on most Acadian menus.

Even if you're not invited into an Acadian home, you're welcome to enjoy the food at Acadian restaurants along La Côte Acadienne (Nova Scotia), Chéticamp (Nova Scotia), the Acadian Coast (New Brunswick), and Région Évangéline (Prince Edward Island).

Background Check: Recommended Books and Movies

Life on the edge of the world has been the inspiration for many Maritimes books and movies. Here are a few of the better known.

The Maritimes in print

A discussion of Maritimes literature can't begin any other way than with *Anne of Green Gables,* by Lucy Maud Montgomery (1877–1942). Born and raised around Cavendish, on Prince Edward Island, Montgomery wrote the children's classic in 1908, using her own childhood as inspiration for the tale of a spunky orphan living on a farm at Avonlea. While the book has been turned into a TV drama *(Road to Avonlea)* and a movie, many places described in the novel still exist, including Green Gables House, which is open as a tourist attraction.

His Majesty's Yankees and *The Governor's Lady,* both by Thomas Raddall (1903–1994), do a wonderful job of delving into Nova Scotia's past using fictional characters. *No Great Mischief* (2001), by Alistair MacLeod, is the story of a Scottish clan that settles on Cape Breton Island in the late 1700s. *Island: The Complete Stories* (2001) showcases MacLeod's florid writing style as he describes rural life in Nova Scotia.

Nova Scotian Thomas Chandler Haliburton (1796–1865) is credited with creating the literary character Sam Slick. In *The Clockmaker,* Haliburton first coined phrases such as "it's raining cats and dogs" and "quick as a wink."

New Brunswick's best-known author is Antonine Maillet, a prolific writer whose book *La Sagouine,* about an Acadian fisherman's wife, has been adapted to a summer stage production in her hometown of Bouctouche. If you're interested in Acadia, do pick up a copy of Clive Doucet's *Notes From Exile* (2000), which explores modern-day Acadian culture by combining Doucet's own experiences with the 1755 deportation. Heartrending yet gritty, *Mercy Among the Children,* authored by David Adams Richards in 2001, is the story of growing up in a rural town along New Brunswick's Miramichi River.

The Maritimes on the big screen

Canada has a well-respected film industry that produces dozens of excellent movies that are little-known even within Canada. While most are obscure, *Shattered City: The Halifax Explosion* (2003) is worth searching out for its realistic portrayal of what was, at the time (1917), the world's largest man-made explosion. More recently, *One More Dead Fish* is a compelling docudrama set in Nova Scotia.

The waterfront precinct of Shelburne was spruced up in 1992 for *Mary Sillman's War,* based on the book *War of Duty,* which was set in Connecticut during the American Revolution. Hollywood producers were so impressed with Shelburne's historical look that they returned with Demi Moore and Robert Duvall to film *The Scarlet Letter.* Modern-day scenes from the 1997 movie *Titanic* were filmed around Halifax. This city has many links to the famous tragedy, including being the resting place of many victims, one of which is J. Dawson, the namesake of Leonardo DiCaprio's character. Halifax Harbour takes a starring role in *K-19: The Widowmaker* (2002), in which Harrison Ford plays a Russian naval captain aboard a nuclear submarine.

Halifax has also stood in for a surprisingly diverse number of cities, including Salt Lake City for the 2005 TV movie *Bring Elizabeth Home: The Elizabeth Smart Story*. Scenes from *Leaving Las Vegas* (1995) were also filmed in the Nova Scotia capital, as were small parts of *The Shipping News,* which was mostly filmed in Newfoundland. The miniseries *Beach Girls*, a teen-angst drama starring Rob Lowe, was filmed in numerous coastal communities south of Halifax. *Outlander,* a science fiction thriller combining Vikings and aliens hasn't hit the big screen as of publication of this book — and I won't be rushing out to see it — but it gives you a good idea of Eastern shore scenery.

Based on a poem by Henry Wadsworth Longfellow, *Évangéline* tells the story of a young woman from Grand Pré who was separated from the love of her life during the Acadian deportation. This classic 1929 silent movie (starring Mexican actress Dolores del Rio) was rereleased on DVD in 2001.

The setting is supposedly an island off New England, but the Fundy Coast around Saint John did just fine for filming of the 1986 movie *Children of a Lesser God,* which won a host of Academy Awards including Best Picture and Best Actress (Marlee Matlin). At the opposite end of the cinematic scale, the backwoods of New Brunswick have provided a backdrop for slasher flicks such as the 1997 hit *I Know What You Did Last Summer* and *Ricky 6* (2000), which was loosely based on the true story of teenaged satanic serial killer from Long Island. Another movie released in 2000 was the thriller *Frozen with Fear,* filmed in and around Fredericton, with Bo Derek as a wife who witnesses her husband's murder. Two years earlier, James Woods and Melanie Griffith were in the New Brunswick capital filming the crime thriller *Another Day in Paradise.*

Lucy Maud Montgomery's florid descriptions of Prince Edward Island came to the small screen in the 1980s TV series *Road to Avonlea,* as well as numerous movies, including *Happy Christmas, Miss King* (1998). Children enjoy watching any of these productions, but don't tell them they were filmed in Ontario. One movie that was filmed on the Island (but you won't want the kids to watch) is *The Ballad of Jack and Rose,* an R-rated drama about a daughter growing up with her father on a remote commune.

Chapter 3

Deciding Where and When to Go

● ●

In This Chapter

▶ Describing the regions

▶ Making the most of your time

▶ Sorting out the seasons

▶ Catching the best festivals and events

● ●

*D*eciding what you want to see and the best time to visit depends on many factors. I begin this chapter with a brief overview of each province, describing spectacular coastal scenery, rural serenity, and the historical appeal of some of North America's oldest towns.

After you have an idea of *where* you want to go on your Maritimes vacation, you need to decide *when* to visit. That's where the second part of this chapter comes to the rescue. I describe the pros and cons of each season and use a table to show monthly temperature differences in a simple format. I end with a round-up of popular festivals and events (along with a few personal favorites).

Going Everywhere You Want to Be

Even though you can include all three provinces in a weeklong vacation, rushing through the Maritimes defeats the purpose of enjoying everything the destination has to offer. Instead, plan your travels around your own interests and needs, using this section to find out the highlights of each region. I go into more detail in the travel chapters of this book.

Nova Scotia

Almost cut off from the rest of Canada by the Bay of Fundy, Nova Scotia (see Part III) is compact and easy to get around, which makes visiting the various regions a breeze. You're never more than 60km (37 miles) from what best defines the province — the ocean. Picturesque fishing villages, abundant seafood, and the stark beauty of Cape Breton Island are highlights of a visit to Nova Scotia.

Halifax (see Chapter 11), capital of Nova Scotia and largest city in the Maritimes, has history and a beautiful location as its major draws. Set around a spectacular harbor, the city radiates from a compact downtown core where you find attractions such as **Halifax Citadel National Historic Site,** world-class hotels, fine dining, and a lively nightlife.

In **southwestern Nova Scotia** (see Chapter 12), **Peggy's Cove, Mahone Bay,** and **Lunenburg** get all the attention for their postcard-perfect oceanfront settings, but many other South Shore villages you don't see in the tourist brochures are equally scenic and a lot quieter. Stroll the waterfront sections of **West Dover, Prospect Point,** or **Blue Rocks** to experience Nova Scotia without the crowds. The **Bay of Fundy** is no scenic gem, but with the world's highest tides and resident populations of **whales,** it's a huge attraction.

Beyond the TransCanada Highway, which cuts through **central Nova Scotia** (see Chapter 13), is a wealth of worthwhile detours. The most intriguing is to watch the **tidal bore** (a wall of water that builds up as the tide comes in against the waters of a river) at **Truro.** You can also drive the **Glooscap Trail** in search of dinosaurs and explore the history of **Pictou** by stepping aboard a replica of the sailing ship that bought the province's first Scottish settlers.

Cape Breton Island (see Chapter 14) is one of Nova Scotia's biggest draws. The island's most spectacular scenery lies within the protection of **Cape Breton Highlands National Park.** The **Cabot Trail,** one of the world's most scenic drives, passes through the park, allowing roadside views of high sea cliffs, endless ocean, white-sand beaches, and occasionally whales frolicking in the water far below.

New Brunswick

The largest of the three Maritime provinces, New Brunswick (see Part IV) is also the most varied in terms of landscape, and it offers diverse experiences to match. An excellent highway system links the three largest cities — **Moncton, Fredericton** (the capital), and **Saint John** — with other excellent destinations close at hand.

The **Acadian Coast** of New Brunswick, northeast of the university town of **Moncton** (see Chapter 15), has long stretches of sandy beaches and some of Canada's warmest ocean water. **Parlee Beach,** near Shediac, is especially popular for its warm water, making it the busiest beach in the Maritimes. If you're after solitude, head northwest from Moncton to the beaches in **Kouchibouguac National Park.**

The world's highest tides are in the **Bay of Fundy,** which is bordered to the west by New Brunswick's **Fundy Coast** (see Chapter 16). **Fundy National Park** and **Hopewell Rocks** are the best spots to view the effects of this natural phenomenon. But a coastal drive must also include the historic port city of **Saint John** and the resort town of **St. Andrews,** which oozes old money.

The capital of New Brunswick, **Fredericton** (see Chapter 17) centers on the **Historic Garrison District,** which has changed little since the mid-1800s, when it was filled with English soldiers defending the Maritimes region from an overland attack. Beyond city limits follow the Saint John River to historic highlights like **Kings Landing Historical Settlement,** and take back roads that lead to dozens of covered bridges.

Prince Edward Island

Usually referred to simply as PEI, Prince Edward Island (see Part V) is Canada's smallest province, just one-tenth the size of Nova Scotia. It's linked to the mainland by a bridge, but is a world away from the rest of the country in look and feel. The Island was immortalized by Lucy Maud Montgomery in her popular *Anne of Green Gables* novel, and in many ways retains the charms she wrote of a century ago.

The centrally located capital is **Charlottetown** (see Chapter 18), which is chock-full of history, inviting bed-and-breakfasts, and a wide range of restaurants.

Few places in the world are as closely associated with a fictional character as PEI is with Anne of Green Gables. Lucy Maud Montgomery, who wrote the classic in 1908, used her childhood home of **Cavendish** (see Chapter 19) as an inspiration for the young girl who comes to live on a farm in the village of Avonlea. Tens of thousands of fans visit Montgomery-related sites annually, including **Green Gables House,** Montgomery's cousin's farm and the principal setting for the book.

Beyond Charlottetown and Cavendish, don't expect dramatic scenery and stunning natural wonders. Instead, you're greeted by a gently rolling landscape of cultivated fields surrounded by stark red cliffs that drop into blue ocean. Many of the Island's most scenic byways, like coastal Route 14 through **Prince County** (see Chapter 20) are unassuming rural roads. Route 2 leads west from Charlottetown through the pretty farmland of Prince County to **North Cape,** a remote point of land jutting into the Gulf of St. Lawrence.

You find more bucolic scenery in **Kings County** (see Chapter 21), especially south from Route 2. This highway provides access to **Prince Edward Island National Park,** protecting a long sliver of the Island's northern coastline that extends west to Cavendish.

Scheduling Your Time

Even though being flexible with your time is fun, having at least an idea of where you want to go before striking out across the Maritimes is important. I lay out some specific itineraries in Chapter 4, which you can combine with the tips laid out in this chapter to create a travel strategy that works best for you.

✔ **Establishing a base.** The vast majority of visitors arriving by air touch down at **Halifax International Airport,** and I recommend that you plan on doing the same. Just a short drive (or cab ride) to the region's largest city, the airport is the terminus of flights from across the continent and beyond. If you only have a few days in the region, Halifax is a good base for day trips that can include Peggy's Cove, Lunenburg, and Annapolis Royal.

✔ **Deciding whether to drive or fly.** Distances are such that driving is the best way to get around the Maritimes. From Halifax, it's only a two-hour drive to New Brunswick, four hours to the farthest point of Prince Edward Island, and five hours to Cape Breton Highlands National Park.

✔ **If your time is limited.** As you see from the itineraries in Chapter 4, hitting the highlights in one week is possible, but don't try to fit too much in. Make all accommodations reservations in advance to save wasting time each afternoon and schedule at least one multi-night stop.

✔ **Considering arriving and departing from different airports.** The way airfares are structured these days, travelers aren't really penalized by purchasing two one-way fares. Rental car drop-off charges may be worthwhile when factoring in the time saved in not backtracking.

✔ **Trying to avoid cities during the week and resort towns on weekends.** This advice is especially apt in July and August, when locals escape the city for resort areas such as St. Andrews and Cavendish.

Knowing the Secrets of the Seasons

Sure, it may be bright and sunny in one province while raining in another. But as a whole, the Maritimes is under the influence of a single weather pattern whose biggest influencing factor is the Atlantic Ocean. In spring, the cold ocean water creates a lag in the warming of land. In fall, the opposite occurs, as the warmth from the ocean delays the onset of cooler temperatures by a few weeks.

Each of the four seasons is very distinct. Summer is far and away the most pleasant time of year to visit. But be forewarned, the vast majority of visitors and local residents take advantage of this season — more visitors arrive in July and August than during the rest of the year combined.

If possible, plan your trip for either late June or early September. Most attractions are already (or are still) open, the crowds are thinner, and lodgings offer discount prices. Which time of year do I prefer? I'll do what all good politicians do and sit on the fence: I like June for the long hours of daylight and September for the better weather.

Handy weather information is provided on the following government Web sites:

- ✔ **Environment Canada** (www.weatheroffice.gc.ca) maintains this Web site with a database of forecasts from across Canada.

- ✔ **Environment Canada Atlantic Region** (www.atl.ec.gc.ca) features general information, such as storm forecasts and details on the hurricane season.

- ✔ **Canadian Hydrographic Service** (www.charts.gc.ca) displays tide charts for the Bay of Fundy.

- ✔ **Marine Services On-Line** (www.marineservices.gc.ca) provides a log of marine forecasts.

The following table shows the average daytime temperatures and precipitation levels in Halifax, which gives you a rough idea for the Maritimes as a whole.

Table 3-1   Halifax's Temperature and Precipitation

Month	Daytime Mean Temperature	Total Monthly Precipitation
January	-5°C (22°F)	147mm (5.8 in)
February	-6°C (21°F)	119mm (4.7 in)
March	-2°C (29°F)	121mm (4.8 in)
April	4°C (39°F)	124mm (4.9 in)
May	9°C (49°F)	111mm (4.4 in)
June	15°C (59°F)	99mm (3.9 in)
July	18°C (65°F)	96mm (3.6 in)
August	18°C (65°F)	109mm (4.3 in)
September	14°C (57°F)	94mm (3.7 in)
October	11°C (52°F)	130mm (5.1 in)
November	3°C (38°F)	155mm (6.2 in)
December	-3°C (27°F)	168mm (6.6 in)

As a general rule, the farther inland you go, the greater the temperature differential over the year. For example, Moncton has a hotter average July temperature than Halifax but is generally colder than Halifax in winter.

Spring

As the long days of spring begin to warm the land, the snow melts quickly, giving way to fresh growth and a certain feeling of optimism in the air.

Spring is wonderful because:

- ✔ The crowds of summer have yet to arrive.
- ✔ Gardens are in full bloom.
- ✔ Days are long, with up to 16 hours of daylight.

But this season can also have its drawbacks, such as:

- ✔ Foggy days, especially along the Nova Scotia coast and the Bay of Fundy
- ✔ A lot of rain, especially on Cape Breton Island
- ✔ Cool temperatures that rule out swimming in the ocean or sunbathing

Summer

The climate from mid-June onward makes travel comfortable throughout the Maritimes. Locals and visitors alike take full advantage of long hours of daylight and temperatures that often reach 30°C (86°F). Sea breezes and moderate temperatures along the coast create an agreeable temperature range.

Summer is the busiest travel season for the following reasons:

- ✔ July and August are the sunniest and warmest months.
- ✔ The Maritimes comes alive with outdoor activities and festivals.

However, keep these points in mind:

- ✔ Crowds are at their peak.
- ✔ Prices are at their highest, and you must make lodging reservations well in advance.

What time is it?

All three provinces are on **Atlantic standard time** (AST), which is one hour ahead of eastern standard time, two hours ahead of central standard time, three hours ahead of mountain standard time, and four hours ahead of Pacific standard time.

Clocks move forward one hour for **daylight saving time** on the second Sunday in March and turn back on the first Sunday in November.

Fall

The ocean climate creates relatively warm temperatures, prolonging fall in the Maritimes. The famous colors begin appearing in mid-September and often linger well into October.

Fall is a favorite time of year because:

- ✔ Temperatures remain pleasant well into October.
- ✔ Turning leaves put on an incredible display of color.
- ✔ Crowds thin out dramatically.
- ✔ Lodging rates are discounted.

But remember:

- ✔ Many summer-only lodgings begin closing in September, and attractions shorten their operating hours.
- ✔ Daylight hours become shorter.
- ✔ You can get caught up in the tail end of a hurricane (like Juan, which hit Halifax in late Sept 2003, leaving 300,000 people without power).
- ✔ Come October, a distinct chill is in the air.

Winter

When winter hits the Maritimes, it does so with a vengeance, dumping up to 300 centimeters (118 inches) of snow on some areas in a single season. The biggest 24-hour snowfall recorded in Halifax was in 1960, when 96 centimeters (38 inches) fell.

Winter is wonderful for the following reasons:

- ✔ Crowds are nonexistent.
- ✔ Airlines lower their prices and hotels offer discounted rooms.
- ✔ Winter temperatures are moderated by the Atlantic Ocean.
- ✔ The snow is great for cross-country skiing.

Keep the following in mind, however:

- ✔ Most outdoor attractions are closed.
- ✔ Blizzards can make driving dangerous.
- ✔ Daylight hours are short.

Hitting the Big Events: A Maritimes Calendar

The Maritimes calendar is brimming over throughout summer, so I focus my efforts there to give you the cream of the crop. However, the other seasons offer their own special taste of Maritimes culture: Spring and fall bring their own festivals and events to the region, while winter is trade show and exhibition time.

The following major annual events are just the tip of the iceberg. Local and regional events take place around the region on a weekly basis, so check individual provincial tourism Web sites (see Appendix) for more information.

May

Nova Scotia

One of the province's most colorful events (literally) is the **Truro Tulip Festival.** Look for tours of private and public gardens, a tulip-themed art display, and an antiques fair. Middle week of May. For details, call ☎ **902-895-9258** or visit www.nstulips.com.

June

Nova Scotia

The **Royal Nova Scotia International Tattoo** is not what you may think. It has nothing to do with body art, but instead brings together military and civilian marching bands for what is billed as the world's largest indoor show. In Halifax over ten days starting on the last Friday in June. Call ☎ **800-563-1114** or 902-420-1114, or visit www.nstattoo.ca.

July

Virtually every town and city across the Maritimes holds **Canada Day** (July 1) celebrations. The typical schedule may include a free breakfast in the morning, a parade at midday, musicians performing on outdoor stages during the afternoon and evening hours, and finally, a fireworks display. Contact the local information center in the town you plan to visit to see what's going on.

Nova Scotia

The biggest Maritimes music gathering, the **Stan Rogers Folk Festival** (best known as "Stanfest"), is hosted by one of the region's most remote towns, Canso. Over 10,000 fans gather for outdoor performances of all genres by Canada's leading musicians, with Celtic music getting an extra-special welcome. First weekend in July. Call ☎ **888-554-7826** or visit www.stanfest.com for details.

New Brunswick

Shediac Lobster Festival: The name alone is tempting. A local tradition for over half a century, it's a culinary salute to the Maritimes' best-known delicacy. You can enjoy the nightly lobster supper, or compete for prizes in the lobster-eating competition. Kids will love the parade, themed especially for them, as well as appearances by Mr. Lobster, the event mascot. Second week of July. Call ☎ 506-532-1122 or visit the Web site at www.lobsterfestival.nb.ca.

The **New Brunswick Highland Games & Scottish Festival** centers on the grounds of Old Government House in Fredericton. Pipe bands, highland dancing, and heavy-duty sports events like caber-tossing are all scheduled. Late July. Call ☎ 888-368-4444 or visit www.highlandgames.ca.

Prince Edward Island

This province is renowned for its beaches, but you can see the famously red-colored sand in downtown Charlottetown during SandLand, when professional sand sculptors create island-themed sculptures that will truly amaze you in their detail. The event opens to the public in early July and is in place until the end of summer. The provincial tourism Web site (www.walkandseacharlottetown.com/sandland) has more information and a schedule.

Historic St. Mary's Church in Indian River provides the perfect setting for the **Indian River Festival.** Various types of music — chamber ensembles, Celtic, jazz, and more — are featured every Friday and Sunday evening through July and August. Call ☎ 902-836-4933 or visit www.indianriverfestival.com for a schedule.

August
Nova Scotia

Hundreds of enthusiasts gather for the **Mahone Bay Classic Boat Festival.** Boat-building demonstrations and finished boats cover the Town Wharf, while the harbor is filled with wooden and homemade boats of all shapes and sizes. Races take place across the weekend, including the Fast and Furious event, in which teams of two have just four hours to build their craft. First weekend of August. Call ☎ 902-624-0348 or log on to www.mahonebayclassicboatfestival.org for details.

The following weekend, the action takes place just down the road at the **Lunenburg Folk Harbour Festival.** Expect traditional and contemporary performances in various venues, including the local churches and a downtown bandstand. For details, call ☎ 902-634-3180, or check out www.folkharbour.com.

Digby Scallop Days celebrate Digby's most famous export. The fun includes scallop-shucking demonstrations and competitions, a parade of scallop boats and, of course, the crowning of the Scallop Queen. Early August. Contact the town office for information, ☎ 902-245-4769, www.digbyscallopdays.com.

New Brunswick

Moncton's **Atlantic Seafood Festival** features celebrity chefs from around the world — whose cooking lives up to their fame. Seafood tasting and demonstrations take place at various city venues, along with a Friday-night street party and a Sunday cooking competition. Middle week of August. Call ☎ 866-584-8585 or check www.atlanticseafood festival.com for information.

For over 100 years, Acadians have celebrated their heritage and rich culture on August 15, but federal and provincial governments didn't officially recognize **National Acadian Day** until 2003. Look for celebrations in downtown Saint John and Moncton.

Prince Edward Island

The first weekend in August, the annual **Tyne Valley Oyster Festival** is in full swing. Everyone is invited to participate in nightly oyster suppers, but the crowd is at its loudest during the Canadian Oyster Shucking Championships. Call ☎ 902-831-3294 for information.

In 2008, the book *Anne of Green Gables* celebrates its 100th anniversary. In recognition, events are held throughout the year. Visit www.anne2008. com for a schedule. Most celebrations take place as they do every year during the annual **L.M. Montgomery Festival** in Cavendish. Join a writing workshop on the grounds of Green Gables, enjoy strawberries and ice cream in the garden of Montgomery's childhood home, or have your children participate in a coloring competition at Avonlea School. Second weekend in August. For details, go to www.lmmontgomeryfestival.com.

September

Nova Scotia

New Scotland Days commemorate the arrival of Pictou's first settlers, who traveled from Scotland aboard the *Hector*. Activities include woodworking demonstrations, walking tours, a children's art center, a reenactment of the arrival of the *Hector,* and a dockside *ceilidh* (a traditional Celtic celebration of singing and dancing). Second weekend of September. Call ☎ 902-485-6057 or go to www.townofpictou.com for details.

New Brunswick

Fredericton's biggest annual event is the **Harvest Jazz & Blues Festival.** Musicians take over downtown, performing on 20 stages, both indoors and out, including the local farmers' market. Second week in September. Call ☎ 506-455-4523 or visit www.harvestjazzandblues.com.

Prince Edward Island

The **PEI International Shellfish Festival,** centered on the Charlottetown waterfront, is a good place to watch the world's fastest oyster shuckers compete, or you can try some shucking yourself under the guidance of a pro. Other event highlights include the International Chowder Championship and boat tours to the shellfish grounds. Third weekend in September. Go to www.peishellfish.com for all the details.

October

Nova Scotia

The **Windsor–West Hants Pumpkin Festival** is a crowd-pleasing event that includes a pumpkin weigh-off (first Sat in Oct), where winning weights regularly top 450 kilograms (1,000 pounds), and a "boat" race (second Sun in Oct) where participants paddle across the Avon River in huge half-pumpkins with the insides scooped out. Visit www.worlds biggestpumpkins.com for a schedule and photos of last year's winners.

Cows and cowboys may seem out of place in Halifax, but the country comes to this port city for the annual **Maritime Fall Fair.** Children will love the Kid's Corral and miniature horses, while all ages will be amazed by the bull riding. Two weekends in early October. Call ☎ 902-876-1811 or go to www.maritimefallfair.com for a schedule of events.

With the stunning colors of fall as a backdrop, Celtic musicians from around the world descend on Cape Breton Island for the **Celtic Colours International Festival.** Performances take place in bandstands, town halls, and theaters at over 40 towns and villages across the island. Second week of October. Call ☎ 877-285-2321 or 902-562-6700, or visit www.celtic-colours.com.

New Brunswick

The winning combination of celebrity chefs and local seafood turns up again at the **Fundy Food Festival**. It's hosted at venues throughout Saint John on the fourth Sunday in October. Call ☎ 506-672-3731 or go to www.fundyfoodfestival.com for details.

November

Nova Scotia

The **Atlantic Christmas Fair,** held at Halifax's Exhibition Park, features over 400 booths filled with antiques and the work of Nova Scotian artisans. First weekend of November. For details, call ☎ 902-679-7177 or visit www.atlanticchristmasfair.com. Similar events take place throughout November across the province, including **Christmas by the Sea,** also the first weekend of November, along the Pictou waterfront.

New Brunswick

The **Silver Wave Film Festival** takes place at theaters around Fredericton. It focuses primarily on New Brunswick filmmakers, but international films fill out a busy screening schedule. Early November. Call ☎ **506-455-1632** or visit www.swfilmfest.com.

The **World Wine & Food Expo,** at the Moncton Coliseum, attracts a blend of connoisseurs and ordinary folks looking to learn more about the world's favorite drink. More than 150 wineries participate, while seminars and gourmet shows add to the mix. First weekend in November. Call ☎ **866-846-9463** or 506-532-5333, or visit www.wineexpo.ca.

Prince Edward Island

The **Charlottetown Christmas Parade** is the biggest in Atlantic Canada. It starts downtown at 1 p.m. on the last Saturday in November.

December

Prince Edward Island

Most cities in the Maritimes organize some sort of family-oriented celebration for New Year's Eve. Charlottetown hosts one of the biggest of these, **Capital New Year in the Park,** with lots of games, sleigh rides, and a mass countdown to midnight in Victoria Park.

Table 3-2	Public Holidays
Date	*Name*
January 1	New Year's Day
March/April	Good Friday and Easter Monday
Monday preceding May 25	Victoria Day
July 1	Canada Day
First Monday in August	Civic Holiday
First Monday in September	Labor Day
Second Monday in October	Thanksgiving
November 11	Remembrance Day
December 25	Christmas Day
December 26	Boxing Day

Chapter 4

Following an Itinerary: Four Great Trips

*E*ven though the Maritimes comprises Canada's three smallest provinces, you can't expect to see everything in a single trip. If you have a specific destination or activity in mind, such as visiting Cape Breton Island for the Celtic Colours International Festival or golfing on Prince Edward Island, then you're well on your way to planning your trip. For those of you who are still pondering the best way to spend your time or which route to take, this chapter's for you. I suggest some itineraries to give you an idea of where you can go and what you can see in the time you have, as well as a trip geared toward families and another specifically designed for seafood lovers.

For each itinerary, I take the liberty of assuming you're flying into Halifax, the transportation hub of the Maritimes, and then renting a vehicle.

Seeing the Maritimes in One Week

If you have one week, you can visit each of the three provinces — but only to hit the highlights.

On **Day 1,** after arriving in **Halifax** (see Chapter 11), plan on making your first stop **Halifax Citadel National Historic Site.** Then wander down to the harbor and enjoy lunch at **Salty's.** Spend the early afternoon browsing the **Historic Properties** or taking in the **Maritime Museum of the Atlantic.** Drive to **Lunenburg** (see Chapter 12), stopping at **Peggy's Cove** to snap the famous **lighthouse** picture without the maddening midday crowds. Spend the night at the **Lunenburg Arms Hotel,** dining in-house on the patio at **Rissers.**

On **Day 2**, strike out early from Lunenburg and cut across southwestern Nova Scotia to **Digby,** walking the docks and then enjoying a scallop lunch at the **Fundy Restaurant.** Catch the ferry across the **Bay of Fundy** to **Saint John** (see Chapter 16). Spend the night at the **Homeport Historic Bed and Breakfast** and ask your friendly hosts for a dinner recommendation.

On the morning of **Day 3,** head north from Saint John to **Moncton** (see Chapter 15). If your mid-morning arrival corresponds with the incoming tide (check at the information center), hang around for the **tidal bore.** Continue north to **Shediac.** Take a dip in Canada's warmest ocean water at **Parlee Beach.** Cross **Confederation Bridge** to **Prince Edward Island** and continue to **Charlottetown** (see Chapter 18). Dinner at **Flex Mussels,** a couple of drinks at **Peake's Quay,** and a bed at the **Shipwright Inn** are an ideal combination for your first night on the Island.

On **Day 4,** drive north from Charlottetown to **Cavendish** (see Chapter 19). Visit the grounds of **Green Gables** and see other "Anne" attractions; then spend the afternoon at your leisure — maybe exploring adjacent **Prince Edward Island National Park** or golfing at **Green Gables Golf Course.** Skip Cavendish's touristy restaurants and enjoy dinner in nearby North Rustico at the **Blue Mussel Café,** and then retire to **Kindred Spirits Country Inn.**

Begin **Day 5** by driving to **Wood Islands** for the ferry trip to **Caribou.** Stop at **Pictou** (see Chapter 13) and visit **Hector Heritage Quay.** Jump aboard Highway 104 and cross Canso Causeway to **Cape Breton Island** (see Chapter 14). Continue along Highway 105 to **Baddeck.** Spend the night at the **Water's Edge Inn.**

On **Day 6,** rise early for the spectacular drive through **Cape Breton Highlands National Park** to **Pleasant Bay,** where you have a mid-morning whale-watching tour booked. Continue along the **Cabot Trail** and take lunch at the **Chowder House** in **Neil's Harbour.** Spend the rest of the afternoon leisurely making your way down the coast to **Glenghorm Beach Resort.**

On **Day 7,** take an early-morning walk along **Ingonish Beach,** or rise at your leisure and begin driving the final stretch of the Cabot Trail to **Baddeck.** Visit the **Alexander Graham Bell National Historic Site,** and then enjoy lunch at an outside table at the **Lakeside Café.** Leave the island and stay overnight at **Truro** (see Chapter 13), which is an hour's drive from Halifax International Airport.

Exploring the Maritimes in Two Weeks

On **Day 1,** fly into **Halifax** and spend the remainder of that day along with **Day 2** enjoying Nova Scotia's capital. Chapter 11 provides a detailed sightseeing plan for Halifax.

On **Day 3,** head southwest from Halifax to **Lunenburg** (see Chapter 12), stopping at **Peggy's Cove** and **Mahone Bay** along the way. That gives you plenty of time to visit the **Fisheries Museum of the Atlantic** and to wander the streets before checking into one of Lunenburg's historic inns.

The destination on **Day 4** is **Shelburne,** an easy two-hour drive from Lunenburg (be sure to hit the road in time to reach Shelburne's **Charlotte Lane Café** for lunch). Spend some time along the waterfront, watching boat-builders at work. Leave Shelburne and continue south to **Whispering Waves Cottages,** where you can order a lobster dinner delivered to your oceanfront cabin.

On **Day 5,** continue around the coast of southwestern Nova Scotia to **La Côte Acadienne,** where Acadian traditions live on in the cooking at **Rapure Acadienne** and in the imposing architecture of **Église de Sainte-Marie.** Continue along the Fundy Coast, explore the **Digby** waterfront, and step aboard the *Lady Vanessa* to see what a scallop boat looks like up close. Pick up fresh seafood from **O'Neil's Royal Fundy Market,** and then check into the **Mountain Gap Inn** where you can cook up a storm on one of the supplied barbecues.

Plan on catching the first ferry of the morning on **Day 6,** crossing the Bay of Fundy to **Saint John** (see Chapter 16) with enough time to go through the **New Brunswick Museum** before lunching at **Market Square.** Continue down the coastline to **St. Andrews.** Soaking up the village's bustling resort atmosphere is easy by walking along the main street (although if you're staying at the upscale **Kingsbrae Arms,** you may not want to leave the grounds).

On **Day 7,** drive to **Fredericton** (see Chapter 17) and join a guided walking tour of downtown sights such as the **Garrison Historic District;** then spend an hour or so on your own exploring the leafy downtown streets of the provincial capital. From Fredericton, follow the **Miramichi River** north to **Miramichi** and hang a right down the **Acadian Coast** (see Chapter 15). With a room booked in **Bouctouche** at **Bellevue sur Mer,** you have time for a beach walk along neighboring **Bouctouche Dune.**

On **Day 8,** take a dip in the warm water off **Parlee Beach** before crossing the **Confederation Bridge** to **Prince Edward Island.** Spend the afternoon catching up with your childhood memories at **Green Gables** in Cavendish (see Chapter 19). Spend the night in a room overlooking **Rustico Bay** at **Barachois Inn.** Nearby, **Fisherman's Wharf Lobster Supper** is a good choice for a casual dinner.

Arrive in **Charlottetown** (see Chapter 18) early on **Day 9,** and park at **Founders' Hall,** which is also home to the city's information center. Walk up the hill to **Province House,** in the heart of the historical precinct. Enjoy a seafood lunch at **Water Prince Corner Shop,** knowing you'd be paying a lot more for the same dishes elsewhere. **Rodd Brudenell River** (see Chapter 21) is a world away from the capital but is easily reached in well under an hour. Make the most of long summer days by fitting in a round of golf at one of the resort's two courses.

On **Day 10,** catch the ferry to **Caribou** and spend the rest of the morning at **Hector Heritage Quay** in **Pictou** (see Chapter 13). Leave Pictou for **Cape Breton Island** (see Chapter 14) and **Baddeck.** Check into the **Water's Edge Inn,** and then walk over to the **Alexander Graham Bell National Historic Site.** Have dinner at the **Lynwood Inn Dining Room.**

The next morning, **Day 11,** drive to **Ingonish.** You have two nights here; choose **Glenghorm Beach Resort** for its casual beachside atmosphere, or the **Keltic Lodge** for its historical grandeur. Spend the rest of the day at your leisure, taking a trip with **North River Kayak Tours,** golfing at **Highland Links,** or just doing absolutely nothing at all down on the beach.

Day 12 is a good one. Rise early to beat the crowds along the **Cabot Trail** in **Cape Breton Highlands National Park.** Drive all the way through the park — stopping at lookouts, maybe doing a short hike or two (the Skyline Trail if you're energetic, Benjie's Lake Trail if it's foggy); take a whale-watching tour at Pleasant Bay; and just generally soak up the magnificent scenery. The turnaround point is **Chéticamp.** Back in Ingonish, dine on creative seafood at **Seascapes Restaurant.**

On **Day 13,** drive back to **Halifax** (443km/275 miles). This is the longest day's drive in this itinerary, but it gets you back to your starting point the night before your flight leaves (and gives you a few extra hours to shop in Halifax). Book a room at the **Quality Inn Halifax Airport** for an early-morning flight, or downtown at the centrally located **Waverley Inn** for last-minute shopping.

On **Day 14,** catch your plane home.

Enjoying the Maritimes with Kids

The attractions and activities incorporated into this itinerary are designed to appeal to traveling families — a combination of learning experiences and fun times at a leisurely pace. Like the first itinerary, it spans seven days.

As with the first two itineraries, **Day 1** starts in Halifax (see Chapter 11). After getting oriented, plan on lunch at the **Harbourside Market,** where everyone can choose their favorite food (seafood, pizza, and so on). Start your vacation off with a splash on a **Harbour Hopper Tour.** If the weather is colder, head to the **Museum of Natural History,** which has a critter-filled nature center. Drive south to **Mahone Bay** (see Chapter 12) and spend the night at the family-friendly **Ocean Trail Retreat.**

On **Day 2,** visit **Lunenburg** (see Chapter 12), and then backtrack through Halifax to Highway 102, reaching **Hopewell Rocks** (see Chapter 16) by mid-afternoon. This natural attraction has to be explored at low tide; if you arrive at high tide, wait till the following morning. From Hopewell Rocks, drive through **Pictou** (see Chapter 13) to **Pictou Lodge Resort,** where the beach and watersports keep everyone busy for the rest of the day.

On **Day 3,** catch the ferry to **Prince Edward Island.** It's a one-hour trip, which is enough time to find your way to the upper observation deck and award a prize to the first one in your family to spot the red-and-white lighthouse beside the ferry dock at **Wood Islands** (see Chapter 21). Stop at **Rossignol Estate Winery** for a bottle of Island wine, and enjoy it on the deck of your cabin at **Lakeview Cottages** in **Cavendish** (see Chapter 19) while the kids burn off energy in the playground.

On **Day 4,** children (and many grown-ups) familiar with *Anne of Green Gables* will want to spend a full morning at **Green Gables House.** Pick one of the many surrounding commercial attractions for an afternoon of fun — **Avonlea** for Anne fans, **Shining Waters Family Fun Park** for the under-12's, or **Sandspit** for the older kids. Spend another night in Cavendish.

Day 5 kicks off with a rural drive to **Charlottetown** (see Chapter 18). For a bit of history, a visit to Founders' Hall is a must, while animal lovers may enjoy a trip searching out seals with **Peake's Wharf Boat Tours**. Stop at **Gateway Village** (see Chapter 18) to pick up last-minute souvenirs before crossing **Confederation Bridge** and heading up New Brunswick's **Acadian Coast** (see Chapter 15) to the **Rodd Miramichi River** at **Miramichi.**

Day 6 mixes nature and fun. Take the boardwalk through **Kouchibouguac National Park** to reach a remote stretch of beach with water warm enough for swimming, and then jump back in the car to head to **Moncton.** Let the kids go crazy at **Magic Mountain Water Park,** and then retire to one of the surrounding family-friendly motels, such as **Holiday Inn Express Hotel & Suites.**

On **Day 7,** the three-hour drive back to Halifax is easy. Depending on your flight time, stagger the drive with a stop to watch the **Tidal Bore** in **Truro** (see Chapter 13) or a visit to **Shubenacadie Wildlife Park.** If your flight doesn't depart until early the next day, make reservations at the **Quality Inn Halifax Airport.**

Cruising the Coast: In Search of Seafood

Even die-hard seafood lovers like myself may not be able to keep up with the following one-week itinerary word for word. It's designed for true devotees of the ocean and all it offers up. But even if you're not a seafood fanatic, this itinerary gives you some ideas for taking advantage of the Maritimes' best-loved export.

Day 1 begins by heading north from Halifax along the **Eastern Shore** (see Chapter 13). Make your first stop the **Fisherman's Life Museum** in **Jeddore Oyster Pond.** In **Tangier,** drop by **J. Willy Krauch & Sons** to stock up on smoked salmon. If the weather is good, take a stroll along the beach in **Taylor Point Provincial Park** before continuing on to the **Salmon River House Country Inn,** where you dine at the in-house **Lobster Shack.**

On **Day 2,** take Highway 7 to **Antigonish,** and then cross to **Cape Breton Island** (see Chapter 14) via the Canso Causeway. At **Baddeck,** check into **Bethune's Boathouse Cottage.** Wander along the waterfront and book an afternoon sailing trip aboard the *Elsie,* returning to shore in time for dinner at **Baddeck Lobster Suppers.**

Day 3 starts out with a short drive along St. Ann's Bay to **Ingonish.** Have some cash on hand for mussels and crab at the **Muddy Rudder,** a unique outdoor restaurant where you can watch your lunch being boiled to order. Then hit the fairways of **Highland Links.** An evening walk to **Middle Head** is a perfect way to walk off dinner from the **Atlantic Restaurant.** Spend the night at the **Keltic Lodge.**

Spend the morning of **Day 4** driving the famous **Cabot Trail** through **Cape Breton Highlands National Park.** Wander down to the docks in **Chéticamp** to watch crab boats unloading their precious catch. Head to the **Restaurant Acadian** for a feast of *croquettes de morue* (codfish cakes) served by women in traditional Acadian dress. From Chéticamp, drive to **Pictou** (see Chapter 13). Learn about the traditions of fishing at the **Northumberland Fisheries Museum,** and spend the night in a waterfront room at the **Consulate Inn.**

Day 5 starts with a ferry trip to **Prince Edward Island.** Drive through **Kings County** (see Chapter 21) and catch a tour boat from **Montague** to visit a large **seal colony,** or take a **kayak tour** at **Brudenell River Provincial Park.** Plan on enjoying the most formal meal of your trip (tuck into Malpeque Bay oysters to start, and then get serious with the seared Atlantic salmon) and a comfortable night's rest at **Dalvay-by-the-Sea.**

Rise early on **Day 6** for the drive to **Shediac** (see Chapter 15) and book a lobster-fishing trip with **Shediac Bay Cruises.** After the traps are hauled up, the lobsters are boiled for an onboard feast. On the way out of town, have someone snap a shot of you in front of the world's biggest lobster. Drive to **Saint John** and cross the **Bay of Fundy,** and then drive along **Digby Neck** (see Chapter 12) to **Brier Island Lodge.**

On **Day 7,** plan on taking an early **whale-watching trip,** returning to **Digby** in time to enjoy a dockside takeout lunch of scallops from **O'Neil's Royal Fundy Market.** This gives you plenty of time to either get back to Halifax for an evening flight home, or to drive only as far as **Annapolis Royal** and stay at the **Garrison House,** where the in-house restaurant does wonders with local seafood.

Part II
Planning Your Trip to the Maritimes

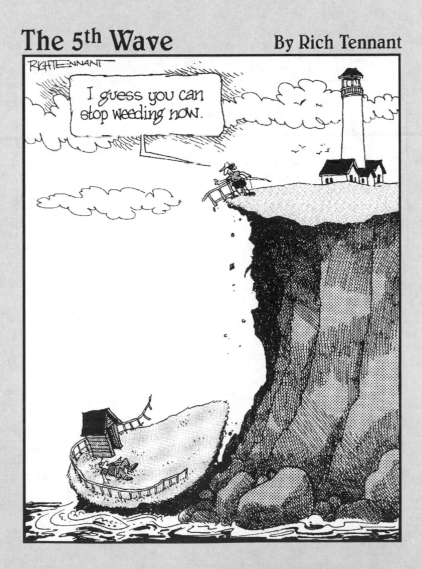

I guess you can stop weeding now.

In this part . . .

You know you're going to the Canadian Maritimes, you're doing some reading, and you have an idea of where you want to travel; now start the actual planning. This section deals with the different ways to get there, your transportation options after you arrive, the types of lodging choices and the rates you can expect to pay, the best ways to deal with your money while on the road, and assorted odds and ends that are easy to ignore — but good to remember.

Chapter 5

Managing Your Money

. . . .

In This Chapter

▶ Estimating your costs

▶ Uncovering hidden charges

▶ Learning about the loonie

▶ Accounting for taxes

▶ Coping with a lost or stolen wallet

. . . .

I kick off this tiresome subject with some good news: Traveling in the Maritimes costs less than anywhere else in Canada. If you're from Europe, throw in a favorable exchange rate, and you have an inexpensive vacation destination.

 Some accommodations and tour companies quote prices in both Canadian and U.S. dollars. This can sometimes work in your favor, other times not, depending on the exchange rate of the day.

Planning Your Budget

Budgeting for your Maritimes vacation isn't hard, and a few hours spent with pen and paper before leaving home will prevent any surprises.

To come up with the total amount that you plan to spend, begin with transportation costs, starting from your front door. Include flight costs (see Chapter 6 for tips on how to fly for less), airport shuttles at both ends, and car rental. Then add in gas, hotel rates, meals, admissions to attractions, and the cost of activities you want to participate in (whale-watching or golf, for example).

Transportation

Costs for transportation, which will likely be the single largest cost associated with your trip, are easy to estimate. If you're arriving by air, begin with the cost of your plane ticket. Next, add your car rental costs (Chapter 7 deals with these in detail), including the rental itself, taxes, and gas expenses. Gas prices can fluctuate quite dramatically, so plan on paying anything between C$1.10 and C$1.30 per liter.

What things cost in the Maritimes

Double room at Halifax's Lord Nelson Hotel ($$$$) on a weekday	C$250
Bed-and-breakfast package for two at the Lord Nelson Hotel ($$$$) on a weekend	C$155
Self-contained unit at Lakeview Lodge & Cottages ($$), Cavendish, PEI, in August	C$127
Self-contained unit at Lakeview Lodge & Cottages ($), Cavendish, PEI, in September	C$65
Dorm bed at Halifax Backpacker's Hostel ($)	C$20
Dinner for two without drinks, tax, or tips at da Maurizio ($$$$) Halifax	C$130
Lobster dinner for one (including a full lobster, mussels, and dessert) at Baddeck Lobster Suppers, Cape Breton Island	C$30
A six-pack of Moosehead beer	C$13.50
A pint of Alexander Keith's beer	C$6.50
Greens fees at Brudenell River golf course in July	C$70
Greens fees *and* accommodations at Brudenell River golf course in October	C$95
Adult admission to Fortress of Louisbourg	C$16.35
Whale-watching in the Bay of Fundy	C$50
Adult admission to Province House, Charlottetown	free

If you are planning to fly from province to province, transportation costs will be an even bigger chunk of your budget.

If you're driving your own vehicle, begin by calculating its fuel consumption. To do this:

1. Fill the gas tank and set the trip odometer to zero.

2. Drive until the tank is nearly empty.

3. Fill the tank again and note the odometer reading.

4. Divide the distance you've driven by the number of gallons (or liters) it took to fill up the second time. This will give you a miles per gallon (or kilometers per liter) amount.

This information may also be available in the owners' manual of your vehicle.

Lodging

Accommodations costs are the biggest variable in your budget. Where you stay and, to a lesser degree, *when* you stay are the determining factors. Staying mid-week at full-service city hotels is going to take a much bigger bite out of your budget than choosing rooms in rural bed-and-breakfasts with shared bathrooms.

In general, rates are at their peak from late June through mid-September. A month on either side is "shoulder season" (intermediate between high and low). The rest of the year is low season, but many bed-and-breakfasts and inns close down completely through the winter. Refer to Chapter 3 for seasonal specifics and see Chapter 8 for lodging categories and costs.

In this book, I use dollar signs ranging from $ to $$$$ to express the approximate cost for a double room in high season (excluding taxes). Hostels and some bed-and-breakfasts outside of cities fall into the $ (under C$75) category. (So do many nondescript roadside motels, but I steer clear of those in this book — you can find them easily enough using the Internet or accommodations guides.) Moving into the $$ range, which runs up to C$150, you have a choice of most bed-and-breakfasts as well as historic inns. In Halifax, the top end of the $$ category will get you a room within walking distance of the harbor. Moving up to the $$$ (C$150–C$225) and $$$$ (C$225 or more) categories, you will find yourself in a fine city hotel or at an upscale oceanfront resort. Very few standard rooms anywhere in the Maritimes cost more than C$250.

Dining

Seafood dominates the restaurant menus across the Maritimes (for the highlights, refer to Chapter 1 or Chapter 4) and is generally well priced, even in the top restaurants. If you can do without the niceties associated with fine dining, seafood is downright inexpensive. When it comes to dishes like lobster, you're really not sacrificing culinary quality by eating at a cheaper restaurant — it doesn't take a master chef to dunk a lobster in boiling water for a few minutes and prepare a side of melted butter.

Attractions

The real reason you're traveling to the Maritimes is to see the sights. Luckily, they're so affordable; in fact, they probably make up the smallest portion of your overall costs. Small town museums often have no admission fee, or else they request a simple donation to cover costs.

Count on paying around half-price admissions for children and teens up to the age of 16, while entry for children under the age of 6 is usually free.

Do-it-yourself dining

Wander down to the docks at most coastal towns and you'll find a fish market of sorts, selling everything from filleted fish to live lobsters. If you're staying in a self-contained unit, cooking fresh lobster, crab, or mussels is as easy as boiling up a big pot of salted water (okay, mussels are better when steamed with wine, but you get the idea), at a fraction of the price of dining out. Some accommodations keep a supply of pots especially for their lobster-boiling guests. Many resorts and smaller bed-and-breakfast inns have barbecues, allowing you to get a little more creative in your selection of seafood. Expect to pay around C$12 to C$15 per pound for fresh lobster, crab, or scallops, and around half that amount for mussels and clams.

The definition of "child" can drop to as low as 2 years old when that child fills an actual seat (on a tour boat, for example), so you can't always expect a deal.

If you plan on visiting lots of national parks and historic sites, consider purchasing an annual pass. After all, the Maritimes has five national parks (out of 39 in all of Canada). An adult day pass costs from C$5.45 to C$67, while entry to each of the Maritimes' 30 national historic sites ranges from C$3.75 to C$16. With these factors in mind, you can decide which, if any, of the following annual passes best serve your interests:

- ✔ The **National Parks of Canada Pass,** valid for entry to all Canadian national parks, is C$62 adults, C$54 seniors, C$32 children aged 6 to 16, to a maximum of C$124 per family.

- ✔ The **National Historic Sites of Canada Pass** is C$49 adults, C$42 seniors, C$25 children aged 6 to 16, to a maximum of C$98 per family.

- ✔ The **Discovery Package** combines annual entry to both national parks and national historic sites for one price — C$77 adults, C$66 seniors, C$39 children aged 6 to 16, to a maximum of C$156 per family.

You can purchase passes at all national parks and national historic sites. For more information, click through the Planning Your Visit link on the Parks Canada Web site, www.pc.gc.ca.

Activities and tours

Although your costs can start adding up if your tastes run to guided tours and sporting endeavors, the Maritime provinces are still a relatively inexpensive destination. A four-hour whale-watching tour in the Bay of Fundy, for example, may cost C$50, but compared to C$80 for a similar trip on the west coast of Canada, it's an excellent value. Golfing is another relative bargain: At Highland Links (Cape Breton Island), which is rated one of the world's top 100 courses, twilight greens fees during peak summer season are a steal at C$53.

 You can save on some tours, golfing, and big-city options like spa treatments if you book them as part of a hotel package. Hotel Web sites are the best place to search out these deals.

Shopping

Shopping can make or break your budget. You can spend anywhere from C$2 on a fridge magnet to well over C$2,000 for an oil painting. Original artwork aside, you can find plenty to buy that doesn't break the bank (or stick on your fridge).

Nightlife

Keeping your costs down when it comes to after-dark entertainment is easy. In the Maritimes, what you wear or which is the hippest nightspot don't matter. The quintessential night out involves simply relaxing with a pint of beer while listening to traditional Celtic music at a local bar (that doesn't charge a cover).

Tips on tipping

Tipping in the Maritimes is no different from anywhere else in North America. A good standard tip for service providers such as waiters and cabdrivers is 15 percent to 20 percent. A smaller tip is enough for a beer at a bar, and C$1 to C$2 per bag is a sufficient tip for a city hotel bellhop.

Cutting Costs — But Not the Fun

 Want to cut vacation costs without cutting corners? Don't we all. Look for the Bargain Alert icon throughout this book for hints on keeping costs down. In addition, here are some general money-saving tips:

- ✔ **Go off season.** Outside of the summer (late June through mid-Sept.) high season, hotel prices are almost half the price of peak months. But don't push it — many smaller places close down completely in winter.

- ✔ **Travel mid-week.** If you can travel on a Tuesday, Wednesday, or Thursday, you may find cheaper flights to the Maritimes. When you ask about airfares, see if you can get a cheaper rate by flying on a different day. For more tips on getting a good fare, see Chapter 6.

- ✔ **Try a package tour.** For many destinations, you can book airfare, hotel, ground transportation, and even some sightseeing just by making one call to a travel agent or packager — and often you pay much less than if you put the trip together yourself. (See Chapter 6 for more on package tours.)

✔ **Reserve a room with a kitchen.** Most motels have a few rooms with cooking facilities, or at the very least a fridge and microwave. Buying supplies for breakfast saves you money (and probably calories).

✔ **Always ask for discount rates.** Membership in the Canadian Automobile Association (CAA, or its American counterpart, AAA), frequent-flier plans, trade unions, AARP (formerly the American Association of Retired Persons), or other groups may qualify you for savings on car rentals, plane tickets, hotel rooms, and even meals. Ask about everything; you may be pleasantly surprised.

✔ **Ask if your kids can stay in the room with you.** A room with two double beds usually doesn't cost any more than one with a queen-size bed, and many hotels won't charge you the additional person rate if the additional person is pint-size and related to you. Even if you have to pay C$10 or C$15 extra for a rollaway bed, you save big bucks by not taking two rooms.

✔ **Try expensive restaurants at lunch rather than dinner.** Lunch usually costs a lot less than dinner at a top restaurant, and the menu often boasts many of the same specialties.

✔ **Get out of town.** In many places, big savings may be just a short drive or taxi ride away. Hotels just outside the city, across the river, or less conveniently located can be great bargains. Outlying motels often have free parking and lower rates than downtown hotels that offer amenities you may never use. Sure, at a motel you carry your own bags, but the rooms are often just as comfortable and a whole lot cheaper. See Chapter 8 for more on accommodations.

✔ **Don't rent a gas-guzzler.** Renting a smaller vehicle is cheaper, and you save on gas to boot. Unless you're traveling with kids and need a lot of space, don't go beyond the economy size offered by most rental companies. For more on car rentals, see Chapter 7.

✔ **Don't use exchange bureaus.** Exchange bureaus give unfavorable rates and then add on a commission. Instead, get your Canadian cash at an ATM, which always gives you the exchange rate of the day.

Handling Money

This section describes the Canadian currency, which is similar to that of the United States, only more colorful and with goofier names. Then, I look at how you can use the Canadian banking system to get your money or to pay for purchases using your hometown financial institution. Finally, I cover what do to if your money or banking cards are lost or stolen.

Making cents of the loonie

Canadian currency is easy to get used to. Coins come in 1-, 5-, 10-, and 25-cent denominations, as well as $1 and $2. The $1 is a gold-colored coin that depicts the loon (a common species of bird), known as the "loonie." The $2 coin has a silver-colored core with a gold-colored rim and is best known as the "toonie." Bills come in the usual denominations of $5, $10, $20, $50, and $100; they're all the same size but vary in color. The $100 bill can sometimes be difficult to cash at smaller businesses or early in the morning, especially if you're only buying something small, like a cup of coffee.

At press time, the Canadian dollar was slightly higher in value than the U.S. dollar. However, exchange rates fluctuate often (and sometimes dramatically), so checking before you go is always a good idea.

 The best online tool I know of for checking exchange rates is the **Universal Currency Converter** at www.xe.com/ucc.

Doting on debit cards

 Using a debit card (also known as an ATM or banking card) is hands-down the easiest way to manage your money while traveling and is extremely popular in Canada (in fact, Canadians are the world's biggest users of this type of banking). You can use your debit card to withdraw cash at ATMs or to pay for purchases at point-of-sale terminals installed at participating merchant locations (over 300,000 in Canada). The national organization responsible for the network in Canada is **Interac** (similar to the **Cirrus** and **Plus** networks elsewhere in the world), so you sometimes hear it referred to as "paying by Interac." Before relying solely on debit and ATMs, check with your bank to find out which Canadian banks honor your card system. The following is a list of the major Canadian banks and the system(s) they use:

- ✔ **Bank of Montreal:** Cirrus

- ✔ **Scotiabank:** Plus

- ✔ **TD Canada Trust:** Cirrus and Plus

- ✔ **CIBC:** Plus

- ✔ **Royal Bank:** Cirrus and Plus

Using ATMs

These days, far more people use ATMs than traveler's checks. Most cities have these handy 24-hour cash machines linked to an international network that almost always includes your financial institution back at home. You can use your debit or credit card to withdraw the money you need every couple of days, which eliminates the insecurity of carrying around a large stash of cash. Of course, many ATMs are little money managers (or dictators, depending on how you look at it), imposing limits on your spending by allowing you to withdraw only a certain amount of money per day.

One important reminder before you go ATM crazy, however: Canadian banks charge a fee of up to C$2.50 whenever a non-account holder uses their ATMs. Your own bank may also charge a fee for using an ATM that's not one of their branch locations. In some cases, you may get charged twice. Check out your bank's policy before ruling out traveler's checks altogether, since they may be a cheaper — though certainly less convenient — option for you.

Do not use privately owned ATMs. Also known as white-label ATMs, these banking machines are most often placed in gas stations, corner stores, restaurants, and bars. Fees can be up to C$4 for a single transaction, in addition to the fee your own bank charges. The businesses that install these machines split the "convenience fee" you pay with the machine owners, making a tidy profit for themselves along the way. Because they are money-makers, some businesses don't use point-of-sale terminals, instead forcing you to withdraw cash from one of these privately owned ATMs hidden away in a corner to pay for your purchase.

Charging ahead with credit cards

Credit cards can be invaluable when traveling: They're a safe way to carry money and they provide a convenient record of all your travel expenses when you arrive home. Of course, the disadvantage is that they're easy to overuse. Credit cards let you indulge in a lot more impulse buying than any other form of payment — taking you as far as your credit limit, which may not bear much relation to your actual financial resources.

You can also get cash advances from your credit card at any ATM if you know your *Personal Identification Number* (PIN). If you've forgotten it or didn't even know you had a PIN, call the phone number on the back of your credit card and ask the bank to send the number to you (you receive the number in about five to seven business days). Some banks can give you your PIN over the phone if you tell them your mother's maiden name or provide some other security clearance.

Use your credit card for a cash advance in emergencies only. Interest rates for cash advances are often significantly higher than rates for credit card purchases. More importantly, you start paying interest on the advance from the moment you receive the cash. On airline-affiliated credit cards, a cash advance doesn't earn frequent-flier miles.

Keep in mind that when you use your credit card abroad, most banks assess a 2 percent fee above the 1 percent fee charged by Visa or MasterCard or American Express for currency conversion on credit charges. But credit cards still may be the smart way to go when you factor in things like exorbitant ATM fees and higher traveler's check exchange rates (and service fees).

Some credit card companies recommend that you notify them of any impending trip abroad so that they don't become suspicious when the card is used numerous times in a foreign destination and block your charges. Even if you don't call your credit card company in advance, you can always call the card's toll-free emergency number if a charge is refused — a good reason to carry the phone number with you. But perhaps the most important lesson here is to carry more than one card with you on your trip; a card may not work for any number of reasons, so having a backup is the smart way to go.

Toting traveler's checks

Traveler's checks are something of an anachronism from the days when people wrote personal checks instead of going to an ATM. Because traveler's checks can be replaced if lost or stolen, they were a sound alternative to cash, and as long as vendors continue to accept them, they are still a viable option to cash or banking cards. Service charges are fairly low, or even nonexistent if you know where to go.

The best way to ensure a fair rate of exchange is to purchase your traveler's checks in Canadian dollars. You can get Canadian-currency traveler's checks at most major banks and organizations such as AAA. **American Express** offers denominations of $20, $50, $100, $500, and (for cardholders only) $1,000. You pay a service charge ranging from 1 percent to 4 percent. You can also get American Express traveler's checks over the phone by calling ☎ 800-221-7282; Amex gold and platinum cardholders who use this number are exempt from the 1 percent fee. **Visa** offers traveler's checks at Citibank locations throughout the United States, as well as at several other banks. The service charge ranges between 1.5 percent and 2 percent; checks come in denominations of $20, $50, $100, $500, and $1,000. Call ☎ 800-732-1322 for information. AAA members can obtain Visa checks without a fee at most AAA offices or by calling ☎ 866-339-3378. **MasterCard** also offers traveler's checks. Call ☎ 800-223-9920 for a location near you.

If you choose to carry traveler's checks, be sure to keep a record of their serial numbers separate from your checks in the event that they are stolen or lost. You get a refund faster if you know the numbers.

Taking Taxes into Account

Two taxes are added onto almost every purchase and transaction made in the Maritimes. (Notable exceptions include liquor and gas purchases, which have taxes built into the posted price.) These taxes are collected in different ways. Each province applies a **Provincial Sales Tax** on top of the Canada-wide 5 percent **Goods and Services (GST) Tax.** In Prince

Edward Island, the provincial tax is 10 percent, for a grand total of 15 percent. In Nova Scotia and New Brunswick, the provincial tax is 8 percent and is blended with the GST to create what is known as a **Harmonized Sales Tax** (HST) of 13 percent. So, since most prices you see quoted do not include tax, you must factor in an extra 13 percent to 15 percent, depending on the province, to come up with a final price.

The Halifax Regional Municipality collects a 2 percent **Halifax Marketing Levy,** which will be added to your Halifax hotel bill.

Dealing with Loss or Theft

While on vacation, there are few events more stressful than losing your wallet. Though you can rarely prevent this from happening, knowing what to do if it does occur can save you a lot of headaches.

Coping with lost credit cards

Most credit card companies have an emergency toll-free number to call if your card is lost or stolen. They may be able to wire you a cash advance immediately or deliver an emergency credit card in a day or two. Make sure you have the numbers with you (but not in your wallet!) so that, if a theft occurs, you can deal with the situation immediately. Check the following Canadian toll-free emergency numbers and note those that apply to you:

- ✔ **American Express** ☎ **800-668-2639**
- ✔ **Diners Club** ☎ **800-363-3333**
- ✔ **Discover** ☎ **800-347-2683**
- ✔ **MasterCard** ☎ **800-307-7309**
- ✔ **Visa** ☎ **800-847-2911**

Be sure to contact all of your credit card companies the minute you discover your wallet has been lost or stolen. Also file a report at the nearest police precinct. Your credit card company or insurer may require a police report number or record of the loss.

If you need emergency cash over the weekend when all banks and American Express offices are closed, you can have money wired to you via **Western Union** (☎ **800-325-6000;** www.westernunion.ca). Agents are scattered across all three Maritime provinces; check the Web site for locations.

Losing your identity

Identity theft and fraud are potential complications of losing your wallet, especially if your driver's license is lost along with your cash and credit cards. Notify the major credit-reporting bureaus immediately; placing a fraud alert on your records may protect you against liability for criminal activity. **Equifax** has offices around the world, including Canada (☎ 800-465-7166; www.Equifax.ca) and the United States (☎ 800-685-1111; www.equifax.com). **Experian** (☎ 888-397-3742; www.experiangroup.com) and **TransUnion** (☎ 888-322-8228; www.transunion.com) are two other U.S. agencies. Finally, if you lose all forms of photo ID call your airline and explain the situation; they may allow you to board the plane if you have a copy of your passport or birth certificate and a copy of the police report you filed.

Chapter 6

Getting to the Maritimes

● ●

In This Chapter

▶ Flying in for less
▶ Traveling by land or by sea
▶ Deciding on a escorted or package tour

● ●

*T*he first steps in vacation planning can be tough. You have to make a lot of commitments early on — and often back them up with your hard-earned money. You probably have questions: Do you want to be totally independent, either because you're a control freak and can't stand even a single detail being out of your hands, or because you're into spontaneity and hate to have things prearranged? Would a self-guided or group tour suit your needs? Which tour company can provide the vacation you're dreaming of? Whatever your goals, this chapter helps you break them down and choose what you really want to do.

If you do decide on a tour, how do you find a deal? I suggest some strategies in the next sections, but every embarkation point and destination province is different, and the tour operators I mention may not offer deals convenient to your city. If that's the case, check with a local travel agent, who likely has a thorough knowledge of your options and how best to bundle packages, such as escorted tours and airline fares.

Flying to the Maritimes

The two major Canadian airlines and several U.S. carriers serve Halifax, the main air hub for the Maritimes. You can also fly into Saint John, Fredericton, Moncton, or Charlottetown. With plenty of competition, prices are usually reasonable and sometimes very good.

Halifax International Airport (www.hiaa.ca), the busiest airport in the Maritimes, handles three million passengers annually in two modern terminals. Direct flights by major Canadian and U.S. airlines (Table 6.1 lists them all) serve this airport from around 30 locations. The Web site www.flyhalifax.com is an excellent resource that allows you to search for flights to Halifax from specific destinations and also check flight arrival and departure times.

Table 6-1	Airlines Serving the Maritimes	
Carrier	*Phone*	*Web Site*
Air Canada	☎ 888-247-2262	www.aircanada.com
Continental	☎ 800-231-0856	www.continental.com
Delta	☎ 800-221-1212	www.delta.com
Northwest	☎ 800-225-2525	www.nwa.com
WestJet	☎ 800-538-5696	www.westjet.com

The other major airports are **Greater Moncton International Airport** (www.gmia.ca), served by Air Canada, and WestJet; **Saint John Airport** (www.saintjohnairport.com), served by Air Canada and WestJet; **Greater Fredericton Airport** (www.frederictonairport.ca), served by Air Canada and Delta; and **Charlottetown Airport** (www.flypei.com), served by Air Canada, WestJet, and Delta.

If you're Maritimes-bound from Europe, your flight will be routed through Toronto or Montreal. Flights originating in Asia and the South Pacific require a plane-change in Vancouver or Toronto.

Now that you know a little about who flies into the Maritimes, start searching out the best fares. Read the advice below, and then do some comparison shopping.

Getting the best deal on your airfare

Competition among major airlines is unlike that of any other industry. Every airline offers virtually the same product (basically, a coach seat is a coach seat is a . . .), yet prices can vary by hundreds of dollars.

 Business travelers who need the flexibility of last-minute changes, or those who want to get home before the weekend, pay (or at least their companies pay) the premium rate, known as the *full fare*. But if you can book your ticket far in advance, stay over a Saturday night, and are willing to travel with restrictions such as non-changeable flights, you can save big bucks.

Air Canada is taking a leading role in streamlining their fare system. They offer four ticket options for North American flights, ranging from a nonrefundable, non-changeable Tango ticket to a flexible Latitude ticket. At the time of publication, a Tango one-way fare from Boston to Halifax was US$154, while the full-fare Latitude option was US$560 for the same flight. The difference shows that you can save a lot by accepting a few restrictions. Go to www.aircanada.com to see more details and tools that allow you to see easily which days have the least expensive flights.

The airlines periodically hold sales, in which they lower the prices on their most popular routes. These fares have advance purchase requirements and date-of-travel restrictions, but you can't beat the prices. As you plan your vacation, keep your eyes open for these sales, which tend to take place in seasons of low travel volume, November to March. You almost never see a sale around the peak summer vacation months of July and August, or around Thanksgiving or Christmas, when many people fly regardless of the fare they have to pay.

Booking your flight online

If you are simply buying a flight from one point to another, you can't beat online prices. Searching out the best online airfares can be more time-consuming than using a travel agent, but it gives you more flexibility and you won't be stuck with any additional charges. Most sites prompt you to enter a departure point and destination along with your dates of travel, so if you're not sure of the specifics of your trip, you can play with the variables until you find the best price. The displayed results usually include a number of flight and fare options.

Most airlines offer online-only fares that even their phone agents know nothing about. So if you're flexible and ready to keep up with your online research, you can get an excellent deal.

Travel Web sites

The "big three" online travel agencies are **Expedia** (www.expedia.com), **Travelocity** (www.travelocity.com), and **Orbitz** (www.orbitz.com). For travelers already in Canada, try www.expedia.ca or www.travelocity.ca; U.K. residents can go for www.expedia.co.uk. Each has different business deals with the airlines and may offer different fares on the same flights, so shopping around is wise.

You have many other options besides the major online travel agencies. To sniff out great deals on airfare, check out **Cheapflights** (www.cheapflights.com), **SmarterTravel** (www.smartertravel.com), and **Priceline** (www.priceline.com), and **Opodo** (www.opodo.co.uk) if you're traveling from the U.K. Also U.K.-based is **Travelsupermarket** (www.travelsupermarket.com), a flight search engine that offers flight comparisons for the budget airlines whose seats often end up in bucket-shop sales (I explain bucket-shop sales later in this chapter).

Consider using *meta-search* sites (which find and then direct you to airline and hotel Web sites for booking) for a cheap ticket. They include **Sidestep** (www.sidestep.com) and **Kayak.com.** Sidestep receives good reviews from users. It's a browser add-on that claims to "search 140 sites at once," although in reality it only beats competitors' fares as often as other sites do. Kayak includes fares for budget carriers like JetBlue and Spirit, as well as the major airlines.

If you're in no rush to book your vacation, you can sign up for sale alerts at some of the major travel Web sites. Two of the big three, Expedia and Travelocity, will send you an e-mail notification when a cheap fare to your favorite destination becomes available.

Opaque fare services

If you're willing to give up some control over your flight details, use an *opaque fare service* such as **Priceline** (www.priceline.com) or **Hotwire** (www.hotwire.com). Both offer rock-bottom prices in exchange for travel on an airline that will remain unknown to you until you purchase your ticket. Be assured that the "mystery airlines" are all major, well-known carriers, and the possibility of traveling from Detroit to Halifax via Vancouver is remote. On the other hand, your chances of getting a 6 a.m. or 11 p.m. flight are pretty high. Hotwire tells you flight prices before you buy; Priceline usually has better deals than Hotwire, but you have to play their "name our price" game.

Last-minute specials

 Great last-minute deals are available through free weekly e-mail services provided directly by the airlines, including **Air Canada** (www.aircanada.ca). Usually, these deals are announced on a Tuesday or Wednesday, and must be purchased online. Most are only valid for travel that weekend, but some can be booked weeks or months in advance. Sign up for weekly e-mail alerts at airline Web sites, or check mega-sites that compile comprehensive lists of last-minute specials, such as **Smarter Travel** (www.smartertravel.com) and **Webflyer** (www.webflyer.com). Also, **LastMinute** (www.lastminute.com) is a great source for last-minute flights and getaways.

 Watch local newspapers for **promotional specials** or **fare wars**, when airlines lower prices on their most popular routes. Also keep an eye on price fluctuations and deals at Web sites such as **Airfarewatchdog** (www.airfarewatchdog.com) and **Farecast** (www.farecast.com).

Consolidators

Also known as **bucket shops, consolidators** are wholesale brokers in the airline ticket game. Consolidators buy deeply discounted tickets ("distressed" inventories of unsold seats) from airlines and sell them to online ticket agencies, travel agents, tour operators, corporations, and, to a lesser degree, the general public.

Several reliable consolidators have worldwide locations and are available on the Internet. In the United States, **STA Travel** (☎ 800-781-4040; www.statravel.com) is a world leader in student travel. The Canadian equivalent is **Travel Cuts** (☎ 866-246-9762; www.travelcuts.com). In both cases, you don't need to be a student to take advantage of their good fares. **Flight Centre** is a large consolidator with offices around the world and competitive online fares. (In the U.S., contact them at ☎ 866-967-5351, www.flightcentre.us; in Canada ☎ 877-467-5302, www.flightcentre.ca; and the United Kingdom ☎ 0870-499-0040; www.flightcentre.co.uk.) London-based **Trailfinders** (☎ 0845-058-5858; www.trailfinders.com) always has competitive fares to North America, along with easy-to-understand rental car and hotel packages. They also produce an informative travel magazine, or you can sign up for their e-mail service.

 On the downside, bucket shop tickets are often rigged with restrictions, such as stiff cancellation penalties (as high as 50 percent to 75 percent of the ticket price). And keep in mind that the availability of most of what you see advertised is limited.

Using frequent flier miles

A **frequent flier membership** doesn't cost a cent, but it can entitle you to better seats, faster response to phone inquiries, and prompter service if your luggage is stolen or your flight is canceled or delayed, or if you want to change your seat. And you don't have to fly to earn points; **frequent flier credit cards** can earn you thousands of miles for doing your everyday shopping. With more than 70 mileage awards programs on the market, consumers have never had more options. Investigate the program details of your favorite airlines before you sink points into any one. Consider which airlines have hubs in the airport nearest you, and, of those carriers, which have the most advantageous alliances, given your most common routes. To play the frequent flier game to your best advantage, consult the community bulletin boards on **FlyerTalk** (www.flyertalk.com) or go to Randy Petersen's **Inside Flyer** (www.insideflyer.com). Petersen and friends review all the programs in detail and post regular updates on changes in policies and trends.

Driving to the Maritimes

You can drive to the Maritimes via numerous highways, all of which enter the region through New Brunswick.

- ✔ **Trans-Canada Highway,** which takes on different numbers as it crosses the country, enters New Brunswick near Edmundston as Highway 2. Using this route, it's 1,238km (769 miles) from Montreal to Halifax and 1,757km (1,092 miles) from Toronto to Halifax. Planning on driving across Canada via the Trans-Canada Highway? Gas up. It's 6,187km (3,846 miles) from Vancouver to Halifax.

- ✔ **Interstate 95** links Portland and Bangor, Maine, with the Maritimes, crossing the Canadian border west of Fredericton at the Houlton/Woodstock crossing.

✔ **Highway 1** winds its way along the Maine coastline to the Calais/St. Stephen border, crossing in the southern corner of New Brunswick. From this point, it's 90km (56 miles) to Saint John, and a little farther to Fredericton.

✔ **Highway 189** branches off Maine's Highway 177km (48 miles) south of Calais. It makes for an interesting approach to New Brunswick. At Lubec, it crosses a bridge to Campobello Island, across the border in New Brunswick. From this point, take a short ferry ride to Deer Island, and then another to reach the mainland. Both ferries are summer-only.

Arriving by Other Means

Though flying is the primary means of getting to the Maritimes, some people enjoy a road trip, or have mobility issues that make flying impossible, or simply prefer not to fly. Here's the lowdown on traveling to the Maritimes by train, bus, and ferry.

Taking the train

VIA Rail (☎ 888-842-7245 or 416-366-8411; www.viarail.ca) operates the *Ocean* between Montreal and Halifax up to six times weekly, with stops in Moncton and Truro en route. The two classes of travel are Comfort (lots of leg room, reclining seats, reading lights, pillows and blankets, and a Skyline Car complete with bar service) and Easterly (daytime seating, nighttime sleeping room, a domed lounge, and a dining car for passengers in this class). A discounted Comfort Class one-way fare between Montreal and Halifax is C$131, while the full fare in Easterly Class is C$485. Discounts of up to 35 percent apply to bookings made more than seven days in advance. Children, seniors, and students also enjoy discounted travel.

If you're planning extensive rail travel in Canada, VIA Rail's **Canrailpass** may be a worthwhile investment. It allows for unlimited rail travel across Canada for 12 days over any given 30-day period for C$837 in high season (June to mid-Oct) and C$523 the rest of the year.

 While the Canrailpass can be a good deal if you plan to do a lot of rail traveling, it comes with a few hitches: If you travel on the Montreal-to-Halifax service, for example, it counts as two days of travel. So check to see that the routes you plan to take don't make this pass a not-so-smart investment.

Bussing it in

Greyhound (☎ 800-231-2222; www.greyhound.com) operates passenger buses throughout North America with only a couple of exceptions, and one of these is the Maritimes. The good news for bus travelers is that connections from Greyhound to the local carrier Acadian (see Chapter 7) are seamless at gateway cities that include Montreal, Toronto, and Bangor (Maine). You can also catch a Greyhound bus to the Maine cities of Portland or Bar Harbor, then jump aboard a ferry to Yarmouth (see the following section), and then rely on Acadian buses to get you around Nova Scotia and beyond.

 Acadian honors all Greyhound passes. Therefore, if you have a 7-day Canada Discovery Pass (C$329) or a 15-day North America Discovery Pass (US$415), no additional costs will apply to your travels within the three Maritimes provinces. Check the Greyhound Web site for pass options.

Arriving by ferry

A glance at a map makes it obvious that catching a ferry from Maine to Yarmouth, on the southwestern tip of Nova Scotia, shortens the journey considerably. **The CAT** (☎ **888-249-7245** or 902-742-6800; www.cat ferry.com) operates along two routes: from Bar Harbor to Yarmouth and from Portland to Yarmouth. Between mid-May and mid-October, ferries run once daily from either Portland or Bar Harbor. It's North America's fastest car ferry, making the journey from Bar Harbor to Yarmouth in under three hours (a traditional ferry takes twice as long). Fares from Bar Harbor are US$63 adults, US$58 seniors, US$43 children 5 to 17, US$125 for vehicles up to 7m (20 feet) long. The slightly higher cost from Portland is US$89 adults, US$85 seniors, US$59 children 5 to 17, US$149 for vehicles. Discounts apply in the shoulder season. Because this service is convenient, vessels fill fast in summer. Therefore, reservations are strongly recommended.

Joining an Escorted Tour

Say the words "escorted tour" and you may automatically feel as though you're being forced to choose between your money and your lifestyle. Think again. Times — and tours — have changed.

An **escorted tour** does, obviously, involve an escort, but that doesn't mean it's constricting. Escorted tours range from cushy bus trips, where you sit back and let the driver worry about the traffic, to adventures that include biking around Prince Edward Island or sea kayaking on Cape Breton Island — situations where most of us can use a bit of guidance. The main point is you travel with a group, which may be just the thing if you're single and want company. In general, your costs are taken care of after you arrive at your destination, but you have to cover your airfare to get there.

Many people love escorted tours. The tour company takes care of all the details and tells you what to expect at each leg of your journey. You know your costs upfront and, in the case of the tame tours, you don't get many surprises. Escorted tours can take you to the maximum number of sights in the minimum amount of time with the least amount of hassle.

 If you decide to go with an escorted tour, I strongly recommend purchasing travel insurance, especially if the tour operator asks you to pay upfront. But don't buy insurance from the tour operator! If the operator doesn't fulfill its obligation to provide you with the vacation you paid for, you have no reason to think that it will fulfill its insurance obligations either. Get travel insurance through an independent agency. (I tell you more about the ins and outs of travel insurance in Chapter 10.)

When considering an escorted tour, find out if you have to put down a deposit, and ask when final payment is due. In addition, ask a few simple questions before you buy:

- ✔ **What is the cancellation policy?** Can the operator cancel the trip if not enough people make reservations? How late can you cancel if you're unable to go? Do you get a refund if you cancel? If they cancel?

- ✔ **How jampacked is the schedule?** Does the tour schedule try to fit 25 hours into a 24-hour day, or does it give you ample time to shop or relax by the pool? If starting your day at 7 a.m. to pack in 10 to 12 hours of nonstop sightseeing sounds like a grind, certain tours may not be for you.

- ✔ **How large is the group?** The larger the group, the more time you spend waiting for people to get on and off the bus. Tour operators may be evasive about this, because they may not know the exact size of the group until everybody has made reservations, but ask them to give you a rough estimate.

- ✔ **What is the minimum group size?** Some tours have a minimum size, and may cancel if they don't book enough people. If a quota exists, find out what it is and how close the tour operator is to reaching it. Again, operators may be evasive in their answers, but the information can help you select a tour that's sure to happen.

- ✔ **What exactly is included?** Don't assume anything. You may have to pay to get yourself to and from the airport. A box lunch may be included in an excursion, but drinks can be extra. Beer may be included, but not wine.

- ✔ **How much flexibility do you have?** Can you opt out of certain activities, or does the bus leave once a day, with no exceptions? Are all your meals planned in advance? Can you choose your entree at dinner, or does everybody get the same chicken cutlet?

Picking the right escorted tour is a very personal choice. I don't pretend to know what you like, but here are a few reputable companies (in alphabetical order) to get you started:

✔ **Ambassatours** (☎ **800-565-7173** or 902-423-6242; www. ambassatours.com) is the Atlantic Canada arm of the Grayline conglomerate. Typical offerings include a three-day Cape Breton Island tour for C$880 and the Atlantic Maritimes tour that hits the hot spots in each of the three provinces over eight days for C$2,400.

✔ **Backroads** (☎ **800-462-2848** or 510-527-1555; www.backroads.com) offers a six-day bike tour of Prince Edward Island for US$2,698. The biking is easy, and upscale accommodations and all meals are included.

✔ **Collette Vacations** (☎ **800-340-5158;** www.collettevacations.com) offers many tours that include the Maritimes. The ten-day Canada's Atlantic Coast tour hits all three provinces as well as Maine for US$1,749 per person.

✔ **Horizon & Co.** (☎ **800-387-2977** or 416-585-9911; www.horizon-co.com) is a Canadian tour company with an excellent reputation. Expect to pay around C$4,495 for a ten-day, all-inclusive Maritimes cruise that begins in New York.

You can also check ads in the travel section of your local Sunday newspaper or in the back of national travel magazines such as *Travel + Leisure*, *Outside*, *National Geographic Traveler*, and *Condé Nast Traveler*.

Choosing a Package Tour

Unlike escorted tours, **package tours** are simply a way to buy the airfare, accommodations, and other elements of your trip at the same time and often at a discounted price. Some companies bundle every aspect of your trip, including tours to various sights, but most deal just with selected aspects. This allows you to get a good deal by putting together an airfare and hotel arrangement, say, or a lodging and greens-fee package. Most packages tend to leave you a lot of leeway, while saving you money.

For the Maritimes, package tours can be a smart way to go. In many cases, a package tour that includes airfare, hotel, and transportation to and from the airport costs less than the price of a hotel alone that you book yourself. That's because packages are sold in bulk to tour operators, who resell them to the public. It's kind of like purchasing your vacation at a bulk store — except the tour operator is the one who buys the 1,000-count box of garbage bags and resells them ten at a time at a cost that undercuts the local supermarket.

Package tours can vary as much as those garbage bags, too. In a comparison of any two tours, one may offer a better class of hotels for the same price, or provide the same hotels for a lower price. Some book seats on scheduled airline flights; others sell charters. In some packages, your choice of accommodations and travel days may be limited. Some let you choose between escorted vacations and independent vacations; others allow you to add on just a few excursions or escorted day trips (also at discounted prices) without booking an entirely escorted tour.

Here are some recommendations (in alphabetical order) for companies offering package tours:

- **Air Canada** (☎ 888-247-2262; www.aircanada.ca), Canada's national airline, offers packages that can be booked through travel agents as well as an online search tool for air-car rental combos.

- **Liberty Travel** (☎ 888-271-1584; www.libertytravel.com) is one of the biggest packagers in the U.S. Northeast. It offers separate package tours to each of the three Maritime provinces.

- **Rodd Hotels & Resorts** (☎ 800-565-7633 or 902-892-7448; www.roddvacations.com) is an upscale Maritimes hotel chain with golf and "leisure" packages that usually include breakfast and passes to local attractions.

- **VIA Rail** (☎ 888-842-7245 or 514-871-6000; www.viarail.ca) and Canadian tour operators combine forces to offer some interesting packages that originate in Toronto and Montreal. Go to www.trainpackages.ca or click on the "Travel Planner" link on the Via Web site for details.

- **WestJet** (☎ 877-737-7001; www.westjetvacations.com) offers its own flights bundled with car rental-hotel packages throughout the Maritimes.

Several big online travel agencies — **Expedia, Travelocity, Orbitz,** and **Site59** — also do a brisk business in packages.

Chapter 7

Getting Around the Maritimes

. . . .

In This Chapter

▶ Exploring the Maritimes by car

▶ Taking the ferry

▶ Flying or riding the rails between provinces

. . . .

So, you know how you're getting *to* the Maritimes: Now you need to know how to get around. This chapter covers driving (really the only way to explore beyond the downtown core of the major cities) as well as two important ferry routes. If you're willing to shell out big bucks, flying between provinces is an option, as is catching the train, although the latter is limited in its options.

Driving Around

Unless you're on an escorted tour, driving is the best way to get around the Maritimes. All you need is a vehicle, a good set of maps, a full tank of gas, and a sense of adventure.

Motoring in the Maritimes is similar to that in other parts of Canada or in the United States. Major thoroughfares are kept in excellent condition, and all towns and minor highways are well marked. Gas stations are regularly spaced — one in almost every town — so running out of gas isn't a problem if you keep an eye on the gauge. Expect to pay around C$1.10 to C$1.30 per liter (US$4.40–US$5.20 per gallon) for gas, though prices can fluctuate quite dramatically.

Apart from other drivers, the most important thing to watch for on the roads is wildlife, most commonly deer, moose, and bears, especially if you're driving at dawn or dusk. Areas with lots of animal activity are usually signposted, but always scan both sides of the road just to make sure. In winter, blowing snow and blizzards can make driving extremely dangerous.

Wearing a seat belt is compulsory in Canada, and the fine for not wearing one is steep. Most drivers voluntarily travel with their headlights on at all times; motorcyclists are required by law to ride with their lights on. Traffic in both directions must stop when school buses have their red lights flashing. Pedestrians have the right of way at crosswalks.

Renting a car

The good news is that every major car rental company is represented in the Maritimes, so you can easily shop around for the best deal. The bad news is that demand is high during the peak summer months (mid-June to early Sept), so prices can be high. Rental car companies and their contact numbers and Web sites are listed in the Appendix.

Getting the best deal

Car rental rates vary even more than airline fares. The price depends on the size of the vehicle, the length of time you keep it, where and when you pick it up and drop it off, where you take it, and a host of other factors. The following tips can help save you hundreds of dollars:

- ✔ Check your rental car company's weekend rates — they may be lower than the weekday rates. If you're keeping the car for five or more days, a weekly rate may be cheaper than the daily rate.

- ✔ Ask about drop-off conditions: Some companies may add a drop-off charge if you don't return the car to the same rental location.

- ✔ Rent your vehicle from some place other than the airport. At Halifax International Airport, for example, a Concession Recovery Fee adds 11.73 percent to all airport rentals. To save this charge, rent a vehicle at one of dozens of downtown agencies.

- ✔ Find out whether age is an issue. Many car rental companies add on a fee for drivers under 25, while some don't rent to them at all.

- ✔ If you see an advertised price in your local newspaper, be sure to ask for that specific rate; otherwise, you may be charged the standard (higher) rate. Don't forget to mention membership in AAA, AARP, and trade unions. These memberships usually entitle you to discounts ranging from 5 percent to 30 percent.

- ✔ Check your frequent flier accounts. Airlines often team up with rental car companies to offer you incentives to use their services. Not only are your favorite (or at least most-used) airlines likely to have sent you discount coupons, but major car rental companies usually add at least 500 air miles to your account.

- ✔ As with other aspects of planning your trip, using the Internet can make comparison shopping for a car rental much easier. You can check rates at most of the major agencies' Web sites. Plus, all the major travel sites, such as **Travelocity** (www.travelocity.com), **Expedia** (www.expedia.com), **Orbitz** (www.orbitz.com), and

Smarter Travel (www.smartertravel.com), have search engines that can dig up discounted car rental rates. Just enter the car size you want, the pickup and return dates, and the location, and the server returns a price. You can even make the reservation through any of these sites.

Adding up the charges

In addition to the standard rental prices, other optional charges apply to most car rentals (along with some not-so-optional charges, such as taxes). The *Loss Damage Waiver* (LDW), which requires you to pay for damage to the car in a collision, is covered by many credit card companies. Check with your credit card company before you go, to see if you can avoid paying this hefty fee (as much as C$30 a day).

The car rental companies also offer additional *liability insurance* (if you harm others in an accident), *personal accident insurance* (if you harm yourself or your passengers), and *personal effects protection* (if your luggage is stolen from your car). Your insurance policy on your vehicle at home probably covers most of these unlikely occurrences. However, if your own insurance doesn't cover you for rentals or if you don't have auto insurance, definitely consider the additional coverage (ask your car rental agent for more information). Unless you're toting around the Hope diamond (and you wouldn't leave that in your trunk anyway), you can probably skip the personal effects insurance, but driving around without liability or personal accident coverage is never a good idea. Even if you're a good driver, other people may not be, and liability claims can be complicated.

 Most companies also offer *refueling packages*, in which you pay for your initial full tank of gas upfront and then return the car with an empty gas tank. The prices are usually competitive with local gas prices, but you don't get credit for any gas remaining in the tank. If you reject this option, you pay only for the gas you use, but you have to return the car with a full tank or face charges that are around 50 percent higher per liter than at the pump to make up for the shortfall. If you tend to run late and a fueling stop may make you miss your plane, you're a good candidate for the fuel-purchase option.

Ferrying Between Provinces

The three provinces are linked not only by road (or bridge, in the case of PEI) but also by ferry. This is a fun, affordable way to travel while cutting down on driving.

Nova Scotia to New Brunswick

The ferry across the Bay of Fundy between Digby, Nova Scotia, and Saint John, New Brunswick, can cut a considerable chunk from your driving mileage if your itinerary takes you either up the Maine coast (and you didn't use the ferry systems detailed in Chapter 6) or on a circuitous route through both Nova Scotia and New Brunswick.

The *Princess of Acadia* plies this route year-round, with up to three sailings daily, depending on the season. The trip takes three hours and is C$30 to C$40 for adults, C$25 to C$30 for seniors, C$20 to C$25 for children 5 to 17, and C$95 to C$100 for vehicles under 6.4m (21 feet). Fare variations reflect seasonal pricing (July to early Oct is high season). Contact **Bay Ferries** (☎ 888-249-7245 or 506-649-7777; www.bay ferries.com) for information and reservations.

Nova Scotia to Prince Edward Island

Although Prince Edward Island is linked to mainland New Brunswick by a bridge, the ferry link between Caribou (north of Pictou, Nova Scotia) and Wood Islands (on the southeastern corner of PEI) is also a viable way of crossing Northumberland Strait.

In July and August, the ferry offers eight sailings daily in each direction, with less frequent service in spring and fall. Drifting ice closes the service down completely between mid-December and April. Once the vessel gets going, the crossing takes little more than an hour. The round-trip fare is C$59 per vehicle including passengers. For walk-on passengers, the cost is C$14 for adults, C$12 for seniors; no charge for children under five. For information, contact **Northumberland Ferries** (☎ 902-566-3838; www.peiferry.com). No reservations are taken, so plan on catching a mid-week (except Fri afternoon) or early morning sailing to avoid a long wait.

 Getting to Prince Edward Island is free, regardless of whether you cross the Confederation Bridge or take the ferry. The bridge toll and ferry fare are only collected when you leave the island. The bridge toll (C$41 for all two-axle vehicles) is less expensive than traveling by ferry, so if you cross to the island aboard the ferry and return to the mainland via the bridge, you'll save a bit of money.

To Newfoundland

I didn't forget about Newfoundland when writing this book. But covering the three Maritime provinces as well as their northern neighbor in the amount of space available is simply impossible. (Collectively, the province of Newfoundland and Labrador and the Maritime provinces are known as Atlantic Canada.)

For those who plan on visiting Newfoundland, this section details ferry routes and rates from Nova Scotia.

Marine Atlantic (☎ 800-341-7981 or 902-794-5200; www.marine-atlantic.ca) operates the following ferries between North Sydney and the Newfoundland docks (reservations are required for all sailings):

✔ **Port aux Basques,** located at the southwestern tip of Newfoundland. This ferry ride takes between five and seven hours, with departures twice daily year-round. Costs are (one-way) C$28 for adults, C$25 for seniors, and C$14 for children 5 to 12. Vehicles up to 20 feet in length cost C$78, and accommodations range from a dorm bed for C$16 to C$99 for a four-berth cabin.

✔ **Argentia**, situated a couple of hours' drive from the capital, St. John's (not to be confused with Saint John, New Brunswick). This route is much longer and more of an adventure, taking around 16 hours and crossing sometimes-rough open ocean. Ferries depart twice a week between mid-June and mid-October. Sample one-way fares are: C$77 adults, C$70 seniors, C$39 children 5 to 12, C$18 reclining chair, C$28 dorm bed, C$138 four-berth cabin, and C$161 for vehicles up to 20 feet in length.

Before leaving home, request an information package from **Newfoundland and Labrador Tourism** (☎ 800-563-6353 or 709-729-2830; www.newfoundlandlabrador.com). The recommended guidebook is *Frommer's Newfoundland and Labrador.*

Getting Around by Other Means

If you aren't on an escorted tour and don't want to drive, your options for travel in the Maritimes are limited to flying between provinces, catching the train along one of two main routes, or taking the bus.

Traveling by plane

Air Canada (☎ 888-247-2262; www.aircanada.ca) flies daily between Halifax, Moncton, Fredericton, Saint John, Charlottetown, and Sydney. At each of these airports, you find transportation to downtown, car rental desks, and an information booth or a bank of phones linked to a directory of local accommodations.

Taking the train

VIA Rail (☎ 888-842-7245 or 514-871-6000; www.viarail.ca) service between Montreal and Halifax stops in Truro, Moncton, Miramichi, and Bathurst, making it a viable intraprovincial transportation option. From the railway station in Moncton, bus connections can be made to Charlottetown, Saint John, and Fredericton. Fares are reasonable, especially if purchased seven or more days in advance.

Catching the bus

As I say in the previous chapter, Greyhound services come close to the Maritimes, but terminate at surrounding cities such as Bangor (Maine), Toronto, and Montreal. From downtown depots in these three places, **Acadian** (☎ **800-567-5151** or 902-454-9321; www.acadianbus.com) provides connecting services to major Maritimes centers and hundreds of towns and villages in between. Acadian services cross the Confederation Bridge to Charlottetown, but beyond the capital there is no public transportation on Prince Edward Island.

Chapter 8

Booking Your Accommodations

- -

In This Chapter

▶ Choosing the best overnight option

▶ Wheeling and dealing for a good night's sleep

- -

*F*inding accommodations that meet the basic criteria of being clean and comfortable is easy — the Maritimes has all the chain hotels and motels you already know. But unless you're traveling there to have the same experience you can have anywhere else, consider my recommended lodgings in Chapters 11 to 21. The chains are sure to lack Maritimes charm, which is why I recommend them only when you have no other options.

Finding the Place That's Right for You

People have different ideas about the type of places they want to stay at, so no lodging I recommend in this book will appeal to everyone. I include a wide cross section of options to suit all tastes and budgets — not hard to do, as the Maritimes has everything from big-city luxury hotels to rustic wilderness cabins. And compared to other North American destinations, hotel rooms in the Maritimes are reasonably priced.

 Remember to add taxes to all quoted prices — the 13 percent Harmonized Sales Tax in Nova Scotia and New Brunswick and 15 percent worth of taxes on Prince Edward Island. Halifax accommodations also collect a 2 percent **Halifax Marketing Levy**.

Hotels and motels

You can find a plethora of luxury hotels in the major cities. Most international chains are represented in each province, along with **Fairmont Hotels and Resorts** (www.fairmont.com) and **Delta Hotels** (www.delta hotels.com), both upscale Canadian chains with impeccable credentials. These hotels have rack rates in the top $$$$ (over C$225) category, but generally offer discounts on weekends or for online bookings.

Reliable mid-priced chains like **Holiday Inn** (www.ichotelsgroup.com) and **Best Western** (www.bestwestern.com) are also plentiful. The Maritimes' own **Rodd Hotels & Resorts** (www.rodd-hotels.ca) is in this same $$-to-$$$ price bracket. On the edge of the cities and in smaller towns, you can find hotels in the middle of the $$ category. Their rooms usually come with fewer amenities and the furnishings may be older.

If you just need somewhere to spend the night or you can't get a room at one of my recommended lodgings, a roadside motel will do. Access to the room is normally from the parking lot. In general, motels don't have attached dining rooms. They are common throughout the Maritimes, other than in Prince Edward Island. Always in the $ or $$ range but rarely over C$100, they're listed in provincial tourism guides, or their brochures are displayed in local information centers.

Bed-and-breakfasts

Some travelers plan their vacations around bed-and-breakfasts; others avoid them like the plague. If you fall into the first category, you have plenty of scope in the Maritimes. Literally hundreds of homes in each of the three provinces have been converted to bed-and-breakfast accommodations, with a wide range of services and prices to match (anywhere from C$50 to over C$200 double). By doing some research and asking the right questions, you can easily avoid unpleasant surprises. If you follow my recommendations, you won't have to worry about ending up in a room left vacant by the owner's college-bound kid. My picks are all proper businesses with more than two guest rooms, not individuals looking to rent an extra room to make some quick cash.

Bed-and-breakfasts are a great place to meet fellow travelers, learn more about the area from knowledgeable hosts, and enjoy a hearty breakfast before hitting the road. A perceived lack of privacy puts most people off this type of accommodations. Most North American travelers don't relish the idea of sharing a bathroom with other guests — which isn't the case at all bed-and-breakfasts. Here are the accepted definitions (I use them throughout this book), but always double-check when reserving your room so you know exactly what you're getting:

- ✔ **En suite bathroom:** A bathroom that is accessed directly from the guest room, and only used by the guests in that room.

- ✔ **Private bathroom:** A bathroom that is for the sole use of one room, but may be down a hallway.

- ✔ **Shared bathroom:** A bathroom that is used by guests in more than one room.

 If you're traveling with children or have a disability, be sure to make the proprietor aware of your situation before making a reservation. Other guests may not appreciate children (since they may be vacationing from their own kids!). Many bed-and-breakfasts are converted residences, so wheelchair access is often limited.

Cottages, cabins, and chalets

This type of accommodations is perfect for families or those who don't need the luxuries of resort living.

The words "cabin" and "cottage" are mostly interchangeable, but "cottage" sounds somehow more inviting (sort of like using "home" rather than "house"). Either way, you can expect a free-standing unit with a bathroom and linen provided. Some may have extras like a kitchen or a private veranda. Generally, a chalet is a larger unit with more amenities and some attention to décor.

Many cabin resorts predate World War II and became increasingly popular as families began to vacation together in the coastal resort towns. These old cabins, loaded with character, remain; some have been combined with newer and bigger units to suit a wider range of budgets and needs, and feature facilities that may include a restaurant or canoe rentals. For this reason, pricing runs the full spectrum. A good example is **Glenghorm Beach Resort** on Cape Breton Island (www.capebreton resorts.com), where the most basic cabins are at the bottom end of the $$ price range while luxurious chalets cost well into the top $$$$ category at C$399.

Expect older, more basic cabins to be in the $ category (under C$75). The addition of cooking facilities doesn't usually affect the price that much, with many self-contained cabins costing around C$100. By the time you reach the $$$ category, you're getting a modern, self-contained cabin with a separate bedroom.

Cabins and cottages are priced seasonally throughout the Maritimes, with peak season in July and August. Many close completely after September and reopen in April or May.

Resorts

While most hotels and motels are set up for overnight stays, resorts are designed to keep you happy for an entire vacation. The Maritimes' top resorts do this well, with golf courses, activity programs, spa services, and a choice of dining rooms. Resorts are generally kid-friendly, with children's programs and menus as well as babysitting services.

Of course, you pay for all this pampering. Rack rates at most resorts are in the $$$-to-$$$$ range, with decent savings for booking a package that may include meals or greens fees. Resorts are the first to offer discounts outside of summer, so look for bargains in June and September, when the property is still functioning fully. My resort recommendations are spread liberally throughout this book, but the Web sites for **Rodd Hotels and Resorts** (www.rodd-hotels.ca), **Cape Breton Resorts** (www.cape bretonresorts.com), and **Signature Resorts** (www.signatureresorts. com) are a good place to decide if this type of accommodations seems suited to your needs.

Finding the Best Room Rate

The **rack rate** is the maximum rate a hotel charges for a room. It's the rate you get if you walk in off the street and ask for a room for the night. You sometimes see these rates printed on the fire/emergency exit diagrams posted on the back of your door.

Hotels are happy to charge you the rack rate, but you can almost always do better. Perhaps the best way to avoid paying the rack rate is surprisingly simple: Just ask for a cheaper or discounted rate. You may be pleasantly surprised.

In all but the smallest accommodations, the rate you pay for a room depends on many factors — chief among them is how you make your reservation. A travel agent may be able to negotiate a better price with certain hotels than you can get by yourself. (The hotel often gives the agent a discount in exchange for steering his or her business toward that hotel.)

Shopping early for the greatest choice

If you're planning on traveling to the Maritimes in summer, start booking your lodging at the beginning of the year. Some chain hotels sell a percentage of rooms at a discounted rate, and when they're gone, they're gone — everyone else pays a higher rate. Booking early doesn't get you a discount at that quaint little bed-and-breakfast, but it ensures that you get the room you want, rather than, say, their smallest room with a bathroom down the hallway, which is always last to go.

Traveling off-peak

As shown as an example in Chapter 5, Lakeview Lodge & Cottages, in Cavendish on Prince Edward Island, rents self-contained cottages for C$127 in July and August. If you make your booking outside of this period — even for the first week of September — the rate drops to C$85. In June and September, the rate drops even further, to C$65, an almost 50% savings. The difference isn't always this abrupt — many accommodations discount a bit during "shoulder season" (June and Sept), then further discount rates the rest of the year (or close altogether).

Luxury hotels and big resorts often charge less than half their peak rates during the off season, which often puts them in competition with midrange chain hotels. Check the Web sites of the major chains as well as of Canadian companies such as **Delta Hotels** (www.deltahotels. com) and **Rodd Hotels and Resorts** (www.rodd-hotels.ca), who lead the way in this regard.

Refer to Chapter 3 for more information on what you can expect during different times of year in the Maritimes.

Asking for discounts

Hotels usually offer discounts for people with travel club or other memberships. In most cases, you can expect a 10 percent to 15 percent discount simply for flashing your AAA card. Going gray has its advantages too — Best Western offers an automatic 10 percent discount to all travelers over 55, with upgrades, late checkouts, and complimentary breakfasts thrown in for good measure. Most major hotel chains have loyalty programs, but usually you don't really need to be loyal to reap the benefits. Members of Holiday Inn's Priority Club and Fairmont's President Club, for example, enjoy daily papers, free local calls, late checkouts, and more, simply for signing up.

Guesthouses and bed-and-breakfasts are a little different. You can ask for a discount if you want to stay more than one night or pay with cash, but don't push it.

Surfing the Web for hotel deals

Shopping online for hotels is generally done one of two ways: You can book through the hotel's own Web site or through an independent booking agency (or a fare-service agency like Priceline). These Internet hotel agencies have multiplied in mind-boggling numbers of late, competing for the business of millions of consumers surfing for accommodations around the world. This competitiveness can be a boon to consumers who have the patience and time to shop and compare the online sites for good deals — but shop they must, because prices can vary considerably from site to site. And keep in mind that hotels at the top of a site's listing may be there for no reason other than that they paid money to get the placement.

Web sites of the chain hotels (see the Appendix) are the best place to search out discounted rates ("Web savers," advance bookings, and last-minute deals). Another way to pay less for your room is to have it bundled as a package with an activity like golfing or with passes to a local attraction. Refer to Chapter 6 for discussion on booking a package.

For smaller places, check out **BBCanada** (www.bbcanada.com) and **Innsite** (www.innsite.com), which list independent establishments you may not otherwise find on your own. Although you can't book online through these sites, you can follow the links to individual lodgings' Web sites and book directly with them.

Although the major travel booking sites, such as **Travelocity** (www.travelocity.com), **Expedia** (www.expedia.com), and **Orbitz** (www.orbitz.com), offer hotel bookings, you may be better off going directly to the source and booking online with the property itself. Also reliable are **Hotels.ca** (www.hotels.ca) and **Quikbook.com** (www.quikbook.com). An excellent free program, **TravelAxe** (www.travelaxe.com) can help you search multiple hotel sites at once — even ones you may never have heard of — and conveniently lists the total price of the room, including the taxes and service charges.

It happens: Travelers arrive at the hotel after making reservations through an online intermediary, and are told that they have no reservation. To be fair, many of the major sites are undergoing improvements in service and ease of use, and Expedia will soon be able to plug directly into the reservations systems of many hotel chains — none of which can be bad news for consumers. In the meantime, **get a confirmation number** and **make a printout** of any online booking transaction.

Getting the most for your money

Now you know how to wrangle a great price, but how about the quality of the room? When making your reservation, ask a couple of pointed questions to make sure you get the best room in the house. Here are some tips that can help, whatever lodging you choose:

✔ **Always ask for a corner room.** They're usually larger, quieter, and have more windows and light than standard rooms, and they don't always cost more.

✔ **Avoid renovations.** If the hotel is renovating, request a room away from the work. Of course, they probably won't offer up this information when you're making your reservation, so you have to ask.

✔ **Inquire about the location of the hotel's restaurants and bars.** This can go either way — fine if you want to be close to the action, but if sleep is what you're after, the hotel's hot nightspots are potential sources of annoying noise.

If you aren't happy with your room when you arrive, talk to the front desk. If they have another room, they're usually happy to accommodate you, within reason.

Chapter 9

Catering to Special Travel Needs

*I*f you have special needs or interests, this chapter makes your travel planning a little easier. So many resources are available now, especially online, that whatever your needs, you can find the information and the support you need to ensure that your trip is safe, stress-free, and most of all, fun!

Traveling with the Brood: Advice for Families

If you have enough trouble getting your kids out of the house in the morning, dragging them thousands of miles away may seem like an insurmountable challenge. But family travel can be immensely rewarding, giving you new ways of seeing the world through more youthful eyes.

Here are a few pre-trip planning tips for families:

▶ **Look for the Kid-Friendly icon.** I mark lodgings, restaurants, and attractions especially suited to children throughout the book.

▶ **Read books set in the Maritimes.** Books such as *Anne of Green Gables* are a great introduction to the Maritimes, and kids will love visiting Cavendish after reading about it (as do thousands of adults).

▶ **Surf the Internet.** Each of the three provincial tourism Web sites has a section devoted to family travel, including kid-friendly attractions or ideas for entire vacations.

Internet Web sites have good family-oriented vacation advice, like **Family Travel Forum** (www.familytravelforum.com), a comprehensive site that offers customized trip planning; **Family Travel Network** (www.familytravelnetwork.com), which offers travel features, message boards, deals, and tips; **Traveling Internationally with Your Kids** (www.travelwithyourkids.com), a comprehensive site that offers customized trip planning; and **Family Travel Files** (www.familytravelfiles.com), which offers an online magazine and a directory of off-the-beaten-path tours and tour operators for families.

✔ **Pack favorite toys and games.** Something simple from home can act as a security blanket for a child traveling in a strange place.

✔ **Reserve a child-safety seat.** If your kids are small, be sure to arrange a car seat for your rental car.

Making Age Work for You: Advice for Seniors

Mention the fact that you're a senior citizen when you make your travel reservations. Many hotels still offer discounts for seniors. In most cities, people over the age of 60 qualify for reduced admission to theaters, museums, and other attractions, as well as discounted fares on public transportation.

Members of **AARP**, 601 E St. NW, Washington, DC 20049 (☎ 888-687-2277 or 202-434-2277; www.aarp.org), get discounts on hotels, airfares, and car rentals. AARP offers members a wide range of benefits, including *AARP: The Magazine* and a monthly newsletter. Anyone over 50 can join.

Elderhostel (☎ 877-426-8056 or 978-323-4141; www.elderhostel.org) arranges study programs for those aged 55 and over (and a spouse or companion of any age) in more than 80 countries around the world, including Canada. The courses in Nova Scotia last five to ten days, and many include accommodations (in modest inns), meals, and tuition.

I recommend these publications that offer travel resources and discounts for seniors:

✔ *Travel 50 & Beyond*, the quarterly magazine (www.travel50andbeyond.com)

✔ *Travel Unlimited: Uncommon Adventures for the Mature Traveler* (Avalon Travel Publishing) and its associated Web site, www.travelwithachallenge.com

✔ *Unbelievably Good Deals and Great Adventures That You Absolutely Can't Get Unless You're Over 50* (McGraw-Hill)

Accessing the Maritimes: Advice for Travelers with Disabilities

The options and resources available to travelers with disabilities are greater than ever before, allowing almost anyone to enjoy a vacation to the Maritimes.

Many travel agencies offer customized tours and itineraries for travelers with disabilities. **Flying Wheels Travel** (☎ 507-451-5005; www.flying wheelstravel.com) is a full-service travel agency that caters exclusively to travelers with disabilities. Similarly, **Accessible Journeys** (☎ 800-846-4537 or 610-521-0339; www.disabilitytravel.com) accommodates the travel needs of slow walkers and wheelchair travelers and their families and friends. The **Access-Able Travel Source** (www.access-able.com) is a comprehensive compendium of travel agents who specialize in travel for people with disabilities. The site also has an extensive database of lodgings around the world, including the Maritimes, which are suited to travelers with disabilities.

The following organizations offer assistance to travelers with disabilities:

✔ The **Moss Rehab Hospital** (www.mossresourcenet.org) provides an online library of accessible-travel resources.

✔ The **Society for Accessible Travel & Hospitality** (☎ 212-447-7284; www.sath.org; annual membership fees: US$49 adults, US$29 seniors and students) offers a wealth of travel resources for people with all types of disabilities, as well as informed recommendations on destinations, access guides, travel agents, tour operators, vehicle rentals, and companion services.

✔ The **American Foundation for the Blind** (☎ 800-232-5463; www.afb.org) provides information on traveling with Seeing Eye dogs. In Canada, **CNIB**, also known as the Canadian National Institute for the Blind (☎ 416-486-2500; www.cnib.ca), offers a wide variety of services from division offices in Halifax (☎ 902-453-1480), Fredericton (☎ 506-458-0060), and Charlottetown (☎ 902-566-2580).

✔ Operated by the Canadian government, **Access to Travel** (www.accesstotravel.gc.ca) is an information clearinghouse of accessible travel information.

✔ Check out the quarterly magazine *Emerging Horizons* (US$16.95 per year, US$21.95 outside the U.S.; www.emerginghorizons.com), a quarterly magazine for travelers with special needs. The book *Barrier-Free Travel: A Nuts and Bolts Guide for Wheelers and Slow Walkers* is published by Emerging Horizons.

Advice for Gay and Lesbian Travelers

The university cities of Halifax, Fredericton, and Charlottetown tend to have the most resources in the Maritimes for gay and lesbian travelers. These centers don't have gay or lesbian neighborhoods, but they do have specific hangouts, like nightclubs, coffee shops, and bookstores. Outside of the cities, attitudes are generally conservative but accepting.

A good source of gay- and lesbian-friendly businesses in Halifax, including accommodations and restaurants, is the Web site http://gay.hfxns.org. **Gay Crawler** (www.gaycrawler.com) is a search engine with a searchable database of over 17,000 gay-themed Web sites, many of which are travel-related. The **International Gay & Lesbian Travel Association** (IGLTA; ☎ 800-448-8550 or 954-776-2626; www.iglta.org) is the trade association for the gay and lesbian travel industry, and offers an online directory of gay- and lesbian-friendly travel businesses. A search feature makes finding local businesses easy.

Some companies offer tours and travel itineraries specifically for gay and lesbian travelers. One of these is **Now, Voyager** (☎ 800-255-6951 or 415-626-1169; www.nowvoyager.com), a well-known San Francisco-based gay-owned and -operated travel service.

The following travel guides are available at most travel bookstores and gay and lesbian bookstores, or you can order them from **Giovanni's Room** bookstore, 345 South 12th St., Philadelphia (☎ 215-923-2960; www.giovannisroom.com):

✔ *Out and About* (www.outandabout.com) offers online travel guides and a monthly newsletter packed with solid information on the global gay and lesbian scene.

✔ *Spartacus International Gay Guide* (Bruno Gmünder Verlag; www.spartacusworld.com/gayguide/) and *Odysseus* (www.odyusa.com) are both good, annual English-language guidebooks focused on gay men.

✔ The *Damron* (www.damron.com) guides feature separate annual books for gay men and lesbians.

Chapter 10

Taking Care of the Remaining Details

*D*on't you hate that feeling that you've forgotten something but can't remember what it is? In this chapter, I discuss a variety of often-overlooked planning elements. So relax and read on — you're all covered.

Getting a Passport

A valid passport is the only legal form of identification accepted around the world. You can't cross an international border without it. Getting a passport is easy, but the process takes some time. U.S. citizens can find an up-to-date country-by-country listing of passport requirements around the world on the "Foreign Entry Requirement" Web page of the **U.S. State Department** Web site (www.travel.state.gov).

Applying for a U.S. passport

If you're applying for a first-time passport, follow these steps:

1. **Complete a passport application.** You can do this in person at a U.S. passport office; a federal, state, or probate court; or a major post office. To find your regional passport office, either check the **U.S. State Department** Web site (www.travel.state.gov) or call the **Passport Services Office** (☎ 877-487-2778) for automated information.

2. **Present a certified birth certificate.** This is proof of citizenship. (Bringing along your driver's license, state or military ID, or social security card is also a good idea.)

3. **Submit two identical passport-sized photos.** They should measure 2 × 2 inches in size. You often find businesses that take these photos near a passport office. Note: You can't use a strip from a photo-vending machine because the pictures aren't identical.

4. **Pay a fee.** For people 16 and over, a passport is valid for ten years and costs US$97. For those 15 and under, a passport is valid for five years and costs US$82.

 Allow plenty of time before your trip to apply for a passport; processing normally takes three weeks, but can take longer during busy periods (especially spring).

If you have a passport in your current name that was issued within the past 15 years (and you were over age 16 when it was issued), you can renew the passport by mail for US$67. Whether you're applying in person or by mail, you can download passport applications from the U.S. State Department Web site at www.travel.state.gov. To find your regional passport office, either check the U.S. State Department Web site or call the **Passport Services Office's** toll-free number (☎ 877-487-2778) for automated information.

Applying for other passports

The following list offers more information for citizens of Australia, New Zealand, and the United Kingdom.

✔ **Australians** can visit a local post office or passport office, call the **Australia Passport Information Service** (☎ 131-232 toll-free from Australia), or log on to www.passports.gov.au for details on how and where to apply.

✔ **New Zealanders** can pick up a passport application at any New Zealand Passports Office or download it from their Web site. For information, contact the **Passport Office** at ☎ 0800-225-050 in New Zealand or 04-474-8100, or log on to www.passports.govt.nz.

✔ **United Kingdom** residents can pick up applications for a standard ten-year passport (five-year passport for children under 16) at passport offices, major post offices, or travel agencies. For information, contact **Identity & Passport Service** (☎ 0870-521-0410; www.ips.gov.uk).

Packing for the Maritimes

To be succinct, pack as lightly as possible but be prepared for a variety of weather conditions. Start by assembling all the clothing you think you'll need. Then put half away, and you have an ideal amount for your vacation.

Knowing what to bring

Pack clothing that is comfortable and practical. In summer, a rain jacket, sweater, and a pair of worn-in walking shoes are sufficient accompaniments to your regular casual clothing choices. Pack fragile items between layers of clothes, and pack things that may leak, like shampoo bottles, in sealable bags. Also remember to bring the following:

- ✔ Tickets, rental car and hotel confirmations
- ✔ Discount membership cards
- ✔ Credit and debit cards
- ✔ Prescription medications and a copy of your prescriptions in case you lose them or run out

Though these are not really essential (believe it or not, you *can* buy film in the Maritimes, too), here's a list of handy items that are good to have on hand:

- ✔ Open-toed shoes, such as sandals
- ✔ Binoculars
- ✔ Spare film and batteries for your camera
- ✔ Insect repellent
- ✔ Extra pair of contacts or glasses and a copy of your prescription

Knowing what not to bring

Disregard everything you've heard about Canada and the cold. In summer, you have no need to carry a down parka or heavy winter boots (as proof, refer to Chapter 3 for average Maritimes temperatures). You can make due with comfortable, casual spring and summer clothing. And unless you plan on attending the theater or dining in the finest restaurants, you don't need a suit or formal wear either. Khakis and a golf shirt for men, and dress slacks or a skirt for women, are sufficiently dressy.

Meeting airline baggage requirements

Security measures at airports vary from country to country and even from airport to airport. All major airlines include up-to-date lists of permitted and prohibited items, as well as procedures for boarding flights, on their Web sites. Another option is to go straight to the source:

> ✔ United States: **Transportation Security Administration,** www.tsa.gov
>
> ✔ Canada: **Canadian Air Transport Security Authority,** www.catsa-acsta.gc.ca

If you need to have medical equipment like syringes or oxygen bottles on your person when you fly, contact your airline at least seven days prior to your departure.

Checked bags

Most airlines allow each passenger two pieces of checked luggage at no charge. Maximum weights and dimensions vary with each airline, but Air Canada's guidelines are typical. They allow a maximum measurement (combined length, height, and width) of 160 centimeters (63 inches) for each piece. The weight of each piece must not exceed 23 kilograms (50 pounds). Bags weighing between 23 kilograms (50 pounds) and 32 kilograms (70 pounds) incur a C$50 surcharge.

Sporting equipment like golf clubs, skis, and snowboards is allowed at no extra cost, but counts as one of your two checked bags. Larger items like bikes and surfboards incur an extra charge. In addition to counting as one of your two checked items, Air Canada charges C$50 each way for every oversize bag. Contact your airline for more details.

 On flights originating in the U.S., checked luggage is often screened by hand. Therefore, make sure your luggage isn't locked when you check in. If you're transporting a gift (as either checked-in or carry-on luggage) and it's wrapped, you may be required to unwrap it. So plan ahead, and carry the wrapping paper separately.

 In addition to an identification tag, tying a piece of ribbon to your suitcase makes spotting it on the baggage carousel easy. I've seen a dozen bags come off the same flight with yellow ribbon, so be creative and tie yellow and red, or a combination of colors that represent your country or favorite football team.

Carry-on luggage

Every airline is different when it comes to carry-on luggage allowances, but Air Canada's guidelines, once again, are typical. Each passenger is allowed one carry-on bag that measures less than 55 × 40 × 23 centimeters (21 × 16 × 9 inches) and weighs a maximum of 10 kilograms (22 pounds), and one "personal article" (like a laptop computer or briefcase). Items like cameras and coats are allowed but aren't included in the allowance. Check with your airline (Web sites are easiest) for specifics.

In your carry-on bag, pack valuables like jewelry and cameras; documents such as return tickets and car rental reservations; prescription drugs; and a sweater. Throw in a magazine or good book, and a snack for good measure.

Keep your boarding pass and photo identification (passport or driver license) handy at all times after checking in your main bags.

Getting through Immigration and Customs

Canada is a welcoming country, but officers at the border are still likely to ask some pointed questions, like the purpose of your stay and what you're bringing into the country.

Crossing the border

All foreign visitors require a valid passport to enter Canada and will be asked to produce onward tickets and sufficient funds when they arrive in Canada. At press time, the U.S. government was developing alternatives to the traditional passport. For current information, visit www.travel.state.gov/travel. If you're driving your own vehicle across the border, be sure you have you vehicle's registration papers.

Citizens from some countries are required to apply for a **Temporary Resident Visa** (TRV) before arriving in Canada. For details, as well as contact information for consulates and embassies around the world, contact **Citizenship and Immigration Canada** (☎ 888-242-2100; www.cic.gc.ca). (If you're from the U.S., Britain, a Commonwealth country, or somewhere in Western Europe, you probably don't need a TRV, but check current regulations on Citizenship and Immigration's Web site before leaving home.)

If you travel with a passport, keep it with you at all times. Only give it up at the border for officers to examine. If you lose your passport while in Canada, go directly to the nearest embassy or consulate of your own country.

Passing through Customs

Although the amount of loot you can take into Canada is unlimited, the Customs authority does have limits on how much you can bring in for free (to separate the tourists from the importers).

Entering Canada

If you're bringing goods other than clothing and personal effects into Canada, you need to fill out a declarations form. Here's the threshold on some common items: 50 cigars, 200 cigarettes, and either 1.14 liters (40 ounces) of liquor or wine or one case (12 bottles or cans) of beer. Bringing more than the equivalent of C$10,000 into Canada is not illegal, but you must report it if you do so.

Temporary visitors are permitted to bring their pet cat or dog into Canada without it being quarantined. The department responsible for overseeing the import of animals is the **Canada Food Inspection Agency** (www.inspection.gc.ca). Check their Web site for current regulations.

Revolvers, pistols, and fully automatic firearms are definitely not allowed, and, needless to say, neither are narcotics. For more information, contact the **Canada Firearms Centre** (☎ 800-731-4000; www.cfc-cafc.gc.ca). For more information on general Customs regulations, check with the **Canada Border Services Agency** (☎ 800-461-9999 or 204-983-3500; www.cbsa-asfc.gc.ca).

Returning home

If you're a citizen of the United States, you may bring home US$400 worth of goods duty-free, providing you've been out of the country at least 48 hours. This includes one liter of an alcoholic beverage, 200 cigarettes, and 100 cigars. You may mail up to US$200 worth of goods to yourself (marked "for personal use") and up to US$100 to others (marked "unsolicited gift") once each day. You have to pay an import duty on anything over these limits.

If you have further questions, or you'd like a list of specific items that you cannot bring into the United States, check the **U.S. Customs and Border Protection** Web site, www.cbp.gov.

Customs regulations are different in every country. Here are some contacts for returning citizens of other countries:

- ✔ **Australian Customs Service** (☎ 1300-363-263; www.customs.gov.au).

- ✔ **HM Revenue & Customs** (☎ 0845-010-9000; www.hmrc.gov.uk) for the United Kingdom.

- ✔ **New Zealand Customs Service** (☎ 0800-428-786; www.customs.govt.nz).

Keeping Up with Airline Security

With the federalization of airport security, security procedures at U.S. airports are more stable and consistent than ever. You can check the average wait times at your airport by going to the Transportation Security Administration (TSA) **Security Checkpoint Wait Times** Web site (www.waittime.tsa.dhs.gov). Generally, you'll be fine if you arrive at the airport **one hour** before a domestic flight and **two hours** before an international flight. If you show up late, tell an airline employee and she'll probably whisk you to the front of the line.

Besides arriving on time, here are a few other ways to make your time at the airport go smoothly.

✔ **Bring a current passport.** Keep this ID at the ready to show at check-in, the security checkpoint, and sometimes even the gate. (Children under 18 do not need government-issued photo IDs for domestic flights, but they do for international flights to most countries.)

✔ **Know what you can carry on and what you can't.** For the latest updates on items you are prohibited to bring in carry-on luggage, go to www.tsa.gov/travelers/airtravel.

✔ **Beat the ticket-counter lines.** Use the self-service electronic ticket kiosks at the airport or even print out your boarding pass at home from the airline Web site. Using curbside check-in is also a smart way to avoid lines.

✔ **Help speed up security before you're screened.** Remove jackets, shoes, belt buckles, heavy jewelry, and watches and place them either in your carry-on luggage or the security bins provided. Place keys, coins, cellphones, and pagers in a security bin. If you have metallic body parts, carry a note from your doctor.

✔ **Use a TSA-approved lock for your checked luggage.** Sold at luggage or travel shops and Brookstone stores (or online at www.brookstone.com), these locks can be opened with a master key by airport security, but deter casual thieves.

Playing It Safe with Travel and Medical Insurance

The cost of travel insurance varies widely, depending on the cost and length of your trip, your age and health, and the type of trip you're taking, but expect to pay between 5 percent and 8 percent of the vacation itself. You can get estimates from various providers through **InsureMyTrip** (insuremytrip.com). Enter information such as your trip cost, travel dates, and your age to get prices from more than a dozen companies.

Three kinds of travel insurance are available: trip cancellation, medical, and lost luggage. Here's my advice on all three:

✔ **Trip cancellation insurance** is a good idea if you signed up for an escorted tour and paid a large portion of your vacation expenses upfront (for information on escorted tours, refer to Chapter 6). Trip cancellation insurance covers three types of emergencies: death or sickness that prevents you from traveling, bankruptcy of a tour operator or airline, or a disaster that prevents you from getting to your destination.

✔ For travel overseas, most health plans (including Medicare and Medicaid) do not provide coverage, and the ones that do often require you to pay for services upfront and reimburse you only after you return home. As a safety net, you may want to buy travel medical insurance from a company such as MEDEX (☎ 410-453-6300; www.medexassist.com) or Travel Assistance International (☎ 800-821-2828; www.travelassistance.com).

✔ **Lost luggage insurance** is not necessary for most travelers. Your homeowner's or renter's insurance should cover stolen luggage if you have off-premises theft coverage. Check your existing policies before you buy any additional coverage. On international flights (including U.S. portions of international trips), baggage coverage is limited to approximately US$9.07 per pound, up to approximately US$635 per checked bag. If you plan to check items more valuable than what's covered by the standard liability, see if your homeowner's policy covers your valuables, or get baggage insurance as part of your comprehensive travel-insurance package.

If your luggage is lost, immediately file a lost-luggage claim at the airport, detailing the luggage contents. For most airlines, you must report delayed, damaged, or lost baggage within four hours of arrival. The airlines are required to deliver luggage, once found, directly to your house or destination free of charge.

Don't pay for more insurance than you need. For example, if you need only trip cancellation insurance, don't buy coverage for lost or stolen property. Trip cancellation insurance costs about 6 percent to 8 percent of the total value of your vacation.

Staying Healthy When You Travel

Getting sick will ruin your vacation, so I *strongly* advise against it (of course, last time I checked, the bugs weren't listening to me any more than they probably listen to you).

If you have health insurance, be sure to carry your insurance card in your wallet. Most U.S. health insurance plans and HMOs cover at least part of the out-of-country hospital visits and procedures if insureds become ill or are injured while out of the country. Most require that you pay the bills upfront at the time of care, issuing a refund only after you return and file all the paperwork.

Talk to your doctor before leaving on a trip if you have a serious and/or chronic illness. For conditions such as epilepsy, diabetes, or heart problems, wear a **MedicAlert Identification Tag** (☎ 888-633-4298 or 209-668-3333; www.medicalert.org), which immediately alerts doctors to your condition and gives them access to your records through MedicAlert's 24-hour hot line. Contact the **International Association for Medical Assistance to Travelers** (IAMAT; ☎ 716-754-4883 or, in Canada, ☎ 519-836-0102; www.iamat.org) for tips on travel and health concerns. The United States **Centers for Disease Control and Prevention** (www.cdc.gov) provides up-to-date information on health hazards by region or country and offers tips on food safety. **Travel Health Online** (www. tripprep.com), sponsored by a consortium of travel medicine practitioners, may also offer helpful advice on traveling abroad.

Staying Connected by Cellphone or E-mail

Communications in the Maritimes have come a long way since the distress signal from the Titanic was received at a remote cable station in Canso, Nova Scotia. Today, the three provinces are connected to the outside world with the latest and greatest technology, making calling home a breeze.

Using a cellphone in Canada

Just because your cellphone works at home doesn't mean it works in Canada. The three letters that define **global wireless capabilities** are GSM (Global System for Mobiles), a big, seamless network that makes for easy cross-border cellphone use in and between around 100 countries worldwide, including Canada. In the U.S., T-Mobile, AT&T Wireless, and Cingular use this quasi-universal system; in Canada, Microcell (Fido) and some Rogers customers are GSM, and all Europeans and most Australians use GSM.

If your cellphone is on a GSM system, and you have a world-capable multiband phone such as many Sony Ericsson, Motorola, or Samsung models, you can make and receive calls throughout built-up areas of the Maritimes. Just call your wireless operator and ask for "international roaming" to be activated on your account. Unfortunately, per-minute charges can be high — usually C$2 to C$3 in Canada.

Using an unlocked cellphone

Because of these high roaming charges, buying an "unlocked" world phone from the get-go is important. Many cellphone operators sell "locked" phones that restrict you from using any other removable computer memory phone chip card (called a **SIM card**) other than the ones they supply. Having an unlocked phone allows you to go to a retailer within Canada and install a cheap, prepaid SIM card. (Show your phone to the salesperson; not all phones work on all networks.) You get a local phone number — and much, much lower calling rates. Getting an already locked phone unlocked can be a complicated process, but it can be done; just call your cellular operator and say you're going abroad for several months and want to use the phone with a local provider. Within the United States, **InTouch Global** (☎ 800-872-7626; www.intouch global.com) sells Canadian-specific SIM cards.

In Canada, **Rogers** (☎ 877-764-3772 or 416-935-5555; www.rogers.ca) is a wireless provider with outlets throughout the Maritimes, including downtown Halifax at 6169 Quinpool Rd. (☎ 902-423-5653). This company sells SIM cards, cellphone accessories, and pay-as-you-go phones.

Renting a cellphone

For many, **renting** a phone that is set up to work in Canada is most convenient. While you can rent from within Canada (through car rental companies is often easiest), I suggest renting the phone before you leave
home. That way you can give loved ones and business associates your
new number, make sure the phone works, and take the phone wherever
you go. In the United States, two recommended wireless rental companies are **InTouch Global** (☎ **800-872-7626**; www.intouchglobal.com)
and **RoadPost** (☎ **888-290-1606** or 905-272-5665; www.roadpost.com).
Tell them you're traveling to Canada, and they can tell you what wireless
products you need. InTouch also advises you — for free — on whether
your existing phone will work overseas; simply call ☎ **703-222-7161**
between 9 a.m. and 4 p.m. EST, or go to www.intouchglobal.com/
travel.htm.

Using a satellite phone

If you're venturing deep into the Canadian wilderness, you may want to
consider renting a **satellite phone ("satphones")**, which are different
from cellphones in that they connect to satellites rather than ground-
based towers. A satphone is more costly than a cellphone but works
without cellular signals or towers. Unfortunately, you pay at least $3 per
minute to use the phone, and it only works where you can see the horizon (that is, usually not indoors). In North America, you can rent Iridium
satellite phones from **RoadPost** (☎ **888-290-1606** or 905-272-5665; www.
roadpost.com) from US$100 per week. InTouch Global offers a wider
range of satphones but at higher rates. As of writing this, satphones are
very expensive to buy.

Accessing the Internet away from home

Travelers have any number of ways to check their e-mail and access the
Internet on the road. Of course, using your own laptop, PDA (personal
digital assistant), or electronic organizer with a modem gives you the
most flexibility. But even if you don't have a computer, you can still
access your e-mail and even your office computer.

Cybercafes

Nowadays, finding a city that *doesn't* have a few cybercafes is hard.
Although no definitive directory for cybercafes exists — these are independent businesses, after all — two places to start looking are at www.
cybercaptive.com and www.cybercafe.com.

With your own computer

More and more hotels, resorts, airports, cafes, and retailers are going
Wi-Fi (wireless fidelity), becoming "hotspots" that offer free high-speed
Wi-Fi access or charge a small fee for usage. Most laptops sold today
have built-in wireless capability. To find public Wi-Fi hotspots within the
Maritimes, go to www.jiwire.com; its Hotspot Finder holds the world's
largest directory of public wireless hotspots.

For dial-up access, all business-class hotels in the Maritimes offer in-room connections for laptop modems, and most have wireless Internet.

Wherever you go, bring a **connection kit** with the right power and phone adapters, a spare phone cord, and a spare Ethernet network cable — or find out whether your hotel supplies them to guests.

Sizing Things Up: Converting to Canadian

Well, actually, I mean converting to **metric**. This section is only relevant to readers from countries that have not adopted the global measurement system — the United States, Liberia, and Myanmar.

Metric works on the decimal system, which means that all measurements have a base of ten. The basic unit of measurement is a meter (a little longer than one yard), which can be divided into 100 centimeters (2.5 centimeters equals 1 inch) or 1,000 millimeters. One thousand meters equals one kilometer (approximately 0.6 miles).

Learning the difference between kilometers and miles when driving is probably the most important conversion you need to know. All speed limits and distance signs in Canada are posted in kilometers. If the sign dictates a limit of 100, that means 60 mph. Also, at the pump, gas is sold in liters. Approximately 3.8 liters equals one U.S. gallon.

In 1975, rain began falling in Canada in millimeters and snow in centimeters. And, while older Canadians still talk in Fahrenheit, **Celsius** is the official scale of measuring temperature, with water freezing at 0°C and boiling at 100°C. To convert from Celsius to Fahrenheit, multiply by 1.8 and then add 32.

The only Canadian holdouts to metric conversion are golfers (golf courses are measured in yards), seamen (boat speeds are measured in knots and distances in nautical miles), and grocery stores (bulk retail food like fresh vegetables is priced in ounces and pounds — but weighed at the cash register in metric).

Part III
Nova Scotia

The 5th Wave   By Rich Tennant

"We had it in the guest bedroom, and then in the hallway, but for now we're leaving it in here until we figure out which room it seems to want to be in."

In this part . . .

*L*ife in Nova Scotia revolves around the ocean, and chances are so will your travels in this fascinating province. In this part, I unveil the best of Halifax with tips on the top sights, the best places to stay, and dining experiences you don't want to miss. I also cover famous shipbuilding towns such as Lunenburg and the spectacular Cabot Trail on Cape Breton Island. Nova Scotia offers more than spectacular scenery and quaint seaside towns, so I throw in a few bonus tips, like where to see the world's largest pumpkins and which outdoor restaurant boils its lobster on barbeques — to make sure you get the full effect!

Chapter 11

Halifax

● ●

In This Chapter

▶ Getting to Halifax
▶ Finding your way around the city
▶ Choosing the best places to stay and dine
▶ Seeing the sights
▶ Taking side trips out of the city
▶ Shopping in Halifax
▶ Spending a night on the town

● ●

*H*alifax may look like any other city as you approach the runway, but after you land, you're obviously in the Maritimes. This port city does a wonderful job of combining work and play. Although industrial endeavors take up large chunks of shoreline, a prime stretch of waterfront is the epicenter for locals and visitors alike. Museums, boutiques, restaurants, and pubs fill historic waterfront warehouses, with a seawall promenade winding past tour boats, tall ships — and even the occasional seal!

Although the harbor dominates the landscape, seeing past the working port areas to uninhabited islands is easy, with glimpses of the Atlantic Ocean in the distance. Overlooking the harbor is a compact downtown core, with no point more than a few blocks from the water. Here, you find all the trappings of a modern metropolis, delicately interspersed with rows of 200-year-old stone buildings and abundant green space. Downtown is first and foremost a business core, but the streets are perpetually alive with friendly faces and the catchy sounds of traditional East Coast music wafting out from darkened drinking holes.

Plan on spending two (preferably three) days in Halifax. Maritime weather will have some bearing on what you do, so check the forecast and plan your time at indoor attractions to coincide with rainy spells.

Getting There

Halifax is a transportation hub for all of the Maritimes. Most visitors arrive by plane at Halifax International Airport or drive into the city on one of four major highways.

Nova Scotia

Halifax

ATTRACTIONS:
Alexander Keith's Brewery **11**
Art Gallery of Nova Scotia **15**
Government House **10**
Halifax Citadel National **1**
Historic Site
Historic Properties **26**
Old Town Clock **20**
Maritime Museum of the Atlantic **14**
Museum of Natural History **2**
Pier 21 **8**
Province House **16**

Public Gardens **3**
Saint Paul's Church **17**

ACCOMMODATIONS:
Delta Barrington **28**
Four Points by Sheraton **29**
Halifax
Halifax Backpacker's Hostel **6**
The Halliburton **7**
Lord Nelson Hotel & Suites **4**
Prince George Hotel **19**
Waverley Inn **5**

DINING:
Bish **9**
da Maurizio **12**
Economy Shoe Shop **13**
Five Fishermen **18**
Harbourside Market **24**
Italian Gourmet **21**
Murphy's on the Water **23**
Salty's **25**
Stayner's Wharf Pub **22**
& Grill
Sweet Basil Bistro **27**

Historic Halifax

The sight of arriving immigrant ships and the echoes of horse-drawn carts down cobbled streets may be long gone, but the port city of Halifax retains its historical appeal. Nowhere are the city's nautical traditions better preserved than at the Maritime Museum of the Atlantic, which is flanked by Canada's oldest waterfront warehouses, aptly named the Historic Properties.

But behind the museum and old buildings lies Halifax's colorful history. Now home to popular boutiques and restaurants, Halifax's stone warehouses once stored pirate booty. The British government commissioned private vessels to confront their enemies (usually the French or the U.S.) and called it "privateering" — really just a pleasant name for piracy.

The story of Halifax is punctuated by intriguing footnotes like this. The 1997 movie *Titanic* brought renewed attention to the world's best-known maritime disaster and its numerous Halifax links, most of which are actively promoted as tourist attractions. Other links are more subtle, such as the Five Fishermen restaurant, located in a former funeral home where the *Titanic's* first-class passengers were embalmed.

By plane

Traveling from **Halifax International Airport** to the heart of downtown takes around 40 minutes by road, but allow slightly longer during the morning rush hour. Public transportation options are

- ✔ **Bus.** Because Metro Transit buses don't reach the airport, try the **Airporter** (☎ 902-873-2091), which offers service between the airport and major downtown hotels. The fare is C$16 one-way, C$28 round-trip. The first bus leaves the airport at 6 a.m., the last at midnight. Heading back to the airport, shuttles depart from most accommodations up to 20 times daily between 5:30 a.m. and 10 p.m. (plan on catching a bus at least 90 minutes before your flight departs). You don't need advance reservations.

- ✔ **Taxi.** After collecting your baggage from the carousels, head through the exit doors to the lineup of taxis out front. The set fare to downtown is C$53.

Most of the major **car rental** companies have check-in counters near the baggage carousels, and vehicles can be picked up in a parking lot within easy walking distance. The exception is Discount, which operates out of the nearby Airport Hotel; if your reservation is with this company, call for a pickup at the hotel phone bank in front of the information booth.

The Web site www.flyhalifax.com is filled with helpful information, including links to airlines serving Halifax and a real-time flight tracker.

By car

Highway 102 cuts across Nova Scotia from New Brunswick, bringing you right into the heart of Halifax. Allow three hours nonstop from the border. You may discover plenty of worthwhile stops en route, but the only one you *must* make is at the tollgates east of Amherst (C$3). As Halifax looms on the horizon, Highway 118 branches left off Highway 102. This alternate route draws traffic into the city of Dartmouth, but also provides a final approach to downtown.

Two highways lead into Halifax from the west: **Highway 101** from along the Bay of Fundy; and **Highway 103,** which runs along the South Shore from Yarmouth. Both routes pick up ferry traffic from farther afield. Ferries from Saint John (New Brunswick) terminate at Digby, a three-hour drive along Highway 101 to Halifax. Travelers arriving by ferry at Yarmouth from either Portland or Bar Harbor, both in Maine, face a four-hour drive on Highway 103.

By train or bus

If you choose to travel into Halifax by train, **VIA Rail** runs into Nova Scotia from Montreal, with the service terminating in Halifax at 1161 Hollis St. (☎ 888-842-7245; www.via.ca), on the southern edge of downtown.

Acadian (☎ 902-454-9321; www.acadianbus.com) provides bus service to Halifax from Moncton (New Brunswick), where connections can be made from Montreal or Maine. These two cities are the closest that **Greyhound** services get to the Maritimes. You can purchase through tickets to Halifax from Greyhound, and connections are seamless. Acadian also runs buses to Halifax from points throughout the province, including the ferry ports of Yarmouth and Digby. The Halifax bus depot is in the VIA Rail station at 1161 Hollis St. and is open daily 6:30 a.m. to 7 p.m.

Orienting Yourself in Halifax

Most of Halifax's attractions and major hotels are within walking distance of the touristy downtown waterfront precinct between Cogswell Street in the north and South Street in, you guessed it, the south. The main thoroughfare along this ten-block stretch is Water Street. This narrow, winding road set back slightly from the harbor is dotted with public parking lots (that's a hint — downtown is compact enough that you can see most sights on foot).

Halifax is small and easy to navigate. The city center clings to a hilly peninsula within Halifax Harbour. From here, built-up areas spread in all directions.

Downtown

Most attractions, accommodations, and restaurants are within walking distance of each other in the downtown core. The basic grid pattern of streets laid out over 200 years ago remains, bounded very roughly by the harbor to the east and Citadel Hill to the west, with Cogswell Street and Spring Garden Road creating man-made boundaries to the north and south respectively. Water Street, as you may suspect, runs along the harborfront. South of Sackville Street, it's known as Lower Water Street, while to the north it's Upper Water Street. Between Water Street and the harbor are numerous pay parking lots, the Maritime Museum of the Atlantic, restaurants, and gift shops.

Dartmouth

Two bridges and a ferry service link downtown Halifax with Dartmouth, across the harbor to the east. Although Dartmouth has its own distinct industrial, business, and residential districts, it is not a separate city, but combines with Halifax to form the Halifax Regional Municipality. Less picturesque than Halifax, it offers parks, lakes, and a few eccentric attractions — head here if Quaker history, ocean research, or rocks from around the world are your thing.

Bedford and Sackville

Bedford is a picturesque community at the head of Bedford Basin and north of Halifax proper. Settled as early as 1749, its streets are lined with well-kept middle- and upper-class homes, many with views back down the harbor. If you detour into Bedford, be sure to find your way down to the water's edge, much of it protected by parkland.

You have little reason to visit Sackville, north of Bedford, but a quick overview may be helpful for highway travelers entering Halifax from the north along Highway 102. If you're heading for the city, follow Highway 102 through Sackville. Don't be tempted by "Halifax via the bridges" signage, which detours through Dartmouth and makes the approach to downtown confusing.

Getting Around Halifax

Although downtown can get congested with traffic, this has more to do with the narrow, hilly streets than any great volume of vehicles. The best advice I can give you is to not plan on driving at all. Public transportation schedules and routes are designed to get residents to and from work so, aside from the ferry to Dartmouth, you can leave this form of transportation to the locals.

Driving (and parking)

If you're staying downtown, park your car and walk. Your best bet is the city-operated parking lots along Upper and Lower Water streets.

With admission to Halifax Citadel, you can include parking for an additional C$3.20. Therefore, you can visit this top-of-the-town attraction early in the day, and then leave your vehicle there while you spend the rest of the day exploring downtown. Just remember, it's an uphill walk (or an inexpensive cab ride) at the end of the day, and keep your Citadel entry receipt.

 If Halifax International Airport is the starting point of your Maritimes adventure, reserve your vehicle to be picked up at a downtown location just before heading out of the city. Not only will you save a few days' rental charge, but you won't pay the airport car rental surcharge.

On foot

Downtown Halifax is a great place to get around on foot. You can easily do without a vehicle and not miss any of the popular attractions. If you're staying downtown, then the main information center and all the best restaurants are within easy reach. If you tire of walking, jump aboard a tour bus or take to the water for a break. Only a few attractions are out of reach by walking — save these up and visit them in one go.

Catching cabs

Cabs are easy to hail anywhere in the downtown area, especially along Upper and Lower Water streets, or head for one of the major hotels where taxis wait. Rates begin at C$3, increasing based on time and distance to around C$7 for a trip across downtown. Cab companies include:

- ✔ Casino Taxi (☎ **902-425-6666**)
- ✔ Co-op Taxi (☎ **902-444-0001**)
- ✔ Maritime Taxi (☎ **902-456-4248**)
- ✔ Yellow Cab (☎ **902-420-0000**)

Transit tips

Metro Transit (☎ **902-490-6600**) provides inexpensive bus and ferry transportation to all parts of the city. The fare for any single sector is C$2 adults, C$1.40 seniors and children, exact change only. The main transit interchange is at the corner of Upper Water and George streets. Call or pick up a schedule from the information center.

 From July to October, every 40 minutes between 10 a.m. and 5:30 p.m. Metro Transit sponsors a free shuttle service known as **Fred** (short for "free rides everywhere downtown"). Hop on and ride the loop through Lower Water Street, Spring Garden Road, South Park Street, and South Street for a free tour of the downtown core.

Staying in Halifax

The following recommendations are a cross section of accommodations choices in various price categories. Prices fluctuate with supply and demand. Most downtown hotels cater to business travelers, with rack rates matching Monday-to-Friday work schedules. Weekend packages are offered year-round, but look for the best deals outside of the summer tourist season. As always, hotel Web sites are the best places to start searching out deals.

Ask about additional charges for parking and local calls, since they may not be included in your room's rate.

To the rate quoted, count on 16 percent in taxes being added to your final hotel bill.

First-choice lodgings

Halifax Backpacker's Hostel
$ Downtown

A ten-minute walk north of the waterfront, this renovated residence is perfectly suited to budget travelers looking for a quieter ambience than is found at the Hostelling International hostel, which is surrounded by the pubs of Barrington Street. Facilities include a well-equipped communal kitchen, a lounge room with television and lots of games, Internet access, and a small garden. Bike rentals are C$15 for a full day. The Airport Shuttle drops hostel guests at the nearby Citadel Hotel.

See map p. 95. 2193 Gottingen St. (north of Cogswell Street). ☎ *888-431-3170 or 902-431-3170.* www.halifaxbackpackers.com. *Parking: Street-side. Rack rates: C$20 dormitory bed, C$58 double, C$80 family room. AE, MC, V.*

The Halliburton
$$$–$$$$ Downtown

Three adjoining town houses, one dating to 1809, make up this well-located accommodations. The inn has 29 guest rooms, each elegantly decked out in period antiques, with in-room coffee and super-comfortable beds topped out with goose-down duvets. Most are at the lower end of the price range; the one-bedroom suite comes with its own wood-burning fireplace (C$225). If you choose one of the other rooms, plan on relaxing in the inviting lounge, which also has a fireplace, or in the private garden courtyard. **Stories**, the downstairs restaurant, serves up a complimentary breakfast and the dinner menu features local seafood and game prepared with a European flare.

See map p. 95. 5184 Morris St. (between Barrington and Hollis streets). ☎ *888-512-3344 or 902-420-0658. Fax: 902-423-2324.* www.halliburton.ns.ca. *Rack rates: C$150–C$350 double. AE, DC, MC, V.*

Inn on the Lake
$$$–$$$$ **Waverly**

Set on 2 hectares (5 acres) of lakefront parkland north of Halifax, this country-style retreat is a world away from the bustle of city living (although I have heard complaints about highway noise). You can sunbathe on a white-sand beach, lounge on chairs surrounded by well-manicured gardens, or crank up the energy level on the tennis courts and then cool off in the large outdoor pool. Some of the standard rooms have poolside patios, while others have lake-view balconies. Upgrade for C$25 to a Deluxe Room and enjoy a king-size bed, jetted tub, a balcony, and Internet access. Dining options include a poolside cafe, an English-style pub, or the more formal Encore dining room. The inn is a ten-minute drive from the airport, a short free shuttle ride away.

3009 Hwy. 2 (take Exit 5 from Highway 102), Fall River. ☎ *800-463-6465 or 902-861-3480. Fax: 902-861-4883.* www.innonthelake.com. *Rack rates: C$169–C$320. AE, MC, V.*

Lord Nelson Hotel & Suites
$$$$ **Downtown**

Dating to 1928, this landmark hotel has a reputation as one of Halifax's finest. Standard rooms are large and elegantly furnished; bathrooms are particularly well equipped. Amenities include a business center, in-room Internet access, free local calls, a concierge, and a British-style pub with good, inexpensive food. Despite its size (260 rooms), service and attention to detail is flawless. As is so often the case, disregard the rack rates and book online to snatch deals such as a room, parking, breakfast, and a city tour for two for around C$160. Make sure you request a room with views of the adjacent Public Gardens.

See map p. 95. 1515 South Park St. (at Spring Garden Road). ☎ *800-565-2020 or 902-423-6331. Fax: 902-423-7148.* www.lordnelsonhotel.com. *Parking: C$10 per day. Rack rates: C$250–C$420. AE, DISC, MC, V.*

Prince George Hotel
$$$$ **Downtown**

This place, halfway between the waterfront and Citadel Hill, is my fave among downtown hotels. Even the standard guest rooms are spacious and well appointed with lots of stylish mahogany furniture. For a few extra dollars, you can opt for a Crown Service room, with upgrades like a CD player, evening turndown service, and breakfast delivered to your door. Other in-house amenities include the classy Gio restaurant (see "Dining in Halifax" later in this chapter), a smallish indoor pool, wireless Internet, and a business center. The personalized service is also a step above what you'd expect from a hotel. Don't be scared off by the rack rates — the hotel Web site offers rooms for well under C$200 year-round, making them an excellent downtown deal.

See map p. 95. 1725 Market St. ☎ ***800-565-1567*** *or 902-425-1986. Fax: 902-429-6048.* `www.princegeorgehotel.com`. *Rack rates: C$269–C$475 double. AE, DISC, MC, V.*

Prospect Bed & Breakfast
$$ Prospect

If you have your own transportation, an overnight stay in seaside Prospect, near Peggy's Cove, is a delightful escape from city living. Housed in a 150-year-old convent, four guest rooms each have a private bathroom and the more expensive ones also have a fireplace. The ocean is nearly always in sight, from your bedroom window, from the dining room, and from the Adirondack chairs scattered around the grounds, or wander down to the private beach and dip your toes in the Atlantic. Hot breakfast and afternoon tea are included in the price of your stay.

1758 Prospect Bay Rd., Prospect. ☎ ***877-850-1758*** *or 902-423-1102.* `www.prospect villagebb.ca`. *Parking: Free. Rack rates: C$125 double. AE, MC, V. Open June to mid-Oct.*

Quality Inn Halifax Airport
$$ Airport

As the name suggests, this hotel is right by the airport, 40km (25 miles) north of downtown. A free shuttle transports guests between the two terminals and the hotel 24 hours a day. The exterior and public areas are a little tired, but spacious, comfortable rooms provide a relaxing stay before or after a long flight. Aside from the adjacent aircraft museum, this property is isolated — meaning you're stuck eating at the in-house restaurant (so-so food at best). On the plus side, facilities include indoor and outdoor pools, a small fitness room, wireless Internet, and a lounge that opens to a pleasant patio.

60 Sky Blvd. (take Exit 6 from Highway 102). ☎ ***800-667-3333*** *or 902-873-3000.* `www. airporthotelhalifax.com`. *Parking: Aboveground, free. Rack rates: C$95– C$150 double. AE, DC, MC, V. Wheelchair-accessible rooms.*

Waverley Inn
$$–$$$ Downtown

Originally home to a society couple, one of Halifax's grandest residences was converted to the Waverley Inn in 1876 and has been taking guests ever since. All rooms come with extravagant Victorian touches such as four-poster beds and lace curtains, while more modern conveniences include wireless Internet. Some rooms have jetted tubs. A deck catches the afternoon sun and the parlor is a wonderful place to relax in the evening. A hot buffet breakfast and afternoon tea are included in the rates.

See map p. 95. 1266 Barrington St. ☎ ***800-565-9346*** *or 902-423-9346. Fax: 902-425-0167.* `www.waverleyinn.com`. *Parking: Free. Rack rates: C$129–C$229 double. AE, DISC, MC, V.*

Runner-up lodgings

Delta Barrington
$$$ **Downtown**

The Delta Barrington is ideally located 1 block from the harbor. The 200 guest rooms are midsize and well appointed. An upgrade to Signature Club (bigger room, continental breakfast, and so on) only costs a few extra dollars.

See map p. 95. 1875 Barrington St. ☎ **888-890-3222** *or 902-429-7410. Fax: 902-420-6524.* www.deltahotels.com.

Fountain View Guest House
$ **Near Citadel Hill**

In a renovated residence, seven guest rooms share three bathrooms and parking is on the street, but at under C$60 for double occupancy, no one complains.

2138 Robie St. ☎ **800-565-4877** *or 902-422-4169.*

Four Points by Sheraton Halifax
$$$$ **Downtown**

One of Halifax's most modern hotels, this glass-sided property features stylish rooms with work desks and large televisions. Other amenities include room service, an indoor pool, a fitness room, and a casual restaurant.

See map p. 95. 1496 Hollis St. ☎ **800-368-7764** *or 902-423-4444. Fax: 902-423-2327.* www.starwoodhotels.com.

Travelers Motel
$–$$ **North of Downtown**

An inexpensive choice along the old highway linking downtown to the airport, this park-at-your-door motel has basic guest rooms and a few cabins to rent in summer only.

773 Bedford Hwy. ☎ **800-565-3394** *or 902-835-3394. Fax: 902-835-6887.* www.travelersmotel.ca.

Dining in Halifax

The eateries along the downtown harborfront are the easiest to find and have the best views. Considering their prime tourist locale, these restaurants are surprisingly popular with Haligonians, both during the weekday lunch hour and for an evening meal, and the reasonable prices are a pleasant treat. If you're in the city for more than one night, I encourage you to get adventurous and move away from the waterfront, where you find pockets of restaurants along Argyle Street and Spring Garden Road.

Halifax has a good range of coffeehouses, but the chains you're familiar with (Starbucks, Second Cup, and others) are almost nonexistent. Instead, head to **Perk's,** at 1781 Lower Water St. (☎ **902-429-9386**). Located right beside the harbor, it offers all the usual coffee concoctions, as well as light meals such as seafood salad croissants.

Bish
$$$–$$$$ **Downtown   GLOBAL**

Aside from the unusual name, a few things make Bish stand apart from Halifax's other waterfront restaurants — it's well away from the crush of the Historic Properties, the setting is elegant, and the menu offers a lot more than seafood. The cooking itself is excellent. The Madras curried lamb shank stars as a main course; or have seafood if you must, with choices such as seared scallops with red pepper and cilantro sauce. An impressive wine list includes Canadian ice wines.

See map p. 95. 1475 Lower Water St. (Bishop's Landing). ☎ *902-425-7993. Reservations recommended. Main courses: C$22–C$31. AE, DC, DISC, MC, V. Open: Mon–Sat 5:30–10 p.m.*

da Maurizio
$$$$ **Downtown   ITALIAN**

Halifax's finest Italian restaurant, da Maurizio, is in the historic Alexander Keith's Brewery building, across from the waterfront. Little has been done to alter the structure, yet the dining room is pleasing to the eye, with clean, simple lines set off by exposed red brick and lots of richly finished woods. Begin with *Melazane Alla San Daniele* (grilled eggplant rolled in proscuitto), and then get serious with upscale pasta presentations or main courses like *veal scaloppine* (thin slices of veal sautéed in a lobster, sherry, and cream sauce). Crème brûlée with fresh fruit is a fitting way to end this decadent splurge. The wine list has many Italian choices, while sensibly also including bottles from around the world.

See map p. 95. 1496 Lower Water St. ☎ *902-423-0859. Reservations recommended. Main courses: C$28–C$32. AE, DC, DISC, MC, V. Open: Mon–Sat 5–10 p.m.*

Economy Shoe Shop
$$–$$$ **Downtown   CONTEMPORARY**

First things first. The unusual name is derived from an old neon sign the owners hung out front when they didn't have the budget for proper signage. Since those simple times, the "Shoe" has become one of Halifax's most popular hangouts and expanded to include four dining rooms, each with a different theme and ambience. One of these, Backstage, has a distinct bohemian vibe and a monastery-like setting of arched walls. Diamond is another funky space, this one the domain of music fans who gather around a juke box packed with an eclectic collection of tunes. The Belgian Bar is so named for the European beers on tap, but with its high glass ceiling and tropical setting, its also a great place to feel more cheerful than

In the market for a cheap meal?

One of the best places to find inexpensive food is **Harbourside Market,** occupying a prime waterfront spot within the Historic Properties complex at 1869 Upper Water St. Seating is inside or out, with the outdoor tables sitting right above the water. This glorified food court is anchored by **Captain John's** (☎ 902-420-9255), where choices range from a halibut burger (C$9) to a full lobster with all the trimmings (C$24). Looking for something to share? Try the mussels, steamed in a tomato broth (C$8). Across the way is **Brisket Boardwalk Deli** (☎ 902-423-7625) with healthy wraps, soups, and sandwiches. The market even has its own brewpub, **John Shippey's** (☎ 902-423-7386), which serves up draft (C$6 a pint) brewed on-site and offers table service inside and at one outside corner. The food outlets are open daily 11 a.m. to 9:30 p.m.

the outside weather may allow. Finally, the restaurant's original space has tables spilling onto the sidewalk. Each room has a similar menu, with lots of choices that are perfect for sharing.

See map p. 95. 1663 Argyle St. ☎ *902-423-8845. Reservations not necessary. Main courses: C$13–C$24. AE, DC, MC, V. Open: Daily 11 a.m.–2 a.m.*

Five Fishermen
$$–$$$ Downtown   SEAFOOD

Five Fishermen is one of Halifax's better seafood restaurants, and the only one housed in a building that once served as a funeral home for some of the Titanic's doomed passengers. Table settings are spread through a number of different rooms (one re-creates a cruise ship's dining room), all with high ceilings and lots of brass and dark woodwork. You can't go wrong with any of the seafood or steak choices, but the baked medley of seafood with saffron risotto is hard to top. Take a break from seafood with any of the Alberta beef dishes, or enjoy the best of both worlds by ordering a half-lobster side. Don't be put off by the price of main courses — they include unlimited salad and steamed mussels.

Little Fish, in the same building (☎ 902-425-4025), is an inexpensive offshoot of the Five Fishermen, with most seafood mains under C$20. It's open weekdays for lunch, with locally themed choices like lobster crepes.

See map p. 95. 1740 Argyle St. ☎ *902-422-4421. Reservations recommended. Main courses: C$28–C$40. AE, DC, DISC, MC, V. Open: Daily from 5 p.m.*

Gio
$$$–$$$$ Downtown   GLOBAL

Within the Prince George Hotel, this dining room is one of the best-regarded in Halifax, renowned for upscale ambience and modern, creative cooking. Kick off with signature tuna fries or pan-fried scallops, leaving room for mains like lamb roasted in a maple and flax-seed crust then smothered in blueberry mustard. At lunch, the Kobe beef burger, the city's most expensive burger at C$15, is a popular choice. Adding to the appeal, service and presentation are as good as anywhere in Halifax.

See map p. 95. 1725 Market St. ☎ 902-425-1987. Reservations recommended. Main courses: C$24–C$38. AE, DC, MC, V. Open: Mon–Sat 11:30 a.m.–2:30 p.m. and 5–11 p.m.

Italian Gourmet
$–$$ Spring Garden Road DELI

Spend the morning at Citadel Hill and the Public Gardens, and then walk down Spring Garden Road back toward the harbor to reach this hidden gem, which is my favorite city lunch spot. It's part cafe and mostly deli, with a long counter along one side filled with goodies such as vegetarian quiche, salmon rolls, and gourmet soups. Across the room is another counter, where you order coffee concoctions, chai lattes, and the creamiest hot chocolate you can imagine.

See map p. 95. 5431 Doyle St. ☎ 902-423-7880. Reservations not necessary. Lunches: C$5–C$11. AE, DC, DISC, MC, V. Open: Mon–Sat 9 a.m.–7 p.m., Sun 10 a.m.–5 p.m.

Murphy's on the Water
$$–$$$$ Downtown SEAFOOD

Located on a wharf jutting into Halifax Harbour, the panoramic water views from this huge restaurant's outside seating area at the very end of the building can't be beat. Though the menu isn't the city's most upscale offering, combined with the location, dining here doesn't disappoint. Keep it simple and stick to classics like seafood linguini or bouillabaisse. Aside from a few additional dinner entrees, the same menu is offered all day, meaning you can order a burger for dinner or share a platter of Nova Scotian seafood for lunch.

See map p. 95. 1751 Lower Water St. ☎ 902-420-1015. Reservations accepted. Main courses: C$10–C$27. AE, DC, MC, V. Open: Daily 11 a.m.–10 p.m.

Salty's
$$–$$$ Downtown SEAFOOD

This popular waterfront eatery is in the heart of the action at the front of the Historic Properties complex. The most sought-after seating is out on the wharf, where, for the price of a bowl of clam chowder, you can watch the watery world of Halifax Harbour go by. The menu is typical pub fare, but with lots of local seafood. Considering the location, it's great value, with choices ranging from simple salads (under C$10) to entrees like baked salmon casserole (C$16). This inexpensive menu is available for both lunch and dinner. An upstairs dining room uses the same menu until 5 p.m., and then things get creative (and more expensive) with feature dishes such as blackened halibut doused in a mango salsa and rack of lamb roasted in a herb crust. Of course, steamed lobster is available any-time. Salty's is a good choice for families looking for waterfront dining — the kids' menu is C$6, including drink and dessert.

See map p. 95. 1869 Upper Water St. ☎ *902-423-6818. Reservations recommended for the upstairs restaurant after 5 p.m. Main courses: C$12–C$34. AE, DC, DISC, MC, V. Open: Daily 11 a.m.–11 p.m.*

Stayner's Wharf Pub & Grill
$–$$ Downtown SEAFOOD/PUB FARE

Head to Stayner's for all the usual East Coast pub fare, like fish and chips or mashed potatoes topped with roasted onions. It's also a good choice if you're in the mood for a more refined take on seafood favorites (think baked salmon glazed with maple syrup or Digby scallops fried in lemon herb butter), but don't want to spend a fortune. Plan on eating before 9 p.m., when live music starts most nights.

See map p. 95. 5075 George St. ☎ *902-492-1800. Reservations not necessary. Main courses: C$9–C$18. MC, V. Open: Daily 11 a.m.–11:30 p.m.*

Sweet Basil Bistro
$$–$$$ Downtown ITALIAN/ASIAN

Casual and brightly decorated, this funky dining room is in a historic brick building across from the Historic Properties. It's the perfect spot for an inexpensive meal when you want a break from seafood. The menu features lots of fresh, healthy cooking with classic pastas balanced by lighter choices. Vegetarians will love the ravioli filled with roasted squash and Parmesan-hazelnut cream, or the tofu pad Thai. After 5 p.m., the menu expands to include creative dishes like Slash 'N' Burn Salmon — blackened salmon served with a mango and basil fritter. Save room for a banana split doused in rum and sprinkled with coconut.

See map p. 95. 1866 Upper Water St. ☎ *902-425-2133. Reservations recommended. Main courses: C$17–C$24. AE, DC, MC, V. Open: Daily 11:30 a.m.–10 p.m.*

Exploring Halifax

In this section, I start out by discussing the major attractions of Halifax and surrounding areas such as Dartmouth. If you like having someone else doing the driving, the section on guided tours will be of special interest, while I also include itineraries to make sure you miss nothing.

In addition to the interest of the attractions themselves, sightseeing in Halifax has two things going for it — most downtown sights are within walking distance of each other and entry fees are well-priced.

The great explosion

On December 6, 1917, Halifax was scarred by the largest man-made explosion prior to the Atomic Age. The *Mount Blanc,* a French munitions ship, collided with a Belgian relief ship in the middle of Halifax Harbour. The accident itself wasn't major, but it started a fire aboard the *Mont Blanc,* and the crew, well aware of the cargo on board, took to the water in lifeboats. As crowds gathered near the waterfront to watch the spectacle, the ship exploded, leveling over 100 hectares (250 acres) at the northern end of Halifax.

The force of the blast was almost incomprehensible: It was felt on Cape Breton Island and heard as far away as Prince Edward Island. The initial explosion was followed by fire, much of it fueled by coal stored in cellars for the approaching winter. The final death toll was 2,000, with an additional 10,000 injured.

Fort Needham Memorial Park, a few blocks north of downtown along Gottingen Street, is dedicated to the disaster. From the 14-bell carillon in the center of the park, you can gaze down to the harbor and the exact spot where the explosion occurred.

The top attractions

Alexander Keith's Brewery
Downtown

When Alexander Keith arrived in Halifax from Scotland, he put his experi-ence brewing beer for British troops in India to work, establishing a brew-ery on the Halifax harborfront in 1820. Keith's signature beer, India Pale Ale, is still brewed at what is now North America's oldest working brewery, along with other English-style ales and seasonal brews. Led by costumed guides, brewery tours are as much about the history of the city as they are about the brewing process, making them popular with everyone. (And the two free mugs of beer presented at the end of the tour have nothing to do with it.)

Keith's legacy is celebrated by the raising of mugs across city pubs, often for no particular reason. Keith's birthday, October 5, is celebrated more officially at nearby Pier 22 with Nova Scotian music, marching bands, danc-ing, and, you guessed it — lots of India Pale Ale.

See map p. 95. 1496 Lower Water St. ☎ *902-455-1474.* www.keiths.ca. *Admission: C$16 adults, C$14 seniors, C$8 children. Open: Tours depart every 30 min-utes May Sun–Thurs noon to 5 p.m., Fri–Sat noon to 8 p.m.; June–Oct Mon–Sat noon to 8 p.m., Sun noon to 5 p.m.; Nov–Apr Fri 5–8 p.m., Sat noon to 8 p.m., and Sun noon to 5 p.m.*

Art Gallery of Nova Scotia
Downtown

Much of the art you see in Maritimes' galleries depicts lighthouses and fishing boats. This gallery proves that regional artists have a much broader range of subject matter. The 5,000-strong permanent collection is displayed in two buildings separated by a courtyard. A highlight is the colorful folk art decorated home of Maude Lewis. The gallery also hosts touring and temporary exhibits and is home to a small cafe serving up tasty lunches.

See map p. 95. 1723 Hollis St. ☎ *902-424-7542.* www.agns.gov.ns.ca. *Admission C$12 adults, C$10 seniors, C$3 children. Open: Daily 10 a.m.–5 p.m. (until 9 p.m. Thurs). Tours depart daily at 2:30 p.m.*

Fairview Cemetery
Fairview

You can read the names and moving tributes on some of the 121 headstones at the back of Fairview Cemetery, but most only have numbers. All, however, have the same date — April 15, 1912. Halifax was the port where many bodies from the *Titanic* were bought for identification. Victims were identified by number, in the order they were pulled from the cold waters of the North Atlantic. Graves of the unknown victims are marked with these numbers.

For almost a century, these tombstones lay quietly at the back of the Fairview Cemetery, seen only by the occasional visitor. Everything changed with the release of the 1997 movie *Titanic*. Suddenly, the final resting place of victim number 227, Joseph Dawson, became very popular. He coincidentally shared a name with third-class seaman Jack Dawson (portrayed by Leonardo DiCaprio in the movie) and has, as a result, garnered his own share of the actor's fan base. The grave is impossible to miss — just look for the fresh flowers left by weeping teenage girls.

Cemetery entrances are on Connaught and Chisholm avenues. Admission: Free.

Government House
Downtown

Completed in 1805, this house has been the official residence of Nova Scotia's lieutenant governor longer than any other North American government residence. Built of Nova Scotian stone, it has been extensively restored inside and out and although access is restricted, feel free to admire the exterior from surrounding gardens.

See map p. 95. 1451 Barrington St. Not open to the public.

Halifax Citadel National Historic Site
Downtown

I recommend starting your exploration of Halifax at the top, literally, by visiting Citadel Hill, which sits atop a high point of land overlooking the harbor. The original fortifications, built in 1749, have been replaced numerous times, with the most recent renovations completed in 1856 as a deterrent to a perceived threat from the United States. The fort was decommissioned in 1906, but has continued to serve as a proud symbol of the Canadian military ever since. History comes alive at the Citadel in summer through the haunting reverberations of bagpipers, a variety of interpretive programs, and colorful kilted soldiers following shouted marching orders. Indoor exhibits are tucked away in rooms built into the walls. A good starting point is the Fortress Halifax display, which tells the story of the complex. Other highlights are the schoolroom and the adjacent magazines, where gunpowder and cannon charges were stored. A trail follows the top of the casement, encircling the courtyard and passing cannon emplacements. Looking outward, views extend across downtown to the harbor. In the middle of the courtyard, the two-story Cavalier Building holds an information center, a cafe, and a gift shop.

The Old Town Clock, below the Citadel's George Street entrance, is a city landmark.

See map p. 95. Enter off Sackville Street, immediately west of Brunswick Street, and follow signs to public parking at the rear of the fortifications. On foot, walk up George Street from the waterfront. ☎ *902-426-5080.* www.www.pc.gc.ca/ halifaxcitadel. *Admission: C$11 adults, C$9.20 seniors, C$5.45 children; fees are reduced during shoulder seasons and admission is free Nov to early May. Open: July–Aug daily 9 a.m.–6 p.m., Sept–June daily 9 a.m.–5 p.m. Although the grounds are open year-round, no services are available Nov to early May.*

Maritime Museum of the Atlantic
Downtown

Just about everyone finds something of interest at this museum, one of Halifax's premier attractions. The exhibits in this restored waterfront warehouse include numerous vessels that once plied the coastline, as well as displays exploring Nova Scotia's seafaring legacy through chronicles of shipwrecks, the Canadian Navy, the Great Explosion, Sable Island, and the fishing industry. Because of Halifax's numerous links to the *Titanic*, a good portion of the museum is dedicated to the tragedy. A highlight is *Titanic 3D,* a 15-minute documentary taken at the wreck site, shown at regular intervals throughout the day.

Moored at the wharf in front of the museum is the 1913 hydrographic steamer **Acadia,** which spent most of its life charting the ocean floor. Parts of the ship are open for public inspection, including the deck area and the chart room. At the next wharf is the **HMCS Sackville**, a speedy escort used during WWII. Admission to both vessels is free with a museum ticket.

Titanic tourism

A brochure detailing *Titanic*-related sights is available at the Maritime Museum and local visitor centers. Included are details and driving directions to Fairview Cemetery, along with Mount Olivet Cemetery, the final resting place of John Clarke, one of the *Titanic* band members famous for continuing to play as the ship was sinking.

See map p. 95. 1675 Lower Water St. ☎ 902-424-7490. www.museum.gov.ns. ca/mma. *Admission: A very worthwhile C$8.50 adults, C$7.50 seniors, C$4.50 children. Open: May–Oct daily 9:30 a.m.–5:30 p.m. (Tues until 8 p.m.); Nov–Apr Tues–Sat 9:30 a.m.–5 p.m., Sun 1–5 p.m.*

McNab's Island
Halifax Harbour

On McNab's Island is an 1888 fort built to defend Halifax Harbour from seaborne attacks. It's also a provincial park that provides a quick escape from the bustle of the city. Enjoy numerous hiking trails leading to lookouts with views back across to the city, sandy beaches, a lighthouse, and an abandoned farm. Bring your own picnic lunch and drinks to one of the many designated day-use areas.

Access is by McNab's Island Ferry, ☎ 800-326-4563 or 902-465-4563, www.mcnabs island.com, *which departs on demand from Fisherman's Cove; C$10 round-trip. Admission: Free. For general island information, visit* www.mcnabsisland.ca.

Museum of Natural History
Downtown

The province's rich natural history is presented here, just west of Citadel Hill. The skeleton of a pilot whale and dinosaur fossils take center stage in the main gallery, with geology, anthropology, human history, and Acadian culture displays filling out an interesting facility. Some exhibits change with the season (it was the geology behind the Fundy tides when I last visited) while the critter-filled Nature Centre is where younger children gravitate.

See map p. 95. 1747 Summer St. ☎ 902-424-7353. www.museum.gov.ns.ca/ mnh. *Admission: C$5.50 adults, C$5 seniors, C$3.50 children. Open: June to mid-Oct Mon–Sat 9:30 a.m.–5:30 p.m., Sun 1–5:30 p.m.; mid-Oct to May Tues–Sat 9:30 a.m.– 5 p.m., Sun 1–5 p.m.*

Pier 21
Downtown

Between 1928 and 1971, over one million immigrants first set foot in Canada at Pier 21. The upstairs portion of this historic locale has since been turned into a museum dedicated to these people and the trials and tribulations they encountered on the journey to Canada. The Exhibition Hall is filled with interactive displays that trace the immigration process. Even if you're not researching your roots, plan on spending a little time here, especially at the compelling audiovisual presentations that relate personal immigrant stories. The Research Department sounds more scholarly than it is. Computers and microfilm hold a database of ship arrivals and some passenger lists (1925–1935).

See map p. 95. 1055 Marginal Rd. ☎ *902-425-7770.* www.pier21.ca. *Admission: C$8.50 adults, C$7.50 seniors, C$5 children. Open: May–Nov daily 9:30 a.m.–5:30 p.m., Dec–Apr Tues–Sat 10 a.m.–5 p.m.*

Point Pleasant Park
Downtown

At the southern end of the downtown peninsula, 75 hectares (180 acres) of prime waterfront is protected by this expansive park. The local ecosystem changed forever in September 2003, when Hurricane Juan swept through the park, destroying 75,000 trees, but it's still an enjoyable place to go walking or biking, or enjoy lunch at one of many picnic areas. You can stroll along the 40km (25 miles) of trails that lace the park, or check out the view from the centrally located Prince of Wales Martello Tower, built in 1862 to defend the city from attack.

2km (1 mile) south along Marginal or Young avenues from downtown. Parking is plentiful, or take Bus 9 from Scotia Centre. Open: Daylight hours. Admission: Free.

Province House
Downtown

Famously described by Charles Dickens in 1842 as "like looking at Westminster through the wrong end of the telescope," this small, symmetrical tree-shaded building is Canada's oldest seat of government, having been used as the meeting place of the provincial legislature since 1819. Inside the rather dour sandstone building are a number of inspiring features, including ornamental plasterwork.

See map p. 95. 1726 Hollis St. ☎ *902-424-4661.* gov.ns.ca/legislature. *Admission: Free. Open: July–Aug Mon–Fri 9 a.m.–5 p.m., Sat–Sun 10 a.m.–4 p.m.; Sept–June Mon–Fri 9 a.m.–4 p.m.*

Public Gardens
Downtown

Generally regarded as North America's finest original Victorian garden, this 7-hectare (17-acre) green space was created as a private garden in 1753, just four years after the founding of Halifax. Carefully tended rose bushes bloom in formal Victorian-style beds, rhododendrons grow so lush they form a canopy over the path, and small streams link ponds inhabited by ducks and swans. In the center of the gardens, an old-fashioned bandstand hosts free Sunday afternoon concerts, but any sunny afternoon of the week is a perfect opportunity to while away some time here. Across Sackville Street from the north side of the gardens stands a sandstone cottage, the home of gardener Richard Power, who designed the original layout.

See map p. 95. Bordered by Sackville Street, Summer Street, South Park Street, and Spring Garden Road. The main entrance is at the corner of the latter two streets. www.halifaxpublicgardens.ca. *Admission: Free. Open: May–Nov daylight hours.*

St. Paul's Church
Downtown

Founded in 1749, St. Paul's was the first cathedral built outside Great Britain. Grand, white, and dotted with stained-glass windows, it's now surrounded by modern high-rises. Above the north-facing porch is a piece of metal embedded during the explosion of the *Mont Blanc* (see "The great explosion" sidebar).

See map p. 95. 1749 Argyle St. ☎ *902-429-2240.* www.stpaulshalifax.org. *Admission: Free. Open: Mon–Fri 9 a.m.–4 p.m.*

Crossing the harbor to Dartmouth

Dating to 1750 (just one year after Halifax was founded), the city of Dartmouth lies across Halifax Harbour from downtown. The working waterfront is dominated by industrial complexes with a population of 66,000 sprawling through to city limits. The city itself lacks the charm of Halifax, but it has plenty of things to see and do.

Getting there and around

Driving to Dartmouth is possible, but arriving by ferry is a more enjoyable option. The ferry from downtown Halifax terminates at the **Alderney Landing** quayside complex. A small visitor's booth dispenses information on local attractions and transit routes and schedules for buses headed to the sights listed below. You can also find numerous shops, an indoor play park, a library with free Internet access, an art gallery, and a Saturday market (7 a.m.–1 p.m.).

From Alderney Landing, a short harborfront walking trail offers views back across the water to Halifax and the impossible-to-miss Imperial Oil refinery. In the adjacent Ferry Terminal Park is the World Peace Pavilion, which includes stones of substance from over 60 countries, including chunks of the Berlin Wall and the Great Wall of China.

Bedford Institute of Oceanography
Dartmouth

This government facility beside the MacKay Bridge is definitely worth checking out. It's Canada's largest ocean research center, targeting a wide range of disciplines, from ocean surveillance techniques for the Department of Defense to monitoring cod fisheries for the Department of Fisheries and Oceans. The public is welcome to take a guided tour of the facility that includes a glimpse of the latest 3-D underwater mapping technology. Within the institute, you can also visit the Sea Pavilion, home to a series of touch tanks holding sea life collected from the Nova Scotia coastline, while another interesting display depicts the *Titanic* on the ocean floor.

1 Challenger Dr. ☎ *902-426-4306.* www.bio.gc.ca. *Admission: Free. Guided tours: May–Aug Mon–Fri 9 a.m.–4 p.m.*

Cole Harbour Heritage Farm Museum
Dartmouth

Children will love this little piece of country life, even though it's surrounded by suburbia. Geese, ducks, and rabbits roam freely around the property while sheep and cows are fenced. The original farmhouse has been converted to a tearoom and you can see "smithies" at work in the blacksmith shop.

471 Poplar Dr. ☎ *902-434-0222. Admission: Donation. Open: Mid-May to mid-Oct Mon–Sat 10 a.m.–4 p.m., Sun noon to 4 p.m.*

Downtown Museums
Dartmouth

Within walking distance of Alderney Landing, **Quaker House**, 57 Ochterloney St. at Edward Street (☎ 902-464-5823), is a good little museum open Tuesday to Sunday mid-June through early September 10 a.m. to 5 p.m. Quakers were drawn to Nova Scotia from New England for the whaling industry and this 1786 home tells their story. Costumed guides lead visitors out back to a herb and vegetable garden planted with the same varieties that were planted there over 200 years ago. Admission is C$2. Keep your receipt, because entry to nearby **Evergreen House** is included. It's a just few blocks away, at 26 Newcastle St. (☎ 902-464-2300); hours are the same as at Quaker House. Displays catalog the human history of the Dartmouth region, including a solid collection of antiques.

Fisherman's Cove
South of Dartmouth

Jump aboard bus 60 at Alderney Gate to reach this photogenic fishing village, 7km (4⅓ miles) south of Dartmouth. Though many of the buildings along the wharf have been renovated or are made to look weathered, an authentic atmosphere prevails, with fishing boats bringing in daily catches of lobster, crab, salmon, and halibut. At the **Fisherman's Cove Marine Interpretive Centre,** at the entrance to the wharf (☎ 902-465-6093), learn about the history of the village and view local marine life in the aquariums. Admission is C$1. The waterfront itself is the main attraction, but you can find plenty of activities, including a sandy beach and kayak rentals.

Seeing Halifax by guided tour

If your time in Halifax is limited, joining a guided tour ensures that you see all the major attractions. You can get an overview of the city in a variety of ways — by land, sea, or a combination of the two. But even if you only have one day in town, plan on spending at least some of it exploring on foot. A trip out onto the harbor is also a must.

By bus

For a quick, complete tour of the city, **Ambassatours** (☎ 800-565-7173 or 902-423-6242; www.ambassatours.com) offers a three-hour Deluxe Historic Halifax City Tour for C$39 adults, C$35 seniors, C$27 children. A kilted guide provides a running commentary as a trolley car whizzes you around the city. While this tour provides a good overview, you may not get to linger as long as you'd like at some of the best stops — Citadel Hill alone (one of the stops; admission included) easily deserves a two-hour visit. Departures are June to mid-October daily at 9 a.m. and 1 p.m. from the kiosk at Sackville Landing, Lower Water Street. Another option is a one-hour downtown loop tour aboard an old British-style double-decker bus with **Double Decker Tours** (☎ 902-420-1155; www.doubledeckertours.com). You can get on and off as you please at any of 12 stops. Tickets are C$43 adults, C$39 seniors, C$21 children, C$88 families. Buses depart every 30 minutes from 9 a.m. mid-June to October. The main ticketing office for these tours is a kiosk at the corner of Duke and Lower Water streets.

By boat

One the most pleasurable ways to get a feel for Halifax is from sea level. Jump on a commuter ferry, ride a tugboat with personality, or sail off into the sunset aboard one of the world's most famous yachts. However you do it, get out on the water for a true feel of this seaside town!

The least expensive way to enjoy Halifax Harbour is from the upper deck of the passenger ferry between Halifax and Dartmouth. Operated by **Metro Transit** (☎ 902-490-4000), ferries depart for Dartmouth every 30 minutes between 6:30 a.m. and 9:30 p.m. from the terminal at the foot of Duke Street. The 12-minute trip costs just C$2 adults, C$1.40 seniors and children each way.

For a wide variety of tour boat options, head to Cable Wharf at 1751 Lower Water St. and the **Murphy's on the Water** (☎ 902-420-1015; www.murphysonthewater.com) ticket kiosk. The *Harbour Queen I* sternwheeler departs for a two-hour cruise daily at 10 a.m. and 2 p.m., costing C$22 adults, C$21 seniors, C$17 children; daily at 4:30 p.m. for a one-hour cruise costing C$18 adults, C$17 seniors, C$15 children; daily at 6:30 p.m. for a two-hour dinner cruise costing C$45 adults, C$30 children; and Friday and Saturday at 9:30 p.m. for a two-and-a-half-hour party cruise complete with live music for C$18 per person. Murphy's also offers nature cruises, fishing trips, and boats to Peggy's Cove.

If the *Bluenose II* is away from Halifax, or you miss one of the precious few spots when this famous schooner is in town (see Chapter 12 for more information), the *Mar II* is a good alternative. Operated by Murphy's, this wooden ketch that has circumnavigated the world now departs Cable Wharf five to six times daily for a 90-minute sailing trip. The cost is C$22 adults, C$21 seniors, C$17 children.

By amphibious craft

I'm sure that the engineers who developed the *Larc V* for transporting supplies and troops in the Vietnam War never imagined one of their boats would end up as a colorfully painted tourist attraction. But that happened in Halifax with **Harbour Hopper Tours,** whose amphibious vehicles can drive you around the streets of Halifax and then plunge into the water for a harbor cruise. The ticket kiosk is on Cable Wharf (☎ 902-490-8687, www.harbourhopper.com). May through October, the bus (or is that boat?) departs up to 20 times daily between 9 a.m. and 9:30 p.m. Rides are C$22 adults, C$21 seniors, C$17 children.

Suggested one-, two-, and three-day itineraries

I show you some of the best ways to spend one, two, or three days in Halifax, assuming you're visiting in summer (along with almost everyone else). For details on the attractions, restaurants, and activities mentioned in these itineraries, see the corresponding sections earlier in this chapter.

One-day itinerary

If you have just a single day in Halifax, start at the top and hit **Halifax Citadel National Historic Site** as soon as it opens (9 a.m.) to get a taste of the city's colorful past. Spend an hour exploring this fort, and then head across to the Public Gardens (the Museum of Natural History is the family alternative). Admire heritage buildings such as **Province House** on the walk down to the harbor. At lunchtime, choose from the many stands at Harbourside Marketplace (bypassing the seafood is hard — splurge and share a lobster platter for two) and find a table outside. Afterward, spend an hour or so at the **Maritime Museum of the Atlantic.** Plan on catching the 4:30 p.m. *Mar II* departure. After returning to the dock, take a short walk to Salty's, where your reservation ensures a waterfront table.

Two-day itinerary

If you have two days in Halifax, you can follow the approach of the one-day itinerary and then plan on rising early for a walk through **Point Pleasant Park** on the morning of the second day. Kick off your official sightseeing with a tour through **Alexander Keith's Brewery** and then wander along the waterfront to **Pier 21.** After lunch, move away from the water and browse the shops of George Street and then stop by the Art Gallery of Nova Scotia. Take a break from seafood at da Maurizio, then if you're still feeling active, head to the **Lower Deck** and catch one of the regular bands entertaining the crowd with traditional Maritimes music.

Three-day itinerary

For the first two days, follow the two-day itinerary. If you happen to be in Halifax on Saturday, squeeze in a visit to **Halifax Farmers' Market** and wander through stands of fresh produce and local arts and crafts. Plan on spending most of your third day on the Dartmouth side of the harbor, visiting the **Bedford Institute of Oceanography,** or keep the kids happy by stopping by **Cole Harbour Heritage Farm Museum.** At **Fisherman's Cove,** travelers of all ages can enjoy soaking up the salty sights and smells of a working village, but probably not as much as tucking into a feast of seafood from one of the local eateries. Back in the city, enjoy dinner at the **Economy Shoe Shop**, and then head over to **Henry House** for a pint or two of the Granite Brewery's Peculiar Ale. If you feel up to it, catch a cab to Spring Garden Road and **The Thirsty Duck** to dance the night away to traditional Celtic music.

Shopping

Shopping in Halifax tends to center around the waterfront, with a couple of notable exceptions. You can buy a wide variety of Maritimes creations — everything from ceramic fishermen to one-of-a-kind art-works. The city has a number of excellent art galleries, as well as quirky shops.

Checking out the scene

Shopping hours in Halifax are generally longer than elsewhere in the Maritimes, but vary greatly depending on the clientele. The touristy waterfront area is busy every day of the week, while many shops (and some restaurants) in the business district follow business hours, closing in the early evening and not opening at all on weekends.

 Don't forget that you must add the 13 percent Harmonized Sales Tax to all quoted prices (actually, sellers add the tax at the cash register).

What to look for

Although Halifax is not renowned for any particular specialty items, these Maritimes cultural products find their way into Halifax's many shops:

  ✔ **Seafood.** The only sensible thing to do is with seafood is to eat it, and which you'll probably do most of time. Some seafood, such as smoked salmon, is prepared to last, allowing you to take it home to hungry relatives. At the airport, you can choose a lobster from the tank and have it boxed specially for airplane travel.

  ✔ **Books and music.** Most bookstores have sections dedicated to Atlantic Canada literature. Secondhand and antiquarian bookstores often have large collections of nautical non-fiction. Traditional folk music is also abundant in music stores as well as nearly all souvenir shops, which often have listening stations so you can get a taste of the music before you buy.

  ✔ **Tacky souvenirs.** Whether you're after a lighthouse Christmas decoration, a city-branded T-shirt, or a fluffy moose, Halifax has plenty of touristy shops to fulfill your needs. Start your search in the Historic Properties along Upper Water Street.

Where to find it

This section details some of my favorite Halifax shopping experiences.

Antiques

Curiosities Antiques & Collectibles, at 1544 Granville St. (☎ 902-422-4717), offers an eclectic mix of antiques from around the world.

At **henhouse,** south of downtown within the Hydrostone Market at 5533 Young St. (☎ 902-423-4499), antiques are mixed with beautiful hand-built furniture constructed using traditional techniques. They also sell hand-dyed cotton linens, ceramic kitchenware, and porcelain dog dishes.

Arts and crafts

Jennifer's of Nova Scotia, 5635 Spring Garden Rd. (☎ 902-425-3119), is Nova Scotian all over. Pottery, fabric patchwork, jewelry, soaps, and just about everything else is handcrafted. Many items are seasonal, focusing on such occasions as Easter or Christmas.

The Historic Properties has a selection of crafty shops. One of these is **Aitkens Pewter,** 1869 Upper Water St. (☎ 902-423-4563). Pewter products are crafted throughout the province, and sold at this outlet in Halifax.

Camping and sporting gear

Halifax's largest outdoor retailer is **Mountain Equipment Co-op,** 1550 Granville St. (☎ 902-421-2667). MEC, as it's best known, is a co-operative owned by its members, similar to the American R.E.I. stores. Expect a range of high-quality clothing and camping gear, canoes and kayaks, field guides and maps, and a huge number of accessories.

For over 40 years, **The Trail Shop,** 6210 Quinpool Rd. (☎ **902-423-8736**), has been outfitting locals and visitors planning to explore the surrounding wilderness. The selection of camping equipment, footwear, and field guides is particularly strong.

Clothing

Island Beach Co. started out selling T-shirts from an old log church, but has since grown into a 30-store chain with outlets across Atlantic Canada. Head to their stores at 1903 Barrington St. (☎ **902-423-0908**) and 1781 Lower Water St. (☎ **902-422-4060**) in downtown Halifax for casual, contemporary clothing in a subtly themed nautical setting.

If you're in the market for a kilt, or maybe a length of tartan to make your own, **Plaid Place** in Barrington Place Shops at 1903 Barrington St. (☎ **902-429-6872**) is a good choice. They also stock other plaid clothing such as ties, scarves, and sweaters. The range of children's tartan products is especially impressive.

Crystal

You can't miss **NovaScotian Crystal,** along the waterfront at 5080 George St. (☎ **888-977-2797** or 902-492-0416), when crowds gather to watch artisans turn molten crystal into delicate masterpieces using century-old techniques. The factory doors open for public inspection daily between 8 a.m. and 4:30 p.m., but the most intriguing part of the process — glass-blowing — takes place Tuesday, Thursday, and Saturday. The adjacent shop sells a wide variety of unique pieces such as glasses, vases, and paperweights.

Halifax Farmers' Market

In 2008, North America's oldest farmers' market moved to a sparkling new waterfront building on Pier 20 (off Terminal Road; ☎ **902-492-4043**). Also known as Seaport Farmers' Market, its hundreds of stands are filled with local produce and crafty creations. Search out Nova Scotian maple syrup, homemade meat pies, and specialty soaps. The market operates every Saturday 7 a.m. to 1 p.m.

Nightlife

Mainly due to a healthy population of students, Halifax has a huge number of pubs and nightclubs. Beer aficionados will love the selection of local brews, most available on tap. Live music is a big part of the local nightlife scene, with bands playing every night of the week somewhere in town. Local bands to watch for include the Kilkenny Krew, the Navigators, McGinty, and Sloan.

Most pubs open at 11 a.m. and close at midnight through the week and at 1 a.m. on weekends. Nightclubs generally stay open later, closing between 2 a.m. and 4 a.m.

For complete listings of everything that's happening after dark, pick up the free *Coast* newspaper (www.thecoast.ca) for a full schedule of music, stage, and film performances as well as club listings. Another source of information is the waterfront visitor center, where a map is dedicated to city drinking holes.

Pubbing and clubbing it

There's no better place to start this exploration of the local bar scene than down at the harborfront. The **Lower Deck,** in the Privateer's Warehouse at 1869 Upper Water St. (☎ 902-425-1501), is part of a three-story restaurant complex, with a few tables spread out on the adjacent wharf. It's the quintessential Halifax pub — good tunes, lots of local beer on tap, and smart, friendly service. Bands belt out traditional East Coast music nightly from 9:30 p.m., with afternoon patio parties scheduled on summer Saturday afternoons from 3 p.m. It's popular with locals, so arrive early to get the best seats. **John Shippey's Brewing Company** (☎ 902-423-7386) is tucked into a corner of the Harbourside Market at 1869 Upper Water St. Beer is brewed on-site, with large brew tanks filling a glass-walled loft. As part of the food court, the beer is served at tables spread inside and outside along the dock. A few are set aside for brewery patrons, with table service available. I recommend the Piper's Pale Ale, a light and refreshing beer that is the perfect accompaniment to a seafood meal. Continuing along the harborfront, **Stayner's Wharf,** 5075 George St. (☎ 902-492-1800), is as popular for its food as it is for its beer. Monday and Tuesday nights are dedicated to improv comedy, and Thursday to jazz, while Maritimes music draws weekend crowds. Continuing south along the harbor is the **Stag's Head,** within Keith's Brewery on Lower Water Street (☎ 902-455-1474). Come here to relax with a pint of India Pale Ale and listen to traditional Maritimes music.

The **Granite Brewery,** two blocks from the water at 1662 Barrington St. (☎ 902-422-4954), pours beer from its in-house brewery in a relaxed, upmarket atmosphere. Upstairs is **Ginger's Tavern,** which is the reincarnation of a pub of the same name that was popular in Halifax during the 1980s. On any given night, it can be the same 1980s crowd, too, listening to the same music. Just down the road, Granite Brewery's original location is now **Henry House,** 1222 Barrington St. (☎ 902-423-5660), with a pub downstairs and a restaurant upstairs. It is as authentic as any of the British-style pubs in town, with an exposed brick and beam interior, cozy nooks, private booths, muted lighting, comfortable seating, and of course the Granite's popular Peculiar Ale on tap.

The **Thirsty Duck,** 5472 Spring Garden Rd. (☎ 902-492-3825) is best noted for its sunken rooftop patio, a pleasant escape from the noisy street below. The decibel level does go up on weekends, when crowds gather and bands strum their stuff inside. ("The Duck," as it's usually known, gets its name from a pond in the nearby Public Gardens where ducks gather for a refreshing drink.) Two blocks west, **Your Father's Moustache,** 5686 Spring Garden Rd. (☎ 902-423-6766), is a big, bright pub, with a rooftop patio complete with its own bar and a summer-only

Local brews

Finding an authentic pint in Halifax is easy, and I really encourage you to forego the big brewery products familiar to most of us (through advertising as much as anything else) and try local brews.

Best-known is **Alexander Keith's** India Pale Ale, brewed in Halifax since 1820 (see "Exploring Halifax," earlier in this chapter, for brewery tour information) and available on tap throughout the city and at liquor stores across Canada. This beer has a distinctive "hoppy" flavor, a hangover (pun intended) from the original recipe. The style of beer was developed in Britain, with extra hops added to preserve the beer during its long journey to troops stationed in India (hence the name).

Propeller and **Garrison** are known as microbreweries. Their output is a fraction of Keith's; look for these beers on tap at many pubs and in local liquor stores.

Ingredients are sourced from as far away as England for **Granite Brewery's** Peculiar Ale. This darker ale has a smooth, malty-sweet taste and is usually served only slightly below room temperature.

menu of fresh lobster. Admiring the ocean-themed mural behind the main stage is a good excuse to visit.

Other bars and nightclubs

Dome, 1746 Grafton St. (☎ 902-422-6907), is Halifax's largest dance club. It also features a separate bar area and a room dedicated to live music on weekends; closed Monday and Tuesday. **The Palace,** at 1721 Brunswick St. (☎ 902-429-5959), is another city-style nightclub popular with the 20-something crowd. **Bitter End,** 1570 Argyle St. (☎ 902-425-3039), is a hip hangout that tries for a European air of elegance. The drink selection is impressive (good martinis and Caesars), cool contemporary art hangs on the walls, and candles create a distinctive atmosphere that sets this pub apart from those I mention earlier. **Niche,** 1505 Barrington St. (☎ 902-423-6632), is another stylish place, this one with a good wine list and an outdoor patio. Jazz is a summer music staple.

Reflections, at 5184 Sackville St. (☎ 902-422-2957), has a reputation as Halifax's premier venue for gays and lesbians, but is also popular with the adventurous mainstream crowd. Through the working week, expect game and theme nights as well as karaoke, while on weekends a DJ spins the latest dance hits.

The arts

Halifax more than makes up for its lack of major theater companies with semi-professional theater groups and a packed schedule of summer arts festivals.

Theater

The **Neptune Theatre** calls a historic theater at 1593 Argyle St. (☎ 902-429-7070) home. The main season runs mid-September to May with a smattering of performances ranging from classic to contemporary throughout the summer. Tickets range from C$15 to C$50.

For lighter theater fare (historically themed musical comedy anyone?) that comes with a substantial three-course meal, make reservations for the **Grafton Street Dinner Theatre**, at 1741 Grafton St. (☎ 902-425-1961). Tickets are adults C$36, children under 13 C$17; plan to be seated by 6:45 p.m.

Fast Facts: Halifax

ATMs

Most banks, along with a growing number of grocery stores and gas stations, have ATMs.

Emergencies

Dial ☎ **911** for all emergencies.

Hospital

The Halifax Infirmary (☎ **902-473-3383**) is the 24-hour emergency department of the **Queen Elizabeth II Health Services Centre**, off Robie Street.

Information

Tourism Halifax operates the Halifax Visitor Centre at 1598 Argyle St. (☎ **902-490-5946**; www.halifaxinfo.com). **Tourism Nova Scotia** (☎ **902-425-5781**; www.novascotia.com) has an information booth by the baggage carousels at Halifax International Airport and another on the waterfront at 1655 Lower Water St.

Internet Access

Downtown, **Ceilidh Connection**, at 1672 Barrington St. (☎ **902-422-9800**) has a bank of public computers with high-speed connections.

Police

For emergencies, dial ☎ **911**.

Post Office

The main post office is between Sackville and Prince streets at 1680 Bedford Row.

Restrooms

Along the waterfront, public restrooms are located in the Harbourside Marketplace and the ferry terminal. The public restrooms in hotel lobbies are also a good bet.

Taxis

See "Orienting Yourself in Halifax" earlier in this chapter for a discussion on using local taxis. One company is **Yellow Cab** (☎ **902-420-0000**).

Transit Info

Public buses are operated by **Metro Transit** (☎ **902-490-6600**). See "Orienting Yourself in Halifax" earlier in this chapter for details.

Weather

Environment Canada maintains a Web site at www.weatheroffice.gc.ca with a link to Halifax's forecast.

Chapter 12

Southwestern Nova Scotia

● ●

In This Chapter

▶ Sightseeing in Peggy's Cove

▶ Strolling the streets of Mahone Bay

▶ Exploring Lunenburg

▶ Stepping back in time at Shelburne

▶ Soaking up Acadian culture

▶ Brushing up on the history of Annapolis Royal

● ●

*T*he southwestern portion of Nova Scotia has a raw magnetism unlike anywhere else in Canada. Envisage an endless line of picturesque seaside villages clinging to the rocky shorelines of sheltered bays. The region is mostly rugged and often remote, yet it holds some of Canada's oldest towns. Unhurried and unchanged for decades, they're living proof of Nova Scotia's nautical traditions.

Glance at a map of Nova Scotia to see that a single highway encircles the southwestern part of the province, rarely more than a few kilometers from the ocean. Drive along this route, beginning and ending in Halifax, to get more than a taste of Maritimes history and charm. In this section, I explore some of the notable towns you encounter on the way.

The farther you travel from Halifax, the less touristy it becomes. This is a good thing when it comes to crowds, but always plan ahead by making accommodations reservations in advance and carrying a small amount of cash — just in case that craft shop with the wooden whale doesn't accept credit cards.

Peggy's Cove

Less than an hour's drive southwest of Halifax is Peggy's Cove, a village of just 60 people, renowned for its postcard-perfect composition. On the way there you encounter several towns — including Prospect, East Dover, and West Dover — that are worth a look.

Taking a tour to Peggy's Cove

If you don't have your own vehicle (or even if you do), consider taking a tour to Peggy's Cove. **Ambassatours** (☎ 902-425-9999; www.ambassatours.com) offers transportation that includes a running commentary for C$42 adults, C$38 seniors, C$30 children. The tour is flexible, with the option to return at your own leisure on buses scheduled to leave Peggy's Cove for Halifax every 90 minutes. An alternative to the bus is the **Peggy's Cove Express** (☎ 902-422-4200; www.peggyscoveexpress.com), with the captain searching out whales, dolphins, and puffins on the two-and-a-half-hour journey down the coast from Cable Wharf in downtown Halifax. This tour departs every Friday and Sunday at 9 a.m. between mid-June and mid-October and costs C$70 for adults, C$63 for seniors, and C$50 for children.

Getting there

Finding your way out of Halifax and onto Highway 103 along the South Shore is simply a matter of map-reading — follow Cogswell Street to Quinpool Road then merge across to Highway 3 (Margaret's Bay Road) at the large traffic circle. After 3km (2 miles), Highway 333 to the left is signposted to Peggy's Cove. Take this route, and you quickly leave the city behind; miss the turn, and you end up on Highway 103, which zips down the coast on an inland route that misses some of Nova Scotia's best scenery.

Between Halifax and Peggy's Cove, Highway 333 passes a turnoff to **East Dover** before reaching **West Dover.** Both are quintessential fishing villages, comprising smartly kept homes separated from the ocean by a rocky shoreline. Even if you don't stop to wander the wharves, at least slow down and soak up the atmosphere.

Exploring Peggy's Cove

Ocean views from the approach to Peggy's Cove are impressive. But don't be tempted to drive to the end of the road. Instead, leave your vehicle in the parking lot to the left as you enter the village. From this point, the road narrows and descends to the harbor, with its boats, nets, and lobster traps. At the end of the road are a restaurant that tries hard not be touristy and an octagonal **lighthouse,** surrounded by rounded granite boulders, that is the center of attention for most visitors. It's also the only lighthouse in North America to have a post office.

Beyond the turnoff into Peggy's Cove is the touching **Swissair Memorial,** dedicated to the 229 passengers and crew who lost their lives when Swissair Flight 111 crashed into the ocean, within sight of land, off Peggy's Cove on the night of September 2, 1998.

Because the village is popular with tour buses, it can get extremely busy after 9 a.m., especially when the cruise-ship crowd is docked in Halifax. Plan on an early morning excursion to miss the worst of the crowds and also to have the best light for photographing the "world's most photographed lighthouse." Of course, if you'd rather join the tourists than fight them, see the sidebar "Taking a Tour to Peggy's Cove."

Mahone Bay

Picturesque Mahone Bay is a small village with a big-time reputation for its charmingly restored private homes and businesses set around a narrow inlet filled with boats. The narrow main street wends its way around the water, passing art galleries, craft shops, cafes, and restaurants housed in historic buildings, many dating from the days when Mahone Bay was a major shipbuilding center. At the head of the inlet, the towering spires of three adjacent churches make for one of Canada's most photographed scenes.

Getting there

Follow Highway 103 southwest from Halifax for 80km (50 miles) and take Exit 10 to reach Mahone Bay. Parking is permitted along the streets, but a better option is the parking lot opposite the churches just before downtown.

Staying in Mahone Bay

While day-trippers from Halifax fill the streets of Mahone Bay, only those smart enough to have made advance reservations are able to take advantage of the limited number of guest rooms in the village.

Amber Rose Inn
$$ **Mahone Bay**

Along the main street, Amber Rose Inn offers three old-fashioned, antiques-filled guest rooms in a historic building that has been used by various commercial enterprises (one section now has an antiques shop). All rooms have robes, coffeemakers, and dataports. The inn has a front veranda that is good for people-watching and extensive gardens, complete with outdoor furniture and a swing, which are perfect for escaping from the main street crowds. Rates include a full breakfast.

319 West Main St. ☎ *902-624-1060 or 902-624-0997.* www.amberroseinn.com. *Rack rates: C$125 double. MC, V.*

Mahone Bay Bed and Breakfast
$$ **Mahone Bay**

Watch the world go by from the veranda of this distinctive yellow-and-white inn along the main street. Constructed in 1860 by a shipbuilder, it's a solid old home that has been spruced up with "gingerbread" trim — elaborate swirls of wood below the roofline and around the veranda. Beyond the photogenic exterior are four adequate guest rooms, two with en suites and two with private bathrooms down the hall. Bathrobes are a nice touch, and rates include a full breakfast.

558 Main St. ☎ 866-239-6252 or 902-624-6388. Fax: 902-624-0023. Rack rates: C$75– C$125 double. MC, V.

Ocean Trail Retreat
$$–$$$ Mahone Bay

You won't find a better setting than this sprawling resort high above Mahone Bay. What the resort's hilltop motel rooms lack in cutting-edge décor, they make up for with stunning water views (two of the rooms have balconies) and reasonable prices. For a splurge, book the Balcony Suite that comes with a jetted tub, expansive deck with barbecue, and full kitchen. Closer to the water, the two-bedroom chalets are more comfortable and each has a kitchen, separate living area with gas fireplace, and a balcony. The outdoor pool is a bonus for children.

Maders Cove (between Mahone Bay and Lunenburg). ☎ 888-624-8824 or 902-624- 8824. Fax: 902-624-8899. www.oceantrailretreat.com. *Rack rates: C$99–C$175 double. Minimum stay applies on some units in July and Aug. AE, MC, V. Open: Apr–Nov.*

Dining in Mahone BayBiscuit Eater
$ Mahone Bay   CAFE

Tucked away at the beginning of a residential street 1 block uphill from the waterfront, this inviting cafe makes the most of local and organic ingredients to produce delicious soups, healthy sandwiches, and tempting desserts. Adding to the appeal is a selection of new and used books and public Internet terminals.

16 Orchard St. ☎ 902-624-2665. Lunches: C$5.50–C$8. MC, V. Open: Summer Mon– Tues and Thurs–Sat 8:30 a.m.–5 p.m., Sun 11 a.m.–5 p.m., the rest of the year closed Tues–Wed.

Innlet Café
$$–$$$ Mahone Bay   SEAFOOD

Slightly separated from the main strip of shops, the Innlet Café makes the most of its location, with big windows and a patio allowing for views extending down Mahone Bay. The kitchen takes full advantage of local seafood, and then presents it in hearty European dishes. I had the Skibbereen (seafood stew with Irish cream), doing well to also finish a slice of rich mud cake.

249 Edgewater St. ☎ 902-624-6363. Main courses: C$13–C$20. MC, V. Open: Daily 11:30 a.m.–9 p.m.

Charming Chester

In the late 1700s, Chester, north of Mahone Bay along Highway 3, was an infamous hub of pirates, privateers, and smugglers. The village matured over time into a resort town dominated by imposing waterfront mansions and sprawling summer estates. Today, Chester still has a distinctive moneyed feel. Local real estate is among the highest priced east of Montreal; well-heeled guests stay at upscale lodges such as **Haddon Hall Resort Inn** (☎ 902-275-3577; www.haddonhallinn.com), and yachters from around the world tie up at the local marina. Through it all, the community itself remains very approachable — children splash around in a tidal swimming pool beside million-dollar boats, locals mix with visitors in downtown's brightly colored **Kiwi Café** (☎ **902-275-1492;** daily 8:30 a.m.–4 p.m.), and a mid-August yachting regatta attracts as many spectators as boat owners.

Exploring Mahone Bay

You can walk easily from one end of Mahone Bay to the other in ten minutes, but that's not the point. Instead, plan on spending at least two hours admiring the fine architecture and making the following stops (listed from the parking lot in front of the churches):

✔ **Jo-Ann's Deli:** Located at 9 Edgewater St. (☎ **902-624-6305;** May–Oct daily 9 a.m.–6 p.m.), this is the place to pick up picnic supplies like baked goodies and healthy wraps, as well as jams and preserves. Of special note are the blueberry scones (delicious!) and the bag of carrots (not for general consumption) used as a counterweight for the front door.

✔ **Tea Brewery:** At 525 Main St. opposite the end of Clairmont Street, the Tea Brewery (☎ **902-624-0566;** weekdays 9:30 a.m.–5:30 p.m., Sat 10 a.m.–5:30 p.m., Sun noon to 5:30 p.m.) is crammed with teas and tea-brewing paraphernalia from around the world. Two tables and a selection of cakes may tempt you to linger longer.

✔ **Bandstand:** Behind the grocery store parking lot is a flower-encircled waterfront bandstand. From this vantage point, you can take the classic Mahone Bay photo of the three churches reflected on the water.

✔ **Mahone Bay Trading Company:** Opposite the bandstand on Main Street (☎ **902-624-8425**). Walk past the potting soil and laundry detergent in this general store to admire the massive boat-shaped counter. It's open Monday to Saturday 10 a.m. to 6 p.m., Sunday 11 a.m. to 5 p.m.

✔ **Amos Pewter:** View the ancient art of casting, spinning, and finishing pewter at this waterfront workshop at 589 Main St. (☎ **902-624-9547;** June–Aug Mon–Sat 9 a.m.–6 p.m., Sun 10 a.m.–5:30 p.m., closed Sun the rest of the year).

✔ **Mahone Bay Settler's Museum:** Admission is free to this small museum in a 150-year-old home across from Amos Pewter. Displays trace the history of the local shipbuilding industry and highlight local architecture. It's at 578 Main St. (☎ 902-624-6263). Open: June to early September Tuesday to Saturday 10 a.m. to 5 p.m., Sunday 1 to 5 p.m. Admission is free.

✔ **Redden's Fine Whale Sculptures:** Stop by the studio of Susan Redden, at 788 Main St. (☎ 902-624-1232; June–Sept), to admire her mahogany carvings, which reflect the enchanting personality of whales and dolphins through clean, polished lines.

Lunenburg

A stay in Lunenburg (population 2,400), famous for its colorful, perfectly preserved private homes and commercial buildings overlooking a bustling harbor, is a Maritimes highlight.

Lunenburg successfully juggles an active working harbor with a prosperous tourism industry — and does it well. The town brims with excellent accommodations, lively restaurants, and artsy shops.

Getting there

Lunenburg is 92km (57 miles) southwest of Halifax. To drive from the capital, take Highway 103 to Exit 10 (if you want to visit Mahone Bay) or Exit 11. From either of these exits, take a ten-minute drive along well-signposted rural roads to Lunenburg.

Orienting yourself in Lunenburg

Commercial enterprises are concentrated on four parallel streets: Bluenose Drive (along the waterfront), Pelham Street, Lincoln Street, and Montague Street. Pelham and Montague streets are of most interest to visitors, with restaurants, boutiques, and craft shops.

The location of the **Lunenburg Visitor Information Centre** (take Pelham Street east through town) on Blockhouse Hill Road (☎ 902-634-8100) affords good views, but is a little inconvenient for arriving visitors. It's open May through October 9 a.m. to 8 p.m. The Web site www.explore lunenburg.ca has lots of information on the town's history and links to tourist services.

Staying in Lunenburg

A couple of factors make staying in Lunenburg more expensive than elsewhere in the province — most lodgings are in grand old homes (no chain motels here) and demand is high for a limited number of rooms. Reservations are a must in July and August, but also recommended for June and September.

Lunenburg Arms Hotel
$$–$$$$ **Lunenburg**

This gracious 18th-century hotel has been renovated inside and out, yet retains its historical character. Original hardwood floors combine well with modern amenities such as plush mattresses, spa services, and high-speed Internet access to create a memorable stay. Bathrooms are well appointed and all 24 guest rooms are air-conditioned. Only some have harbor views (404 is the least expensive room with a view of the water). Breakfast (extra) is served in the downstairs restaurant, and relaxing in the adjacent lounge is easy.

94 Pelham St. ☎ *800-679-4950 or 902-640-4040. Fax: 902-640-4041.* www.lunenburg arms.com. *Rack rates: C$129–C$269 double. AE, MC, V.*

Lunenburg Inn
$$–$$$ **Lunenburg**

An attractive Victorian home in a leafy setting, this bed-and-breakfast is away from the bustle of Old Town yet within a five-minute walk of the waterfront. Built in 1893, the inn features seven guest rooms, some opening to a second-floor sun deck, all richly decorated with lots of polished wood. The two suites are extra-large and come with jetted tubs. This inn has five rate levels over a six-month season, with rooms dipping as low as C$85 in April. Rates include a cooked breakfast.

26 Dufferin St. ☎ *800-565-3963 or 902-634-3963. Fax: 902-634-9419.* www.lunenburg inn.com. *Rack rates: C$155–C$195 double. MC, V. Open: Apr–Sept.*

Lunenburg Oceanview Chalets
$$$–$$$$ **Lunenburg**

These chalets are a better option for families than the historic downtown inns, which make up the bulk of Lunenburg's lodgings. The complex comprises six newish log chalets, each with a full kitchen, a fireplace, separate bedrooms, and a deck with gas barbecue. One is wheelchair accessible. From the lofty location atop a high ridge behind town, it's a ten-minute walk to the waterfront.

78 Old Blue Rocks Rd. ☎ *902-640-3344. Fax: 902-640-3345.* www.lunenburgocean view.com. *Rack rates: C$149 one-bedroom cottage, C$199 two-bedroom cottage. MC, V.*

Smugglers Cove Inn
$$–$$$ **Lunenburg**

Simple, practical, and almost motel-like guest rooms in a historic downtown location. Some of the 20 rooms have small balconies, and a few have water views. All have a coffeemaker, air-conditioning, and a dataport. An elevator (rare in Lunenburg) provides access to rooms on the second and third floors.

139 Montaque St. ☎ *888-777-8606 or 902-634-7500. Fax: 902-634-8219.* www. smugglerscoveinn.ca. *Rack rates: C$119–C$169 double. AC, MC, V.*

Spinnaker Inn
$$$ Lunenburg

Similar in personality to Smugglers Cove Inn, the good news is the water views and its central location. The bad news is Spinnaker Inn has only four units, so book well in advance for summer. The rooms' highlights are the big windows and the expansive views (the best in town). The rooms themselves are simply furnished with antique-style beds and hardwood floors, and the bathrooms have been thoroughly updated. The more expensive units are split-level and have a jetted tub and kitchenette (although Suite 4 has limited views). The Spinnaker is one of the fewer small inns open year-round; rates drop as low as C$69 as soon as fall arrives.

126 Montague St. ☎ *888-634-8973 or 902-634-4543. Fax: 902-640-2022.* www. spinnakerinn.com. *Rack rates: C$99–C$170 double. AE, MC, V.*

Dining in Lunenburg

Big Red's
$–$$ Lunenburg   FAMILY DINING

If you're traveling with a family in tow and looking for an inexpensive meal, you can't beat Big Red's, a big restaurant with great views. The menu has seafood, of course, but you can also choose from hamburgers, pizza, and an extensive kids' menu.

80 Montague St. ☎ *902-634-3554. Main courses: C$9–C$23. AE, DC, MC, V. Open: Daily 9 a.m.–10 p.m.*

Old Fish Factory
$$–$$$$ Lunenburg   SEAFOOD

Overlooking Lunenburg Harbour from a converted fish factory (also home to the fisheries museum), this touristy yet stylish restaurant has a varied menu, with plenty of seafood choices. Mussels or oysters are a good choice to start, with mains ranging from fish cakes with baked beans to memorable Atlantic Seafood Supreme. The pricing is a little higher than comparable seafood restaurants, but the tables on the enclosed patio are a pleasant place to relax over an evening meal.

68 Bluenose Dr. ☎ *800-533-9336 or 902-634-3333. Reservations recommended for dinner. Main courses: C$14–C$30. AE, DC, DISC, MC, V. Open: Daily 11:30 a.m.–9 p.m.*

Rissers
$$–$$$ Downtown   SEAFOOD/MODERN CANADIAN

Rissers is away from the water, which isn't necessarily a bad thing — you're not paying for a view and the atmosphere is distinctly more mellow than down the hill along the waterfront. Dining is in a casually elegant room or on a tiered patio. The quality of food is equal to anywhere else in town, with choices running the gamut of Canadian cuisine from lamb to lobster. Rissers has no dessert menu. Instead, samples of each are presented to your table, which makes them almost impossible to resist.

Lunenburg Arms Hotel, 94 Pelham St. ☎ *902-634-3333. Main courses: C$13–C$24. AE, DC, MC, V. Open: Daily 7:30 a.m.–10 p.m.*

Rum Runner Restaurant
$–$$$ Lunenburg   SEAFOOD

Set on the lower level of the Rum Runner Inn, this restaurant is a little bit old-fashioned in décor and cuisine, but the menu is well priced and the unobstructed harbor views are unbeatable. The prime seats are outside on the covered veranda. Local seafood takes precedence on the menu. Lobster is served in various ways, including in a bisque. A seafood platter for two is only C$34, or take your pick from any of a variety of non-seafood mains, like chicken curry and Vienna schnitzel.

66 Montague St. ☎ *902-634-8778. Main courses: C$8–C$25. AE, DC, MC, V. Open: Daily 11 a.m.–9 p.m.*

Exploring Lunenburg

Lunenburg's biggest attraction is the town itself, so take some time to stroll around and appreciate its historic architecture. Or, soak up authentic Maritimes fishing culture at the Fisheries Museum. If you run out of things to do in town, find plenty to see and do out on the water or at any of the nearby attractions — this section's got it all covered.

Fisheries Museum of the Atlantic
Downtown

If wandering along the waterfront doesn't give you a good enough feeling for the region's heritage, this harborside museum in a former fish-processing plant will. As the name suggests, it highlights the fishing industry, using exhibits of boat-building (including a shop where you can watch carpenters at work), whales and whaling, commercial fishing equipment, and rum-running during the era of prohibition. In the Millennium Aquarium, commercially important fish species, super-sized lobsters, and a variety of crabs reside in large tanks, and a touch tank allows you to get up close and personal with tidal pool species such as starfish. And the museum takes advantage of its harborfront location — a small fleet of historic vessels is tied up out front, including the *Teresa E. Connor,* a wooden schooner that spent her life on the famous Grand Banks fishery. You can also take your pick from a busy schedule of daily events such as knot-tying and seafaring storytelling out on the dock.

68 Bluenose Dr. ☎ *902-634-4794.* www.museum.gov.ns.ca/fma. *Admission: C$9 adults, C$7 seniors, C$3 children. Open: May–Oct daily 9:30 a.m.–5:30 p.m., Nov–Apr Mon–Fri 9:30 a.m.–4 p.m.*

Historic buildings of note

Some buildings in the oldest part of town (known as Old Town) date to the 18th century, but most are pre-1900. Aside from the colorful palette of paint, restoration work is unpretentious (no fancy woodwork or fake facades). What you see is what you would have seen a century ago, which creates a real visual sense of history. Although most of the restoration has been done by individual owners, the town as a whole achieved the ultimate accolade in 1995 — when the Old Town was declared a World Heritage Site by UNESCO for being "the best example of a British colonial settlement in North America."

While it was Old Town as a whole that was recognized by UNESCO as a World Heritage Site, the following individual buildings are especially noteworthy:

- ✔ **Scotia Trawler Shipyard.** The *Bluenose* was built at this sprawling complex at 250 Montague St. (☎ **902-634-4914**). Today, it also incorporates boat construction and repair with the Yacht Shop, primarily serving the needs of local seamen but with a range of marine-themed souvenirs unlike anything in the more touristy shops. The actual shipyards are off-limits, but access to the adjacent Government Wharf is permitted.

- ✔ **Knaut Rhuland House.** Aside from commercial enterprises, this historic home at 125 Pelham St. (☎ **902-634-3498**) is the only historic building in Old Town Lunenburg open to the public. Considered to be the finest example of Georgian architecture anywhere in the Maritimes, it's open mid-June through mid-October, Monday to Saturday from 11 a.m. to 5 p.m. Admission costs C$1.

- ✔ **Bailly House.** Built in 1780, this privately owned home at 134 Pelham St. is the oldest building in Lunenburg. It's owned by the brother of artist Earl Bailly, whose work is displayed in civic buildings (including the library and museum) throughout town.

- ✔ **St John's Anglican Church.** Tragically destroyed by fire in November 2001, this 1753 Lunenburg landmark on the corner of Duke and Cumberland streets has been carefully rebuilt in its Gothic Revival grandeur.

- ✔ **Lunenburg Academy.** This striking building at 97 Kaulbach St. is a rare example of a large wooden school. Dating to 1895, it still operates as a center for education. The black-and-white turreted structure is easy to recognize from anywhere around the harbor.

Other cool things to do in and around Lunenburg

In addition to browsing nautically themed shops and walking the fairways of **Bluenose Golf Club** (☎ **902-634-4260**), here are a few other activities to keep you busy in and around Lunenburg.

The *Bluenose*

The dime is the only Canadian coin that doesn't feature one of the country's flora or fauna. It depicts the *Bluenose*, a famous sailing ship that represents East Coast nautical traditions and is about as Canadian as the maple leaf. Built as a fishing schooner, the *Bluenose* was actually designed for winning the International Fishermen's Trophy, an America's Cup–style racing series between working ships from Canada and the U.S. After its launch from Lunenburg in 1921, the *Bluenose* enjoyed a tremendously successful career, retiring from racing after 17 undefeated years, and was then ingloriously lost on a reef off Haiti in 1946.

Back in Lunenburg, construction of the *Bluenose II* began in the 1960s, using the original plans to create an exact replica of her predecessor, right down to the sails and rigging. The *Bluenose II* now spends June through September mixing public cruises with appearances at festivals and events around the Nova Scotian coast. The public cruise portion of her schedule is divided between Lunenburg and Halifax. Half of all tickets are allotted for advance sales (☎ 866-579-4909 or 902-634-4794), with the remainder sold dockside 90 minutes prior to sailing. For tickets in Lunenburg, go to the fisheries museum; in Halifax, look for the booth on the waterfront beside the Maritime Museum of the Atlantic. The cost is C$35 for everyone aged 13 and over, C$20 children 3 to 13. The *Bluenose II* sailing schedule is posted on the Web site, www.museum.gov. ns.ca/bluenose. To ensure a spot, either make advance reservations at least three months prior to sailing or be in line for the standby tickets at least two hours before the posted departure time. Don't say I didn't warn you.

Wondering where the boat's unusual name originated? So do the experts, but I like one theory in particular — local fishermen would wipe their noses when wearing blue mittens, and in the cold, wet conditions onboard, the dye would often run.

Boat tours

The following tours depart May through October, although outside July and August they do run on a limited schedule.

If the *Bluenose II* is out of port, or you missed a spot, don't despair, you have another option. The ***Eastern Star***, a classic 15m (48-foot) wooden ketch, departs Lunenburg up to four times daily for a sailing trip around the harbor (the 7 p.m. Sunset Cruise is two hours and travels to Ovens Natural Park). Buy tickets from the dockside booth at the foot of King Street (☎ 902-634-3535). The cost is C$24 to C$27 adults, C$11 to C$14 children.

Exactly as the name suggests, **Lobstermen Tours** (☎ 866-708-3434 or 902-634-3434), are trips in a working fishing boat. Led by local fishermen, you get to learn firsthand about lobsters and the industry from the experts before pulling traps (hopefully) filled with lobsters. The two-hour tour departs four times daily from the foot of King Street, and the cost is C$32 adults, C$12 children.

If you're not planning on traveling as far as Digby or Cape Breton Island, then Lunenburg is the next best option for a whale-watching trip. **Lunenburg Whale Watching Tours** (☎ 902-527-7175) has an excellent record for spotting humpback, finback, minke, and pilot whales. Regular sightings of sunfish, turtles, porpoises, dolphins, seals, and puffins round out what can be a very exciting tour. The cost is C$45 adults, C$30 children.

Blue Rocks

In this picturesque hamlet is a jumble of fishing cottages clinging to a rocky shoreline, with small fishing boats in a protected bay, and the shoreline dotted with fishing nets and lobster traps. In other words, this is exactly what Nova Scotia is supposed to look like — minus the crowds of Peggy's Cove. Take Pelham Street eastbound through Lunenburg and follow Blue Rocks Road.

Ovens Natural Park

The "ovens" are sea caves that have been carved into cliffs over thousands of years by the ocean's waves. A trail leads to various overlooks, while another ends at the mouth of one of the larger caves. Also at the site are a small gold rush museum and a restaurant. To get to this commercialized natural attraction, take Route 332 south from Lunenburg for 16km (10 miles) (☎ 902-766-4621; www.ovenspark.com). Admission is C$8 adults, C$4 seniors and children. View the caves from sea level on a boat tour for C$27 adults, C$20 children. Open: Mid-May to early October daily 8 a.m. to 9 p.m.

Shelburne

The small South Shore town of Shelburne is as attractive and interesting as its better-known counterparts to the north, but because it's that much farther from Halifax, it remains untouristy.

Founded in 1783, by 1900 Shelburne had grown into one of the most important shipbuilding centers in North America. Local boat builders were renowned for quality wooden boats, with some of the world's first and fastest yachts coming from local shipyards (some consider Shelburne the birthplace of the yacht). The waterfront remains remarkably unchanged from its halcyon years.

Getting there

Take Exit 26 from Highway 103 to access downtown Shelburne. This turnoff is 133km (83 miles) southwest of Lunenburg and 123km (76 miles) east of Yarmouth.

Staying in and around Shelburne

Loyalist Inn
$ **Shelburne**

Don't anticipate too much from this 200-year-old hotel. You get the basics —
budget rooms with private bathroom, television, and air-conditioning. On
weekends, request a room as far away from the downstairs bar as possible
if you want a good night's sleep. The in-house dining room is open Tuesday
to Sunday 7:30 a.m. to 8:30 p.m., or use the money you save on a room for
dinner at Charlotte Lane Café.

160 Water St. ☎ *888-253-1133 or 902-875-2343. Fax: 902-875-1473.* www.loyalist
innshelburne.com. *Rack rates: C$65–C$89 double. MC, V.*

Whispering Waves Cottages
$$$ **Ingomar**

If you want a modern, well-equipped cottage with panoramic ocean views,
Whispering Waves is hard to beat. Beautifully located on the ocean south
of Shelburne, the property runs right down to the rocky shoreline, with
sandy beaches and mackerel fishing within easy walking distance. The cot-
tages are in three subtle themes — wilderness, seaside, and romance —
and are carefully designed to take advantage of ocean views while also
offering a certain amount of privacy. Inside, the practical layout includes
a separate bedroom, small kitchen, and living area with electric fireplace.
Sliding doors open to a veranda. Congenial hosts Jo-Anne and Paul
Goulden go out of their way to make you feel comfortable. They can organ-
ize sea kayaking with a local operator, tee times at the local golf course,
appointments at a nearby spa, and evening beachside bonfires. When I'm
on the road researching a book, I don't have time for golfing or the like,
but I enjoy taking the Gouldens up on one option — a lobster dinner (com-
plete with strawberry shortcake) delivered to my cottage.

Black Point Road, Ingomar (take Exit 27 or 28 from Highway 103). ☎ *866-470-9283 or
902-637-3535.* www.whisperingwavescottages.com. *Rack rates: C$149–C$165
double. AE, MC, V. One cottage is wheelchair accessible.*

Dining in Shelburne

Charlotte Lane Café
$$–$$$ **Shelburne** SEAFOOD/FUSION

Tucked between Shelburne's main street and the waterfront, this delight-
ful dining room is a great find. The Swiss chef concentrates on combining
local seafood with cooking styles from around the world. Starters range
from a rich but simple chowder (with real scallops and shrimp) to a cre-
ative East-meets-West fish sampler, which includes smoked salmon and
sushi. The biggest concern is finding room for dessert (the almond fruit
torte is a must).

13 Charlotte Lane. ☎ *902-875-3314. Main courses: C$15–C$24 Open: Tues–Sat 11:30 a.m.–2:30 p.m. and 5–8 p.m.*

Exploring Shelburne

Head down to Dock Street, which runs along the waterfront, and you're in the middle of **Shelburne Historic District,** which is the largest concentration of wooden buildings from the late 1700s remaining in Canada. Many are private residences, while others are still home to a variety of boat-building endeavors. Four buildings are open to the public. Admission to each is C$3, or buy a combined pass for C$8. They are as follows:

- ✔ **Shelburne County Museum,** 8 Maiden Lane (☎ 902-875-3219; June to mid-Oct daily 9:30 a.m.–5:30 p.m., mid-Oct to May Mon–Fri 2–5 p.m.), is the best place to learn about the earliest Loyalist settlers and the subsequent years of shipbuilding fame.

- ✔ John C. Williams **Dory Shop Museum,** 11 Dock St. (☎ 902-875-3219; June to mid-Oct daily 9:30 a.m.–5:30 p.m.), has been churning out dory boats since the 1880s, when they were first used on the Grand Banks to help lay fishing nets from a mother ship.

- ✔ **Muir-Cox Shipyard,** south end of Dock Street (☎ 902-875-5310; June–Sept daily 9:30 a.m.–5:30 p.m.), has been in continuous operation since 1820. Inside, the Shipbuilding Interpretive Centre describes the history of the industry while the Boatshop, which once turned out enormous full-rigged barques, now takes orders for smaller wooden boats (viewing year-round Mon–Fri 8 a.m.–4 p.m.).

- ✔ **Ross-Thomson House,** 9 Charlotte Lane (☎ 902-875-3141; June to mid-Oct daily 9:30 a.m.–5:30 p.m.), a general store built by Loyalist brothers in 1784. The interior re-creates the time (complete with staff in period costume behind the counter) when locals flocked in to purchase goods such as salted cod and tobacco.

La Côte Acadienne

The French place names, the soaring church spires, and the numerous Acadian flags (red, white, and blue strips with a yellow star) tell you that this is Nova Scotia's largest Francophone enclave. La Côte Acadienne (Acadian Coast) is home to descendants of Acadians who resettled here after returning from their 1755 expulsion, which you can find out all about up the road at Grand Pré National Historic Site (see later in this chapter).

Getting there

La Côte Acadienne stretches for 50km (31 miles) along the Bay of Fundy between Yarmouth and Digby. Highway 101 zooms through the region, but take coastal Highway 1 to hit the highlights that I detail in the upcoming sections.

Staying along La Côte Acadienne

La Côte Acadienne is decidedly untouristy, but scattered through the small towns are a number of roadside motels like the **Bluefin Motel**, along Highway 1 in Meteghan (☎ **902-645-2251**), which falls into the $$ price range and has a restaurant.

Cape View Motel & Cottages
$$ Mavillette

What would normally be a rather nondescript complex of ten motel rooms and five self-contained cottages is enlivened by sweeping water views and an adjacent provincial park that protects a sandy beach. Across the road is an affiliated restaurant where the menu includes locally inspired dishes such as a lobster omelet.

124 John Doucette Rd., Mavillette Beach. ☎ *902-645-2258. Fax: 902-645-3999.* www.capeviewmotel.ca. *Rack rates: C$89–C$149 double. MC, V. Open: Apr–Nov.*

Dining along La Côte Acadienne

You find small cafes in most towns along La Côte Acadienne, and restaurants in the motels, but for a fully Acadian dining experience, nowhere beats Rapure Acadienne.

Rapure Acadienne
$ Point de Église   ACADIAN

More of a bakery than a restaurant, this roadside outlet specializes in *rappie* pie, a simple and hearty Acadian dish. The filling — shredded potato, chunks of chicken, and bacon — is delicious, but it has an unusual texture that may take some getting used to. The pies here are massive (plan on sharing one between two people) and come with a side of molasses. Order at the inside window and plan on eating at one of the outdoor picnic tables off to the side.

1443 Hwy. 1, Point d'Eglise (Church Point). ☎ *902-769-2172. Main courses: C$6. Open: Mon–Sat 8 a.m.–5:30 p.m.*

Exploring La Côte Acadienne

The drive along Highway 1 is scenic, and also takes in each of the attractions that I describe in this list, which are detailed from south to north.

✔ **Mavillette Beach Provincial Park.** La Côte Acadienne's nicest stretch of sand is within this small park on the south side of Mavillette. The sun warms the shallow water on summer days, but swimming isn't compulsory — you can also comb the beach for seashells and follow a boardwalk that leads across a salt marsh.

✔ **Smuggler's Cove Provincial Park.** The name is a giveaway. From a cliff-top parking lot, a path leads down through a wind-blown coastal forest to a cove where, the story goes, rumrunners stored their goods during the Prohibition era.

✔ **La Vielle Maison.** This homestead in Meteghan has been restored and converted to a museum. It allows a glimpse inside an Acadian home, with furnishings dating back 200 years and interpreters in traditional dress. It's along Highway 1 (☎ 902-645-2389). Open: July to August daily 9 a.m. to 7 p.m., and admission is by donation.

✔ **Église de Sainte-Marie.** This, the tallest wooden church in North America, towers above all else in the aptly named village of Church Point. Completed in 1905, the church is laid out in the shape of a cross, with the steeple rising 56m (175 feet). Inside is a small museum open weekdays through summer.

Digby and Digby Neck

Best-known for its plump, sweet-tasting scallops, this bustling town of 2,300 has been an important fishing center since Loyalists founded it in 1783.

Getting there

Digby is near the entrance to the Annapolis Basin, just off Highway 101, halfway between Yarmouth and Wolfville.

Bay Ferries (☎ 888-249-7245 or 902-245-2116; www.nfl-bay.com) operates the *Princess of Acadia* year-round between Saint John (New Brunswick) and Digby, with one or two daily departures in each direction. The crossing takes between two and three hours. Depending on the time of year (July to early Oct is high season) the one-way cost is C$30 to C$40 adults, C$25 to C$30 seniors, and C$20 to C$25 children aged 5 to 17. The fare for regular sized vehicles under 6.4m (21 feet) is C$75 to C$80 one-way.

Staying in and around Digby

Bayside Inn
$–$$ Digby

Overlooking the bay and within walking distance of downtown Digby, you can't go wrong at this small lodging that has been taking in guests for over 100 years. Historic character blends with modern touches in the 11 rooms, some outfitted with antiques and others in a floral theme. Every room has a television and en suite bathroom, while an enclosed porch awaits you downstairs. Rates include a cooked breakfast.

115 Montague Row. ☎ *888-754-0555 or 902-245-2247.* www.baysideinn.ca. *Rack rates: C$58–C$98 double. AE, DC, DISC, MC, V.*

Brier Island Lodge
$–$$ **Brier Island**

Nature lovers ought to plan on spending at least one night on Brier Island, preferably at Brier Island Lodge, perched atop sea cliffs and surrounded by native woodlands. Staying here, you can spot whales from your room, go bird-watching, or hike down to a narrow cove where seals haul themselves onto the rocks. The 40 motel-like rooms are a little plain, but they are clean and comfortable and most have ocean views. The more expensive rooms have either a king-size bed or a jetted tub.

The restaurant is casual (open 7 a.m.–9:30 p.m.) featuring lots of exposed wood and snappy-colored fabrics. Mains are mostly under C$20, including smoked pollock, a local delicacy that is poached in milk and served with a creamy white sauce.

Westport, Brier Island. ☎ *800-662-8355 or 902-839-2300. Fax: 902-839-2006.* www. brierisland.com. *Rack rates: C$75–C$145 double. MC, V. Open: Apr–Oct.*

Mountain Gap Inn
$$–$$$$ **Smith's Cove**

Set along the edge of Annapolis Basin, this sprawling resort does a good job of keeping guests occupied. Activities include hiking, biking, tennis, and swimming at the beach or in the outdoor heated pool; or you can just relax in the hot tub or at tables spread throughout the grounds. The least expensive motel rooms need renovations, but many of the remaining rooms and older cottages have kitchens and water views. The dining room is contained in the original 1915 lodge building and is open daily 7:30 a.m. to 9:30 p.m. For something more casual, pick up seafood at the fish market in Digby and boil or grill it at one of the resort's barbecue areas.

Smith's Cove (Exit 25 from Highway 101 east of Digby). ☎ *800-565-5020 or 902-245-5841. Fax: 902-245-2277.* www.mountaingapinn.ca. *Rack rates: C$99–C$340 double. AE, MC, V. Open: May–Oct.*

Summer Solstice Bed and Breakfast
$$ **Long Island**

One night may not be enough. Energetic host Deb Tobin encourages you to make the most of your time at Summer Solstice by suggesting activities such as hiking, bird-watching, and whale-watching. Within this renovated home overlooking the ocean, the Meadow Room has an en suite bathroom while the three other guest rooms — two with ocean views — share two bathrooms. Rates include a cooked breakfast, which may include pancakes filled with local berries. To get there from Digby, drive along Digby Neck, catch the ferry to Long Island, and then drive 17km (11 miles) to Overcove Road.

325 Overcove Rd., Long Island. ☎ *902-839-2170.* www.summersolstice.ca. *Rack rates: C$75–C$95 double. V. Open: June–Sept.*

Dining in Digby

Fundy Restaurant
$$–$$$$ Digby   SEAFOOD

With a harbor full of trawlers, finding fresh seafood in Digby is not an issue. What really matters is the view, and the Fundy Restaurant wins hands down. Located right on the harborside boardwalk, choose from an upstairs dining room that opens to a wide deck or the downstairs Dockside Restaurant with tables spread right to the water's edge. For an evening meal, stick to the upstairs section. The menu is scallop-centered, whether you're looking for breakfast (scallop omelet), lunch (scallop wrap), or dinner (scallop stir-fry, fettuccini, or casserole).

34 Water St. ☎ 902-245-4950. Main courses: C$15–C$28. MC, V. Open: Daily 7 a.m.– 11 p.m.

O'Neil's Royal Fundy Market
$–$$ Digby   SEAFOOD

Primarily a fish market, a few tables are set aside for in-house dining at this family-run business that also operates a fleet of fishing boats. Scallops (pan- or deep-fried) and chips is the obvious choice, but you can also order steamed mussels, lobster, or a platter of fish, scallops, and shrimp. The market also sells a wide variety of seafood (fresh scallops are around C$12 per pound), perfect if you are staying somewhere with cooking facilities. Otherwise, grab Digby chicks (smoked herring) for C$1 each and eat them on the go.

Prince William Street. ☎ 902-245-6528. Main courses: C$6–C$15. Open: Mon–Fri 9 a.m.–5:30 p.m., Sat 10 a.m.–5 p.m.

Exploring Digby

Although Digby offers a couple of worthwhile sights, the main local attraction is the drive out along Digby Neck.

Along the Harborfront

The **Admiral Digby Museum**, an 1850s home at 95 Montague Row (☎ 902-245-6322), documents a local history dominated by the ocean. On display are model ships, re-created 1880s living quarters, and a large collection of photographs. Open: Mid-June to August Tuesday to Saturday 9 a.m. to 5 p.m., Sunday 1 to 5 p.m.

In front of the Fundy Restaurant at 34 Water St., the *Lady Vanessa,* a retired wooden scallop boat, is open for inspection June to September daily from 9 a.m. to 7 p.m. In addition to simply clambering over and into the boat, a video shows footage of fishermen at work, and displays include the claws of a 20-kilogram (45-pound) lobster. Admission is a worthwhile C$2.

Driving Digby Neck

Digby Neck is a narrow finger of land that extends around 50km (31 miles) into the Bay of Fundy. Most visitors are drawn to the end of the road by its diversity of wildlife.

Along the way you encounter a string of villages. The most picturesque is **Sandy Cove**, overlooking a beach with good swimming. Ask directions to the local waterfall, one of the highest in the Maritimes.

Highway 217 reaches right to the end of Digby Neck. From there it's a short ferry ride to **Long Island**, then an 18km (11-mile) drive to another ferry that crosses to **Brier Island**. Both ferries run 24 hours per day, year-round. Departures are timed to link up with drivers who don't stop in-between. The fare on either ferry is C$4 round-trip, per vehicle (including passengers).

The ferry from the mainland docks on Long Island at Tiverton, a small fishing village with a couple of whale-watching operations and a museum. Around 2km (1¼ miles) beyond the village is a trail to the **Balancing Rock**. This striking natural feature is an outcrop of igneous (volcanic) rock that rises 7m (22 feet) from a narrow ledge above the ocean. The 2km (1.2-mile) trail leading to the lookout platform is somewhat tricky to negotiate, but you can make the round-trip easily in 90 minutes.

If you're feeling hungry as you approach the far end of Long Island, make a stop in Freeport at **Lavena's Catch Café** (☎ **902-839-2517**; mid-May to mid-Dec daily 9 a.m.–8 p.m., until 11 p.m. in summer) for well-priced fresh seafood without a deep fryer in sight.

Around the world in 1,160 days

Born near Digby in 1844 and raised on Brier Island, **Joshua Slocum** left home at 16 for a life on the high seas. After a distinguished career as captain, he set off on April 24, 1895, in the 11m (37-foot) sloop *Spray* on a journey that would make him famous well beyond the sailing community. He was at sea for over three years, returning to his starting point on June 27, 1898, thus becoming the first person to sail single-handedly around the world.

Although Slocum remains one of the world's best-known sailors of all time, his feat is not well-promoted in Annapolis County — a plaque on Brier Island makes note of his Nova Scotian links; the ferry to Brier Island is named in his honor, as is a bar at Mountain Gap Inn; and the one-room school he attended in Hanley is now a museum. You won't find his grave around these parts — he was lost at sea in the southern Atlantic in 1909.

The ferry from Freeport docks at **Westport**, the only settlement on **Brier Island**. The island is renowned for high populations of seabirds and excellent hiking.

Whale-watching

The Bay of Fundy teems with plankton, which attracts an abundance of marine life — fish, whales, and dolphins are all common in the area. Of course, that means the whale-watchers aren't far behind. Finback, minke, and humpback are the most common types of whales, but right and sperm whales are also present. The main whale-watching season is June through mid-October, with August considered the prime month.

A number of companies based along Digby Neck and on the two islands take people to see the whales. Most use ex-fishing boats, with the captains keeping in contact with each other by radio to help track down the whales. Trips last three to five hours (depending on how quickly whales are found) and cost around C$50 adults, C$40 seniors, and C$26 children. Tours with **Ocean Explorations,** at Tiverton (☎ **877-654-2341** or 902-839-2417; www.oceanexplorations.ca), are led by biologist Tom Goodwin in large, stable Zodiac boats. The advantage of this type of craft is speed — reaching the whales takes less time. In August, when North Atlantic right whales (the world's rarest whale) congregate in the middle of the Bay of Fundy, this is the only company that can get out far enough to see them. Also recommended is Westport-based **Brier Island Whale and Seabird Cruises** (☎ **800-656-3660** or 902-839-2995) and **Mariner Cruises** (☎ **800-239-2189** or 902-839-2346).

Annapolis Royal

The site of Canada's first permanent settlement, Annapolis Royal is under the grand delusion that it's still the Victorian era. The French and British fought for control of this town for over a century. In 1710, the British finally took control and renamed it in honor of Queen Anne. Despite its age, fewer than 1,000 people call Annapolis Royal home, although the streets swell with summer visitors wandering the compact downtown core.

Getting there

Annapolis Royal is 29km (18 miles) northeast of Digby Neck. Take Exit 23 from Highway 101 to follow the Annapolis Basin shoreline to town or Exit 22 for a more direct approach.

Staying in Annapolis Royal

Garrison House Inn
$$ Annapolis Royal

Unlike most local bed-and-breakfast inns, the 1854 Garrison House was designed originally as a guesthouse. Careful renovations have restored its Victorian-era feel. In total, there are seven guest rooms, each with a private bathroom and shower, and some with canopy beds. Choose Room 2 for its spaciousness and views across to Fort Anne, or Room 4 for its quiet, nicely cozy feel. The in-house restaurant is Annapolis Royal's premier dining room.

350 St. George St. ☎ *902-532-5750. Fax: 902-532-5501.* www.garrisonhouse.ca. *Rack rates: C$79–C$149 double. AE, MC, V. Open: Mid-May to Oct.*

Queen Anne Inn
$$–$$$ Annapolis Royal

Named for the Queen of England at the time the British were ceded Acadia, this 1865 landmark lodging is set back from the road and surrounded by expansive gardens. A grand stairway leads from the lobby and parlor to ten guest rooms, all of which are extremely spacious (except Number 10). While furnishings and fabrics reflect the Victorian era, the rooms have been thoroughly modernized, some featuring amenities like a jetted tub. An adjacent carriage house holds an additional two units, each with two bedrooms. Rates include a full breakfast and nice touches, such as plush bathrobes and the use of a DVD player on request.

494 St. George St. (across from the Historic Gardens). ☎ **877-536-0403** *or 902-532-7850. Fax: 902-532-2078.* www.queenanneinn.ns.ca. *Rack rates: C$119–C$209 double. AE, MC, V. Open: May–Nov.*

Dining in Annapolis Royal

Fort Anne Café
$–$$ Annapolis Royal   CAFE FARE/SEAFOOD

The décor may not have changed since the 1970s, but that's not a concern to the locals who gather here for hearty and well-priced, no-frills food. Served until noon, breakfast choices include a three-filling omelet for just C$5; even the biggest, meanest cooked breakfast is only C$8. The rest of the day, tuck in to a clam burger for C$6.50 or pay C$14 for a pile of juicy Digby scallops.

298 St. George St. ☎ **902-532-5254.** *Main courses: C$7–C$16. Open: Daily 8 a.m.–8 p.m.*

Keji what?

Pronounced "Kedge-im-a-*koo*-jik" (and sensibly known simply as "Keji"), **Kejimkujik National Park** protects a remote inland region of Nova Scotia. Scarred by glacial action from the last Ice Age, the ancient landscape combines barren rock, dense forests, and an extensive network of rivers and shallow lakes.

A single road penetrates the park, branching off Highway 8 halfway between Annapolis Royal and Liverpool. Along its length are numerous easy hikes, a lookout tower with expansive views, a large campground, and supervised swimming at Merrymakedge Beach. The park's waterways ideal for canoeing. Rentals are available at **Jakes Landing**, 8km (5 miles) from Highway 8 (☎ **902-682-2196**) for C$5 per hour and C$25 per day, including paddles and life jackets.

Stop at the **Visitor Reception Centre** by the park entrance (☎ **902-682-2772**; www. pc.gc.ca; daily 8:30 a.m.–4:30 p.m., until 8 p.m. in summer) for schedules of guided walks and paddles and the evening interpretive program. A Day Pass costs C$5.45 adults, C$4.70 seniors, C$2.70 children.

Garrison House Restaurant
$$–$$$ Annapolis Royal   SEAFOOD/GLOBAL

At this lovely three-room restaurant in the lodging of the same name, seafood and local produce are served in all kinds of creative ways. The menu changes every few weeks, but usually includes a rich Acadian seafood chowder and mains ranging from the simple (pan-fried haddock) to Greek-inspired (Digby scallops, feta cheese, and olives on a bed of pasta) to Asian (chicken and shrimp coconut milk curry). Most dishes are accompanied by local, farm-fresh produce.

350 St. George St. ☎ *902-532-5750. Main courses: C$17–C$23. AE, MC, V. Open: Mid-May to Oct daily 5:30–8:30 p.m.*

Exploring Annapolis Royal

Make your first stop the generating station, home to the **Annapolis Visitor Centre** (☎ 902-532-5769; May to mid-Oct daily 9 a.m.–5 p.m.). Here you can pick up the brochure *Footprints with Footnotes,* an excellent reference for a self-guided tour of **St. George Street,** one of Canada's oldest streets. Of dozens of historic buildings, the most notable is the **Sinclair Inn,** at 230 St. George St. Built in 1710, it's the oldest wooden building in Canada.

Annapolis Tidal Generating Station
North of downtown

The Bay of Fundy's record-breaking tides are used to generate electricity at the world's second-largest tidal generating station (actually, only three exist, but it's bigger than the one in Russia) on a causeway north of Annapolis Royal. Although it continues to generate electricity, the station was originally built as an experiment, a precursor to a more ambitious project that has been stalled by environmental concerns. An upstairs interpretive center explains the generation process in a straightforward manner, with large picture windows allowing views of the holding pond.

236 Prince Albert Rd. (Highway 1). ☎ *902-532-5769. Admission: Free. Open: Mid-May to mid-Oct daily 9 a.m.–5 p.m.*

Fort Anne National Historic Site
Downtown

Preserving the site of settlements dating back to 1629, this accessible attraction is centrally located on a low-rise beside the main street. Star-shaped earthen fortifications and a moat dating to 1702 are the oldest visible remains of 200 years of struggles between the French and British. In a more modern building is a midsize museum with rooms representing different eras, including the period between 1713 and 1749 when the settlement was the capital of Nova Scotia. If you are staying overnight in town, ask at the museum about entertaining nighttime tours of the Garrison Graveyard, led by a top-hatted "undertaker."

St. George Street. ☎ *902-532-2397. Admission: C$4 adults, C$3.50 seniors, C$2 children, C$9.90 families. Open: Mid-May to mid-Oct 9 a.m.–5:30 p.m.*

Historic Gardens
Downtown

These "historic" gardens were actually created in the 1980s, but they have been laid out to represent distinct eras in the history of Annapolis Royal, including Acadian (pre-1700s), British (early 1700s), and Victorian (late 1880s). Also on the grounds is a rose garden that comes alive with color in midsummer, a small maze to keep children on their toes, and a marshland trail dotted with interpretive panels explaining Acadian dyking techniques. A restaurant with a pleasantly shaded patio serves lunch.

441 St. George St. ☎ *902-532-7018.* www.historicgardens.com. *Admission: C$8.50 adults, C$7.50 seniors and children. Open: May to mid-Oct daily 9 a.m.–5 p.m. (8 a.m.–dusk July–Aug).*

Port-Royal National Historic Site

This is the actual site of Canada's first permanent settlement, which was founded in 1605 by French explorer Samuel de Champlain. Destroyed by the British eight years later, the fort has been reconstructed using Champlain's original plans, complete with costumed interpreters. One of the most interesting exhibits describes how the Mi'Kmaq helped the settlers adapt to the new land.

Follow Granville Road for 10km (6¼ miles) from the north side of the causeway. ☎ *902-532-2898. Admission: C$4 adults, C$3.50 seniors, C$2 children, C$9.90 families. Open: Mid-May to mid-Oct 9 a.m.–5:30 p.m.*

Continuing toward Halifax from Annapolis Royal

From Annapolis Royal, Highway 101 continues to make its way along the southern edge of the Bay of Fundy. It's just over 200km (125 miles) back to Halifax along this direct route. A more enticing option is Highway 1, which heads in the same direction, but at a more relaxing pace. Reach the following from both highways:

✔ **Cape Split.** Reaching the end of this narrow finger of land extending almost across the Minas Channel entails an 8km (5-mile) one-way hike, but you're rewarded with magnificent views down to the Bay of Fundy. On the protected eastern side of the spit, **Blomidon Provincial Park** protects an impressive lineup of red cliffs. To get to either spot, take Exit 11 from Highway 101 and follow the signs from Highway 358.

✔ **Wolfville.** This university town (home of the well-respected Acadia University) has an impressive array of Victorian-era homes, the **Randall House Museum** at 259 Main St. (☎ 902-542-9775), which catalogs the colonists who came after the Acadians had been expelled, and a pleasant waterfront area where interpretive boards describe the natural and human history of Minas Basin. Built by an apple baron, **Victoria's Historic Inn** at 600 Main St. (☎ 800-556-5744 or 902-542-5744; www.victoriashistoricinn.com) can be an inexpensive overnight stop or a decadent splurge, depending on your room choice. Regardless of how much you pay, everyone enjoys the same gourmet breakfast. Rates are C$118 to C$245, which is in the $$-to-$$$$ range.

✔ **Grand Pré National Historic Site.** Once the principal population center of Acadia, this outdoor museum east of Wolfville off Highway 1 (☎ 902-542-3631) remembers the expulsion of Acadians in 1755. Although the English burned their villages, the clever dyking system Acadians developed to farm land below sea level is still present. Also on the grounds are a church, various statues and monuments, and a blacksmith's shop. While the outdoor attractions are the main draw, it's well worth also spending time in the main interpretive center to learn a little about Acadian culture and the deportation. Admission C$7.15 adults, C$5.90 seniors, C$3.45 children. Open: Mid-May to mid-October daily 9 a.m. to 6 p.m.

✔ **Howard Dill Enterprises.** If you're tiring of history, take a detour to one of Nova Scotia's quirkiest, yet most impressive, attractions. Howard Dill is famous for developing pumpkin seeds that go on to produce some of the world's largest pumpkins, including the current world record of 681 kilograms (1,502 pounds). The best time to visit his farm at 400 College Rd. (☎ 902-798-2728) is late September through early October, when the pumpkins are at their biggest.

Chapter 13

Central Nova Scotia

● ●

In This Chapter

▶ Watching the tidal bore in Truro

▶ Poking around Pictou

▶ Exploring the wild and rugged Eastern Shore

● ●

"*C*entral" Nova Scotia is a somewhat arbitrary designation that encompasses the region north of Halifax and extends east to Cape Breton Island. This portion of the province is served by main highways that lead to major population centers like Truro, New Glasgow, and beyond. In this chapter, I encourage you to explore towns and attractions that lie beyond the highways but are still close at hand. Highlights are as varied as watching the tidal bore created by massive tides in the Bay of Fundy, clambering over a replica of the boat that transported early Scottish settlers to North America, and learning to surf in the Atlantic Ocean.

Truro

Two major highways merge at Truro, which is Nova Scotia's third-largest city with a population of 12,000, but many tourists pass right on by. That's a shame, because the Truro area offers a few notable attractions that make a visit worthwhile.

Getting there

Highway 102 from Halifax (90km/56 miles to the south) passes west of Truro, while the east–west Trans-Canada Highway, here called Highway 104, passes north of it. To get downtown from Highway 102, take Exit 14; if you're on Highway 104, take Exit 15 to Highway 102 and then Exit 14.

Staying in Truro

Truro lodgings are designed to fill the needs of overnighting highway travelers. You can find some decent, well-priced motel rooms along the roads linking downtown to the main highways.

Comfort Inn Truro
$$ **Truro**

This low-slung, two-story chain motel is handy to Highway 102, but far enough away from it for traffic noise to be at a minimum. The midsize rooms come with lots of amenities (wireless Internet, free local calls, in-room coffee, hair dryers, ironing facility), and a light breakfast is included in the rates.

12 Meadow Dr. (Exit 14 from Highway 102). ☎ *800-424-6423 or 902-893-0330. Fax: 902-897-0176.* www.choicehotels.ca. *Rack rates: C$127–C$147. AE, DC, DISC, MC, V.*

Palliser Motel
$$ **Truro**

The older-style rooms are certainly not the attraction here: It's quite simply the location. Set on a low bluff above the Salmon River, this is the prime local spot for viewing the tidal bore (the river in front of the motel is lit at night for this purpose). The Palliser also has a restaurant, where motel guests are offered a complimentary hot buffet breakfast and a 15 percent discount on all other meals.

Tidal Bore Road (Exit 14 from Highway 102). ☎ *902-893-8951. Fax: 902-895-8475. Rack rates: C$75–C$99 double. AE, DC, MC, V.*

Dining in Truro

Give all the usual chain restaurants on the outskirts of Truro a miss, and take the time to search out the only local restaurant I recommend.

Murphy's
$ **Truro SEAFOOD**

Who says it's all about location? One of Nova Scotia's best-known seafood restaurants is in Truro, which isn't even on the ocean — and it's in a strip mall to boot. Inside, the fish nets, model boats, and bright maritime murals leave no one guessing at this restaurant's specialty. The menu offers a wide range of all the usual seafood suspects, but the perfectly cooked deep-fried fish (usually cod) brings in a constant flow of locals and travelers in the know.

88 Esplanade St. ☎ *902-895-1275. Main courses: C$11–C$23 dinner. AE, MC, V. Open: Daily 11 a.m.–8 p.m.*

Exploring Truro

Start your visit at the **Visitor Information Centre** (Victoria Square; ☎ **902-893-2922;** open May–Oct daily 9 a.m.–5 p.m.; in July–Aug extended to daily 8 a.m.–8 p.m.), and take a downtown walking tour that focuses on an unfortunate history with a silver lining. A few years back, Dutch elm disease struck many of the stately elm trees lining Truro's streets. While trees afflicted with the same disease in other towns were destroyed, an imaginative group of locals commissioned a woodcarver to create art from the trunks. Today, over 30 tree-trunk sculptures dot the downtown streets. Ask for a map detailing each at the information center.

Truro doesn't give you many reasons to linger too long, though. See the tidal bore, and then hit the road for some quick out-of-town sightseeing.

Tidal Bore
Truro

Some of the world's highest tides rise through the Bay of Fundy. When the ocean water in the bay is forced up adjacent low-lying rivers, a wall of water surges across the mudflats and funnels into the local river systems, and you can actually see the water changing direction. Truro's location beside the Salmon River at the far end of the "funnel," combined with easy access from the highway, make the local **Tidal Bore Park** a favorite viewing spot for this intriguing sight.

Tides change just over every six hours, so the bore occurs twice daily. It arrives approximately 50 minutes later each day, so be sure to check at the visitor center (☎ 902-893-2922) for tide times.

Tidal Bore Road (Exit 14 off Highway 102 or west from downtown along Prince Street). Admission: Free.

Balmoral Grist Mill
Balmoral Mills

Step back in time at this underrated, off-the-beaten-path attraction that was built in 1874 and has been restored to working order. Within a bright-red wooden building nestled in a lush valley, water tumbles through a water wheel linked by a pulley system to a solid granite millstone that grinds wheat and oats. Various demonstrations take place daily, with the finished product used in a variety of baked goodies sold at the site. Not only is Balmoral Grist Mill worth visiting for its historical interest, but the location is delightful. Plan on enjoying a picnic lunch in the adjacent park.

Matheson Brook Road, 38km (24 miles) north of Truro off Highway 311. ☎ 902-637-3016. Admission: C$3.25 adults, C$2.25 seniors and children, C$7.50 families. Open: June to mid-Oct Mon–Sat 9:30 a.m.–5:30 p.m., Sun 1 p.m.–5:30 p.m.

Glooscap Trail
West from Truro

Named for a mythical Mi'Kmaq spirit who controlled the tides, this route (Highway 2) follows the northern shoreline of Cobequid Bay and Minas Basin west from Truro to Parrsboro before taking a jog north to rejoin the Trans-Canada Highway (104) near Springhill. Although the Glooscap Trail is in the geographical center of the Maritimes, it passes through a relatively remote region, with verdant forests running down to sea cliffs and tiny fishing villages.

An obvious attraction along this stretch of highway is the scenery, but the most interesting features are less obvious. In the 1980s, this region came into the paleontological spotlight when more than 100,000 bone fragments from dinosaurs were unearthed. The **Fundy Geological Museum** in Parrsboro (☎ 902-254-3814) explains the importance of the 200-million-year-old fossil beds. In addition, agate and amethyst are common along this stretch of coast. **Parrsboro Rock and Mineral Shop** (☎ 902-254-2981), operated by local dinosaur-hunting legend Eldon George, displays various fossils (including thumbnail-sized dinosaur footprints) along with lots of gemstones. Eldon sells you rock-collecting gear or, if he's not busy, takes you out to his favorite collecting grounds for around C$30 per person.

The 1893 **Maple Inn**, at 2358 Western Ave. in Parrsboro (☎ 877-627-5346 or 902-254-3735; www.mapleinn.ca) is a good overnight choice for travelers looking to soak up local history. Rates for the nine guest rooms range C$90 to C$150 double, including breakfast.

Pictou

In 1773, about 250 hardy Scottish settlers stepped ashore at Pictou Harbour after a treacherous trans-Atlantic journey aboard the *Hector*. They were brought to the area by a Philadelphia company looking to fulfill the terms of a land grant. Few people from North America were willing to move to the area, so the company began to look farther afield; Acadia was renamed Nova Scotia ("New Scotland" in Latin) in a desperate effort to attract Scots.

Getting there

Pictou lies on a protected harbor 12km (7½ miles) north of Highway 104. The road to Pictou is busier than you may expect, because it continues through town to the Caribou ferry terminal, one of two gateways to Prince Edward Island.

Staying in Pictou

This town has a good selection of historic properties that offer comfortable lodging without going over-the-top in décor or price.

Consulate Inn
$$–$$$ Pictou

This ivy-covered 1810 building was once a consulate for the United States, and later a prominent local judge called it home for 50 years. Perhaps as a result, it has a somewhat jaded air of having been-there, done-that. The cheaper rooms may not be designer-chic, but you get a good night's rest. The Lower Garden Suite with basic cooking facilities is good value, but has a low ceiling (C$79). Rooms in the modern annex all have a jetted tub and varying water views. Out back, the garden runs all the way to the water's edge, with outdoor furniture, a gazebo, and a barbecue area. For families on a budget, the adjacent house can be rented through the Consulate Inn for C$119. All rates include breakfast.

115 Water St. ☎ *800-424-8283 or 902-485-4554. Fax: 902-485-1532.* www.consulate inn.com. *Rack rates: C$75–C$159 double. AE, MC, V.*

Pictou Lodge Resort
$$–$$$$ East of Pictou

This sprawling resort occupies a prime position on Northumberland Strait. Pictou Island is visible in the distance and water surrounds the property on three sides, with a man-made pond thrown in for good measure. Activities include canoeing, sea kayaking lessons, horseback riding, hiking along nature trails, biking, or just relaxing on the private beach. The oldest units date to the 1920s and were last renovated in 2006; some have been given a thorough going-over (the one-bedroom deluxe cottages, complete with kitchen and screened veranda, are my favorite), but more modern motel units and snazzy log cabins have the better views. A summer activity program makes the lodge a great place for families.

Braeshore Road. (5km/3 miles east of Pictou). ☎ *800-495-6343 or 902-485-4322. Fax: 902-485-4945.* www.pictoulodge.com. *Rack rates: C$135–C$289 double. AE, DISC, MC, V. Open: Mid-May to mid-Oct.*

Dining in Pictou

Pictou Lodge Resort Dining Room
$$–$$$$ East of Pictou   NORTH AMERICAN

Even if you're not staying here, take the short drive just for a meal. While the rest of the resort has undergone numerous upgrades through the years, the restaurant hasn't, which is a good thing. Breakfast and lunch are taken on the screened-in veranda, while the main dining room, with its high ceiling, exposed log work, and massive fireplace, has a distinctly historical charm. The menu also reflects an earlier era, with steak, chicken, and seafood dishes cooked to perfection and served without frills. The salmon, basted in maple syrup and herbs and broiled on a cedar plank, is a real treat. Sunday brunch is also popular.

Braeshore Road. ☎ *902-485-4322. Reservations recommended for dinner. Main courses: C$17–C$30. AE, DISC, MC, V. Open: Mid-May to mid-Oct daily 7 a.m.–9 p.m.*

Exploring Pictou

Pictou's biggest draw is the waterfront. Plan on spending at least half a day poking around the harbor.

Hector Heritage Quay
Pictou

This harbor complex is anchored by a full-sized floating replica of the 34m (110-foot) *Hector*, the sailing ship that transported Nova Scotia's first

Scottish settlers across the Atlantic. The three-masted ship was constructed using traditional tools and techniques, making it the most faithful reconstruction project of its kind ever undertaken in North America. Admission includes access to the ship itself, but spending time "on land" is worthwhile to read interpretive panels that narrate the story of the original ship and its passengers and watch blacksmiths and carpenters at work in their dockside shops. Guided tours at 10 a.m. and 2 p.m. are offered free with admission. This attraction is perfect for families — interesting for adults, but the kids will have fun, too.

33 Caladh Ave., Pictou. ☎ *902-485-4371. Admission: C$7 adults, C$5 seniors, C$2 children 6–12. Open: Mid-May to Oct Mon–Sat 9 a.m.–5 p.m., Sun 10 a.m.–5 p.m.*

Northumberland Fisheries Museum
Pictou

At one time, this red-brick railway station was the eastern end of the rail line across Canada. Now it's an unassuming museum that's actually pretty interesting. The museum has an impressive collection of exhibits on diverse ocean-related topics ranging from local marine life to the whaling and fishing industries and racing boats. Kids will love the model boats and tank of live lobsters. Spending an hour at this museum is easy, even if you're not a maritime buff.

71 Water St., Pictou. ☎ *902-485-4972. Admission: C$4.50 adults, C$3.50 seniors, C$2 children 6–12. Open: Mid-June to mid-Oct Mon–Sat 9 a.m.–7 p.m., Sun noon to 5 p.m.*

Not Jost another winery

Everyone loves promoting a local product — that's why you see wines from **Jost Vineyards** (pronounced "yost") featured in many Nova Scotia restaurants. Though it's situated well away from Canada's better-known wine-producing regions, Jost has produced some award-winning products. They're only available in Nova Scotia, so be sure to get a sample while you're here, especially of their award-winning **ice wine**. Frost is the enemy in most vineyards, but at Jost it's a vital part of the ice wine process. The frozen grapes are left on the vines for a few days, and then gently pressed to extract just a few drops of concentrated juice from each grape. The result of this low-yield process is an intensely sweet dessert wine that sells for around C$40 per bottle. Ice wine is only a small part of the Jost repertoire. Many classic European varietals that reflect the owner's German roots, including a classic Riesling, are picked at a more traditional time of year to produce bottles of wine mostly in the C$10-to-C$20 range.

Free winery tours are offered daily at noon and 3 p.m. throughout the summer. Afterward, you can browse the wine shop, pick up some gourmet goodies at the deli, and enjoy a picnic on the patio.

Jost Vineyards is at Malagash, east of Pictou along Highway 6 (☎ **902-257-2636**; www.jostwine.com). Open: June to mid-Sept daily 9 a.m.–6 p.m.

Touring along Northumberland Strait

East of Pictou, Northumberland Strait is bordered by a convoluted coast-line that extends all the way to Canso Causeway, gateway to Cape Breton Island. Highway 104, the main route to Cape Breton, sensibly follows a direct route well away from the coastline, leaving a variety of options for casual touring. Here are some suggested detours along the way:

- ✔ **New Glasgow.** East of Pictou along Highway 104, this sprawling town has a pleasant downtown core centered on a river. An 1841 building constructed from ship ballast has been converted to the **Dock, Food, Spirits, and Ales** pub, at 130 George St. (☎ 902-752-0884). Its historical origins are ignored by most patrons, who gravitate to the sun-drenched patio.

- ✔ **Stellarton.** New Glasgow and Stellarton are separated by Highway 104, though linked by commercial sprawl. Take Exit 24 on Highway 104 to get to Eastern Canada's largest museum, the **Museum of Industry** (☎ 902-755-5425). This may not sound like an exciting stop, but kids will love every minute of it — from the opportunity to talk with a retired coal miner to printing their own bookmarks. In keeping with the theme, you must punch a time card upon entry. Allow at least an hour to explore. Open: Monday to Saturday 9 a.m. to 5 p.m., Sunday 10 a.m. to 5 p.m. (closed weekends outside of summer). Admission: C$7.50 adults, C$4.50 seniors, C$3.25 children.

- ✔ **Antigonish.** Pronounced An-*tee*-gun-ish, this busy highway town becomes even busier during the middle weekend of July for the **Highland Games,** the biggest and oldest such games outside of Scotland. Heavyweight events like tug-o'-war and caber-tossing are balanced by pipe-bands and performances by some of the biggest names in Celtic music.

- ✔ **Arisaig Provincial Park.** This park protects coastal cliffs that tell the 400-million-year-old story of a time when Nova Scotia was part of a shallow sea. What makes this place particularly interesting to scientists is that layers of sediment laid down over millions of years have become exposed along a single cliff line, revealing a neck-straining timeline of ancient life on earth. Digging into the cliff for fossils is not permitted, but you are allowed to search through fallen rubble along the beach.

Eastern Shore

Promoted as the **Marine Drive** (Highway 7, and then highways 211 and 316), the route between Halifax and Canso looks relatively tame on a big map, but when it comes to negotiating the narrow, winding 320km (200-mile) route you should allow a full day — *without* stops. But don't let the pace put you off: The slow going is the perfect excuse to take your time and spend the night in one of the charming villages en route.

Getting there

From Dartmouth, across the harbor from downtown Halifax, take Exit 7 from Highway 111. The highway is occasionally in sight of the ocean, but the most scenic areas are along side roads. Consult a good map, and enjoy!

Staying along the Eastern Shore

The Eastern Shore has a few excellent lodging options, but reserve ahead of time so you don't end up spending the night in a nondescript roadside motel.

Liscomb Lodge
$$$ Liscomb Mills

Its location halfway between Halifax and Canso makes Liscomb Lodge a good place for an overnight stop. Standard rooms are comfortable but unexceptional. Paying extra for the much larger cottages is worthwhile, even if you don't have a family in tow. Activities like hiking and boating will tempt you to stay longer. The resort restaurant is one of the few dining choices along this stretch of coast, so inquire about meal packages when booking a room (although breakfast is included in the rates).

Highway 7, Liscomb Mills. ☎ *800-665-6343 or 902-779-2307. Fax: 902-779-2700.* www.liscombelodge.ca. *Rack rates: C$155 double. AE, DISC, MC, V. Open: Mid-May to late Oct.*

Salmon River House Country Inn
$$ Salmon River Bridge

Less than an hour's drive from Halifax, this lodging has been a popular get-away for almost 100 years. The rooms have been modernized, but décor remains a bit old-fashioned. Still, the additions of en suite bathrooms and televisions aren't a bad thing. Close-up river views and a wonderful restaurant are the real reason this place makes the cut. The self-contained guesthouse may appeal to those looking for a little more privacy.

Highway 7, Salmon River Bridge. ☎ *800-565-3353 or 902-889-3353. Fax: 902-889-3653.* www.salmonriverhouse.com. *Rates: C$108–C$144 double. AE, MC, V. Open: Apr–Oct.*

Seaboard Bed and Breakfast
$$ East Lawrencetown

Popular with active travelers on a budget, this converted 1912 farmhouse is less than 1km (½ mile) from the waves of Lawrencetown Beach. Guests are welcome to use bikes or the canoe the hosts leave at a lake across the road. Seaboard offers basic, comfortable accommodations, a communal television room, a small library, and a lounge with fireplace. A hearty breakfast with lots of homemade baked goodies gets you going in the morning.

2629 Crowell Rd. ☎ *866-599-8094 or 902-827-3747.* www.seaboardbb.com. *Rack rates: C$100–C$115 double. MC, V.*

St. Mary's River Lodge
$$ **Sherbrooke**

The seven guest rooms in this renovated residence all have private bathrooms and television, and all but one are air-conditioned. The rooms are a little cutesy for my liking, but the price is right and it's handy to historic Sherbrooke Village, which is right next door. Rates include a cooked breakfast.

21 Main St., Sherbrooke. ☎ *902-522-2177. Fax: 902-522-2626.* www.riverlodge.ca. *Rack rates: C$76–C$106 double. MC, V.*

Dining along the Eastern Shore

J. Willy Krauch & Sons Ltd.
$ **Tangier SEAFOOD**

You'll often see salmon in restaurants referred to as "Krauch" salmon, and this is where it comes from. Krauch salmon is cold-smoked, which means the fish has been salted and then smoked for up to a week at very low temperatures. The process is very different from normal smoking, where the fish literally cooks as it is smoked. Cold-smoking creates a subtle, savory flavor and a firm texture — perfect for slicing thinly and serving on crackers (it's the most divine smoked salmon you'll ever taste). If you worry about consuming your purchase before it makes it home, you'll be pleased to know that the company ships worldwide.

Highway 7, Tangier. ☎ *902-772-2188. Open: Mon–Fri 8 a.m.–6 p.m.*

Lobster Shack
$$–$$$ **Salmon River Bridge SEAFOOD**

Ahoy, matey! Even landlubbers feel at home in this small-town restaurant with a big-time reputation. The dining room is part of the Salmon River House Country Inn and has a pleasant riverside deck. The interior walls are decorated in all manner of maritime memorabilia — the sort of stuff you'd expect to find washed up on the beach after a big storm. As the name suggests, lobster is a menu feature. To start, choose from super-creamy lobster chowder or rich seafood dip with pita bread. If you're serious about your lobster, choose one from the tank and order it as a main course. Boiled lobster is boiled lobster; what sets the Lobster Shack apart from other restaurants is the variety of sizes — up to 5 pounds on my last visit (I was told they often hold them up to 10 pounds).

Highway 7, Salmon River Bridge. ☎ *902-889-3353. Main courses: C$13–C$25. AE, MC, V. Open: Apr to Oct 8 a.m.–9 p.m.*

Exploring the Eastern Shore

Like the rest of the province, the Eastern Shore has a long and interesting history, which can be relived at numerous attractions. But the smell of salt in the air, the long stretches of sandy beach, and the quiet coves are the real draw.

Fisherman's Life Museum
Jeddore Oyster Pond

Life for an East Coast fisherman and his family 100 years ago was not easy. This museum re-creates the simple, self-sufficient lifestyle of one such family. Ervin Myers, the husband, spent long days at sea while his wife Ethelda raised 13 daughters in this small green and white house. Details such as the family's woodstove and small pipe organ and the surrounding gardens planted with root vegetables add to the museum's authentic quality.

58 Navy Pool Loop, Jeddore Oyster Pond. ☎ 902-889-2053. Admission: C$3.25 adults, C$2.25 seniors and children. Open: June to mid-Oct Mon–Sat 9:30 a.m.–5:30 p.m., Sun 1 p.m.–5:30 p.m.

Canso Islands National Historic Site
Canso

The Canso Islands, within sight of the small town of Canso, have a long history, but today sit empty beyond the end of one of Nova Scotia's most remote roads. The British established an outpost on one of them, Grassy Island, in the early 1700s, harvesting and processing 8 million cod annually. They also made a lackadaisical attempt at fortifying the settlement, but were unable to protect it against a 1774 attack by the French, who destroyed the entire town. The National Historic Site has two parts; stop by the Visitor Reception Centre along Union Street in Canso to learn more about the history, and then take the free 15-minute boat ride across to the island, where an interpretive trail leads past various foundations and a well. It's an interesting trip for the stark, end-of-the-world feel surrounding the site.

Access by boat from Canso ☎ 902-366-3136. Admission: Suggested donation of C$5 includes admission to the Visitor Reception Centre and boat ride. Open: June to mid-Sept daily 10 a.m.–6 p.m.

Sherbrooke Village
Sherbrooke

What makes this historic park stand out from others is that the village is an actual community, with real live Nova Scotians going about their daily business. Sherbrooke was the site of an 1860s gold rush, and many of the original buildings have been faithfully restored in the style of this era. Costumed guides are on hand to talk about the village and its history, or to give demonstrations of traditional crafts such as candle-making and old-time photography. One of the most interesting displays is the workshop, where carpenters combine traditional skill with modern technology to produce reproductions in demand at historic sites across the province. On Thursdays at 7:30 p.m., the village courthouse hosts the Courthouse Concert Series, which may be anything from Celtic to country.

Highway 7, Sherbrooke. ☎ *888-743-7845 or 902-522-2400.* www.museum.gov.ns.ca/sv. *Admission: C$9 adults, C$7.25 seniors, C$3.75 children. Open: June to mid-Oct daily 9:30 a.m.–5 p.m.*

More cool things to do along the Eastern Shore

While the historic sites are worth a stop, the ocean takes center stage along the Eastern Shore. Apart from the coastal scenery, it's a great area for trying your hand at surfing or sea kayaking, and boasts some great beaches:

- ✓ **Surfing:** After surfing on both coasts of Canada, I can't say if one is better than the other. One thing is for certain, though: Lawrencetown Beach, a half-hour drive from Halifax, is Canada's best-known surf spot. Waves break along a rocky point as well as on the beach, with the biggest swells rolling through in winter. **Dacane Surf Shop** (☎ 902-431-7873) charges around C$50 per day for rental of surfboard and wet suit (you'll need one, even in summer). Lessons are also offered from their beachside outlet.

- ✓ **Sea kayaking:** Even if you've never been near a sea kayak, the guides at **Coastal Adventures,** based at Tangier (☎ 877-404-2774 or 902-772-2774; www.coastaladventures.com), make you feel comfortable in the water. The full-day beginner course (C$120 per person) is as much a tour as a lesson, with an introduction to basic paddling skills followed by a trip to an uninhabited island and lunch. You're in safe hands with co-owner Dr. Scott Cunningham, who could write a book on the subject — and in fact has *(Sea Kayaking in Nova Scotia).*

- ✓ **Beach walking:** Okay, this activity is a little less adventurous than the others, but nothing's like feeling sand between your toes and breathing in the smells of the ocean. Best of all, it's free. As Nova Scotia's longest stretch of sand (5km/3 miles), **Martinique Beach,** south of Musquodoboit Harbour, is a good option for an extended beach walk. It's protected as a provincial park and is dotted with day-use areas and access paths. Continuing north from Martinique Beach, **Taylor Head Provincial Park** protects a narrow spit of land lined by glorious white-sand beaches along its protected eastern side.

Chapter 14

Cape Breton Island

• •

In This Chapter

▶ Taking in the life and times of Alexander Graham Bell at Baddeck
▶ Driving the Cabot Trail through Cape Breton Highlands National Park
▶ Stepping back in time at the Fortress of Louisbourg

• •

*C*ape Breton Island is a Maritimes gem. It offers plenty of breathtaking coastal scenery and a dash of Canadian history, coupled with that unmistakable down-home East Coast charm you hear so much about. Joined to the mainland by a causeway, the island is renowned for its rugged coastline, although mountains, lakes, and salmon-filled rivers add to the diversity inland. The Cabot Trail, a 300km (186-mile) road that winds its way around Cape Breton Highlands National Park, is the island's top attraction.

History buffs will be satiated at Canada's largest historical reconstruction, the Fortress of Louisbourg National Historic Site. It reminds us that the French once held sovereignty to the island after ceding the rest of the province to the British in 1713.

A big part of this region's appeal is the people ("Cape Bretoners"), many of them proudly descended from Scots who were attracted by the island's strong resemblance to their homeland. The island's most famous resident was born in Scotland himself: Alexander Graham Bell. He, like so many others, was captivated by this unique part of the country and called Baddeck home for much of his life.

You need your own vehicle to make the most of a visit to Cape Breton Island.

Plan on spreading the wealth around when it comes to lodging. One night at a historic inn at Baddeck and another at a beachy resort along the Cabot Trail is the perfect combination for a two-night stay.

Cape Breton Island

Baddeck

Halfway up the island, the delightful resort town of Baddeck is a good central location to plan an overnight (or longer) stay. The town's most famous resident was Alexander Graham Bell, who spent summers and then the last three decades of his life at a stately waterfront mansion across the bay from Baddeck. Bell's descendants own the home, but one of the province's best museums that tells his interesting life story is in town. Down on the waterfront, a free ferry shuttles visitors to Kidston Island for hiking and swimming, while other tour boats can take you to search out nesting bald eagles.

Getting there

Take Highway 105 north from the Canso Causeway, and in less than an hour you're greeted by a bombardment of Baddeck billboards.

Staying in Baddeck

Whether you're looking to spend your day at a waterfront resort or a character-laden historic lodging, you can find your perfect accommodations in Baddeck.

Summer is very busy in Baddeck, so reservations are necessary for local lodging. If you do arrive without having booked a room, stop at the centrally located **Baddeck Welcome Centre** (☎ 902-295-1911) for suggestions.

Bethune's Boathouse Cottage
$$ **Baddeck**

The name says it all: This small cottage is a converted boathouse on the Baddeck waterfront. Inside is a double bed, bathroom, and living area with a television and radio. Do your cooking on an outside barbecue. The cottage sits on its own small lot but is not particularly private. If you feel like getting away, simply take to the water in the complimentary rowboat.

49 Water St. ☎ *902-295-2687. Rack rates: C$120 double. No credit cards. Open: Mid-May to mid-Oct.*

Inverary Resort
$$–$$$$ **Baddeck**

Kids in particular enjoy this resort on the south side of Baddeck. It's not really within walking distance of town, but why would you want to leave when you've got tennis courts, a spa facility, an indoor pool, a fitness center, a large playground, boat and kayak rentals, and sailing trips aboard a boat once owned by Alexander Graham Bell? The rooms vary from those of the original building to modern, fully equipped suites with private balconies. The resort also has two restaurants and a lounge. Golf and meal packages can be a good deal.

Shore Road. ☎ *800-565-5660 or 902-295-3500. Fax: 902-295-3527.* www.capebreton resorts.com. *Rack rates: C$119–C$390 double. AE, DISC, MC, V. Open: Apr–Dec.*

Telegraph House
$–$$$ **Baddeck**

Built in 1861 and now run by the fifth generation of the same family, this imposing gray-and-white inn on a main street was once a telegraph office. Rooms in the main lodge are basic and some are very small, but all are clean and comfortable, and the location can't be more central. Alexander Graham Bell often stayed in Room 1 when in town — do you need a better recommendation? Behind the main lodge is a wing of more modern motel rooms decorated in a vaguely Victorian décor. They may lack the history of those in the original building but are good value, especially the extra-large ones which are ideal for families. Finally, a self-contained cabin is available for those who like to really spread out.

9 Chebucto St. ☎ *888-263-9840 or 902-295-1100. Fax: 902-295-1136.* www.baddeck. com/telegraph. *Rack rates: C$79–C$199 double. AE, MC, V.*

Water's Edge Inn
$$–$$$ **Baddeck**

Water's Edge Inn overlooks the lake and Kidston Island, and is just a couple of blocks downhill from the main street. Paying extra for one of the four rooms with private balconies and water views is worthwhile, although all six are well-appointed and come with niceties such as DVD players, air-conditioning, and original art. A lounge is stocked with books and a computer for guest Internet access. The inn is also home to a cafe (open daily for breakfast and lunch) and an art gallery.

22 Water St. ☎ *866-439-2528 or 902-295-3600. Fax: 902-295-1382.* www.thewaters edgeinn.com. *Rack rates: C$140–C$170 double. AE, MC, V. Open: May–Oct.*

Dining in Baddeck
Restaurants line the main street through Baddeck, but some of the better dining choices are associated with local lodgings.

Baddeck Lobster Suppers
$$ **Baddeck**   **SEAFOOD**

In typical lobster-supper style (or lack of it), this traditional Maritimes feast is replayed for tourists in a dining hall across from the waterfront. At dinner, pay C$30 for one full lobster and all-you-can-eat mussels, seafood chowder, salad, bread rolls, dessert, and non-alcoholic drinks. Lunch offers similar choices from a regular menu, such as a lobster roll for C$9.

Ross Street. ☎ *902-295-3307. Lobster supper: C$30. MC, V. Open: June–Oct daily 11:30 a.m.–1:30 p.m. for lunch and 4–9 p.m. for dinner.*

Lakeside Café
$$ Baddeck   CAFE

Drive down through the Inverary Resort to reach this casual waterfront restaurant, which has lots of outdoor tables. The lunch menu is made up of fancy sandwiches such as a Lobster Clubhouse and appetizers from the dinner menu. The evening menu takes its roots from around the world, with an emphasis on local produce. Choose from dishes such as a Thai stir-fry tossed with scallops, or go Greek with grilled halibut topped with feta cheese and olives.

Inverary Resort, Shore Road. ☎ *902-295-3500. Main courses: C$12–C$20. AE, MC, V. Open: May–Oct daily 11 a.m.–3:30 p.m. and 4:30–10 p.m.*

Lynwood Inn Dining Room
$$–$$$ Baddeck   CANADIAN

Tucked inside a historic residence that has been converted to an inn, this smallish dining room features a crisp Victorian color scheme with the modern addition of a deck wrapped around two sides. For starters, the menu covers all bases, with nachos, mussels, and chicken soup (with loads of chicken). Entrees are no less diverse, with choices ranging from a charbroiled T-bone to grilled rainbow trout splashed with a corn salsa.

23 Shore Rd. ☎ *902-295-1995. Main courses: C$14–C$23. AE, MC, V. Open: Daily 11 a.m.–9 p.m.*

Exploring Baddeck

Baddeck isn't big on traditional official "sights," but it's still a delightful town to visit. Chebucto Street is the main thoroughfare, but walk 1 block down Jones Street to reach the waterfront and find yourself in the real heart of the town.

Alexander Graham Bell National Historic Site
Baddeck

Like most kids, I learned in school that Alexander Graham Bell invented the telephone, but it wasn't until I spent a few hours in this museum that I realized the extent of his contribution to the world of science and engineering. The first exhibit explains Bell's achievements in teaching the deaf (including Helen Keller) to speak, using a phonetic alphabet developed by his father. Spend some time at this display, as the interpretive panels go on to explain how this early work was inextricably linked to his later experimenting with transmitting sound along wire using voice pulsations. This, of course, led to Bell's patenting of the world's first telephone in 1876. The rest of the museum is devoted to his lesser-known inventions, such as the world's first hydrofoil and first seaplane. Among the various replicas and original parts on display is the *Silver Dart*, with which Bell broke the world speed record on Bras d'Or Lake. As a symbol of Bell's work with children, part of the museum is set aside for kids, with puzzles, experiments, and kite-making.

Cape Bretoners and their music

Wherever you travel on Cape Breton Island, you hear Celtic-based music. It's incredibly popular with the local population, and so catchy that you can't help but be captivated by its spirit and energy. Cape Bretoners Natalie MacMaster, Ashley MacIsaac, The Rankins, and The Irish Descendants have introduced this music to the world, but visiting the island itself is the best way to immerse yourself in the traditions of Celtic song and dance. To find great places to go for a night out, ask a local, check entertainment listings in newspapers, or simply wander the streets listening for live music.

One event worth noting is the **Celtic Colours International Festival** (☎ 877-285-2321 or 902-562-6700; www.celtic-colours.com), held the second week of October with the magnificent backdrop of fall's blazing colors. Celtic musicians from around the world perform in over 40 island towns in churches, halls, and theaters.

Chebucto Street. ☎ *902-295-2069.* www.pc.gc.ca/lhn-nhs/ns/grahambell. *Admission: C\$7.15 adults, C\$5.90 seniors, C\$3.45 children. Open: May daily 9 a.m.–5 p.m., June daily 9 a.m.–6 p.m, July to mid-Oct daily 8:30 a.m.–6 p.m., last two weeks of Oct daily 9 a.m.–5 p.m.*

Other cool things to see and do in Baddeck

Relax at an outdoor cafe, wander down to the waterfront or, if you're feeling more active, consider one of the following:

✔ **Set Sail.** The *Elsie* (☎ 902-295-3500) is a gracious sailing boat once owned by Alexander Graham Bell. It departs the Inverary Resort daily at 10:30 a.m. and 2:30 p.m. for a three-hour tour on Bras d'Or Lake. Keep an eye out for Alexander Graham Bell's mansion, and you may spy a bald eagle along the way. The cost is C\$65 per person.

✔ **Paddle over to Kidston Island.** Protected as a park, this uninhabited island lies just across a narrow channel from Baddeck. It has a beach, nature trails, and even a lighthouse. A free ferry departs Government Wharf for the island every 20 minutes, but renting a canoe or kayak from **Harvey's** is more enjoyable, which is beside Government Wharf (☎ 902-295-3318).

✔ **Take a drive through the Margaree Valley.** West of Baddeck, the southernmost section of the Cabot Trail follows the Margaree River, famed in fishing circles for its high concentrations of salmon. At the **Margaree Salmon Museum** in North Margaree (☎ 902-248-2848) find out about the salmon's lifecycle from guides or on your own. It's open mid-June to mid-October daily 9 a.m. to 5 p.m., and entry is just C\$1. North of the museum, potter Bell Fraser sells her distinctive ocean-inspired pieces at **Cape Breton Clay** in the village of Margaree Valley (☎ 902-235-2467).

 ✔ **Dance the night away.** The **Baddeck Gathering Ceilidhs** is a
 nightly performance by local musicians in St. Michael's Parish Hall
 on Main Street (☎ **902-295-2794**). Entry costs just C$8 for adults
 and C$4 for children; tea, coffee, and oatcakes are each C$2. All the
 action gets underway at 7:30 p.m., July and August only.

Cape Breton Highlands National Park and the Cabot Trail

Everyone falls in love with this spectacular national park, which
stretches across the top of Cape Breton Island. Sea cliffs and rocky
coves dominate the west side and long sandy beaches run down the east
side, with a vast plateau of wilderness in between. The Cabot Trail, one
of Canada's most scenic drives, loops through the park and weaves
along both coasts, ensuring that you miss nothing. Wildlife viewing is
excellent: Most visitors spot moose, whales, and bald eagles, often without even leaving their vehicles.

Getting there

Unless you plan to traverse the Cabot Trail by bike, you need your own
vehicle. To reach the main park gate, turn off Highway 105 south of
Baddeck.

Paying entrance fees

The **park entry fee** of C$6.90 adults, C$5.90 seniors, C$3.45 youths, to a
maximum of C$17 per vehicle, is good until 4 p.m. the day following its
purchase. Passes can be purchased at the information center north of
Chéticamp or at the tollbooths at both park entrances. If you have a
National Parks of Canada Pass (refer to Chapter 5), you'll be waved
right on through.

Arriving at the park's main entrance

Make your first stop the **Chéticamp Visitor Centre** (☎ **902-224-2306**),
5km (3 miles) north of Chéticamp. It's open May to June and September
to mid-October daily 9 a.m. to 5 p.m., July to August daily 8 a.m. to 8
p.m. Inside, natural history exhibits provide a good introduction to the
park, and posted activities schedules help in planning your time.
Friendly staff at the information desk supply free maps and help you
decide which hiking trails best suit your abilities. Off to one side is **Les
Amis du Plein Air** (☎ **902-224-3814**), a bookstore that stocks park-
related literature and a wide selection of general outdoor and nature
guides.

Staying along the Cabot Trail

Cliff Waters Wilderness Retreat
$$$$ **Pleasant Bay**

Cliff Waters comprises two units that are rented as one, making this the perfect accommodations for two couples traveling together or families with older children. The Spinning Jenny Guest Cabin, an old tool shed that has been transformed into a contemporary space, overlooks the ocean and has wood floors, a three-piece bathroom (or the option of an outdoor shower). The larger cottage features a cathedral ceiling, full kitchen, and a deck with ocean views. The emphasis throughout the property is on eco-friendliness (think solar-powered lanterns, organic coffee, and more).

1773 Red River Rd., 9km (5.6 miles) north from Pleasant Bay. ☎ *902-224-1130. Fax: 902-422-1711.* www.cliffwaters.com. *Rack rates: C$249 for both units. AE, MC, V. Open: Mid-May to mid-Nov.*

Glenghorm Beach Resort
$$–$$$$ **Ingonish**

Set on a sprawling property that extends from the Cabot Trail to a beautiful sandy beach, this resort has activities for the whole family and accommodations to suit all tastes. It offers canoe and kayak rentals, an outdoor pool, volleyball courts, a large playground, a fitness room, an aesthetics salon, and nightly beachside bonfires. The least expensive units are roadside motel rooms. Older cottages come with a kitchen and up to two bedrooms; some are within sight of the ocean. The Deluxe Suites are among the best guest rooms in all of the Maritimes: Luxuriously appointed, they still manage to maintain a casual air — you can happily tramp sand in without feeling guilty. Each air-conditioned unit has a private veranda or balcony, separate sleeping quarters, a jetted tub, a kitchen, and comfortable couches set around a gas fireplace. Resort dining includes a restaurant open for three meals and the charmingly named Thirsty Hiker Pub with live Celtic music most nights.

Ingonish Beach. ☎ *800-565-5660 or 902-285-2049. Fax: 902-285-2395.* www.cape bretonresorts.com. *Rack rates: High season C$109–C$399 double, low season C$80–C$295 double. AE, MC, V. Open: May to mid-Oct.*

Keltic Lodge
$$$–$$$$ **Ingonish Beach**

Sharing a narrow peninsula that juts into Ingonish Bay with the famous Highland Links golf course, the Keltic Lodge is one of Canada's most fashionable resorts. A short drive from the Cabot Trail leads to the perfectly positioned main lodge, on an isthmus high above the ocean and with water views to the north and south. The nationalistic red-and-white exterior contrasts starkly with the surrounding blues and greens. Dating to the 1940s, this is the original lodge, with older rooms, a restaurant and lounge, and the main lobby. Guests also have the use of a heated outdoor pool, and spa services; and the concierge can make bookings for tennis, whale-watching, and fishing. You don't need to be a registered guest to get a tee time at Highland Links or to hike out to the tip of Middle Head, but you feel more like you belong if you are. The rooms are a little on the small side, but are outfitted in smart heritage color schemes. Regardless, you'll find yourself enjoying the outdoors for much of your stay. Rooms in the main lodge are a little old-fashioned, while those in the Inn at Keltic are motel-like, but air-conditioned and just steps away from a grassy area with a gazebo and colorful Adirondack chairs. The four-bedroom cottages can be rented as an entire unit or with guests sharing a communal living area.

Ingonish Beach. ☎ 800-565-0444 or 902-285-2880. Fax: 902-285-2859. www.keltic lodge.ca. *Rack rates: High season C$190–C$340 double, low season C$100–C$160 double. AE, DISC, MC, V. Open: Mid-May to mid-Oct.*

Parkview Motel
$$ Chéticamp

Choose from older rooms or upgrade to air-conditioned creek-side deluxe rooms at this motel complex within walking distance of the park informa-tion center. The on-site restaurant and lounge save you from having to drive anywhere.

West entrance, 5km (3 miles) north of Chéticamp. ☎ 902-224-3232. Fax: 902-224-2596. www.parkviewresort.com. *Rack rates: C$89–C$109 double. AE, MC, V. Open: May to mid-Oct.*

Seascape Coastal Retreat
$$$ Ingonish

Set on a grassy slope that ends at a private beach on Ingonish Bay, this resort is a little piece of heaven beside the busy Cabot Trail. The well-tended grounds are dotted with outdoor seating and a hot tub. In one corner, a garden produces vegetables and herbs used in the adjacent restaurant. The cottages have solid, modern furnishings; amenities such as jetted tubs and fireplaces; and special touches like bathrobes add to their charm. All cottages have a veranda with an ocean view. Prices include seafood hors d'oeuvres upon arrival, a cooked breakfast, and the use of kayaks and mountain bikes.

36083 Cabot Trail, Ingonish. ☎ 866-385-3003 or 902-285-3003. www.seascape coastalretreat.com. *Rack rates: High season C$224–C$249 double. MC, V. Open: May–Oct.*

Dining along the Cabot Trail
It's seafood and more seafood along the Cabot Trail. If you feel like a break from the catch of the day, try the major resorts, most of which have restaurants with wide-ranging menus.

Atlantic Restaurant
$$–$$$ Ingonish Beach   SEAFOOD/CANADIAN

Looking in, this place could be an upmarket family restaurant anywhere in North America. Looking *out*, the drop-dead gorgeous ocean view through big windows could only be Cape Breton. Low prices are the only real surprise on the seafood-dominated menu. You can order favorites like beer-battered fish and chips for as little as C$10, but I encourage you to be more adventurous. The grilled salmon, bookended by crab cakes to start and a slice of blueberry shortcake for dessert, sets you back around C$38. The extensive salad bar, complete with mussels and chowder, is an additional C$9, or you can have it as a meal in itself for C$13.

Keltic Lodge, Ingonish Beach. ☎ *902-285-2880. Main courses: C$12–C$25. AE, DC, DISC, MC, V. Open: Mid-May to mid-Oct 11 a.m.–9 p.m.*

Chowder House
$–$$ Neil's Harbour   SEAFOOD

This is casual Cape Breton dining at its very best. The Chowder House is in a weather-beaten building on a headland through the village of Neil's Harbour. Don't be put off by the pine-paneled décor: The food is super-fresh and very well priced. The clam chowder is chockablock with juicy clams and costs just C$5 per bowl; a lobster burger costs C$10; or you can order the most expensive item on the menu board, a full lobster with fries and coleslaw, for C$22. After you decide, order at the counter and listen for your number. The restaurant is totally enclosed, which is a bit of a shame — if it's a nice day, I recommend spreading a blanket out on the grassy headland.

Neil's Harbour, beside the lighthouse. ☎ *902-336-2463. Main courses: C$5–C$22. Open: May–Sept 11 a.m.–8 p.m.*

Muddy Rudder
$–$$ South Ingonish Beach   SEAFOOD

The delightfully named Muddy Rudder is part restaurant, part attraction, and totally unique. It's simply a roadside shanty at the head of Ingonish Harbour with a few plastic outdoor table settings off to one side. Choose from lobster, crab, mussels, or clams, all of which are cooked to order in big pots of boiling water out front. Prices are a little higher than at a local seafood market, but a lot lower than at a regular restaurant. While researching this edition, my wife and I enjoyed the biggest plate of mussels I've ever seen (C$7), followed by a full crab that came with tea cakes and coleslaw (C$19), and we just happened to have a bottle of red from Jost Vineyards (refer to Chapter 13) in the car, which the owner happily opened for us.

Cabot Trail, South Ingonish Beach. ☎ *902-285-2266. Main courses: C$7–C$19. Cash only. Open: May–Sept 10 a.m.–7 p.m. (later if the owner doesn't have other engagements).*

Restaurant Acadian
$–$$ Chéticamp ACADIAN

Attached to a craft shop, this casual restaurant is a wonderful place to try Acadian cuisine. Adding to the charm, the women who work there all dress in traditional clothing. Mains like *Croquettes de Morue* (codfish cakes) and *Chaudrée au Poisson* (haddock chowder) are mostly under C$10. Plan on saving room for dessert — the raisin pudding (C$3.75) is as good as it gets.

15067 Main St., Chéticamp. ☎ *902-224-3207. Main courses: C$8–C$17. AE, DISC, MC, V. Open: Mid-May to mid-June daily 11 a.m.–7 p.m., mid-June to late Oct daily 7 a.m.–9 p.m.*

Seascapes Restaurant
$$$ Ingonish SEAFOOD

Attached to the resort of the same name, missing this small oceanfront dining room is easy to do as you scoot along the eastern side of the Cabot Trail. It has no menu as such; the chef simply uses available seafood to create a half-dozen dishes (along with at least one vegetarian option), which are written up on a blackboard. I picked a creamy lobster linguini (C$22), and the lobster was boiled especially for my order. A rather refined-looking couple seated next to me were gleefully tucking into snow crab — complete with bibs (on them, not the crabs).

Seascape Coastal Retreat, 36083 Cabot Trail, Ingonish. ☎ *902-285-3003. Reservations recommended. Main courses: C$18–C$28. MC, V. Open: May–Oct daily 6–9 p.m.*

Exploring the Cabot Trail

The Cabot Trail, parts of which I cover elsewhere in this chapter, is a 300km (186-mile) route that takes in not just Cape Breton Highlands National Park, but also the coastal drive south from the park to St. Ann's and on to Baddeck, and then through the Margaree Valley to Chéticamp. Here I detail the spectacular 110km (68-mile) section inside the park.

Highlights along the way

Although the distance is only a little over 100km (62 miles) between Chéticamp and Ingonish, allow at least one full day for this stretch of highway, simply due to the number of interesting stops en route. The road is steep and narrow in some sections but is not difficult to drive. Pullouts and viewpoints are spaced along the entire route. Do not use the narrow shoulder as your personal parking space.

My description of the Cabot Trail follows a clockwise direction. I could have gone either way, but by following this course, you hit the main information center first up and complete the drive on the east side of the peninsula, where you find most of my recommended accommodations and restaurants.

The most dramatic section of the entire Cabot Trail is the 45km (28-mile) stretch along the west coast. The scenery kicks off in a big way almost immediately, with the road hugging the shoreline, ascending precipitous sea cliffs, and then dropping back down to sea level. Stop at as many overlooks as your time allows; take in the scenery and read the interpretive boards.

 One particularly scenic overlook is the **Veterans Monument,** 18km (11 miles) north of the park entrance. When I last made the stop, a moose and her calf were grazing in the open meadows below while a whale could be seen in the ocean beyond and a black bear foraged on the high hills behind.

After an inland detour, the road descends steeply via a series of switchbacks to reach sea level at **Pleasant Bay,** just outside the park boundary. This small village, which existed well before road access was possible, now takes full advantage of summer traffic with a variety of tourist services. It tries hard to function primarily as a fishing village, but the harbor is filled with whale-watching boats and sea kayakers. The **Whale Interpretive Centre,** at 104 Harbour Rd. (☎ 902-224-1411; open June to mid-Oct daily 9 a.m.–5 p.m.) has displays on the various species you may see out on a whale-watching trip. Admission is C$5 for adults, C$4 for seniors and children.

From Pleasant Bay, the Cabot Trail begins its ascent to a high plateau, reentering the national park after a few minutes' drive. Just inside the boundary is **Lone Shieling,** the stone replica of a Scottish crofter's hut. It is also the starting point for a short trail leading to a grove of 350-year-old sugar maple trees. Continuing eastward, the road traverses a stunted *taiga* (mostly evergreen) forest before reaching a turn off to **Cape North.** This side road skirts **Aspy Bay,** where a plaque and statue commemorate John Cabot's 1497 landfall. It then crosses to the northern tip of the island and the picturesque fishing communities of **Bay St. Lawrence, Capstick,** and **Meat Cove** — Cape Breton living in its rawest state.

After a side trip to Cape North, you have no choice but to backtrack before rejoining the Cabot Trail for its final push across the peninsula. Although the landscape on the east coast is less dramatic than the west, it's no less captivating, with long stretches of sand broken by rocky headlands. Highlights include the beach at **Black Brook Cove** and **Lakies Head Lookout.** Continuing south, the Cabot Trail leaves the park again. Along this section, it passes four villages with Ingonish in their names, although in reality, they merge into one long strip broken only by Middle Head, a narrow peninsula that holds one of Canada's finest golf courses and the grand Keltic Lodge. Beyond Ingonish, the Cabot Trail leaves the national park for a final time, making its last grand ascent to **Cape Smokey,** one of the most dramatic lookouts along the entire trail.

Hiking the highlands

You can enjoy the park's spectacular scenery from the inside of your vehicle easily enough, but to really appreciate the place, get out onto the hiking trails (free trail maps at the information center). Stray away from the road to experience the park's natural beauty on my favorite of the park's trails:

- ✔ **Le Buttereau Trail:** An easy trail to get you started. This 1.6km (1-mile) loop starts just north of the tollbooth, with views across a large lagoon and across a meadow cleared by early Acadian settlers. Plan a dawn walk for the best bird-watching, or wait until dusk to watch the sun set over the Gulf of St. Lawrence.

- ✔ **Skyline Trail:** The Skyline is a high ridge with a long but easy trail leading to a magnificent viewpoint where you can often spot whales frolicking below. The trail head is on the left as the Cabot Trail heads inland beyond French Mountain. Allow three hours for the 9.2km (5.7-mile) round-trip.

- ✔ **Benjie's Lake Trail:** You can reach this small lake easily in 30 minutes from a parking lot 6km (3.7 miles) beyond the Skyline Trail. As most visitors spend their time along the coastline, visiting this lake is a good way to escape the crowds — and you may even spy moose along the way.

- ✔ **Fishing Cove Trail:** Two trails make the steep descent to this small bay along an otherwise inaccessible stretch of coastline. The first, beginning 3km (1.9 miles) north of Benjie's Lake Trail, is 8km (5 miles) each way. Farther north, another trail is much shorter (4km/2.5 miles) but a lot steeper. Either way, pack a lunch and something to drink.

- ✔ **Jigging Cove Lake Trail:** On the park's east coast, 4km (2.5 miles) south of Neil's Harbour, this lake lies just out of sight of the highway. It's encircled by a 2.4km (1.5-mile) trail that you can hike in well under an hour.

- ✔ **Jack Pine Loop:** Escape the crowds at Black Brook Cove by scrambling through the boulders at the north end of the beach to reach the beginning of this 2.3km (1.4-mile) loop which weaves through coastal forest. You'll be back on your beach towel in less than an hour, even if you stop to read the interpretive boards along the way.

- ✔ **Middle Head Trail:** Drive as far as you can through the grounds of the Keltic Lodge, and then walk for 1.9km (1.2 miles) to the very end of a narrow peninsula surrounded by dramatic cliffs. If you're staying at the Keltic Lodge, join a 9:30 a.m. guided walk to learn about the flora and fauna as you go.

✔ **Freshwater Lake Loop:** As the trail head is Ingonish Beach, one of Canada's finest stretches of sand, you may find that motivating yourself to leave the beach is the hardest part of taking this easy 2km (1.2-mile) loop trail. Walking the path at dusk is a good opportunity to watch beavers hard at work — and you won't feel so bad about not being on the beach.

Other cool reasons to stop along the Cabot Trail

Apart from driving and hiking, consider the following options:

✔ **Whale-watching:** From the village of Pleasant Bay, you can take a tour boat to see whales frolicking along the coast. Commonly sighted species are pilot, humpback, and minke whales. The following operators are Coast Guard–certified, have partly covered vessels, and are run by experienced captains who have a wealth of knowledge: **Cabot Trail Whale Watching** (☎ 902-224-1976), **Captain Mark's Whale & Seal Cruise** (☎ 888-754-5112 or 902-224-1316), and **Fiddlin' Whale Tours** (☎ 866-688-2424). Typically, tours last 90 minutes and cost C$25 to C$30 for adults and C$12 to C$15 for children. Each operator has a booth along the marina at Pleasant Bay, but advance reservations are recommended. All cruises are weather permitting — if the captain decides not to go sail because of rough seas, you probably don't want to be out on the water anyway.

The advantage of choosing a whale-watching trip at Pleasant Bay over other locations throughout the Maritimes is that it's only a short ride to where the whales are, so you get to spend more time watching and less time traveling.

✔ **Sea-kayaking:** The protected water of St. Ann's Bay, south of Ingonish, is an ideal place to kayak. You're likely to spot eagles and whales while visiting inaccessible-by-foot beaches, sea caves, and tidal pools. Twice daily, **North River Kayak Tours** (☎ 888-865-2925 or 902-929-2628; www.northriverkayak.com) offers a half-day (actually, around a three-hour) trip for C$55 and a full-day trip for C$99. I recommend the full-day option. Great for first-timers and families, you practice basic paddling techniques and then head off to a sea cave; keep a lookout for eagles and mink along the way. The turnaround point is a remote beach where lunch is prepared. The cost includes kayak rental, instruction, lunch (steamed mussels if you're lucky), and maybe a friendly wave from the lighthouse keeper as you pass his posting. Overnight and multi-day trips explore more remote waters, including the Roughing It and Romance overnight excursion, which includes camping gear, all meals, and guidance to a remote beach for C$249 per person.

✔ **Beaching it:** The best beaches are on the eastern side of the park. **Black Brook Cove** is somewhat protected from wind and ocean swells, creating a safe swimming spot. This sandy beach is backed by a grassy picnic area. Continuing south, **Ingonish Beach** is a long stretch of sand, well protected by Middle Head. The shallow water is warm, and a short section is patrolled through summer daily from noon.

✔ **Golfing:** A 1939 Stanley Thompson layout, **Highland Links,** near Ingonish (☎ **800-441-1118** or 902-285-2600; www.highlandlinks golf.com) is consistently rated as one of the world's top 100 courses by *Golf Magazine.* Although not overwhelming by today's standards, it's a classic links-style course with a dramatic coastal setting. In keeping with the Scottish theme, each hole has a name, with both English and the Gaelic translation signed at the teebox (Hole 6, for example, is Mucklemouth Meg, the nickname for a girl with a big mouth, in reference to a pond that swallows wayward golf balls). Greens fees are C$73 to C$100 during peak season, dropping to just C$45 for twilight golfing during the shoulder season (June and Oct).

Shopping

Shopping? In a national park? Well, sort of. Cape Breton Island is known for its artists and, with the large number of tourists, many have set up shop in the tiny villages that lie on the edge of the park. Most are open long hours through summer, shorter hours during the shoulder seasons, and then close completely for winter.

I list the following in a clockwise direction from Chéticamp: Beyond the top of the park at Dingwell, **Arts North** (☎ 902-383-2732) showcases the driftwood whale carvings of owner Linda Doyon, the jewelry of Johanna Padelt, and the hooked rugs of Maggie Miller. One of the island's best-known painters is Christopher Gorey, whose oil and watercolor landscapes are sold at **Lynn's Craft Shop & Christopher Gorey Gallery,** at Ingonish (☎ 902-285-2845). **Tartans and Treasures** at South Harbour (☎ 902-383-2005) claims to have North America's largest collection of tartan scarves and blankets. Most products come directly from the mother country, so you know you're buying the real thing. **Iron Art & Photographs,** south of Ingonish at Tarbot (☎ 902-929-2318), combines the hand-forged ironwork of Gordon Kennedy with the striking hand-tinted black-and-white photography of his wife, Carol, to make a worthwhile stop on the road back to Baddeck.

Louisbourg

Over 250 years ago the French were driven from the lonely outpost of Louisbourg, on the remote eastern tip of Cape Breton Island. Today, it's one of the most interesting historical sites in all of the Maritimes, with lodging and other tourist services in an adjacent town of the same name (population 1,200) and an ambitious C$300-million resort development taking shape along the adjacent coastline.

Getting there

Louisbourg is 45km (28 miles) southeast of Sydney along Highway 22. No public transportation reaches the town.

Staying in Louisbourg

Even though it's at the end of the road, Louisbourg has several comfortable lodgings within walking distance of the fort, including these two recommendations.

Cranberry Cove Inn
$$-$$$ Louisbourg

You can't miss this three-story, cranberry-red inn as you head out to the fortress. Inside, the décor is a little tamer. Each of seven guest rooms has its own theme. The top-floor Captain's Den, for example, has a quirky layout (thanks to the gabled roof), a cheery maritime color scheme, wireless Internet, a gas fireplace, and a jetted tub. Downstairs is a parlor, in which three generations of the same family used to spend their evenings during the inn's former life. Breakfast is included in the rates and is served on the sunny side of the house.

12 Wolfe St. ☎ *800-929-0222 or 902-733-2171.* www.cranberrycoveinn.com. *Rack rates: C$105–C$160 double. AE, MC, V. Open: May–Oct.*

Point of View
$$-$$$ Louisbourg

This modern oceanfront property hogs the prime spot on a high headland within walking distance of both the town and the fortress. It sprawls over 1.6 hectares (4 acres) of well-maintained grounds, with a private beach at one corner of the property. Inside, the units have a sleek, contemporary styling, hardwood floors, and sliding doors that open to either a balcony or veranda. The apartments are much larger than the suites and come with a full kitchen.

At the front of the property is a beach house where the owners host a nightly Feast for the Senses. It's a casual gathering of guests, who are served steamed lobster and crab with all the trimmings and entertained with storytelling or a singalong. Breakfast isn't included in the rates, but is available, eggs, bacon and all, for just C$4 per person.

15 Commercial St. Extension. ☎ *888-374-8439 or 902-733-2080.* www.louisbourg pointofview.com. *Rack rates: C$125 double, C$199 apartments. MC, V.*

Dining in Louisbourg

Plan on eating lunch at one of the three restaurants at the Fortress of Louisbourg. If you're staying at Point of View Suites, reserve a spot at their nightly lobster supper. If not, this single recommendation is a good one.

Grubstake Restaurant
$$–$$$ Louisbourg   SEAFOOD

Over 35 years ago a group of well-traveled friends got together and opened this restaurant that serves local cuisine to visitors from around the world. Not much has changed since, and no one seems to mind. The restaurant is casual and cozy, and the seafood is done without a deep fryer in sight. If you order the oversize Seafood Pasta Extreme, plan to give dessert a miss; or, for something lighter, try halibut poached in milk and white wine, fish cakes with baked beans, or a vegetarian stir-fry.

7499 Main St. ☎ 902-733-2308. Dinner reservations accepted. Main courses: C$10–C$25. MC, V. Open: Daily noon to 8:30 p.m., later in July and Aug.

Exploring Louisbourg

Even if you don't like history lessons, a little background is necessary to set the scene for a visit to the Fortress of Louisbourg National Historic Site. After the 1713 Treaty of Utrecht, all the land the French were left with in the Maritimes were Prince Edward Island and Île Royale (Cape Breton Island), the latter a base for a lucrative codfishing industry. Wary of an attack on their sovereignty, the French established a massive fortress around the Louisbourg village to repel an attack from the ocean, but in 1745, the British came from behind and took it in a little more than six weeks. After the fortifications changed hands on two more occasions, the British destroyed them and burned the village to the ground in 1760. Two hundred years later, with many Cape Breton coal mines closing, the federal government decided to begin the daunting task of rebuilding the entire village and fort as a make-work project. The result is Canada's largest historical reconstruction — a must-see for anyone traveling around Cape Breton Island.

Fortress of Louisbourg National Historic Site

Plan on spending the better part of a full day on the grounds. Start by watching the video at the interpretive center, and then catch the shuttle to the back of the fort to get going on your exploration of the site. Every detail of the original fort and village has been re-created, down to the construction techniques and materials. Even the social structure is historically correct, with ostentatious homes of the rich filled with fine china and French wines, while ramshackle working-class abodes have earthen floors and wood stoves for heating. Around 100 costumed interpreters do a wonderful job of playing their parts. Actually, if you ask them, they won't admit they're playing a part at all — a military officer may sternly ask if you're spying for the British, or a carpenter may complain about how much harder it is to get materials in Canada than back in France, while vendors peddle their wares on cobblestoned streets.

Traditional menus and costumed servers depict 1700s life at three eateries. **Hotel de la Marine** and **Grandchamps Inn** are where regular folk eat; no meat is served on days of abstinence (Fri and Sat), and customers eat with only a large spoon. Expect to pay around C$15 ($$) for lunch at either of these two restaurants. If you arrive at the settlement with limited funds, head to **King's Bakery,** where a loaf of heavy bread and a hunk of cheese cost less than a single appetizer at the other eateries.

Louisbourg. ☎ *902-733-2280.* www.pc.gc.ca/louisbourg. *Admission: C$16 adults, C$14 seniors, C$8.15 children, C$41 families. Open: Mid-May to June and Sept to mid-Oct daily 9:30 a.m.–5 p.m., July–Aug daily 9 a.m.–5:30 p.m.*

Fast Facts: Cape Breton Island

ATMs

ATMs aren't as common as they are elsewhere in Nova Scotia. Most towns have at least one, including Baddeck (Royal Bank) and Ingonish (Scotiabank).

Emergencies

Dial ☎ 911 for all emergencies.

Hospitals

Options include **Cape Breton Regional Hospital**, 1482 George St., Sydney (☎ 902-567-8000), and **Victoria County Memorial Hospital**, Baddeck (☎ 902-295-2112).

Information

If driving to Cape Breton Island, make your first stop over Canso Causeway at the provincial **Visitor Information Centre**, Port Hastings (☎ 902-625-4201). It's open June to September daily 9 a.m. to 5 p.m. The **Baddeck Welcome Centre** (☎ 902-295-1911) maintains similar hours through the summer season.

Internet Access

You can retrieve your e-mail at **Cape Breton Regional Library**, 526 Chebucto St., Baddeck (☎ 902-295-2055).

Police

For emergencies, dial ☎ 911; the non-emergency number in Baddeck is ☎ 902-295-2350.

Post Office

The post office in Baddeck is on Chebucto Street.

Weather

Environment Canada maintains a Web site at www.weatheroffice.gc.ca with links to the forecast for major Cape Breton Island towns.

Part IV
New Brunswick

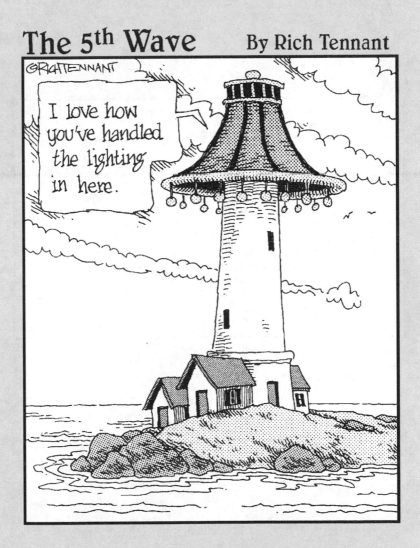

In this part . . .

New Brunswick is a quiet achiever — though it's the biggest of the Maritime provinces, it's not so familiar to outsiders as a tourist destination. Spend any time there and, like me, you'll wonder why it's not more popular. Here, I cover New Brunswick's three main cities: Moncton, with its distinct Acadian flavor; historic Saint John, Canada's oldest city; and the stately provincial capital, Fredericton. Follow my lead to go swimming in the warm waters off the Acadian Coast, fishing for lobsters in Northumberland Strait, searching out "kissing bridges" along the Saint John River, and marveling at the Fundy tide phenomenon.

Chapter 15

Moncton and the Acadian Coast

- -

In This Chapter

▶ Finding your way to and around Moncton

▶ Deciding where to stay and eat

▶ Hitting the town

▶ Relaxing on the beaches of Shediac

▶ Immersing yourself in Acadian culture

- -

*M*oncton, which due to its location at the geographic center of the Maritimes serves as a transportation and business hub, began in the 1720s as an Acadian settlement. Today, a third of its 97,000 residents are French-speaking, and it's the only officially bilingual city in Canada. The influence of Acadian culture is everywhere you go — all signage is in both English and French, and residents greet you in both official languages. Moncton University is the largest French university outside Quebec in Canada.

The nearest stretch of coastline is along Northumberland Strait, near the resort town of Shediac, which is renowned for long beaches and warm water. The region north of Shediac is known as the Acadian Coast for its long association with Acadians who returned to the Maritimes after being expelled from Nova Scotia by the British in 1755. The city itself has two quirky natural attractions: a tidal bore, which moves up the Petitcodiac River twice daily, and a hill with a seemingly magnetic pull.

Getting To Moncton

Moncton is an excellent starting point for a Maritimes vacation. In addition to its location at the geographic center of the region, flights there are often cheaper than they are to Halifax, which is just a three-hour drive to the southeast. You can also roll into the city by rail or bus.

New Brunswick

Moncton

2 mi
2 km

Airport
Golf Course
Information

ATTRACTIONS:
Bore View Park **13**
Moncton Museum **11**
Musée Acadien **16**
Thomas Williams Heritage House **7**
Magic Mountain **2**
Magnetic Hill Zoo **3**
The Boardwalk **4**

ACCOMMODATIONS:
Bonaccord House **8**
Château Moncton **14**
Holiday Inn Express Hotel & Suites **5**
Ramada Plaza Moncton **15**
Restwell Motel **1**
Wild Rose Inn **17**

DINING:
Maverick's **6**
Mexicali Rosa's **9**
Pump House **12**
t-bones **10**

By plane

Greater Moncton International Airport (www.gmia.ca) is off Champlain Street (Route 132), 8km (5 miles) east from downtown. It's served by Air Canada, CanJet, and WestJet (see the Appendix for toll-free numbers and Web sites), with direct flights originating in Halifax, St. John's, Montreal, Ottawa, Toronto, Calgary, and Newark (New Jersey). Fares between airlines are generally competitive, but check each for specials.

All passengers departing Greater Moncton International Airport must contribute C$15 to the Airport Improvement and Reconstruction Fund. Unlike for most other airports, the fee is not included in the ticket price and you must make payment at a booth inside the main terminal.

Air Cab (☎ 506-857-2000) is one of many local cab companies serving the airport. You don't need to call, as taxis always wait out front of the main terminal. The metered fare to downtown is around C$18. Avis, Budget, Hertz, and National have desks at the airport (see the Appendix for the toll-free numbers and Web sites of major car rental agencies).

By car

If you're driving around the Maritimes, chances are you'll pass through Moncton at some stage of your travels. Here's how to enter the city from a variety of directions:

- ✔ **Route 2 from Nova Scotia:** Take Exit 467 for downtown or Exit 450 for Magnetic Hill.

- ✔ **Route 15 from Shediac and the Confederation Bridge:** Pass under Route 2 and follow the signs right into downtown.

- ✔ **Route 114 from Hopewell Rocks:** Cross the Petitcodiac River via one of two bridges — the first to reach downtown, the second to loop around the western edge of the city to Magnetic Hill.

- ✔ **Route 2 from Fredericton:** Take Exit 466 (Route 128) for downtown or Exit 450 for Magnetic Hill.

By train or bus

VIA Rail's *Ocean* train passes through Moncton on its daily (except Tues) run between Montreal and Halifax. The station is off Main Street, on the southwest side of downtown (☎ 888-842-7245; www.viarail.ca).

Acadian (☎ 800-567-5151 or 506-859-5060; www.acadianbus.com) buses arrive and depart from a centrally located depot at 961 Main St. (corner of Bonaccord Street). The building is open Monday to Friday 7:30 a.m. to 8:30 p.m. and weekends 9 a.m. to 8:30 p.m. Some destinations linked to Moncton that are served by Acadian include the Acadian Coast, Prince Edward Island, Halifax, Fredericton, and Saint John.

Getting Around Moncton

Except for morning and evening weekday rush hours, driving around Moncton is easy. The downtown core spreads out around a bend in the Petitcodiac River. Main Street, which runs parallel to the river, is the main thoroughfare. To the east is suburban Dieppe, while south across the Petitcodiac is Riverview. The city's fun sights are 9km (5½ miles) northwest of downtown at Magnetic Hill, on the north side of Route 2.

Parking

Finding parking in downtown Moncton isn't too difficult if you know where to look. The best bet for a spot is Moncton Market, on Westmorland Street south of Main Street, where parking costs C$1 per hour to a maximum of C$7 per day (free on weekends). Metered street parking is C$1 an hour, but it's not monitored weekdays after 6 p.m. or on weekends.

Cabbing It

Hailing a cab from the street is possible, but it's easier in front of a major hotel such as the Delta Beausejour, 750 Main St. (at Westmorland Street). From downtown, expect to pay around C$18 to reach either Magnetic Hill or the airport. Cab companies include:

- ✔ Air Cab (☎ 506-857-2000)
- ✔ Trius Taxi (☎ 506-858-0000)
- ✔ White Cab (☎ 506-857-3000)

Taking transit

Codiac Transit (☎ 506-857-2008) serves Moncton with a bus network running Monday through Saturday 6:30 a.m. to 7 p.m. (extended to 10:30 p.m. on Thurs and Fri). Buses run east along Main Street to a major interchange at Champlain Place, from where they head out in all directions, including to Magnetic Hill. Bus fare is C$2 per sector for all passengers over age 5.

Staying in Moncton

As the hub of the Maritimes, Moncton can meet every lodging need and budget. Accommodations are available all over the city, with the two main concentrations being downtown and out on Route 2 near Magnetic Hill.

As in the rest of the Maritimes, July through August is high season in Moncton — this is when lodging is in most demand and rates are highest.

As always, if you're planning on staying in a chain hotel, check its Web site for package deals and discounted rates.

 ### Bonaccord House
$ **Downtown**

Centrally located Bonaccord House is halfway between downtown and the university campus. The 100-year-old home has a common lounge area with fireplace and four guest rooms with private bathrooms.

See map p. 182. 250 Bonaccord St. (at John Street). ☎ *506-388-1535. Fax: 506-853-7191. Rack rates: C$65–C$75 double. AE, MC, V.*

Château Moncton
$$–$$$$ **Downtown**

This four-story downtown hotel is difficult to miss with its bright red roof. The rooms have a vaguely European feel and are comfortably sized. Some have views of the Petitcodiac River, which flows right by the back door. All guests can enjoy views of the river and the tidal bore from Le Galion, a first-floor lounge with a south-facing deck that catches the afternoon sun. A light breakfast is included in the rates, but no other meals are served.

See map p. 182. 100 Main St. ☎ *800-576-4040 or 506-870-4444. Fax: 506-870-4445.* www.chateau-moncton.nb.ca. *Parking: Free. Rack rates: C$139–C$259 double. AE, MC, V.*

 ### Holiday Inn Express Hotel & Suites
$$–$$$ **Magnetic Hill**

This modern lodging comes exactly as you'd expect from the well-known chain — a handy highway location; an indoor pool, sauna, and hot tub; spacious rooms packed with basic amenities; and a complimentary breakfast bar off the lobby. A few rooms are themed especially for children, and a family-style Italian restaurant is open Monday to Saturday at 5 p.m. From Route 2, take Exit 450; from downtown Moncton, follow Mountain Road northwest for 9km (5½ miles).

See map p. 182. 2515 Mountain Rd., Magnetic Hill. ☎ *888-561-7666 or 506-384-1050. Fax: 506-859-6070.* www.hiemoncton.com. *Parking: free. Rack Rates: C$135–C$195 double. AE, DC, DISC, MC, V.*

Ramada Plaza Moncton
$$$–$$$$ **Dieppe**

This modern hotel, which is part of the Crystal Palace Amusement Park complex and a short walk from the largest shopping mall in the Maritimes, is popular with vacationing Maritimers year-round — so don't expect any great off-season bargains. The surroundings are parking-lot plain, but the hotel itself is centered around a tropical atrium with a pool and restaurant. The business rooms are adequately appointed, while 12 "Themed Suites" are devoted to diverse themes ranging from rock 'n' roll to the Victorian era.

See map p. 182. 499 Paul St., Dieppe. ☎ *800-561-7108 or 506-858-8584. Fax: 506-858-5486.* www.crystalpalacehotel.com. *Parking: free. Rack rates: C$159–C$249 double. AE, DC, DISC, MC, V.*

Restwell Motel
$–$$ **Magnetic Hill**

This nondescript roadside motel close to Magnetic Hill provides better value than the nearby chain hotel properties. Some rooms share bathrooms, but the more expensive ones are surprisingly attractive and overlook pleasant grounds with a small outdoor pool and barbecue area. To get there, take Exit 450 (Magnetic Hill) north from Route 2, and then go 4km (2½ miles) west along Ensley Road.

See map p. 182. 12 McFarlane Rd., Magnetic Hill. ☎ *506-857-4884.* www.restwell motel.com. *Rack rates: C$59–C$99 double. MC, V. Open: May–Oct.*

Wild Rose Inn
$$–$$$$ **Lakeville**

The Auberge Wild Rose Inn is set on 15 hectares (38 acres) of beautifully landscaped gardens on the north side of Route 2. The inn has a dignified ambience, but is far from formal. The 15 guest rooms have modern amenities, such as cable TV and Internet access, as well as thoughtful touches, like bathrobes and plush comforters. Those in the C$145 to C$155 range, with jetted tubs and either a private entrance or balcony, are the best deal. On the premises is a restaurant that serves full breakfasts (included in the rates) and fixed-price dinners in a charming French Provincial atmosphere.

See map p. 182. 17 Baseline Rd. (off Route 134), Lakeville. ☎ *888-389-7673 or 506-383-9751. Fax: 506-870-7547.* www.wildroseinn.com. *Rack rates: C$99–C$229 double. AE, DC, MC, V.*

Dining in Moncton

Moncton bustles with chain restaurants, which can be found along all major arteries and concentrated around Magnetic Hill. For something more original, head to Main Street, the busy thoroughfare that runs through downtown Moncton. It's lined with pubs, cafes, and restaurants, many with tables set out on the sidewalk.

Maverick's
$$–$$$$ **Downtown   STEAK**

Finding this lovely restaurant is well worth the effort. In a modern hotel away from the main restaurant strip, it's a little pricey for the college population and, aside from in-house guests, is mostly the haunt of locals in the know. The winsome menu combines the best cuts of beef with local seafood — lobster-stuffed mushrooms to start, for example, and then rib-eye with a side of garlic prawns. The wine cellar is one of the best in town.

See map p. 182. Future Inns Moncton, 40 Lady Ada Blvd. ☎ *506-855-3346. Reservations recommended. Main courses: C$18–C$30. AE, MC, V. Open: Daily 6:30 a.m.–10 p.m.*

Mexicali Rosa's
$-$$ Downtown MEXICAN

A central location and inexpensive food make this place hugely popular with the college-aged crowd. The décor is bright and attractive, blending red-brick walls with orange paint and head-high cactuses. The menu is mostly Mexican, with a "California influence" (their words, not mine) and a tip of the hat to Italy (pasta dishes served with tortilla chips). The kitchen prepares a delicious Mexicali dip as well as combo platters for around C$16. Save room for the deep-fried ice cream.

See map p. 182. 683 Main St. ☎ *506-855-7672. Reservations recommended on weekends. Main courses: C$9–C$23. MC, V. Open: Daily 11:30 a.m.–10:30 p.m.*

Pump House
$-$$ Downtown PUB FARE

Locals come to this brewpub for its convivial atmosphere and well-priced food, and in-house beers like Blueberry Ale. The menu is mostly pub fare, with the emphasis on beer (think beer-steamed mussels and "brewschetta"), but you can also order the usual westernized Mexican dishes good for sharing and single-serve pizzas from a wood-fired oven. Explore the pub before settling down at a regular table — choices include booths contained within cut-off wine barrels, a sunny sidewalk deck, and tables in front of the brew tanks.

See map p. 182. 5 Orange Lane. ☎ *506-855-2337. Reservations not necessary. Main courses: C$8–C$21. AE, MC, V. Open: Daily 11 a.m.–10 p.m.*

t-bones
$$-$$$ Downtown NORTH AMERICAN

Hotel restaurants are the same the world over. They offer wide-ranging menus that don't offend anyone, they are open long hours, and the service is efficient. Which, along with signature T-bone steaks cooked exactly as ordered, is exactly what you get at t-bones, off to one side of the lobby at the downtown Crowne Plaza Hotel. This is one of the best places in town for breakfast; expect to pay around C$10 for a cooked breakfast, or C$13 if you opt for the exotic lobster eggs Benedict.

1005 Main St. ☎ *506-854-6340. Main courses: C$12–C$37. AE, DC, MC, V. Open: Daily 6 a.m.–2 p.m. and 5–10 p.m.*

Exploring Moncton

Moncton's location makes it a perfect base from which to explore the region. It's central to the beachy resort town of Shediac, the culturally intriguing Acadian Coast (both covered later in this chapter), and the Bay of Fundy (see Chapter 16).

The city itself features two interesting natural phenomena (maybe a little less exciting than the tourist brochures claim, but interesting nevertheless), as well as a mix of museums and cultural pursuits.

Downtown

Bore View Park, home to the main visitor information center, is the best starting point for exploring downtown. West of the park, Main Street has been the focus of a rejuvenation program in recent years — red-brick sidewalks, ornate benches, old-fashioned lampposts, and the like.

Bore View Park
Downtown

Twice daily, the Petitcodiac River drains dry of water as the huge Fundy tide recedes; then the tide turns, literally, and water rushes up the muddied riverbed, led by a "wave" up to 50 centimeters (20 inches) high. The river takes an hour to fill completely. The phenomenon is interesting rather than exciting, but well worth watching. You can see the bore anywhere along the river (as well as many other places, including Truro in central Nova Scotia), but Bore View Park is the most accessible and has interpretive boards describing the how's and why's of the tide. Look for the clock at the park's Main Street entrance to see when the bore is next due.

Bore View Park is linked to the **Riverfront Promenade**, a wheelchair-accessible walkway extending east to Hall's Creek and west to the Gunningsville Bridge, a total distance of 2km (1.2 miles). Take the path upstream to quickly leave the city high-rises behind and be rewarded with panoramic views across the river to undeveloped wetlands.

The park is also home to the **Moncton Visitor Information Centre** (☎ 800-363-4558 or 506-853-3540; open mid-May to early October daily 9 a.m.–8 p.m., the rest of the year Mon–Fri 8:30 a.m.–4:30 p.m.).
See map p. 182. Main St. (at Lewis Street). Admission: Free.

Moncton Museum
Downtown

Housed in the former city hall, the Moncton Museum gives a good general overview of local history. Its displays concentrate on the region's first inhabitants, the Mi'Kmaq First Nations people, as well as industries such as shipbuilding that have long since disappeared. The museum also hosts several touring exhibits a year.

Beside the museum is the Free Meeting House, used by various religious congregations. Dating to 1821, it's Moncton's oldest remaining building. *See map p. 182. 20 Mountain Rd. (at Belleview Street).* ☎ *506-856-4383. Admission: Donation. Open: July–Aug daily 9 a.m.–5 p.m.; Sept–June Mon–Sat 9 a.m.–4:30 p.m., Sun 1–5 p.m.*

Musée Acadien
North of downtown

Founded by Father Camille Lefebvre in 1886, this museum focuses on historic events and aspects of Acadian life. Over 35,000 pieces are on display, making it Canada's largest collection of Acadian culture. The oldest is an ax dating to 1645, which was recovered from the site of a trading post along the Acadian Coast. Of special historical importance is the original Acadian flag; also of interest are the original register of donated pieces and displays of Acadian art and religious sculptures. The museum is on the sprawling grounds of Moncton University, well worth walking around in summertime for the peaceful student-free setting. *See map p. 182. Clément-Cormier Building, Moncton University.* ☎ *506-858-4088. Admission: C$2 adults, C$1 children. Open: July–Aug Mon–Fri 10 a.m.–5 p.m., Sat–Sun 1–5 p.m.; Sept–June Tues–Fri 1–4:30 p.m., Sat–Sun 1–5 p.m.*

Thomas Williams House
Downtown

Tucked away on a quiet residential street eight blocks from downtown is a grand home built in 1883 for Thomas Williams, treasurer of the Intercolonial Railway. Period furnishings and gardens reflect the Victorian era. The house is worth visiting for afternoon tea alone, which is served on the veranda. It's not particularly traditional (coffee and muffins, by golly!), but the parklike setting and unpretentious ambience lend to an enjoyable time out from sightseeing. *See map p. 182. 103 Park St. (at Highfield Street).* ☎ *506-856-4383. Admission: Free. Open: July–Aug Mon–Sat 9 a.m.–5 p.m., Sun 1–5 p.m.*

Magnetic Hill
Take Exit 450 from Route 2 or follow Mountain Road northwest from downtown to reach the Magnetic Hill area, a crunch of commercialism that has grown around an optical oddity.

Upon arrival, you must first take care of business and pay C$3 per vehicle at the tollbooth. Continuing a short distance along a rural-type stretch of road, signage directs you to come to a complete stop. Then, when you take your foot off the brake, your vehicle seemingly rolls *uphill.* The illusion is compelling: Basically, the entire lower hillside of a larger mountain is tilted at an angle to the surrounding countryside, creating the impression that the top of the hill is lower than the bottom. It has puzzled folks for generations, including early farmers who were forced to pull their wagons "down" the hill to town.

A magnet for commercial attractions

The magnetic appeal of Magnetic Hill extends well beyond one quirky stretch of road. Many local entrepreneurs have set up theme-park style businesses around the bottom (or is that the top?) of the hill. Here are the highlights:

- ✔ **Magic Mountain** (☎ 506-857-9283) is the largest water park in the Maritimes. Expect wild water rides, a wave pool, kid slides, and an oversize hot tub. Admission is C$23 for everyone over 48 inches high, with the exception being seniors aged 70 and older who pay just C$7. It's open mid-June through early September daily 10 a.m. to 6 p.m.

- ✔ **Magnetic Hill Zoo** (☎ 506-877-7718) is home to around 100 species of mostly exotic animals. It also has a small petting zoo of farm animals. Admission is C$9.50 adults, C$8.50 seniors, C$6.50 children. It's open mid-May through mid-October daily 9 a.m. to 6 p.m.

- ✔ **The Boardwalk** (☎ 506-852-9406) features go-cart rides, batting cages, minigolf, a golf driving range, and butterflies flying freely in their domed habitats. It's open June through mid-September daily 10 a.m. to 9 p.m.

Nightlife

Despite its outwardly staid appearance, Moncton has a number of happening pubs and clubs. You can find entertainment listings through **Tourism Moncton** (☎ 800-363-4558 or 506-853-3590; www.gomoncton.com). This organization also publishes a list of annual festivals and events.

Bars and live music

Le Galion, an elegant lounge in the Château Moncton at 100 Main St. (☎ 506-870-4444), is a pleasant place to unwind, with a bar that opens to a deck overlooking the Petitcodiac River.

The stretch of Main Street between Botsford Street and Lutz Street has an active nightlife, with crowds of college-aged drinkers spilling onto sidewalk tables. **Doc Dylan's** at 841 Main St. (☎ 506-382-3627) awaits, with one of the best ranges of draft beer in town and bands on some nights. A half-block off Main, the **Pump House Brewery,** 5 Orange Lane (☎ 506-855-2337), brews a delicious range of beers, which can be enjoyed indoors or out on a small porch with parking lot views. For something a little different, try the Blueberry Ale, which comes complete with floating blueberries.

For live music, head to **Club Cosmo,** 700 Main St. (☎ **506-857-9117**), a multi-room venue that also attracts the under-25 crowd to Moncton's largest dance floor. The music is as hip as it gets in New Brunswick, with a crowd to match. Open Wednesday through Sunday only. Nearby **Ivory's Piano Bar,** at 706 Main St. (☎ **506-854-8679**), is a little more subdued, while **Oxygen,** at 125 Westmorland St. (☎ **506-854-0265**), is a groovy nightclub attracting more of the college-aged crowd.

The arts

The **Capitol,** at 811 Main St. (☎ **800-567-1922** or 506-856-4377), is an old vaudeville house that has been devotedly restored to its 1920s grandeur, right down to gold-leaf stenciling and renovated opera boxes. It provides a home for Theatre New Brunswick and the Symphony New Brunswick, as well as a stage for a wide range of touring acts. Check a schedule at their Web site, www.capitol.nb.ca.

Acadian Coast

The French-flavored Acadian Coast stretches north from Moncton along Northumberland Strait. Separating Prince Edward Island from the mainland, this narrow waterway is lined along the New Brunswick side by beaches galore, where shallow water warms quickly under the summer sun. The center of beach culture is Shediac, although the place to get away from the crowds is to the north in Kouchibouguac National Park.

Shediac

Beach lovers will feel right at home in laid-back Shediac. The coast here borders Northumberland Strait, a shallow stretch of water between the mainland and Prince Edward Island, where the water reaches a pleasant 22°C (72°F) in summer. So even when the Bay of Fundy is foggy, or the water along the Nova Scotia coast is too cold for swimming, the stretch of coast fronting Shediac sparkles in the sun. But don't expect to have the place to yourself through the warmest months of the year — the town gets packed with college students on summer break and retirees who can afford to kick back for a few months.

Getting there

From Moncton, follow Route 15 in a northeasterly direction for 20km (12 miles) to Exit 31B. Head north along Route 11 for a 400m (½ mile), and then take Exit 1. This road leads past the main information center and Shediac Harbour, and then along the long main street. The turnoff to Parlee Beach is through the town to the east.

Expulsion, and then a cultural explosion

Most of the French-speaking population in the Maritimes today is Acadian, a culture that differs from that of its better-known francophone cousin, Quebec, not only in history but in dialect, cuisine, and customs.

When the French began colonizing the Maritimes in the 1630s, most settled in the Annapolis Valley, which came to be known as Acadia (and its settlers, hence, as Acadians). In 1713, the British claimed sovereignty to Nova Scotia, and the Acadians were encouraged to swear an oath of allegiance to England. Most refused, and in 1755 the British reacted by confiscating their property and expelling them. With no place to call home, the Acadians scattered — some returned to France, others moved west to Quebec, and some settled in Louisiana (where they became known as Cajuns); a small percentage escaped into the remote forests of what is now New Brunswick and to the far corners of Prince Edward Island.

A decade after their expulsion, many who had been exiled came out of hiding and returned to the region. They resettled and built new communities as far from the British as possible. In 1884, at an Acadian convention held in Miscouche, Prince Edward Island, these once displaced people officially adopted their own flag and anthem ("Ave Maris Stella") — the seeds of a distinct and unique culture that thrives to this day.

New Brunswick, Canada's only bilingual province, has a large Acadian population centered in Moncton and stretching up the coast. Acadian heritage and traditions remain strong, and visitors are offered many opportunities to experience it firsthand through museums, historical reenactments, and, of course, the food!

Staying in Shediac

Many of the accommodations near the water are rented by the week or the month, making them impractical for the casual visitor. If hanging out at the beach for a week fits into your schedule, **Complexe Domaine Parlee Beach,** a short walk from the water at 642 Main St. (☎ **800-786-5550** or 506-532-5339; www.complexedomaine.ca) is the place to do it. Cottages rent for C$1,100 per week; suites are C$1,200 to C$1,450, with daily rates from C$125 offered from early September through late June.

Auberge Belcourt Inn
$$ Shediac

This stately residence was built in 1911 for a local doctor and was the home of a former New Brunswick premier for a time. Today, it provides a refined and relaxing retreat from the sun and sand (spend some time on the covered veranda for the full effect). The seven guest rooms are filled with Victorian charm and period antiques. All have en suite bathrooms. The rate includes a full breakfast served between 8 and 9:30 a.m.

310 Main St. ☎ *506-532-6098. Fax: 506-533-9398. Rack rates: C$95–C$110 double. AE, DC, MC, V.*

Dining in Shediac

You can enjoy lobsters at most restaurants along the main street, or buy them live or cooked from **Shediac Lobster Shop,** a seafood market at 261 Main St. (☎ 506-532-4302). Expect to pay around C$15 per pound.

Captain Dan's
$–$$ Shediac   SEAFOOD

This boisterous restaurant/bar is away from the best beaches but attracts hordes of tanned bods for fresh seafood, cold beer, and live music Tuesday to Sunday throughout the summer. The food is exactly what you'd expect from a seafood house, with prices that may pleasantly surprise you: For example, the substantial three-piece fish-and-chips entree comes with freshly made tartar sauce for C$11. The lobster bisque and maritime chowder are also both under C$10. Take a table either downstairs, upstairs on the tiered deck — with views across to the marina — or in the Lobster Hut, where you can order full lobster, chowder, coleslaw, and dessert for just C$32.

50 Pointe-du-Chêne Wharf. ☎ *506-533-2855. Main courses: C$8–C$21. AE, MC, V. Open: Daily 11 a.m.–10 p.m.*

Cool things to do in and around Shediac

Don't come to Shediac looking for cultural stimulation. This is a place to lie on the beach, swim in the warmest ocean water north of Virginia, and feast on lobster.

The swimming season is short — July and August only. **Parlee Beach,** accessed from the east side of town, is by far the most popular spot for sunning and swimming. A large complex behind the dunes holds change rooms, a concession, and a lively bar/restaurant with a huge deck. Mid-May through mid-September, beach access costs C$9 per vehicle (it's free the rest of the year). Farther east, **Ocean View Beach** and **Gagnon Beach** are quieter and just as pleasant.

When you've had enough sun, sand, and salt, consider the following:

✔ **Go lobster fishing.** With Eric LeBlanc at the helm, **Shediac Bay Cruises** (☎ 888-894-2002 or 506-532-2175; www.lobstertales.ca) takes visitors on a 2½-hour fishing trip that culminates in an onboard lobster feast. The cost is C$55 adults, C$35 children. From the Reception Centre at Pointe-du-Chene Wharf, departures are daily between late April and early November.

✔ **Drive to Cape Jourimain.** The easternmost point of New Brunswick, 80km (50 miles) east of Shediac, is protected by a national wildlife area that is home to 170 species of birds. A 13km (8-mile) system of hiking trails branches out from **Cape Jourimain Nature Centre** (☎ 506-538-2220; open mid-May through early Oct daily 9 a.m.– 5 p.m.). One trail ends at the cape itself, where views extend north along the Confederation Bridge. Admission is C$6 adults, C$5 seniors, C$4 children.

✔ **Climb on the world's largest lobster.** This 10m-long (33-foot) cast-iron crustacean stands guard at the mouth of the Scoudouc River, at the west entrance to town. Kids love clambering over its massive claws, while adults are usually content with a photograph.

✔ **Enjoy the Shediac Lobster Festival.** Held over five days in early July, this annual festival celebrates everything related to Shediac's favorite feast, including nightly lobster suppers and a lobster-eating contest. For details call ☎ **506-532-1122** or visit www.lobsterfestival.nb.ca.

Bouctouche and beyond

Imagine spending the morning exploring a seemingly endless sand dune, followed by an afternoon immersing yourself in Acadian culture in a make-believe island village. You can do this at Bouctouche, a small coastal town 20km (12 miles) north of Shediac along Route 11.

Staying in Bouctouche

Accommodations in Bouctouche are limited. If the recommendation here doesn't sound like your scene, continue north to the Acadian Peninsula, or plan on visiting the region as a day trip from Moncton.

Bellevue sur mer
$$ **Bouctouche**

A small inn catering to guests who value a homey atmosphere over a room full of fancy amenities, this lodging is in an 1870s farmhouse that was home to three generations of the same Acadian family. Set on the water, it's a five-minute drive from La Dune de Bouctouche, so you can rise early and enjoy the spit before the crowds arrive, or walk to Le Pays de la Sagouine. The four guest rooms are decorated with soothing pastel colors and each has an en suite bathroom. Rates include cooked breakfasts such as crepes with maple syrup.

539 Rte. 475. ☎ *506-743-6575. Rack rates: C$75–C$99 double. V.*

Exploring Bouctouche

It may not be much more than a lot of sand, but **La Dune de Bouctouche** is one of the natural highlights of New Brunswick. It's an extremely narrow spit of sand, extending 12km (7½ miles) into Northumberland Strait. Plant life, such as beach heather, has a stabilizing effect, but tidal action and wind still manage to move the sand around, ever so slowly extending the spit while also making it narrower. To learn more about the unique ecosystem, stop by **Irving Eco Centre,** along Route 475 at the start of the spit (☎ **506-743-2600;** open July–Aug 10 a.m.–8 p.m.). To protect the fragile environment from overuse in the busiest months (July and Aug), only the first 2,000 visitors to arrive each day after 10 a.m. are allowed access. A boardwalk extends for the first 2km (1¼ miles); to continue farther, walk along the high tide mark.

Located on a small island in the Bouctouche River, **Le Pays de la Sagouine,** accessed by footbridge from Acadie Street (☎ **800-561-9188** or 506-743-1400; www.sagouine.com), is a fun place to immerse yourself in the rich culture of Acadia. Part theme park, part learning experience, it centers on a fictional Acadian village created by writer Antonine Maillet. Costumed performers put on musical and theatrical presentations throughout the day. Storytelling neighbors, young pranksters, and Acadian bands encouraging singalongs are just a taste of what you can expect. Admission is C$15 adults, C$14 seniors, C$11 children. On Saturday and Sunday nights in July and August, *Pelagie-la-Charrette,* a magnificent dinner theater featuring up to 70 actors, costs C$69 for adults and C$48 for children. Tuesday through Friday a variety of less ambitious dinner theater productions are C$69 adults and C$45 children, which includes general park admission.

Kouchibouguac National Park

Although the entire Acadian Coast offers similar coastal scenery, the section between Bouctouche and Miramichi is particularly appealing because it's protected as a national park and, therefore, remains in its natural state. Kouchibouguac (pronounced *Koo*-she-*boo*-gwack), meaning "river of long tides," is dominated by a ribbon of barrier islands composed entirely of sand. Extending for 25km (16 miles), these islands have formed lagoons that attract a wide variety of bird life (over 200 bird species have been recorded in the park). The rest of the park is a mix of forest, slow-flowing rivers, peat bogs, and marshland. Deer, moose, black bears, and beavers are all residents, while you can often spot seals in the surrounding waters.

To experience the best of Kouchibouguac, explore beyond the paved roads. Here's how:

✔ **Hiking.** This isn't the place for grueling all-day hikes. Instead, visitors have a choice of short trails, many lined with interpretive panels describing the surroundings. If you take just one trail, make it **Kelly's Beach Boardwalk,** which crosses a lagoon to sand dunes and open water. Don't be perturbed by the name of the Bog Trail — a boardwalk leads through the marshland.

✔ **Biking.** You can find a 60km (37-mile) system of crushed-gravel bike trails. The main loop — taking in the river, the forested interior, and the coast — is 23km (14 miles). Complete the circuit in two hours, or spend all day stopping at its points of interest. Bikes can be rented at **Ryans Recreation Equipment Rental Centre,** based at Ryans day-use area (☎ **506-876-8918**), for C$6 per hour or C$30 per day.

✔ **Canoeing.** If you are comfortable out on the water on your own, canoes can be rented from Ryan's (see earlier), which is beside the calm waters of the Kouchibouguac River. Just as enjoyable is joining park staff on a three-hour guided paddle in a large voyageur canoe, which seats up to nine people. The cost is C$30 per person. Reserve a seat at the visitor center (☎ **506-876-2443**).

✔ **Swimming.** The water on the ocean side of the dunes at Kelly's Beach is supervised throughout the summer. Although the water temperature is comfortable, it's even warmer to the south at Callender's Beach, along a tidal lagoon.

Get to the park by taking Exit 75 from Route 11, 35km (21 miles) north of Bouctouche. Just inside the park boundary is the **Visitor Reception Centre** (☎ **506-876-2443**), holding displays on the park ecosystem and including a small theater, a gift shop, and an information desk. This is also the place to pick up a park **day pass,** which costs C$6.90 adults, C$5.90 seniors, C$3.45 children, to a maximum of C$17 per vehicle. The center is open mid-June through early September daily 9 a.m. to 5 p.m., with extended hours in July and August of 8 a.m. to 8 p.m daily. Access to the park is possible year-round, but everything closes down in September, and the entry fee isn't collected out of season.

Check the bulletin board at the visitor center for a schedule of events, which may include interpretive hikes, campfire talks, slide presentations, and a puppet theater.

Acadian Peninsula

Extending northeast from Miramichi along Baie des Chaleurs, the Acadian peninsula is a hotbed of Acadian culture. You can experience this unique culture by exploring local museums, sampling the cuisine, or simply taking a drive through the many small villages where traditions run deep.

At Miramichi, you have two options for onward travel: Either cut south through the heartland of New Brunswick to Fredericton, or follow Route 11 around the Acadian Peninsula, which is dotted with farms and fishing villages.

Staying on the Acadian Peninsula

Use Miramichi as a base for a day trip around the Acadian Peninsula, or push on and spend the night at the recommended accommodations in Caraquet (the region's largest town) or Miscou Centre.

Governor's Mansion Inn
$–$$ Miramichi (Nelson)

The lovely location and budget-priced rooms alone make this lodging a good choice. But best of all is the historical atmosphere — pull up a chair on the covered veranda, look across to the river, and imagine yourself transported back in time. Formerly the home of a provincial lieutenant governor, this stately 1860 mansion has been given a bright yellow coat of paint on the outside and undergone a rigorous restoration inside. Rooms are divided between the main home and the adjacent Beaubear Manor. Antiques and convivial hosts make up for slightly threadbare furnishings. Some rooms share bathrooms (the Eagles Eyrie, with water views, is the pick of these), but at just C$79 for the most expensive (the Lord Beaverbrook Room, which comes complete with a four-piece bath and fireplace), you can afford to splurge. Within sight of the inn is Beaubears Island; tours depart the nearby dock Tuesday and Thursday at 6:30 p.m. and Sunday at 1:30 p.m.

62 St. Patrick's Dr. ☎ *877-647-2642 or 506-622-3036. Fax: 506-622-3035.* www.governorsmansion.ca. *Rack rates: C$59–C$99 double. AE, MC, V.*

Hotel Paulin
$$$–$$$$ **Caraquet**

Modern development has encroached on the water views at this 1891 hotel, but it still offers a level of intimacy you just can't get at a motel. Operated for three generations by the same family, the Paulin has a Christmasy red-and-green exterior and a cheerful interior to match. The 12 guest rooms have been given a serious overhaul and feature a contemporary slant on the heritage theme, comfortable beds, and en suite bathrooms. The four top-floor suites are massive and come with upgraded everything. In the evening, guests congregate in a lounge, where local musicians occasionally stop by to play the piano.

143 Blvd. St-Pierre West, Caraquet. ☎ *866-727-9981 or 506-727-9981.* www.hotel paulin.com. *Rack rates: C$195–C$315 double. AE, MC, V.*

Plage Miscou Chalets
$$ **Miscou Centre**

Situated on Miscou Island, which is linked to the mainland by a bridge, this complex is part cottages, part campground, and all fun. It lies behind a long sandy beach, with water warm enough for swimming. And plenty of other activities keep everyone busy — fishing trips, canoeing (rentals available), volleyball, minigolf, horseshoes, and more. The six cabins each have two bedrooms and a fully equipped kitchen, making them excellent value.

22 Allée Alphonse, Miscou Centre. ☎ *506-344-1015. Fax: 506-344-7444. Rack rates: C$105 double. MC, V. Open: Mid-May to mid-Sept.*

Rodd Miramichi River
$$–$$$ **Miramichi (Chatham)**

Located right on the Miramichi River, this modern motel has a distinctive lodge feeling to its rooms, which are decorated in earthy tones and have fish prints on the walls. The specialty at the in-house Angler's Reel Restaurant is salmon, while the adjacent lounge spreads onto a riverside deck. Request a room with a river view when booking.

1809 Water St., Chatham. ☎ *800-565-7633 or 506-773-3111. Fax: 506-773-3110.* www. rodd-hotels.ca. *Rack rates: C$115–C$155 double. AE, DC, MC, V.*

Dining on the Acadian Peninsula

Most villages have a choice of cafes or restaurants, and you may consider taking a chance at any of them. I recommend two very different restaurants that showcase the charm of the region in their own unique ways. As alternatives, the Hotel Paulin or Rodd Miramichi River (earlier in this chapter I recommend both as places to stay) have dining rooms worthy of a visit.

La Fine Grobe Sur Mer
$$–$$$ Nigadoo   FRENCH

Translating to "fine grub by the sea," this fine restaurant provides some of the best cooking in New Brunswick, with spectacular views of Chaleur Bay. The seasonal menu offers a great variety of traditional French dishes, relying on local seafood and produce from the garden to create a memorable meal. The super-smooth lobster bisque and herb-crusted leg of lamb are both noteworthy. For dessert, the cheese plate is tempting, but, seriously, can you choose anything but the chocolate cake?

289 Main St., Nigadoo (north of Bathurst). ☎ *506-783-3138. Main courses: C$17–C$29. AE, DC, MC, V. Open: Daily 5–10 p.m.*

Old Town Diner
$ Miramichi (Chatham)   DINER

Chances are you'll be the only out-of-towner at this small-town, super-friendly diner on the south side of the Miramichi River in Chatham. The menu is exactly what you may expect — breakfast served all day, deep-fried seafood, and a couple of token salads. A full-cooked breakfast costs just C$5, including bottomless coffee.

1724 Water St., Chatham. ☎ *506-773-7817. Main courses: C$6–C$9.50. Open: Daily 7 a.m.–7 p.m.*

Exploring the Acadian Peninsula

To fully appreciate the peninsula's natural and cultural appeal, plan on spending at least a day in the region. Visiting the following two top Acadian attractions alone will fill the better part of a day.

Route 11 parallels the Gulf of St. Lawrence all the way from Miramichi to Bathurst, a total distance of 170km (106 miles). From Bathurst, it's a short hop back across the peninsula to Miramichi.

Village Historique Acadien
Route 11 west of Caraquet

Definitely a highlight of the Acadian Coast, this park re-creates Acadian life between 1770 and 1890. The 40 restored buildings include simple homes, a chapel, a farmyard, a schoolhouse, various workshops, a lobster hatchery, and a tavern. Costumed staff bring the village to life as they go about their daily business — tending to their animals, overseeing auctions, spreading gossip, attending marriages, and more. Visitors can also watch as artists ply their trade, or dine on Acadian food in one of two restaurants.

Route 11 between Caraquet and Grand-Anse. ☎ *877-721-2200 or 506-726-2600. Admission: C$15 adults, C$13 seniors, C$10 children, C$30 families. Open: June to late Sept daily 10 a.m.–6 p.m.*

Acadian Museum
Caraquet

Founded by Acadians fleeing the British in 1755, the village of Caraquet has evolved into the unofficial center of the peninsula's French-speaking community. This small museum does a wonderful job of representing the town and its residents, many of whom have donated items to display. Taking in the water view from the second floor balcony is worthwhile.

15 Blvd. St-Pierre West, Caraquet. ☎ *506-726-2682. Admission: C$3 adults, C$1 children. Open: June to mid-Sept Mon–Sat 10 a.m.–6 p.m., Sun 1–6 p.m.*

Newcastle

Now incorporated as part of Miramichi, this bustling river town is more attractive than at first glance. Make your way down to **Ritchie Wharf Park** (Leddon Street) and let the children go wild on the maritime-themed playground and splash park; take lunch at one of the cafes; and learn more about the region at the riverside information center.

In the heart of downtown is a memorial to Lord Beaverbrook (1879–1964), a British press baron who spent his childhood in Newcastle. His boyhood home, at 518 King George Hwy., is a few blocks west of the memorial (☎ 504-622-5572). It's open to the public June to August Monday to Friday 9 a.m. to 5 p.m. and Saturday 10 a.m. to 5 p.m. Admission is free.

From the south, cross the Miramichi River via Route 8 and follow King George Highway to the southeast.

Metepenagiag Heritage Park
Red Bank

At a riverside location that has been home to the Mi'Kmaq for 3,000 years, this park protects two National Historic Sites: Augustine Mound, a sacred burial site, and Oxbow, the location of an ancient village. While walking trails link the two and meander along the river, the main interpretation center really brings the Mi'Kmaq culture to life. To get to the park from Miramichi, head west for 26km (16 miles) along Route 425 to Red Bank. *2202 Micmac Rd., Red Bank.* ☎ **506-836-6118.** *Admission: C$8 adults, C$6 seniors and children. Open: Mid-May to mid-Oct daily 9 a.m.–6 p.m., mid-Oct to mid-May daily 10 a.m.–3 p.m.*

Fast Facts: Moncton

ATMs

Most banks have ATMs, including the **Bank of Montreal** at 633 Main St., **CIBC** at Church and Main streets, and **Scotiabank** at 780 Main St.

Emergencies

Dial ☎ **911** for all emergencies.

Hospital

Moncton Hospital is at 135 MacBeath Ave. (☎ **506-860-2378**).

Information

Tourism Moncton (☎ **800-363-4558** or 506-853-3590; www.gomoncton.com) operates an information center at Bore Park, Main Street. It's open June to August daily 9 a.m. to 8 p.m., the rest of the year Monday to Friday 8:30 a.m. to 4:30 p.m.

Internet Access

Moncton Public Library, 644 Main St. (☎ **506-869-6000**), has free public Internet access.

Pharmacy

Drugstore Pharmacy is at 165 Main St. (☎ **506-852-2069**).

Police

For emergencies, dial ☎ **911.** For other police matters, call ☎ **506-857-2400.**

Post Office

The main post office is at 281 St. George St. (at Highfield Street).

Restrooms

The main Visitor Information Centre, in Bore View Park, has public restrooms.

Taxis

Reliable cab companies include **Air Cab** (☎ **506-857-2000**) and **White Cab** (☎ **506-857-3000**).

Transit Info

Public buses are operated by **Codiac Transit** (☎ **506-857-2008**) daily, except Sunday.

Weather

For the local weather forecast, call **Environment Canada** at ☎ **506-851-6610** or check the Web site www.weather office.gc.ca.

Chapter 16

Saint John and the Fundy Coast

● ●

In This Chapter

▶ Getting to Saint John and finding your way around the city

▶ Deciding where to stay and dine

▶ Seeing the sights and spending a night on the town

▶ Visiting St. Andrews and exploring Fundy National Park

● ●

*S*aint John is a gritty industrial city with a striking waterfront enhanced by the Harbour Passage, a municipal beautification project. With a population of 120,000, Greater Saint John is New Brunswick's largest city and offers all the benefits of big-city life — like upscale accommodations and creative dining — at affordable small-town prices.

Established in 1785 by *Loyalists* (American colonists who wished to remain loyal to the British crown after the birth of the United States), Saint John was Canada's first incorporated city, prospering as a port and shipbuilding center. In 1877, a fire destroyed almost the entire downtown, which was then rebuilt with fine brick and stone buildings, most of which remain today.

Saint John is always spelled out. It is never abbreviated to "St. John," thereby avoiding confusion with St. John's, Newfoundland.

Saint John may be the biggest name on the map, but in this chapter I give you plenty of reasons to explore the rest of the Fundy Coast. Take Route 1 west from Saint John to reach St. Andrews, a one-time retreat for the wealthy that now welcomes everyone. Up the Bay of Fundy from Saint John, a rugged section of the coast is protected by Fundy National Park. Beyond the park is Hopewell Rocks, intriguing towers of sandstone that have become separated from the mainland.

Getting To Saint John

Most travelers arrive in Saint John by road, but options include flying in or coming from Nova Scotia by ferry.

By plane

Saint John Airport (www.saintjohnairport.com) is along Route 111 toward St. Martins, 16km (10 miles) east of downtown. Air Canada flies into Saint John from Halifax, Toronto, and Montreal. WestJet links Saint John with Toronto. Rental car companies with desks at the airport are Avis, Budget, Hertz, and National.

The least expensive way to travel between the airport and downtown is on a **Saint John Transit** bus (☎ 506-658-4700). The service departs the airport four times daily and costs C$2.25, exact change only. The cab fare between the airport and downtown is C$30 for the first person, and C$2 for each additional person.

All passengers departing Saint John Airport are required to pay a **Passenger Facility Fee** of C$15. The fee is incorporated into the price of your airline ticket.

By car

The most direct route between Moncton and Saint John is Route 1, a distance of 155km (96 miles) that takes about 90 minutes to drive. A more scenic option is Route 114 along the Bay of Fundy, which passes two of New Brunswick's most appealing natural attractions — Hopewell Rocks and Fundy National Park. Taking this route doubles the driving time.

The provincial capital of New Brunswick, Fredericton, is 105km (65 miles) north of Saint John via Route 7. If you're willing to do a longer course with scenic appeal, take Route 102 via Gagetown.

By ferry

If you're visiting both southwestern Nova Scotia and New Brunswick, it makes sense to take advantage of the ferry service between Digby and Saint John. **Bay Ferries** (☎ 888-249-7245 or 506-649-7777; www.nfl-bay.com) runs this passage year-round, up to three times daily in each direction. The one-way fare is C$30 to C$40 adults, C$25 to C$30 seniors, C$20 to C$25 children ages 5 to 17, and C$75 to C$80 for vehicles under 6.4m (21 feet). Reservations for the three-hour trip are highly recommended in summer.

Getting Around Saint John

Saint John is very spread out, with downtown (and the best attractions) centered on a peninsula at the mouth of the Saint John River. Exit 122

Saint John

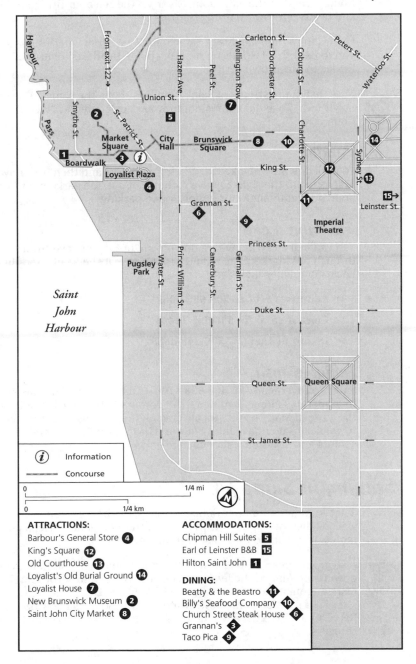

ATTRACTIONS:
Barbour's General Store **4**
King's Square **12**
Old Courthouse **13**
Loyalist's Old Burial Ground **14**
Loyalist House **7**
New Brunswick Museum **2**
Saint John City Market **8**

ACCOMMODATIONS:
Chipman Hill Suites **5**
Earl of Leinster B&B **15**
Hilton Saint John **1**

DINING:
Beatty & the Beastro **11**
Billy's Seafood Company **10**
Church Street Steak House **6**
Grannan's **3**
Taco Pica **9**

from Route 1 leads right into the heart of downtown. Immediately west, Route 1 crosses the Saint John River via the Harbour Bridge (C25¢ toll) and heads out toward Irving Nature Park.

Ferries from Digby arrive in Saint John West, from where signage directs you to Exit 120 of Route 1. From this point, head east over the Harbour Bridge to downtown.

Note that many streets of Saint John West have the same names as those downtown. To avoid confusion, they are designated as "West," as in Church St. W.

Parking

To park downtown, take Exit 122 from Route 1 and then turn down the first street to the right to have a choice of outside parking for C$1 per hour, or slightly more for underground parking.

Grabbing a cab

You can hail a cab anywhere downtown, but if you have trouble, walk through the Market Square and wait for one at the Saint John Hilton. Local companies include:

- ✔ **Century Taxi** (☎ 506-696-6969)
- ✔ **Coastal Taxi** (☎ 506-635-1144)
- ✔ **Diamond Taxi** (☎ 506-648-8888)

Taking transit

Saint John Transit (☎ 506-658-4700) is a highly efficient bus system that operates along 22 routes to all corners of the city, including out to the airport. Many buses run at ten-minute intervals from the main downtown pickup point at King's Square. The fare is C$2.25 for adults, C$2 for seniors and children, exact change only.

Staying in Saint John

Saint John has a number of historic inns, the best of which are within walking distance of downtown. Concentrations of mid-priced chain motels lie along Route 1 east and west of the city.

A string of cheap motels is spread along Manawagonish Road, west of downtown. Among the least expensive is the **Island View Motel,** 1726 Manawagonish Rd. (☎ **888-674-6717** or 506-672-1381; www.islandview motel.ca), which comes with water views and a small outdoor pool. Rates are C$75 to C$85, which puts it at the lower end of the $$ price category.

Chipman Hill Suites
$–$$$$ Downtown

Set up for long-term rentals, but with nightly rates offered for short-stay visitors, this collection of units in buildings spread through the Uptown section of downtown Saint John is a good choice for those who like to do their own cooking. All offer a stylish heritage theme, en suite bathrooms, private entrances, TV/DVD combos, and all but the smallest have full kitchens. The more expensive suites have three bedrooms.

Office at 9 Chipman Hill. ☎ *506-693-1171. Fax: 506-657-5950.* www.chipmanhill. com. *Parking: On the street. Rack rates: C$49–C$249 double. AE, MC, V.*

Earl of Leinster B&B
$$ Downtown

Inside this red-brick, downtown building, are seven inviting guest rooms, each with a smallish en suite bathroom, phone, fridge, and television. Those out back in a converted coach house have kitchenettes. Guests have access to a games room and laundry, and a cooked breakfast is also available (C$13 per person).

See map p. 203. 96 Leinster St. ☎ *506-652-3275. Parking: On the street. Rack rates: C$92–C$96 double. AE, DC, MC, V.*

Hilton Saint John
$$$–$$$$ Downtown

Located right on the water and linked by a covered walkway to Market Square, this hotel has the best location of any downtown Saint John accommodations. The 197 rooms are spacious and comfortable, and most have water views. The menu at the Turn of the Tide Restaurant doesn't offer any surprises, but it offers good, solid, contemporary Canadian cooking (and a daily buffet breakfast for C$17), while the Brigantine Lounge is one of the best places in town to enjoy a quiet drink. Both the restaurant and lounge have water views. The hotel also has a swimming pool and exercise room.

See map p. 203. 1 Market Sq. ☎ *800-445-8667 or 506-693-8484. Fax: 506-657-6610.* www.hilton.com. *Parking: C$15. Rack rates: C$180–C$320 double. AE, DC, DISC, MC, V.*

Holiday Inn Express Hotel & Suites
$$–$$$$ West of Downtown

A good choice for families, this modern hotel comes with no surprises. The 96 midsize rooms are filled with all the usual amenities. The Kids' Suites come with a separate bunk room complete with their own TV and PlayStation. A light breakfast is included in the rates.

400 Main St. (at Chesley Drive). ☎ *888-465-4329 or 506-642-2622.* www.ichotels group.com. *Parking: Free. Rack rates: C$145–C$285 double. AE, DC, MC, V.*

Homeport Historic Bed & Breakfast
$$–$$$ **West of downtown**

This large and luxurious bed-and-breakfast lies on a high ridge overlooking the harbor and is within walking distance of downtown via the Harbour Passage promenade. The creation of the inn, a subtle amalgamation of two side-by-side mansions built for shipbuilding brothers, was a labor of love for owners Ralph and Karen Holyoke. The inn is full of appropriate antiques sourced by Ralph throughout the Maritimes; big windows, high ceilings, and ornate furnishings add to the grandeur. The ten guest rooms are all very different, but each is outfitted with a large bathroom. The Veranda Room (C$140) is my favorite. The centerpiece of this unit is an 1850s walnut bed, while the adjacent sitting area has views across to Saint John Harbour. The parlor is a popular place to relax, especially in the afternoon when refreshments are laid out. A big breakfast gets you going each morning.

80 Douglas Ave. ☎ *888-678-7678 or 506-672-7255. Fax: 506-672-7250.* www.homeport.nb.ca. *Rack rates: C$95–C$175 double. AE, MC, V.*

Inn on the Cove & Spa
$$$–$$$$ **Irving Nature Park**

This sprawling property well away from the bustle of the city has 11 stylish guest rooms, all with stunning ocean views and some with private balconies. Centered on a 1907 mansion that has been thoroughly modernized by gracious owners Ross and Willa Mavis, the place is sophisticated but has a wonderfully carefree feeling about it. The perfect way to follow up a walk in the adjacent Irving Nature Park (which was once part of the estate) is by spending time in the inn's day spa. A gourmet breakfast is included in the rates, while dinner, available Monday to Saturday, revolves around seafood and seasonal produce (reservations required).

1371 Sand Cove Rd. (take Exit 119A from Route 1). ☎ *877-257-8080 or 506-672-7799. Fax: 506-635-5455.* www.innonthecove.com. *Rack rates: C$159–C$235 double. MC, V.*

Dining in Saint John

In Saint John, many of the better restaurants are tucked away and easy to overlook. One place you can't miss is **Market Square,** down on the waterfront, where a string of restaurants take full advantage of summer warmth by setting out tables along a cobbled plaza.

Beatty & the Beastro
$$–$$$ **Downtown EUROPEAN**

This restaurant overlooks King's Square from beside the historic Imperial Theatre. Lunch is extremely popular — mussels steamed open in white wine, "Bowl of the Beast" soup, Caesar salad, and a curried chicken wrap are all good. In the evening, the curry of the day is a local favorite (as is the accompanying freshly made mango chutney), but my last visit coincided with a delivery of spring lamb from a local farm, so choosing anything else wasn't even an issue.

See map p. 203. 60 Charlotte St. ☎ *506-652-3888. Reservations recommended. Main courses: C$20–C$22. AE, DC, MC, V. Open: Mon–Fri 11:30 a.m.–3 p.m. and 5–9 p.m., Sat 5–10 p.m.*

Billy's Seafood Company
$$–$$$$ **Downtown** **SEAFOOD**

Tucked away at the back of the Saint John City Market, Billy's enjoys a stellar reputation for fresher-than-fresh seafood, which can also be bought market-style at the front counter. The restaurant itself is a sleek, old-fashioned room with comfortable booths, dim lighting, and lots of dark polished wood. You can start by sharing steamed mussels and crab cakes with mango dipping sauce, and then move on to cedar plank salmon, broiled halibut in blueberry balsamic sauce, or a full lobster from the tank. The wine list complements the food well but is a bit expensive. Lunchtime is a good time to try the lobster roll, packed with a combination of the delicious meat and mayonnaise (C$14).

See map p. 203. 49 Charlotte St. (Saint John City Market). ☎ *888-933-3474 or 506-672-3474. Reservations recommended. Main courses: C$18–C$32. AE, DC, DISC, MC, V. Open: Mon–Thurs 11 a.m.–10 p.m., Fri–Sat 11 a.m.–11 p.m., Sun 4–9 p.m.*

Church Street Steak House
$$–$$$$ **Downtown** **STEAK**

Saint John is a long way from the rangelands of Alberta, but this popular steakhouse does an excellent job of sourcing the best cuts of beef and cooking them exactly as you ordered them. The appetizers are mostly seafood-oriented, a perfect complement to a beef entree. The setting is a historic red-brick building that remains virtually unchanged in appearance since it was built following the 1877 fire that destroyed most of downtown.

See map p. 203. 10 Grannan St. ☎ *506-672-3463. Reservations recommended. Main courses: C$17–C$32. AE, MC, V. Open: Mon–Thurs 4 p.m.–11 p.m., Fri–Sat 4 p.m. to midnight, Sun 4 p.m.–10 p.m.*

Grannan's
$$–$$$$ **Downtown** **SEAFOOD**

My favorite of the many Market Square restaurants. Grannan's has lots of outdoor seating, but the interior is also appealing, with a stylish mix of maritime-themed artifacts, including brass ship lamps and an antique diving suit. A blackboard menu is the place to search out seasonal seafood, but you won't go wrong with a pick from the Features section of the regular menu (my seafood casserole was delicious). For a splurge, consider the Seafood Brochette, a lobster tail with skewered scallops and shrimp sautéed at your table.

See map p. 203. Market Square. ☎ *506-634-1555*. Reservations recommended for dinner. Main courses: C$15–C$37. AE, DC, MC, V. Open: Mon–Thurs 11:30 a.m.–11 p.m., Fri–Sat 11:30 a.m. to midnight, Sun noon to 10 p.m.

Taco Pica
$–$$ **Downtown   GUATEMALAN/MEXICAN**

Look no farther than Taco Pica for a unique and inexpensive meal in cheerful surroundings. The flavorful dishes are impressive, such as pepian, a spicy beef stew, and chimichanga, a minty-flavored pork tortilla. Seafood offerings include a Spanish-style paella and a garlic shrimp dish. The dessert menu goes beyond the confines of Central America to include Pavlova, an Australian meringue cake topped with cream and fruit.

See map p. 203. 96 Germain St. ☎ *506-633-8492*. Reservations recommended. Main courses: C$9.50–C$18. AE, DC, MC, V. Open: Mon–Sat 10 a.m.–10 p.m.

Exploring Saint John

Earlier, this chapter discusses your accommodations and dining options. Here I get into the real reason for spending time in Saint John — to soak up the sights, sounds, and smells of a port city that has changed little in appearance in over a century.

All of the attractions discussed in this section (except Carleton Martello Tower) are within walking distance of each other. Pick up the *Three Historic Walking Tours* brochure (free) from the information center to learn more about the most notable buildings as you explore downtown.

Barbour's General Store
Downtown

This late-1800s shop is preserved as a museum, its shelves stocked with merchandise sold a century ago, like candy and tobacco.

See map p. 203. Market Square. ☎ *506-658-2939*. Admission: Free. Open: Mid-June to early Sept daily 9 a.m.–6 p.m.

Carleton Martello Tower
Saint John West

Built in 1812 to protect the then-fledgling Loyalist city of Saint John from attack, the tower is similar in design to circular towers built along the British coastline during the Napoleonic Wars. Over the years, this solid stone structure has also been used for ammunition storage, as a soldiers' barracks, as a detention center for deserters, and as an anti-aircraft position. Today, protected as a National Historic Site, it's all tourist attraction.

454 Whipple St. (at Fundy Drive; take Exit 120 from Route 1). ☎ *506-636-4011*. Admission: C$3.95 adults, C$3.45 seniors, C$1.95 children. Open: June–Sept daily 10 a.m.–5:30 p.m.

Walking the walk

Harbour Passage, along Saint John's downtown foreshore, is an ambitious project that will eventually see the entire waterfront area linked by pathways and dotted with green space, benches, and interpretive panels that extend all the way to Reversing Falls. At this stage, the 2.7km (1.7-mile) paved trail extends around the harbor from the Hilton Saint John to Reversing Falls. Along the way it passes by the Gathering Garden, planted with the same species used by native peoples long ago; the site of a 1600s Acadian fort; a pavilion with sweeping city views; and a power substation with interpretive panels describing what goes on behind the wire fence.

Fort Howe Lookout
North of Downtown

The best place to get a feel for the layout of Saint John is Fort Howe Lookout, a two-minute drive north of downtown, off Main Street. The Loyalists established a fort here in 1778 to defend their new settlement against attack by Americans. Looking out to the mouth of the harbor, which affords unobstructed views of incoming vessels, the reason they chose this lofty location is clear.

Magazine Street off Main Street.

King's Square
Downtown

From the waterfront, take a steep walk up King Street to reach King's Square, which was laid out in the shape of a Union Jack to reflect the loyalty to the British monarchy held by those who escaped the American Revolution to settle in Saint John. The most intriguing of numerous monuments is a lump of melted metal salvaged from a hardware store that was destroyed by the fire that raced through downtown in 1877.

Across Sydney Street from King's Square are a couple of other historical diversions. Inside the 1829 County Courthouse, at King and Sydney streets, is a massive spiral staircase built of unsupported stones. Across King Street is the Loyalist's Old Burial Ground, the final resting place of the city's founding fathers.

See map p. 203. At King and Charlotte streets.

Loyalist House
Downtown

Dating to 1817, this Georgian-style Loyalist House is Saint John's oldest building and is well worth visiting. Lived in by six generations of the same family, it is furnished with authentic Georgian antiques and has a total of eight fireplaces, an indication of the wealth of its original owner, David Daniel Merritt.

See map p. 203. 120 Union St. ☎ 506-652-3590. Admission: C$3 adults, C$1 children. Open: Mid-May to June Mon–Fri 10 a.m.–5 p.m., July to mid-Sept daily 10 a.m.–5 p.m.

New Brunswick Museum
Downtown

One of the largest museums in the Maritimes, this modern facility is part of the Market Square complex down on the harborfront. Every gallery has something different and interesting: The Shipbuilding Gallery catalogs the city's first industry, the Hall of Great Whales is dominated by a full-size right whale skeleton, the Birds of New Brunswick Gallery features displays describing some of the province's 370 recorded species, and the Discovery Gallery is filled with kid-friendly learning experiences.

See map p. 203. Market Square. ☎ 506-643-2300. www.nbm-mnb.ca. Admission: C$6 adults, C$4.75 seniors, C$3.25 children. Open: Mon–Sat 9 a.m.–5 p.m. (Thurs until 9 p.m.), Sun noon to 5 p.m.; closed Mon Nov–Apr.

Saint John City Market
Downtown

The 1876 City Market, the oldest in Canada, occupies a full block between Charlotte and Germain streets. The handsome building was designed by local shipbuilders, whose influence is obvious when you look up at the inverted-keel ceiling. The collection of stalls is varied — an old-fashioned butcher, produce, fresh seafood, and touristy knickknacks. Instead of eating at the unappealing food court along one side, choose some cheeses from the dairy bar, some smoked salmon and a cooked lobster from the seafood counter, and some crusty rolls from the bakery and then head out to Irving Nature Park for a picnic lunch.

See map p. 203. 47 Charlotte St. ☎ 506-658-2820. Admission: Free. Open: Mon–Thurs 7:30 a.m.–6 p.m., Fri 7:30 a.m.–7 p.m., Sat 10 a.m.–5 p.m.

Other cool things to see and do
After you finish exploring downtown, expand your horizons and consider the following attractions.

Reversing Falls
Another Fundy phenomenon, this is Saint John's most hyped natural attraction. As the massive Fundy tide rises, the flow of the Saint John River reverses as ocean water pushes upstream. When the tide recedes, the water flows in the opposite direction. The "falls" are a series of rock ledges at the base of a narrow gorge, which form rapids where the water tumbles in opposite directions just before and after low tide. You really need to visit at both high and low tides to appreciate the difference in water level — 4.4m (15 feet).

To get to Reversing Falls from downtown, cross Route 1 via Main Street and take Chesley Drive off to the left. You can also get there by taking Exit 119 from Route 1 and turning right onto Bridge Road.

Overlooking the gorge is the **Reversing Falls Visitor Centre,** part of a restaurant complex at 200 Bridge Rd. (☎ **506-658-2937**). Displays describe the effect of the tides, out back is an observation platform, and you can watch a film about the falls (C$2.50). The center is open from mid-May through early October, daily 8 a.m. to 8 p.m. Or cross to **Fallsview Park,** on the east side of the gorge. Access is via Douglas Avenue.

Boats can navigate the gorge safely, but only when the tide reaches a certain level and the current slows. The only people who avoid this "slack" tide are folks at **F1 Reversing Falls Jet Boat Rides** (☎ **888-634-8987** or 506-634-8987), who wait until the rapids are at their roughest to take you out for a 20-minute ride through the churning water. The cost is C$34 adults, C$27 children. The departure point is Fallsview Park. The same company runs a regular one-hour boat tour through the gorge and around the harbor for C$34 adults, C$27 children. These trips depart from downtown's Market Square to coincide with calm slack tide.

Rockwood Park

The Maritime's largest urban park (810 hectares/2,000 acres) encompasses native forests and numerous lakes northeast of downtown Saint John. Everyone can find plenty to do, including:

- ✔ **Monkey around** at **Cherry Brook Zoo,** Foster Thurston Road (☎ 506-634-1440), where you can see lions, tigers, and over 30 other exotic species. It's open 10 a.m. to 6 p.m., and admission is C$8 adults, C$7 seniors, and C$6 children.

- ✔ **Take a hike** along 25km (15.5 miles) of pathways. One popular trail begins from Lake Drive South and encircles pretty Crystal Lake.

- ✔ **Aim for the water hazard** at **Rockwood Park Golf Course,** on Sandy Point Road (☎ 506-634-0090), which has the Maritimes' only aquatic driving range. Greens fees are C$35.

- ✔ **Swim and splash** in one of the park's 12 lakes. **Fisher Lakes,** off Lake Drive South, has supervised swimming, canoe rentals, and a sandy stretch of beach.

The easiest way to get to Rockwood Park is to take Foster Thurston Drive north from Exit 128 of Route 1, 3km (2 miles) east of downtown. This road leads all the way around the park. If you're feeling confident in your route-finding ability, cross Route 1 via Somerset Street and hook a right on Churchill Boulevard. For park information, dial ☎ **506-658-2883.**

Irving Nature Park

A rocky peninsula jutting into busy Saint John Harbour has escaped development and is protected as Irving Nature Park. This 243-hectare

(600-acre) park has a sandy stretch of beach near the entrance, rocky coves, pleasant hiking trails, and tidal pools filled with colorful critters. At the park's highest point, reached along the **Squirrel Trail**, an observation tower offers sweeping views back across the mud flats linking the peninsula to the mainland. Between early June and late October the park becomes home to hundreds of seals, which haul themselves out of the water and onto the rocky shoreline. Bird life is prolific year-round — over 200 species have been recorded in the park.

Irving Nature Park is west of downtown. To get there, take Exit 119 from Route 1 and follow Bleury Street and then Sand Cove Road into the park. Cross the mud flats to reach an information booth that is staffed late May through October. For park information, call ☎ 506-653-7367. Admission is free.

Nightlife

If you feel like enjoying a tipple and some local music but want to avoid the hard-drinking, dimly lit downtown bars, you have plenty of options. Stop by either of the city information centers for a schedule of what's on, or check with **Tourism Saint John** (☎ 866-463-8639 or 506-658-2855; www.tourismsaintjohn.com) directly.

Pubs and clubs

All the restaurants in Market Square, including **Grannan's** (☎ 506-634-1555), have a section of the public plaza cordoned off for outdoor seating. You're welcome to stop by for just a refreshing drink in the sun at any of these places. Also here is **Saint John Ale House** (☎ 506-657-2337), with British-style beers on tap and a full menu. In the vicinity, the **Brigantine Lounge** in the Hilton Saint John at 1 Market Square (☎ 506-693-8484) has unobstructed harbor views from its outdoor patio.

The Trinity Royal area, up King and Princess streets, is a good place to look for local color and live music. **O'Leary's Pub,** 46 Princess St. (☎ 506-634-7135), is a jumping Irish pub, with Guinness on tap and Celtic bands most nights. **Tapps Brew Pub,** 78 King St. (☎ 506-634-1957), attracts an older crowd.

The arts

The **Imperial Theatre** on King's Square (☎ 506-674-4100) is a meticulously restored 1913 vaudeville theater. It's home to local theater, opera, ballet, and music productions, with programs that usually run from September through to April. Theater tours are available in summer Monday through Saturday 10 a.m. to 6 p.m. for C$2 per person.

Fundy Coast

Beyond Saint John, you can head west to the resort town of St. Andrews, back toward Moncton via Fundy National Park, or inland to the provincial capital of Fredericton. The following sections detail the first two options, while I cover Fredericton in Chapter 17.

Fundy National Park

The massive Fundy tides are the most dramatic aspect of this popular coastal park northeast of Saint John, but the rugged interior dotted with lakes along with the network of hiking trails brings in the summertime crowds. The park even has a covered bridge, which lies near the end of Point Wolfe Road.

Wildlife is prolific on the land, in the air, and out in the Bay of Fundy. At dawn or dusk you have an excellent chance of spying moose, beavers, or black bears, while bird-watchers delight in spotting peregrine falcons.

Getting there

You need a vehicle to reach Fundy National Park. It's bisected by Route 114, which branches off Route 1 84km (51 miles) northeast of Saint John. From this junction, it's 25km (16 miles) to the park gate and a farther 17km (11 miles) to the main facility area.

Park entry fees

The daily entry fee to Fundy National Park is C$6.90 adults, C$5.90 seniors, C$3.45 children, to a maximum of C$17 per vehicle. Fees are collected at booths located at both park entrances.

Gathering more information

The **Visitor Reception Centre** (☎ **506-887-6000;** www.pc.gc.ca) is just inside the east park gate. It's open mid-June through August daily 8 a.m. to 10 p.m. and from mid-May to mid-June and September to mid-October daily 8 a.m. to 4:30 p.m.

If you're coming in from the west, make a stop at the **Wolfe Lake Visitor Centre,** open mid-June through mid-August daily 10 a.m. to 6 p.m.

Staying in Fundy National Park

Most people staying in Fundy camp out in one of four park campgrounds. Campsites and indoor accommodations are limited, so reserve as far in advance as possible.

Fundy Highlands Inn & Chalets
$$ Fundy National Park

Perched on a grassy slope 2km (1¼ miles) from the main facility area, this comfortable lodging offers views across the Bay of Fundy that make it worth every cent of the already reasonable rates. Units within the main complex are slightly dated, but each comes with cooking facilities and opens to a large patio with ocean views. The 24 chalets are smaller, but have kitchenettes and private decks, as well as a little more character.

Route 114, Fundy National Park. ☎ *888-883-8639 or 506-887-2930. Fax: 506-887-2453.* www.fundyhighlandchalets.com. *Rack rates: C$85–C$105 double. MC, V. Open: May–Oct.*

Fundy Park Chalets
$$ Fundy National Park

These fresh little cottages lie in a grove of trees adjacent to hiking trails, the swimming pool, the golf course, a restaurant, and the main information center. Each has basic cooking facilities and a bathroom. In the shoulder seasons, you can enjoy accommodations, a round of golf, and a lobster dinner for just C$80 per person. Book well ahead for July and August.

Fundy Park Chalet Road, Fundy National Park. ☎ *877-887-2808 or 506-887-2808. Fax: 506-887-2282.* www.fundyparkchalets.com. *Rack rates: C$99 double. MC, V. Open: May to mid-Oct.*

Dining in Fundy National Park

The park has just one restaurant, but as both accommodations have cooking facilities, preparing your own meal is an easy option. In adjacent Alma, **Butland's Seafood** on Main Street (☎ 506-887-2190) sells cooked lobsters for around C$12 per pound, with the price clearly displayed in black marker on their claws. You can also buy fresh shrimp, mussels, scallops, and a variety of fish.

Seawinds Dining Room
$$–$$$ Fundy National Park   SEAFOOD

This restaurant is exactly what you'd expect in the popular park — family-friendly and informal, with well-priced, unfussy food. Three massive chandeliers, a large stone fireplace, and a 6-kilogram (14-pound) lobster shell dominate the main dining room. The menu is short and simple, ranging from a traditional roast beef dinner to sautéed scallops. All children's dishes are under C$6.

Fundy Park Chalet Road, Fundy National Park. ☎ *506-887-2808. Reservations not necessary. Main courses: C$9.50–C$23. MC, V. Open: May–Oct daily 11 a.m.–9:30 p.m.*

Exploring Fundy National Park

The main facility area, just inside the east gate, is a good place to get oriented. Stop by the visitor center for a park map and hiking trail description brochure, and then wander down to the water's edge for panoramic views across the Bay of Fundy.

Hiking

Within the park are 120km (74.6 miles) of hiking trails designed for all fitness levels. Head to either visitor center for a trail map and to ask advice about which trails would suit your fitness level and interests.

At low tide, you can walk along the beach below the main visitor center, but don't expect to have it to yourself. To escape the crowds, drive west along Point Wolfe Road From the end of this road, a 0.6km (0.4-mile) path leads through a lush spruce forest to **Point Wolfe Beach** at the braided mouth of the Point Wolfe River. From the same trail head, the **Coppermine Trail** leads 2.3km (1.4 miles) farther west along the coast to the site of an abandoned mine. Allow two hours for the round-trip. Backtrack along Point Wolfe Road and then take Herring Cove Road to reach **Herring Cove Trail,** a 15-minute jaunt down to a rocky cove with a tidal cave off to one side. From the cove, the **Matthews Head Trail** leads off to the south, traversing to a high headland with stunning ocean views. Allow 90 minutes for this 4.5km (2.8-mile) circuit.

An easy introduction to the park's interior forest is the **Caribou Plain Trail,** a 3.4km (2.1-mile) circuit that loops around a beaver pond. The trail head is just east of Bennett Lake. **Third Vault Falls** tumbles over a 16m-high (53-foot) ledge in the eastern portion of the park. The falls are reached via a 3.7km (2.3-mile) trail that braches off Laverty Road. Allow 60 to 70 minutes each way.

Other things to do and see in Fundy National Park

Hiking is the major attention-getter in the park, but you can also do the following:

- ✔ **Swim.** A unique **saltwater pool** is filled with water pumped up from the Bay of Fundy and then heated to a comfortable temperature. Entry is C$3.45 adults, C$2.95 seniors, C$1.90 children. It's open July through August, daily 11 a.m. to 7 p.m.

- ✔ **Golf.** The fairways of a short nine-hole golf course wind their way along Dickson Brook, beside the main facility area. A pro shop (☎ **506-887-2970**) rents clubs and collects greens fees of C$1780, or golf all day for C$32.

- ✔ **Paddle.** Rent a canoe (C$9 per hour) at **Bennett Lake,** halfway along the park road, to explore the shoreline of this tranquil body of water.

- ✔ **Watch the tide.** Okay, watching tidal movements is not very exciting, but at low tide, **Alma Harbour** is devoid of water, leaving fishing boats high and dry on the ocean floor.

Hopewell Cape

Around halfway between Fundy National Park and Moncton, Route 114 rounds Hopewell Cape. Turn here to reach Hopewell Rocks, a cluster of rock towers that were once part of the mainland but became separated by erosion caused by the tides. Known as "flower pots" (many have trees and shrubbery growing on top), they're partly covered at high tide, but when the massive Fundy tide recedes, they rise starkly from the muddy shoreline.

Plan on arriving one to three hours before low tide. Tidal charts are published in all local newspapers and are available at information centers. The visitor's guide to Fundy National Park (you get one at the park entrance) has a tide chart on the center page.

Staying and dining at Hopewell Cape

Most visitors to Hopewell Rocks spend two to four hours poking around and then move on to Moncton or Fundy National Park. Alternatively, you can stay overnight at the Hopewell Rocks Motel & Country Inn, within walking distance of the attraction.

Hopewell Rocks Motel
$$ **Hopewell Cape**

Located at the entrance to Hopewell Rocks, this adequate motel has large air-conditioned rooms and a small outdoor pool. The hanging baskets of colorful flowers out front are a nice touch. Rooms 11 through 20 face away from the road and are quieter. Summer rates include a pancake breakfast.

Ignore your hunger pangs down at Hopewell Rocks and plan on taking a meal back out on the highway at this motel's **Log Cabin Restaurant.** The lobster dinner is well priced; or choose one of the daily specials, which are discounted from the main menu. The dining room is open May through October, daily 8 a.m. to 9 p.m.

Route 114. ☎ *888-759-7070 or 506-734-2957. Fax: 506-734-2252.* www.hopewell rocksmotel.com. *Rack rates: C$95 double. AE, MC, V. Open: May–Oct.*

Exploring Hopewell Rocks

At the end of the access road off Route 114 are a massive parking lot and a fee station where the entry charge is collected. Admission is C$8 adults, C$6.75 seniors, C$5.75 children.

The gates are open mid-May to mid-June daily 9 a.m. to 5 p.m., mid-June to mid-August daily 8 a.m. to 8 p.m., mid- to late August daily 8 a.m. to 6 p.m., September to mid-October 9 a.m. to 5 p.m., and are closed the rest of the year.

Beyond the fee station, make your way down to the large **Interpretive Centre** (☎ 506-734-3552). This is a good place to get an overview of these geological oddities, as well as to learn more about the Fundy tides.

The rock towers are scattered along a 2km (1¼-mile) stretch starting immediately below the interpretive center, but the most impressive concentration is a 30-minute walk away, along a wooded trail. The alternative to walking is to catch a ride in an oversize golf cart. This costs just C$1.50 each way; buy tickets at the main entrance or at the cart turnaround point.

At the end of the trail/cart path, a steep metal stairway descends to the muddy shoreline and the **Flower Pot Rocks.** To escape the summer crowds, walk west along the beach (to the right from the bottom of the stairs). Hoses are provided back at the top to clean the sticky, red mud from the soles of your shoes.

 The time of day you visit is restricted by the tide, but early morning is best if you want to avoid the crowds. For shutterbugs, an early-morning visit also offers more favorable light for photography. Check the Web site www.thehopewellrocks.ca for a tide chart.

St. Andrews

On the Fundy Coast west of Saint John, St. Andrews is New Brunswick's most famous resort town. Laid out by Loyalists in 1783, the oldest part of town has remained remarkably untouched by modern encroachment and is protected as a National Historic Site.

St. Andrews was mainly a port city until it was discovered in the late 1880s by wealthy Americans looking to escape the summer heat of the Eastern Seaboard. They stayed in grand resorts like the Algonquin or in their own private estates, and St. Andrews was transformed.

Today, St. Andrews, population 2,000, is popular not only with vacationing New Englanders, but also with Canadians who come to celebrate special occasions, spend time out on the water, or simply stroll the streets browsing through the many galleries and boutiques.

Getting there

Although St. Andrews is across the St. Croix River from Maine, access from the United States is via the Calais/St. Stephen border crossing, 24km (15 miles) northwest.

From elsewhere in New Brunswick, the most direct access to St. Andrews is Route 1 west along the Bay of Fundy from Saint John, a distance of 100km (62 miles). From Fredericton, 133km (83 miles) away, the most direct way is Route 3 via St. Stephen.

Just before entering the town proper, make a stop at the **St. Andrews Welcome Centre,** in a converted residence at 46 Reed Ave. (☎ **506-529-3556**). It's open May through September daily 9 a.m. to 6 p.m. (and until 9 p.m. in July and Aug).

Staying in St. Andrews

Many of St. Andrews' lodgings are upscale inns and bed-and-breakfasts, priced higher than elsewhere in the Maritimes. I include the best of these and dig out a cheapie and a family favorite to keep everyone happy.

Inn on Frederick
$$$–$$$$　Downtown

This centrally located structure started life in the 1840s as home to a Loyalist family. Now beautifully restored to create a historical and welcoming ambience, the building is also home to a fine-dining restaurant (open for dinner daily 5–9 p.m.). The seven guest rooms are big and bright, with even the smallest featuring a canopy bed and luxurious bathroom. Rates include a cooked breakfast.

58 Frederick St. ☎ *877-895-4400 or 506-529-2603. Fax: 506-529-4460.* www.innon frederick.ca. *Rack rates: C$195–C$495 double. AE, MC, V. Open: Apr–Dec.*

Kingsbrae Arms
$$$$　Downtown

Staying at this country estate, the only Relais & Châteaux property in the Maritimes, is an unforgettable experience. Built by a Boston businessman in 1897, the Kingsbrae was originally part of a sprawling estate that is now Kingsbrae Garden (see later). Today, the gracious home is still surrounded by beautifully landscaped grounds, and has been converted to an inn with an impeccable pedigree. The eight rooms have marble bathrooms, gas fireplaces, and canopy beds, topped with luxurious linens. Although bed-and-breakfast rates are offered, most guests stay as part of a package that includes a memorable cooked breakfast, picnic lunch, and four-course table d'hôte dinner, inclusive of wine.

219 King St. ☎ *506-529-1897. Fax: 506-529-4311.* www.kingsbrae.com. *Rack rates: C$585–C$985 double. AE, MC, V. Open: May–Oct.*

Picket Fence Motel
$$　North of downtown

If all you want is a regular motel room, consider this lodging on the edge of town.

102 Reed St. ☎ *506-529-8985.* www.picketfencenb.com. *Rates: C$80–C$95. AE, MC, V. Open: Mid-May to mid-Oct.*

Seaside Beach Resort
$$　Downtown

Located at the far end of the main street, this is a good choice for families who are looking for a waterfront setting at a reasonable price. Each of the 24 units in this historic miscellany of cottages and apartments is different, but most have cooking facilities and bright, practical furnishings. The two-bedroom Seagull apartment is right on the water and opens to a boardwalk dotted with Adirondack chairs, while the Sandpiper cottage is a cozy space set back from the water. Barbecues and picnic tables dot the grounds.

339 Water St. ☎ *800-506-8677 or 506-529-3846. Fax: 506-529-4479.* www.seaside. nb.ca. *Rack rates: C$120–C$200 double. AE, MC, V. Open: Apr–Dec.*

Treadwell Inn
$$–$$$$ Downtown

The seven-room, olive and burgundy-colored lodge, built in the 1820s for a ship chandler, combines a waterfront setting with comfortable rooms to make it one of the nicest places to stay in St. Andrews. The current owner's faultless taste shines through without taking away from the historical charm. Of the well-furnished rooms, only two don't have ocean views. My fave? Room 5 (C$250), with a king-size bed, a bathroom with a soaker tub, and wide doors that open to a private balcony with sweeping views across Passamaquoddy Bay.

129 Water St. ☎ *888-529-1011 or 506-529-1011. Fax: 506-529-4826.* www.treadwell inn.com. *Rack rates: C$145–C$250 double. MC, V.*

Dining in St. Andrews

Dining in St. Andrews compares favorably with much larger centers across the Maritimes — a combination of an abundance of seafood and a century of demand from well-heeled visitors.

The Gables
$$–$$$ St. Andrews   SEAFOOD

This restaurant lies down a narrow alley, beyond a giant woodcarving of a lobster. It's a casual affair, liberally decorated with netting and the like, all salvaged from the sea. Seating is inside or out on a deck that extends to above the high-tide mark. The cooking is simple but tasty. Plan on starting with a plate piled high with steamed mussels. For mains, peruse the blackboard offerings, which feature whatever seafood is in season — lobster, scallops, halibut, and haddock are all staples. The Gables opens for breakfast in summer, with full cooked breakfasts costing a reasonable C$8.

143 Water St. ☎ *506-529-3440. Reservations recommended for dinner. Main courses: C$14–C$24. AE, MC, V. Open: July–Aug daily 8 a.m.–11 p.m., Sept–June daily 11 a.m.–9 p.m.*

Garden Cafe
$$–$$$ St. Andrews   CAFE

A century-old home at the top of this famous garden has been converted to an inviting cafe, complete with a patio offering sweeping views across the manicured lawns and colorful flower beds. Traditional afternoon tea, complete with finger sandwiches, loose-leaf tea, and sweet treats, is C$12 per person. Lunch choices include a steaming bowl of seafood chowder (C\$9.50), hearty sandwiches, a daily quiche, and a lobster roll.

220 King St. ☎ *506-529-3335. Reservations not neccesary. Lunch: C\$8–C\$15. AE, MC, V. Open: Mid-May to mid-Oct daily 10 a.m.–5 p.m.*

Niger Reef Tea House
\$\$–\$\$\$ St. Andrews   CANADIAN

This historic teahouse is my favorite spot in St. Andrews for lunch, although I have dropped by just for a piece of the melt-in-your-mouth strawberry shortcake. Choose to dine in a cozy room and enjoy the wonderful aromas that waft in from the kitchen, or sit out on the weathered deck and take in the view across Passamaquoddy Bay. In the evening, you can indulge in the rich seafood chowder or skewered scallops, grilled with a ginger and curry glaze. If you weren't here at lunch, end your meal with the shortcake; otherwise, go for the triple chocolate brownie sundae. The salmon eggs Benedict (C\$13), served at Sunday brunch, is to die for.

1 Joe's Point Rd. ☎ *506-529-8007. Reservations recommended for dinner. Lunch: C\$7–C\$14. MC, V. Open: Mid-June to early Sept daily 11 a.m.–5 p.m.*

Exploring St. Andrews

If you'd like to take a self-guided walking tour of St. Andrews, pick up a map highlighting points of interest from the Welcome Centre. If you're heading out on your own, here are some sights you don't want to miss.

Atlantic Salmon Interpretive Centre

Very different from St. Andrews' historical attractions, this is the public portion of a research station that studies one of Canada's most important fishing exports. The modern interpretive center nestles in a lush forest, right over a stream where salmon spawn. Inside the timber-frame building are displays on the life cycle of the salmon and the ongoing fight to save its habitat, as well as some old fly-fishing equipment. A trail leads downstream to Chamcook Harbour and upstream to shallow gravel beds where the fish spawn.

Route 127 (6km/3¾ miles toward Saint John). ☎ *506-529-1384. Internet:* www.asf. ca. *Admission C\$5 adults, C\$4 seniors, C\$3 children. Open: Mid-May to Sept daily 9 a.m.–5 p.m.*

Kingsbrae Garden

Once part of the sprawling Kingsbrae Arms Estate, this 11-hectare (27-acre) plot is generally regarded as one of the top ten gardens in Canada. The Rose Garden, filled with fragrant old varieties, is from the original estate; the White Garden is composed entirely of white and silver blossoms; and the Scents and Sensitivity Garden allows visually impaired visitors to experience distinct smells and textures up close. And new gardens are always being added — the Gravel Garden addresses modern environmental concerns by using a minimum of water. In other parts of the grounds, you'll find a scaled-down working windmill, a wooden maze, and fish-filled ponds. Complement your visit with a bowl of steaming seafood chowder in the Garden Café. Kingsbrae is a ten-minute walk up King Street from the waterfront.

220 King St. ☎ 866-566-8687 or 506-529-3335. Admission C$9 adults, C$7.50 seniors and children over 5. Open: Mid-May to mid-Oct daily 9 a.m.–6 p.m.

Minister's Island

Once the summer retreat of William Van Horne, the driving force behind the completion of Canada's transcontinental railway, this small island holds one of the finest private residences that you are likely to come across in Canada. Built of locally quarried sandstone, the mansion is notable for its 50 rooms, including a massive drawing room and a billiard room with the original table. On the grounds is a sandstone bathhouse with a tidal swimming pool.

Getting to the island is an adventure in itself. The only access is at low tide (ask at the visitor center or dial ☎ 506-529-5081 to hear a recorded message with exact tide and tour times), at which time everyone meets at the end of Bar Road from where an escort is provided across the dry sea floor to the island. You must have your own vehicle.

Bar Road (off Mowat Drive). ☎ 506-529-5081. Admission C$12 adults, C$10 seniors and children over 5. Tours: June to mid-Oct; times vary with the tide.

Ross Memorial Museum

Formerly the summer retreat of a wealthy American family named Ross, this neat two-story 1824 home was deeded to the town to help preserve local history. It offers a glimpse into the life of the Rosses, with rooms that remain much as they left them, filled with fine furnishings and original paintings.

188 Montague St. ☎ 506-529-5124. Admission: Donation. Open: Early June to early Oct Mon–Sat 10 a.m.–4:30 p.m.

Other cool things to do in and around St. Andrews

Several companies run sightseeing trips on Passamaquoddy Bay, or you can go whale-watching or kayaking. The **Day Adventure Centre,** beside Market Wharf (☎ 506-529-2600), represents various operators, or choose from one of these options:

- ✔ **Whale-watching: Fundy Tide Runners,** Market Wharf (☎ 506-529-4481), uses a stable Zodiac to reach whale-watching grounds out in the Bay of Fundy. Tours last two hours and cost C$50 adults, C$35 children. The whale-watching season is June through September.

- ✔ **Sea kayaking:** Even if you've never kayaked before, the guides at **Seascape Kayak Tours,** 165 Water St. (☎ 866-747-1884 or 506-747-1884), will make you feel at ease on a two-hour introductory paddle from their seafront headquarters; C$50 per person.

✔ **Tide watching:** Walk north along Water Street to reach St. Andrews Blockhouse National Historic Site. Built in the early 1800s to protect the town from attack, the grassy bank in front of this wooden building is the perfect place to watch the tide receding.

✔ **Golfing:** It will *feel* like you're out at sea as you stand on the 12th tee at **Fairmont Algonquin Golf Club,** Brandy Cove Road (☎ 506-529-7142), aiming for a tiny patch of green perched on a nub of land surrounded by water. High season greens fees are C$99.

Shopping

Artisans are attracted to St. Andrews for the inspiration of its scenic setting, and you can't deny that the area is beautiful. But the more cynical may say that affluent visitors with pockets full of cash are the real draw. Regardless, the end result is a street lined with galleries and boutiques, including the following:

✔ **Jarea Art Studio & Gallery,** 166 Montaque St. (☎ 506-529-4936), displays the unusual art of Geoffrey David-Slater, whose work features a single line that changes color but remains unbroken.

✔ **Serendipin' Art,** 168 Water St. (☎ 506-529-3327), features colorful hand-blown glass fish and creative wood turning.

✔ **The Whale Store,** 173 Water St. (☎ 506-529-3926) is highlighted by stylish whale woodcarvings.

✔ If you want to find that perfect nautical-themed painting, start your search at the **Seacoast Gallery,** 174 Water St. (☎ 506-529-0005).

✔ **Gumushel's Tartan Shop,** 183 Water St. (☎ 506-529-3859), sells tartan ties, berets, and jackets — but you guessed that from the name, didn't you?

✔ **St. Andrews Hardware,** 189 Water St. (☎ 506-529-3158), is filled to the rafters with a hodgepodge of hardware and nautical-themed knickknacks.

Fundy Isles

Spending time on one or more of the Fundy Isles is a unique and memorable addition to your travels along the Fundy Coast. The three main islands, Deer, Campobello, and Grand Manan, are all linked to the mainland by ferry and easily visited in a day. You can explore the islands or, if you prefer, head out to the water to marvel at marine life or try your hand at some of the area's popular watersports.

Deer Island

It may be named for a land mammal, but life on this small island revolves around the ocean. The importance of the lobster industry is clear — you'll see the pounds used to hold live lobsters scattered around the shoreline. To get to the island, catch the free ferry (departures year-round, every

30 minutes) from Letete, south of St. George. You can explore the island in just a few hours, but allow two extra hours to take a whale-watching trip with **Billy Mac Tours** (☎ 506-747-2307). **Sunset Beach Cottage & Suites,** on the west side of the island at 21 Cedar Grove Road (☎ 506-747-2972; www.cottageandsuites.com), is right on the beach and has an outdoor pool; rates for the five kitchen-equipped suites and one cottage are C$70 to C$100 double, which is in the $-to-$$ range. Open May to October.

Campobello Island

A summer-only ferry links Deer and Campobello Islands, but most visitors cross to the island by bridge from Lubec, Maine — even those visiting from New Brunswick, as St. Stephen is just 70km (43 miles) away by road. Franklin Roosevelt's family members were perhaps the most notable of the many wealthy people who have spent their summers here. His 34-room cottage is protected as part of **Roosevelt Campobello International Park** (☎ 506-752-2922). The grounds are open year-round while the home is open for inspection late May through mid-October daily 10 a.m. to 6 p.m. Admission is free.

An adjacent property, once owned by Roosevelt's cousin, has been converted to **Lupine Lodge** (☎ 888-912-8880 or 506-752-2555; www.lupine lodge.com), with 11 woodsy rooms in two log cottages. Rates are C$85 to C$150 per unit ($$). The restaurant here is recommended for its simple presentations of local seafood. A good source of island information is the Web site www.campobello.com.

Grand Manan Island

Grand Manan is larger than the other Fundy Isles and much farther from the mainland. Bird-watchers in particular are drawn to the island — famed naturalist John James Audubon spent time here painting. Other draws are seal and whale-watching, biking, hiking, and a string of sandy beaches.

Coastal Transport (☎ 506-662-3724; www.coastaltransport.ca) operates ferries year-round, four to seven times daily between Blacks Harbour (take Exit 60 from Route 1) and the island. The crossing takes two hours. The round-trip fare is C$11 adults, C$5.20 children, C$31 vehicles. Reservations are only taken for the return journey from the island to the mainland.

Don't look farther than the **Swallowtail Inn,** at 50 Lighthouse Rd. near the ferry dock (☎ 866-563-1100 or 506-662-1100; www.swallowtail inn.com), for a gorgeous setting high atop a rocky bluff. Formerly a lighthouse keeper's residence, the six guest rooms (C$85–C$115; $$) have en suites and ocean views.

Island Coast Whale Tours (☎ 877-662-9393 or 506-662-8181) takes visitors on five-hour boat tours searching out humpback, finback, and minke whales. Whale sightings are guaranteed through the July to mid-September season. The cost is C$50 adults, C$25 children. **Sea Watch**

Tours (☎ 877-662-8552 or 506-662-8552) has onboard naturalists who are especially knowledgeable about local bird life. **Adventure High,** based near the ferry dock (☎ 506-662-3563), takes visitors kayaking (C$55 for three hours), rents bikes (C$22 per day), and rents cabins scattered through the island (from C$100 per night). In addition to being a wonderful way to explore the island, using a bike means you don't need to bring a vehicle across on the ferry, saving both the expense and, more important, a possible long wait in line to board.

Fast Facts: Saint John

ATMs
All banks along King Street have ATMs accessible 24 hours daily.

Emergencies
Dial ☎ 911 for all emergencies.

Hospital
Saint John Regional Hospital is at 400 University Ave. (☎ 506-648-6000).

Information
Tourism Saint John (☎ 866-463-8639 or 506-658-2855; www.tourismsaint john.com) operates an information center downtown in Market Square (open daily 9 a.m.–6 p.m., July–Aug until 8 p.m.) and along Route 1 as you approach the city from the west (open mid-May to mid-Oct daily 9 a.m. until at least 6 p.m.).

Internet Access
Internet access is free at **Saint John Free Public Library,** in Market Square (☎ 506-643-7220); closed Sunday.

Police
For emergencies, dial ☎ 911. For other police matters, call ☎ 506-757-1020.

Post Office
Downtown drugstores such as the one in Brunswick Square have postal services. The main post office is at 125 Rothesay Ave.

Restrooms
Public restrooms are located at street level in Market Square.

Taxis
Local cab companies include **Diamond Taxi** (☎ 506-648-8888) and **Royal Taxi** (☎ 506-652-5050).

Transit Info
Saint John Transit (☎ 902-490-6600) is discussed earlier in this chapter under "Getting Around Saint John."

Weather
The **Environment Canada** Web site (www.weatheroffice.gc.ca) has links to the Saint John forecast.

Chapter 17

Fredericton

*F*redericton (population 50,500), the capital of New Brunswick, is an appealing and practical stopping place with classic Victorian architecture, interesting museums, riverfront pathways, and an excellent range of lodging and dining options.

In 1793, at the end of the American Revolution, around 2,000 Americans loyal to the British crown made their way north into the Saint John River Valley. They set up camp at a site that had been the one-time capital of Acadia. These Loyalists set out to create a gracious town, and this sense of style remains today.

Getting to Fredericton

Fredericton is accessible by plane and bus, but most people arrive by automobile, driving in via an excellent provincial highway system.

By plane

Greater Fredericton Airport (www.frederictonairport.ca) is 14km (8¾ miles) southeast of downtown via Route 102. Air Canada and its subsidiary Air Canada Jazz fly in daily from Halifax, Toronto, Ottawa, and Montreal. Delta Air Lines links Fredericton with Boston.

Taxis line up out front of the main terminal and charge around C$20 to take you downtown. Car rental companies that maintain desks at the airport are Avis, Budget, Hertz, and National.

By car

Route 2 (Trans-Canada Highway) is the main highway from Moncton and all points east, including Halifax. The drive from Moncton is 174km (108 miles), or around two hours.

Entering New Brunswick near Edmundston, Route 2 follows the winding Saint John River all the way to Fredericton for 290km (180 miles), which means you should allow at least four hours.

If you're traveling up the Acadian Coast from Moncton, take Route 8 from Miramichi south through the heart of New Brunswick to reach Fredericton in two hours.

Route 7 is the most direct road between Saint John and Fredericton (105km/65 miles), but Route 102 along the Saint John River is a more scenic alternative.

By bus

Acadian (☎ 506-458-6007) buses arrive at 101 Regent St. (at Brunswick Street), the same location as a Discount car rental agency (☎ 506-452-7620) and within walking distance of downtown hotels.

Getting Around Fredericton

Downtown Fredericton lies on the inside of a bend in the Saint John River. King and Queen streets, running parallel to the river, are the main thoroughfares. North Fredericton, on the north side of the river, is mostly residential. It's linked to downtown by the Westmorland St. Bridge. Farther east, the Trail Bridge, starting at the corner of Brunswick Street and University Avenue, is for pedestrians only. Even if you don't need to get to the other side, consider crossing the bridge just for the views that extend back across downtown — you can see the higher buildings rising above the tree-lined riverbank.

Parking

You've gotta love a city that welcomes visitors with free parking. At the visitor center at the corner of Queen and York streets, show proof that you are from out of province — such as a driver's license — and the staff will issue you a two-day parking permit valid at all parking meters and at the lot at the north end of York Street, immediately behind the visitor center.

Catching cabs

Hailing a taxi is easy along Queen and King streets. If you're really stuck, you can always go to the Lord Beaverbrook Hotel and have the front desk attendant call one for you. Among the local companies are **Checker Cabs** (☎ 506-450-8294), **Loyal Taxi** (☎ 506-455-6789), and **Standard Taxi** (☎ 506-450-4444).

Riding transit

Fredericton Transit (☎ 506-460-2200) operates city buses along 12 routes Monday through Saturday 6:30 a.m. to 11 p.m. The fare is C$1.75 per sector (children 6 and under ride free). Exact change is required.

Fredericton

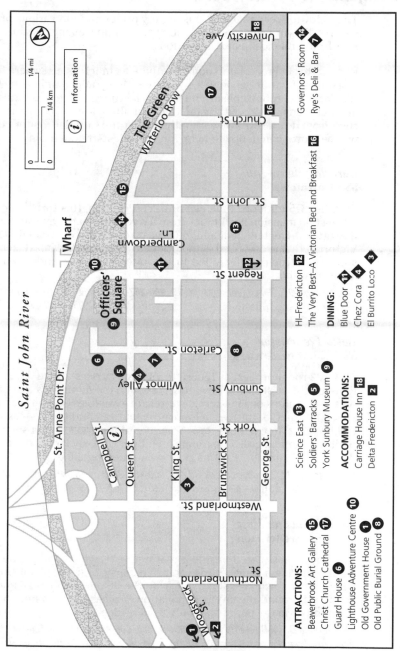

Staying in Fredericton

The following recommendations are my preferences in various price categories. Downtown accommodations are within walking distance of the riverfront and most major attractions.

Room rates in Fredericton don't fluctuate as much as elsewhere in the Maritimes, but offer good value year-round. If you're just looking for a regular motel room, consult the provincial tourism guide, or cruise the arterial roads for posted vacancies (start along Route 105, across the river from downtown). The friendly staff at the City Hall visitor center will be more than happy to help you find a last-minute room.

Carriage House Inn
$$ Downtown

Built in 1875 for a one-time mayor of Fredericton, this three-story Queen Anne-style mansion lies 1 block from a riverfront pathway leading right to downtown. The ten medium-sized guest rooms are decorated in a subtle Victorian theme and filled with antiques. A cooked breakfast, served in a sunny side room, is included in the rates. Children under ten are not allowed at this inn.

See map p. 227. 230 University Ave. ☎ *800-267-6068 or 506-452-9924. Fax: 506-452-2770.* www.carriagehouse-inn.net. *Rack rates: C$95–C$105. AE, MC, V.*

Delta Fredericton
$$–$$$ Downtown

This 222-room property, Fredericton's largest, rises above the Saint John River on the west side of downtown (about a ten-minute walk to City Hall). All the amenities of a full-service hotel are available — room service, high-speed Internet, bathrobes, a lounge/restaurant, and so on — as well as a few bonuses: free parking, indoor and outdoor pools, and a summer-only poolside bar and grill. The rooms aren't particularly large but are smartly designed. Request one with a river view when booking.

See map p. 227. 225 Woodstock Rd. ☎ *800-462-8800 or 506-457-7000. Fax: 506-457-4000.* www.deltahotels.com. *Rack rates: C$159–C$199 double. AE, DC, MC, V.*

Fort Nashwaak Motel
$ North Fredericton

This motel is situated beside a restored fort, where the Nashwaak and Saint John rivers meet. The 54 rooms are fairly large but plainly furnished; what makes this place stand out from the 30-odd other roadside motels scattered around the city is its location, a pleasant 15-minute walk from downtown via the pedestrian-only Trail Bridge.

15 Riverside Dr. (at Route 10). ☎ *800-684-8999 or 506-472-4411. Fax: 506-450-8586.* www.fortnashwaakmotel.com. *Parking: Free. Rack rates: C$75 double. AE, MC, V.*

HI–Fredericton
$ **Downtown**

Nestled on a peaceful tree-lined street six blocks up Regent Street from downtown, this hostel is in a converted residence hall. Thoughtful renovations have created more atmosphere than you may imagine a hostel would offer. All the expected amenities are available, including a communal kitchen, laundry, and Internet access. Beds are available in both dormitories and lots of private rooms (two with en suites), but outside of summer, you can find yourself a private room for the price of a dorm. Check-in is 7 a.m. to noon and 6 to 10 p.m.

See map p. 227. 621 Churchill Row. ☎ *506-450-4417.* www.hihostels.ca. *Parking: Free. Rack rates: C$20–C$25 members of Hostelling International, C$23–C$30 non-members. MC, V.*

On the Pond
$$ **Mactaquac**

Set on a forested waterfront property well beyond city limits, this European-style country lodge is inviting and relaxing rather than luxurious. Stress-reducing facilities include a wide range of spa services and a beautiful library. You can also grab a bike or canoe and pedal or paddle to your heart's content. The eight spacious guest rooms are richly handsome in an old-fashioned way. Breakfast and dinner are served in the dining room. Check the Web site for packages that include meals and activities.

Route 615 (off Route 105, 21km/13 miles west of Fredericton). ☎ *800-984-2555 or 506-363-3420. Fax: 506-363-3479.* www.onthepond.com. *Rack rates: C$155. MC, V.*

Ramada Fredericton
$$ **North Fredericton**

Yes, it's part of a chain, but the Ramada Fredericton offers excellent value. It's also right by the river and adjacent to a par three golf course and a complex of tennis courts. The 116 rooms are set around a tropical atrium that contains a swimming pool, hot tub, and poolside bar. The standard guest rooms face the atrium and have small balconies. They are tastefully decorated and all units have coffeemakers, irons, comfortable couches, and wireless Internet. Executive rooms are larger and overlook the golf course. The on-premise restaurant serves typical hotel fare in Mediterranean-style surroundings.

480 Riverside Dr. (Route 105). ☎ *800-596-4656 or 506-460-5500. Fax: 506-472-0170.* www.ramadafredericton.com. *Rack rates: C$105–C$145 double. AE, DC, MC, V.*

The Very Best — A Victorian Bed and Breakfast
$$ **Downtown**

On a quiet street at the eastern edge of downtown, this elegant 1840 home, run by friendly owners Yolande and Sam Rubenstein, is a wonderful retreat from the surrounding city. Inside, welcoming public areas open onto five guest rooms that mix modern conveniences like air-conditioning and wireless Internet with antiques and historical charm. The sunny rear garden has a heated pool and plenty of space to stretch out and relax. You can have your breakfast in the formal dining room or outdoors under a gazebo.

See map p. 227. 806 George St. (at Church Street). ☎ *506-451-1499. Fax: 506-454-1454.* www.bbcanada.com/2330.html. *Rack rates: C$119–C$129 double. AE, MC, V.*

Dining in Fredericton

You can indulge in a surprising range of cuisine in this outwardly staid city, thanks in part to the population of worldly university students. Outdoor dining is a treat that locals take full advantage of throughout the summer.

Blue Door
$–$$$ **Downtown FUSION**

It's difficult to miss this casual and colorful downtown restaurant — just look for the historic brick building with bright red shutters, distinctive white trim and yes, a blue door. In good weather, enjoy your meal (or just a martini) on the large patio. The energetic owners have brought their West Coast experiences to Fredericton, offering dishes that combine Canadian produce with spices and cooking styles from around the Pacific Rim. You'll be hooked on the flavorful seafood stew, which is full of shrimp, mussels, haddock, and salmon. Other choices are varied: Try the sake-marinated salmon or pork ribs smothered in house-made barbecue sauce. Non-meat-eaters (as well as meat-eaters) will love the pad Thai, a filling noodle dish.

See map p. 227. 100 Regent St. ☎ *506-455-2583. Reservations recommended for dinner. Main courses: C$15–C$26. AE, MC, V. Open: Mon–Sat 11:30 a.m.–10 p.m., Sun 4–10 p.m.*

Chez Cora
$–$$ **Downtown BREAKFAST**

The story sounds good — a Quebec woman makes good with a local cafe that serves up healthy breakfasts in a cheery environment, and then franchises the concept across eastern Canada. In reality, you get a Denny's-style breakfast with a couple of slices of fruit on the side. Your best bet is the crepes, which range from an adventurous spinach/cheddar combo to a sweet and creamy Strawberry Satisfaction. This place stands out because of its bright color scheme, fun-loving furnishings (lots of stuffed chickens), and walls graffitied with the names of dishes. Kids will love the fun atmosphere, and parents will fall for the reasonable prices. Breakfast is served all day; lunch is from 11 a.m. until the mid-afternoon closing.

See map p. 227. 476 Queen St. ☎ *506-472-2672. Reservations not taken. Main courses: C$7.50–C$13. AE, MC, V. Open: Mon–Sat 6 a.m.–3 p.m., Sun 7 a.m.–3 p.m.*

El Burrito Loco
$-$$ Downtown   MEXICAN

Locals are drawn in droves to this smallish restaurant for one reason: the authentic Mexican cooking of owner Carlos Perez Huerta. Everything from the guacamole to the taco shells is created in-house. In warmer weather, you'll need to reserve ahead to snag a table on the patio. Occasional live entertainment creates a fun vibe.

See map p. 227. 304 King St. ☎ 506-459-5626. Reservations recommended. Main courses: C$9.50–C$20. AE, MC, V. Open: Daily 9:30 a.m.–10:30 p.m.

Governors' Room
$$$-$$$$ Downtown   CONTINENTAL

The intimate setting and consistently high quality of food make the Governor's Room popular with locals celebrating a special occasion and business travelers dining on expense accounts (it's ensconced in a bustling business hotel). The kitchen concentrates on classic European cooking. For starters, try shrimp bisque topped with brandied croutons. Then move on to grilled venison topped with black currant and port sauce, or roasted rack of lamb brushed with Dijon mayonnaise. End the meal with a rum-based, nut-topped ice cream Bananas Foster.

Also in the hotel is the informal **Terrace Room,** with a wide-ranging hotel menu and a large deck overlooking the river, and the **Maverick Room,** an upscale steak and seafood restaurant.

See map p. 227. Crowne Plaza Fredericton, 659 Queen St. ☎ 506-455-3371. Reservations essential. Main courses: C$18–C$38. AE, DC, MC, V. Open: Daily 6–9:30 p.m.

Rye's Deli & Bar
$-$$ Downtown   DELI/PUB FARE

The combination of healthy deli food and traditional pub fare may seem a little strange, but Rye's does it well. The interior is publike, but if the weather is warm, you'll want to be on the street-front trellised patio. The specialty is smoked meat on rye or in a wrap (all under C$12), a perfect lunchtime meal, although the portions are huge and can pass for dinner. Other notable offerings include Cajun-spiced chicken nachos and a tangy Thai chicken and bacon burger. The most popular breakfast dish — with good reason, as I found out after dining here — is huevos rancheros.

See map p. 227. 73 Carleton St. ☎ 506-472-7937. Reservations not necessary. Main courses: C$8–C$17. AE, MC, V. Open: Mon–Fri 8 a.m.–11 p.m., Sat from 9 a.m., Sun from 10 a.m.

Exploring Fredericton

Queen Street, 1 block from and running parallel to the Saint John River, is lined with historic sights and attractions. Most major sights are within walking distance of the City Hall at 397 Queen St., which houses the **Visitor Information Centre** (☎ 506-460-2129), open April through October daily 8:15 a.m. to 4:30 p.m. (July and Aug 8 a.m.–8 p.m.).

Historic Garrison District

Due to its status as the capital of New Brunswick and to the proximity of the United States border, Fredericton was the headquarters to a large contingent of British military personnel. After Confederation in 1867, the military moved on, but much of the character remains within the walls of the old military compound, now protected as the Historic Garrison District National Historic Site, located right downtown. Inside the precinct's wrought-iron fence are a number of historic buildings. In addition to the two attractions discussed later, one room in the imposing Soldiers' Barracks is open to the public (July and Aug daily 10 a.m.–7 p.m.). The cellars of this same building provide a summer home for local artists selling their wares.

A troupe of costumed performers lead free, one-hour theatrical walking tours of the historic precinct in July and August. The meeting place and time is City Hall, 397 Queen St., daily at 10 a.m., 2:30 p.m., and 5 p.m. Call ☎ **506-460-2129** for details.

Guard House
Downtown

The interior of this solid stone building looks much as it did when occupied by garrison guards in the mid-1800s, complete with muskets at the ready and uniforms hanging along one wall. The adjacent windowless cellblock is also open for inspection. Try to time your visit with the outdoor musical presentations, which take place on the veranda through summer on Wednesdays at 12:30 p.m.

In July and August, daily at 11:15 a.m., children have the opportunity to dress up as a soldier, parade through the grounds, and, of course, have their picture taken out front of the Guard House. The cost is C$8 per child.

See map p. 227. Carleton St. ☎ 506-460-2129. Admission: Free. Open: July–Aug daily 10 a.m.–6 p.m.

York Sunbury Museum
Downtown

Finding a home in the Officer' Quarters, this old-fashioned museum spills from the room with an eclectic display of memorabilia. Much of the space is devoted to telling the story of the Mi'Kmaq and the early European settlers, but expect a couple of surprises, including a stuffed 17-kilogram (37-pound) frog.

See map p. 227. 571 Queen St. ☎ 506-455-6041. Admission: C$3 adults, C$1 children. Open: Mon–Sat 10 a.m.–5 p.m., Sun noon to 5 p.m.

Other Fredericton sights

Beaverbrook Art Gallery
Downtown

A gift to the city from the late press baron Lord Beaverbrook, this is one of Canada's premier art galleries. The building's rather dour exterior belies the treasures inside, most notably Salvador Dalí's *Santiago el Grande*. The gallery is also home to an impressive collection of works by other European masters — J. M. W. Turner, John Constable, and Augustus John, as well as works of Canada's best-known artists from all eras, including Emily Carr.

Kids are encouraged to try their hand at painting and drawing in a special summer program operated by the gallery. Children aged 5 to 8 are invited to the 10 a.m. session, while those aged 9 to 12 attend the 2 p.m. sitting. Classes last around two hours and cost C$15 per child.

See map p. 227. 703 Queen St. ☎ *506-458-2028.* www.beaverbrookartgallery. org. *Admission: C$8 adults, C$6 seniors, C$3 children. Open: June–Sept daily 9 a.m.–5:30 p.m.; Oct–May Tues–Sat 9 a.m.–5:30 p.m., Sun noon to 5:30 p.m.*

Christ Church Cathedral
Downtown

For over 150 years, the single spire of this compact Gothic Revival church has dominated the Fredericton skyline. Rising regally from the surrounding residences and the tree-lined riverbank, the building was modeled on the 1340 St. Mary's Church in the village of Snettisham, Norfolk.

The most beautiful of many stained-glass windows is on the east side and is best viewed from the nave. From this central location, the morning sun illuminates a seven-paneled scene depicting Christ on the cross, flanked by three apostles on either side. Facing the nave from the northern transept is a massive organ comprising 1,500 pipes.

See map p. 227. 168 Brunswick St. ☎ *506-450-8500.* www.christchurch cathedral.com. *Church tours (free) are offered mid-June through Aug Mon–Fri 9 a.m.–6 p.m. July–Aug chamber music recitals are held every Fri 12:10–12:50 p.m.*

Old Government House
Downtown

An impressive stone structure set on the banks of the Saint John River, this mansion was built in 1826 as the official residence of the governor, and served as such until 1892. In the ensuing years, it housed a school for the deaf, functioned as a hospital, and was the headquarters of the RCMP in New Brunswick. In the late 1990s, a massive overhaul of the grand old building saw it return to its original use as the home of the lieutenant governor, the representative of the Queen Elizabeth II in New Brunswick. Great care was taken in the restoration work to properly replicate the original

234 Part IV: New Brunswick

look, right down to the carpet and draperies. The governor's living quarters are on the top floor, away from the eyes of the public, but the rest of the building is open for tours throughout the year. Rooms restored to their former look include the library, formal dining room, and drawing room. *See map p. 227. 51 Woodstock Rd. ☎ 506-453-2505. Admission: Free. Open: Mid-June to mid-Sept daily 10 a.m.–5 p.m., mid-Sept to mid-June Mon–Fri 10 a.m.–4 p.m.*

Science East
Downtown

Set in a stone jail that dates to 1840 and was used as a prison until 1996, this fun attraction will keep enquiring minds occupied for at least a few hours. Everywhere you turn are interesting displays and interactive activities — an oversize kaleidoscope, an insectarium, and the chance to create a mini-tornado are the more popular ones. Outdoor amusements center on a large playground. The building's former life has been preserved in the grim dungeon, where displays describe the most notorious inmates and tell the story of the last hanging. *See map p. 227. 668 Brunswick St. ☎ 506-457-2340.* www.scienceeast.nb.ca. *Admission: C$6 adults, C$5 seniors, C$3 children. Open: July–Aug Mon–Sat 10 a.m.–5 p.m., Sun 1–5 p.m.; Sept–June Mon–Sat noon to 5 p.m.*

Other cool things to see and do in Fredericton

Fredericton has a well-marked trail system, good for walking or biking. The downtown section extends east from the front of the Fredericton Sheraton to the Princess Margaret Bridge. Along the way is the Trail Bridge, originally built for trains but which now provides a pleasant link to North Fredericton for cyclists and pedestrians.

You can also take a break from sightseeing to:

- ✔ **Climb a lighthouse.** The nationalistic red-and-white **Lighthouse Adventure Centre,** at the foot of Regent Street (☎ 506-460-2939), was built as a tourist attraction. To climb to the top costs C$2 adults, C$1.50 seniors and children. At street level is a booking desk for attractions throughout the region. You can also rent bikes and canoes here. It's open July and August daily 10 a.m. to 9 p.m., September daily noon to 7 p.m.

- ✔ **Take a river cruise.** The *Carleton II* takes up to 100 passengers on one-hour cruises along the downtown shoreline. The cost is a very reasonable C$10 adults, C$5 children. The departure point is Regent Street Wharf, behind the Lighthouse Adventure Centre (☎ 506-454-2628). Tours run June through August, up to five times daily.

- ✔ **Explore an urban forest.** At 175-hectare (430-acre) **Odell Park,** ducks frolic on a small pond, trails lead through various forest environments, and large grassy areas are perfect for stretching out and doing absolutely nothing. In the southern section (access from Waggoner's Road) is an arboretum containing all of New Brunswick's native tree species.

✔ **Wander among headstones.** Walk up Carleton Street to Brunswick Street to reach the **Old Public Burial Ground,** the final resting place of the city's earliest residents.

✔ **Head back to school.** Founded in 1785, the **University of New Brunswick,** Bailey Drive (☎ 506-453-4666), is North America's oldest public university. Feel free to walk the grounds.

✔ **Go golfing.** Picturesque **Kingswood Park Golf Course,** south of downtown along Hanwell Road (☎ 800-423-5969 or 506-443-3333), stretches over 7,000 yards from the back markers. Big bunkers, rolling fairways, and a 10m (33-foot) waterfall on the signature 14th hole define the layout. Greens fees are C$65.

Shopping

You may be surprised at the diversity of shops in the downtown area, especially along the lower end of York Street, where an old-fashioned drug store, trendy import stores, and secondhand clothing shops sit side by side.

Fredericton has mall shopping along Prospect Street, including the **Fredericton Mall,** at 1150 Prospect St. (☎ 506-458-9226).

Antiques

Old Tyme Collectibles, 40 Main St. (☎ 506-451-9218), is the largest of Fredericton's antiques shops. Across the road is **This Old Thing Antiques,** at 173 King St. (☎ 506-454-4317). Both have solid collections of Maritimes furniture and knickknacks from the late 1800s and early 1900s.

Arts and crafts

The centrally located **Gallery Connexion,** at 453 Queen St. (☎ 506-454-1433) is an artist-operated, not-for-profit outlet where artists work *in situ.* Open Tuesday through Friday only. Also within the Garrison Historic District is **River Valley Fine Crafts,** a string of vendors with summer-only outlets on the lower level of the Soldier's Barracks (☎ 506-460-2837). Look for handmade soaps and candles, jewelry, knitted clothing, and more. **Aitkens Pewter** has a more traditional setting, at 408 Queen St. (☎ 506-453-9474), along with free tours of their workshop. The **New Brunswick Crafts Council** displays an eclectic range of its members' work at a gallery within the **Charlotte Street Arts Centre,** at 732 Charlotte St. (☎ 506-450-8989).

Gallery 78, at 796 Queen St. (☎ 506-450-8989), housed in a converted century-old residence just a few blocks east of the main downtown core, is worth visiting to view the building itself. But the art is worth a peek, too — the gallery sells mostly contemporary Canadian work at prices that aren't as high as you may expect.

Books

Westminster Books, 445 King St. (☎ **800-561-7323** or 506-454-1442) is Fredericton's premier independent bookstore. You can pick up everything from the latest bestsellers to local fiction, along with maps and specialty guidebooks. For secondhand and rare books, browse the floor-to-ceiling shelves at **Owl's Nest Bookstore,** at 390 Queen St. (☎ **506-458-5509**).

Market

The **W.W. Boyce Farmers' Market,** 665 George St. at Regent Street (☎ **506-451-1815**), is open year-round, Saturday 6 a.m. to 1 p.m. It attracts hordes of locals who come for fresh produce, meats, and cheeses, as well as local arts and crafts.

Nightlife

Fredericton isn't particularly known for its nightlife, but warm summer nights keep numerous decks and patios busy, while the populations of two universities keep the downtown spots busy the rest of the year.

Pubs and clubs

Most pubs and clubs are within walking distance of each other in the downtown core. Here are a few options:

- ✔ The **Lunar Rogue,** 625 King St. (☎ **506-450-2065**), is an English-style pub with lots of draft beer choices. The patio hops on hot nights.

- ✔ **Rye's Deli & Bar,** 73 Carleton St. (☎ **506-472-7937**), has a small outdoor patio, and books jazz and blues music acts on weekends.

- ✔ **Dolan's Pub,** 349 King St. (☎ **506-454-7474**), has a traditional pub atmosphere and live East Coast music.

- ✔ The **Dip Pool Bar,** set beside an outdoor swimming pool, is located in the Delta Fredericton at 225 Woodstock Rd. (☎ **506-457-7000**), and offers a resort atmosphere.

- ✔ **After Dark Club,** at 87 York St. (☎ **506-457-9805**) is a two-level complex where younger crowds gather to drink (downstairs) and dance (upstairs).

- ✔ **Nicky Zee's,** 375 King St. (☎ **506-455-6408**), is another of the city's hottest nightclubs, but more intimate than After Dark.

The arts

Fredericton Playhouse, at 686 Queen St. (☎ 506-458-8344; www.the playhouse.ca), is the capital's main venue for performing arts and live music. Symphony New Brunswick and Theatre New Brunswick regularly perform here.

Side Trips from Fredericton

The Saint John River flows past Fredericton, draining into the Bay of Fundy at Saint John. If you're traveling between these two cities, the detour to pretty Gagetown is well worthwhile.

Upstream of Fredericton are a string of historic riverside towns, along with Kings Landing Historical Settlement, which re-creates a Loyalist village from 200 years ago.

Gagetown

Historic Gagetown is regarded by many as one of the picturesque villages in all of the Maritimes. Laid out by Loyalists in 1783, the streets lie parallel to Gagetown Creek and are lined with stately trees and carefully restored buildings, some over 200 years old. The surrounding countryside is equally appealing — think apple orchards, grazing cattle, and the wide Saint John River dotted with islands.

To get to Gagetown from Fredericton, follow Route 2 (Trans-Canada Highway) east for 50km (31 miles) and take Exit 330 to the south. Following Route 102 from the capital takes a little longer, but the scenery is more eye-catching.

In the center of the village, **Queens County Museum** is a whitewashed home at 69 Front St. (☎ 506-488-2966) filled with Loyalist antiques. It's open June to mid-September daily 10 a.m. to 5 p.m. Admission is C$2. Gagetown is a fertile ground for shopping. One of my favorite stores is **Jugglers Cove Fine Arts & Crafts,** 32 Tilley Rd. (☎ 506-488-2574), which displays a colorful range of pottery and paintings. **Loomcrafters,** 23 Loomcraft Lane (☎ 506-488-2400), located in a structure dating to 1761 at the east end of Tilley Road, is the place to pick up handmade woven items.

Mactaquac and area

The highlight of the Mactaquac area, west of Fredericton, is King's Landing Historical Settlement, but **Mactaquac Provincial Park** is also worth exploring. Protecting the shoreline of a reservoir formed by the Mactaquac Dam, which spans the Saint John River, activities on offer include canoeing (rentals available), golfing (greens fees C$48; ☎ 506-363-4926), and hiking. To get to the park, cross the Saint John River via

Kissing bridges

If your travels include driving around New Brunswick, you'll no doubt notice that an abundance of covered wooden bridges dot the province. Now a symbol of New Brunswick, the enclosures, affectionately referred to as "kissing bridges," were originally created to protect the wood from weathering by sun and rain — not to provide an opportunity for a romantic rendezvous. It was estimated that uncovered bridges lasted around ten years, while those that were covered would last many times longer. The fact that 66 covered bridges remain is a testament to their durability.

Some of the easiest bridges to find are along the upper Saint John River Valley. Heading north from Kings Landing, the **Nackawic Siding Covered Bridge** straddles Route 585 west of Millville, while in Benton, west of Meductic, the **Benton Village Covered Bridge** is in a particularly scenic locale.

Farther north, the **Hartland Covered Bridge,** in the town of Hartland, stretches for 390m (1,280 feet) across the Saint John River, making it the world's longest covered bridge. The visitor center on the east side of the bridge has displays telling the story of this and other bridges in the province.

Fredericton's Westmorland St. Bridge and follow Route 105 west for 24km (15 miles). Park gates open daily at 8 a.m. and entry costs C\$7 per vehicle per day.

From the park, retrace your path and drive south across the Mactaquac Dam to reach Route 2.

Kings Landing Historical Settlement
King's Landing

Fleeing the American Revolution in 1783, around 15,000 people loyal to Britain headed north to New Brunswick. They established settlements throughout the region, including Saint-Anne, on the site of present-day Fredericton. King's Landing is a re-creation of one of these villages, historically accurate down to the last detail and fun for the whole family. Over 100 costumed staff "live" here, transporting visitors along dirt roads in horse-drawn carts, tending to crops, picking apples in the orchard, crafting horseshoes in the blacksmith shop, and cooking simple meals for visitors in the King's Head Inn. Children will love the outdoor theater program, while all ages will enjoy the ice-cream shop.

20 King's Landing Rd., King's Landing (Exit 253 from Route 2). ☎ *506-363-4999.* www . kingslanding.nb.ca. *Admission C\$15 adults, C\$13 seniors, C\$10 children. Open: June to mid-Oct daily 10 a.m.–5 p.m.*

Fast Facts: Fredericton

ATMs
Look for ATMs at all downtown banks. Try **CIBC**, at 448 Queen St., and **Bank of Montreal**, at 505 King St.

Emergencies
Dial ☎ **911** for all emergencies.

Hospital
Dr. Everett Chalmers Hospital is at 700 Priestman St. (☎ **506-452-5400**).

Information
Contact **Fredericton Tourism** at ☎ **888-888-4768** or 506-460-2041; www.tourism fredericton.ca. The main visitor center is in **City Hall**, at 397 Queen St. It's open mid-May to mid-October daily 8 a.m. to 5 p.m., extended hours July and August until 8 p.m.

Internet Access
Fredericton Public Library, at 12 Carleton St. (☎ **506-460-2800**), has free Internet access on a first-come, first-served basis.

Police
Dial ☎ **911** in an emergency. For non-emergencies, dial ☎ **506-452-3400**.

Post Office
The main downtown post office is at 570 Queen St.

Restrooms
Militia Arms Store, Historic Garrison District, Carleton Street.

Taxis
Call **Checker Cab** (☎ **506-450-8294**), **Loyal Taxi** (☎ **506-455-6789**), or **Standard Taxi** (☎ **506-450-4444**).

Transit Info
The information line for **Fredericton Transit** is ☎ **506-460-2200**.

Weather
Click through the links at the Environment Canada Web site (www.weatheroffice. gc.ca) for local forecasts, or call ☎ **506-446-6244** for a recorded message.

Part V
Prince Edward Island

The 5th Wave   By Rich Tennant

"THAT'S NOT WHAT I MEANT!"

In this part . . .

Potatoes, lobsters, and an orphan girl named Anne are the best-known exports from Prince Edward Island, a serene oasis unlike anywhere else in Canada. Usually referred to simply as "PEI," it may be the country's smallest province, but for many visitors it's the most memorable. Beyond the historic capital of Charlottetown, a patchwork of fields extends in all directions, ringed by red cliffs that descend to often calm ocean waters. Dotted throughout this landscape are painted farmhouses, quaint towns, and fishing villages. The Island became more accessible in 1997 with the completion of the Confederation Bridge that links it to the mainland, yet the atmosphere on the Island remains mellow. The summer visiting season attracts visitors from around the world to Cavendish, the setting for *Anne of Green Gables,* while vacationing families from throughout the Maritimes are drawn to surrounding beaches.

Chapter 18

Charlottetown

∙∙

In This Chapter

▶ Making your way to Charlottetown
▶ Getting to know the city
▶ Learning about the top places to stay and eat
▶ Checking out the prime attractions and activities

∙∙

*W*ith a population of 33,000, Charlottetown is Canada's smallest provincial capital and like no other city in the country. A distinct lack of pretense and an unhurried feel make it decidedly un-capital–like, while its tree-lined downtown streets and incredibly rich history only add to the charm.

In summer, downtown Charlottetown bustles with activity. Its central location makes it a natural draw for visitors and its well-priced lodgings and cultural events make the city a perfect base for day trips to other island destinations (Cavendish, for example, less than an hour's drive away).

Getting There

Sitting in the central portion of Queens County, Charlottetown is at the hub of a varied road system that includes everything from the major thoroughfares to narrow back roads. The most important of these roads is the Trans-Canada Highway, which links Charlottetown to the mainland by bridge and ferry.

By plane

Air Canada has direct flights to Charlottetown from Halifax, Montreal, and Toronto. **WestJet** flies in from Toronto and **Northwest** connects Charlottetown to Detroit through summer only. **Charlottetown Airport** (www.flypei.com) is 8km (5 miles) north of downtown. A Passenger Facility Fee of C$15 is incorporated into the fare for departing flights. Charlottetown has no airport shuttle service, but a row of taxis waits out front of the arrivals terminal, charging C$11 per person plus C$3 for every extra person for the ride downtown.

Confederation Bridge

Completed in 1997, the Confederation Bridge links Prince Edward Island to the rest of Canada. It's the world's longest single-span bridge — 13km (8 miles) from Cape Jourimain, New Brunswick, to Borden-Carleton, just an hour west of Charlottetown in PEI. Built at a cost of almost C$1 billion, it comprises 44 spans, each as long as a city block, and extends up to 20m (66 feet) above Northumberland Strait.

Driving to the Island is free. The toll (C$41 for all two-axle vehicles) is only collected on the return journey.

Avis, Budget, Hertz, and **National** car rental companies have airport desks and vehicles are parked within easy walking distance of the arrivals area. The number of vehicles is limited, so make reservations as far in advance as possible. For information on contacting major car rental companies, see the Appendix.

By car

The **Trans-Canada Highway** (Highway 1) crosses to Prince Edward Island via the Confederation Bridge, 60km (37 miles) from the capital. If you cross to the Island via the ferry, it's a similar distance from the dock to downtown.

By bus

Acadian (☎ **800-567-5151** or 902-628-6432; www.acadianbus.com) has service three times daily between Moncton and Charlottetown, with connections in Moncton from throughout the Maritimes. The Charlottetown bus depot is at 156 Belvedere Ave. **PEI Express Shuttle** (☎ **877-877-1771** or 902-462-8177; www.peishuttle.com) offers van service between Halifax and Charlottetown for adult C$55, senior C$50, child C$45 each way. The trip takes five hours, with pickup and drop-offs made at major hotels in Halifax.

Getting Around Charlottetown

The downtown core of Charlottetown is very compact. Almost all the accommodations recommended here are within walking distance of the best restaurants. Scattered throughout are the main city attractions, including the very central **Province House,** with other buildings of historical interest, the best shops, and the harbor all within 6 blocks.

Downtown streets are laid out in a grid pattern. Those running northwest to southeast end at Water Street, which runs along the harborfront. At its north end, Water Street merges with the eastbound Trans-Canada

Prince Edward Island

Charlottetown

River

Riverside Dr.

Mt. Edward Rd.

St. Peter's Rd.

Esher St.

Allen St.

Lapthorne Ave.

Longworth Ave.

St. Edward St.

Orlebar St.

Cumberland St.

Pond St.

Walthen Dr.

Upper Prince St.

Weymouth St.

Grafton St.

Summer St.

Euston St.

Hillsborough St.

Queen St.

University Ave.

Prince St.

Richmond St.

Hillsborough

Spring Park Rd.

Bayfield St.

Fitzroy St.

Kent St.

Church St.

Peake's Wharf

Queen St.

Great George St.

Sydney St.

Dorchester St.

King St.

Water St.

Greenfield Ave.

North River Rd.

Rochford Sq.

Euston St.

Pownal St.

Pond Rd.

Grafton St.

Rochford St.

West St.

Information

0   1/4 mi
0   1/4 km

York Ln.

Brighton Rd.

Park Driveway

Old Battery Point

Park Roadway

Duchess Point

Charlottetown Harbour

ATTRACTIONS:
Beaconsfield Historic House **4**
Confederation Centre **10** of the Arts
Founders' Hall **22**
Government House **5**
Victoria Park **6**
Province House **11**
St. Dunstan's Basilica **16**

ACCOMMODATIONS:
Aloha Tourist Home **21**
Charlotte's Rose Inn **7**
Dundee Arms **2**
Inn on the Harbour **8**

Inns on Great George **17**
Rodd Charlottetown **3**
Shipwright Inn **1**

DINING:
Café Diem **12**
Claddagh Oyster House **15**
Fishbones **13**
Flex Mussels **19**
Lucy Maud Dining Room **9**
Mavor's **10**
Meeko's Mediterranean Cafe **14**
Merchantman Pub **18**
Peake's Quay **20**
Water Prince Corner Shop **23**

Highway. University Avenue is the major northbound artery. North of the university, you can take Malpeque Road to Route 2 toward Cavendish and the North Shore, or head west along the Trans-Canada Highway to the Confederation Bridge.

Parking

Public parking is spread along Water Street. Parking meters and pay lots cost C50¢ per hour on weekdays. Look for free street parking on the outskirts of downtown (try northeast of Prince Street). Parking is free everywhere on weekends.

The best place to park and start your exploration of the city is the main information center along Water Street at Hillsborough Street. Don't forget to pick up a voucher for one hour's free parking in the adjacent lot at the information center.

Transit and tours

Charlottetown Transit (☎ **902-566-9962**) serves mostly residential areas along seven routes Monday through Saturday. The fare is C$2 per sector.

Jump aboard the red double-decker bus operated by **Abegweit Sightseeing Tours** (☎ **902-894-9966**) to see all the downtown highlights as well as outlying attractions, such as the lieutenant governor's mansion, the University of Prince Edward Island campus, and Victoria Park. The tour takes one hour and is bargain-priced at C$10 for adults and just C$1 for children. The bus departs June through mid-September up to six times daily, with pickup points in front of the Rodd Charlottetown and the Queen Street side of the Confederation Centre of the Arts.

Staying in Charlottetown

Accommodations in Charlottetown are generally well priced and fall within one of two categories: hotels or historic inns. Don't associate the city's lower rates with a lack of services or charm — you get excellent value for your money in Charlottetown, especially during non-summer months.

Because the city is compact, you can plan on walking to all the top attractions and restaurants from your room.

Aloha Tourist Home
$ Downtown

A centrally located home has been converted into accommodations for travelers on a budget. The house has a shared bathroom, lounge with cable TV, and fully equipped kitchen. Local calls are free. The three guest rooms are brightened by a coat of colorful paint and all are clean and well-maintained. The property is open year-round, with discounts outside the summer months.

See map p. 246. 234 Sydney St. ☎ *902-892-9944.* www.alohaamigo.com. *Rack rates: C$56 double.*

Charlotte's Rose Inn
$$–$$$ **Downtown**

This cozy 1884 Victorian residence is on a quiet, tree-lined street close to everything. The four guest rooms are decorated with period antiques and lots of frilly fabrics. Each has an en suite bathroom, a TV/DVD combo, original artwork on the walls, and comfortable wingback chairs. The top floor loft apartment has a small kitchen and opens to a private rooftop deck. Downstairs has a parlor stocked with cookies and coffee, and a richly decorated breakfast room. Rates include a full breakfast.

See map p. 246. 11 Grafton St. ☎ *888-237-3699 or 902-892-3699. Fax: 902-894-3699.* www.charlottesrose.ca. *Rack rates: C$145–C$195 double. AE, MC, V.*

Dundee Arms
$$–$$$ **Downtown**

Built in 1906 for a local entrepreneur, this elaborate Queen Anne Revival building has housed an inn since 1972. It has gone through many changes over the years, including the additions of an English-style pub, a dining room, and a wing of motel rooms (known as the Annex). Through it all, the Dundee Arms remains a charming choice for your stay in Charlottetown. Guest rooms in the original building range from cutesy (Anne's Room) to staid (Chandler Suite), but all come packed with niceties, such as bathrobes and Internet access.

See map p. 246. 200 Pownal St. ☎ *877-638-6333 or 902-892-2496. Fax: 902-368-8532.* www.dundeearms.com. *Rack rates: C$155–C$300 double. AE, DC, MC, V.*

Inn on the Harbour
$$–$$$$ **Downtown**

Opposite Founders' Hall and the main information center, this restored heritage home is close to everything. The seven stylish heritage-style rooms have hardwood floors, wireless Internet, and TV/DVD combos, although the more expensive ones come with a fireplace, jetted tub, and water view. A light breakfast is included.

See map p. 246. 3 Hillsborough St. ☎ *877-333-9933 or 902-651-2191. Fax: 902-651-3733.* www.innontheharbourpei.com. *Rack rates: C$99–C$219 double. AE, MC, V.*

Inns on Great George
$$$–$$$$ **Downtown**

Dating to the early 1800s, three adjoining town houses bookended by two hotels and a smattering of surrounding buildings make up this grand lodging complex 1 block from Province House. In its heyday, the Pavilion Hotel at Dorchester Street was the fashionable social center of the city and the accommodations of choice for delegates attending the 1864 Charlottetown Conference. This property now holds the most guest rooms (24) along with the reception area and a sofa lounge — a comfortable gathering spot where a light breakfast is served each morning. The layout and décor of the guest rooms varies greatly, but all are thoroughly modern (en suites, air-conditioning, high-speed Internet access, and so on). For a splurge, consider one of the four Deluxe Stable House rooms, especially Room 222, which features a kitchen, luxurious bathroom, original art, separate bedroom, and lounge area with leather furniture and a fireplace. My favorite rooms can be found in the Wellington Hotel, which combines historical charm with modern styling at a reasonable price. Family Efficiencies, with one to four bedrooms, are set up for families or small groups.

See map p. 246. 58 Great George St. ☎ *800-361-1118 or 902-892-0606. Fax: 902-628-2079.* www.innsongreatgeorge.com. *Rack rates: C$199–C$384 double. AE, DC, MC, V.*

Rodd Charlottetown
$$ **Downtown**

A distinctive 1931 red-brick building with grand colonnades flanking its entry, this downtown hotel is perfectly located for the tour group crowd. The marble-floored lobby gives way to 115 elegant guest rooms decorated with period reproductions. Amenities include a largish indoor pool, a fitness room, and a sauna. You can take a break from seafood with the finest cuts of beef in Chambers Restaurant, or relax with a cocktail in the adjacent lounge before searching out dinner at one of the many nearby restaurants. Weekend discounts are standard year-round, but the best deals are packages advertised on the Rodd Web site.

See map p. 246. 75 Kent St. ☎ *800-565-7633 or 902-894-7371. Fax: 902-368-2178.* www.rodd-hotels.ca. *Parking: Free. Rack rates: C$145 double. AE, DC, DISC, MC, V.*

 ### Royalty Maples Cottages
$$ **North of Downtown**

On the north side of downtown, close to the airport and perfect for getting an early-morning start to Cavendish, this lodging is about as un-city-like as you'll ever find. It's comprised of a collection of ten neat cottages and six motel rooms set around a sprawling green space — perfect for children.

The cottages come with one or two bedrooms and each has a kitchen and cable TV.

Malpeque Road (north of the Trans-Canada Highway). ☎ *800-381-7829 or 902-368-1030. Fax: 902-566-9242.* www.royaltymaples.com. *Rack rates: Motel rooms C$75 double, cottages C$95–C$105 double. AE, MC, V.*

Shipwright Inn
$$–$$$$ Downtown

The water views that the original owner, a local shipbuilder, enjoyed from this 1860s home are long gone, but the building's solid timber construction — including the original hardwood floors — remains through extensive restoration work. The end result is one of Charlottetown's premier accommodations. Each of the nine guest rooms has its own character and configuration, but what they have in common is a distinct historical charm and a subtle maritime theme. The rooms have amenities you expect in a hotel — TV, air-conditioning, telephone, wireless Internet — as well as many you don't, like goose down duvets and nautical-themed antiques. Even the smallest unit, the Chart Room (which really isn't that small) has a fireplace, a walnut four-poster bed, and, of course, nautical charts on the walls. Breakfast is taken in a communal dining area, although I found myself sneaking back through the day for the complimentary homemade goodies and freshly squeezed lemonade.

See map p. 246. 51 Fitzroy St. ☎ *888-306-9966 or 902-368-1905. Fax: 902-628-1905.* www.shipwrightinn.com. *Rack rates: C$149–C$289 double. MC, V.*

Dining in Charlottetown

Charlottetown's local dining scene is surprisingly vibrant, thanks to a healthy student population and thriving tourism industry.

Café Diem
$ Downtown   CAFE

Of Charlottetown's small selection of cafes, this is the best. You can take advantage of the tree-shaded tables out front or check your e-mail on computer terminals lined along the narrow indoor loft. The blackboard menu is crammed with healthy choices — salads, soups, curries, and more — all under C$10.

See map p. 246. 128 Richmond St. ☎ *902-892-0494. Lunches: C$6–C$10. MC, V. Open: Daily 9 a.m. to midnight.*

Claddagh Oyster House
$$$–$$$$ Downtown   SEAFOOD

Owner Liam Dolan named this restaurant for a fishing village in his Irish homeland, and naturally the menu features mostly seafood with a small selection of other dishes. As the name suggests, oysters are the specialty,

A moolicious treat

Wowie Cowie. Deja Moo. Gooey Mooey. These are three of over 30 flavors you'll be confronted with at **COWS**, an Island institution whose ice cream holds up against the best Ben & Jerry's can offer (I've "researched" both). COWS uses handmade waffle cones and an old-fashioned recipe that calls for the freshest Island cream. Started from a single outlet in Cavendish, the company now has two stores in Charlottetown (one at 150 Queen St. and another at Peake's Wharf), one in Gateway Village (at the north end of Confederation Bridge), another onboard the Caribou–Wood Islands ferry, and others as far away as Park City (Utah).

The ice cream may be traditional, but the associated COWS fashion line is anything but — the distinctive and colorful T-shirts make a wonderful souvenir. Look for them in all COWS stores or purchase online at www.cows.ca.

and the tasting plate of ten for C$17 is a good starter to share. Or dive right into typical mains like sesame-seed-crusted salmon or honey-mustard lamb chops. A contemporary dining room, sharp service, and a delicious dessert selection round out what many consider to be Charlottetown's finest restaurant.

See map p. 246. 131 Sydney St. ☎ *902-892-9661. Main courses: C$16–C$32. AE, MC, V. Open: Mon–Fri 11:30 a.m.–2 p.m., Mon–Sat 5–10 p.m.*

Fishbones
$$–$$$ Downtown   SEAFOOD

This glorified oyster bar is on Victoria Row, a short section of Richmond Street that is designated pedestrian-only throughout the summer months. Choose to dine at tables out on the sidewalk, or inside at regular tables and in very private booths. Malpeque Bay oysters are a natural starter. They sit on a massive bed of ice, accompanied by your choice of sauces for C$2 each. Other sample starters are a rich seafood chowder and steamed mussels broiled in a garlic broth; mains include seafood harvest salad and delicious chicken and lobster casserole. Lunches are mostly under C$15, including tangy lemon-peppered haddock.

See map p. 246. 136 Richmond St. ☎ *902-628-6569. Reservations not necessary. Main courses: C$15–C$23. MC, V. Open: Mon–Sat 11 a.m.–1 a.m., Sun 11 a.m.–11:30 p.m.*

Flex Mussels
$–$$$ Summerside   SEAFOOD

Wow! For those who like mussels, no place in the Maritimes is like this simple cafe, where the island delicacy is steamed to order in 50 different ways. Take your pick from Bombay (ginger, lime, curry, mango, and cream), Maine (baby clams, white wine, cream, and parsley), Wild Turkey (roast corn, green onions, kumquats, and bourbon), and more, many more.

A pound of mussels costs C$10 to C$12, with fries cut from Island potatoes and a freshly baked baguette extra. And if you've always wondered what a growing mussel looks like, check out the Mussel Cam at www.flex mussels.com.

See map p. 246. 2 Lower Water St. ☎ 902-569-0200. Main courses: C$7.50–C$22. Open: Late May to mid-Oct daily noon to 9 p.m.

Lucy Maud Dining Room
$$–$$$ **Downtown   MODERN CANADIAN**

Second-year students at the highly regarded Culinary Institute of Canada prepare lunch and dinner, and then enthusiastically serve it to the public as part of their training at this large restaurant. Dining here is a wonderful opportunity to enjoy fine food at reasonable prices. Snag a window seat to enjoy views that extend over Charlottetown Harbour. The menu changes each semester and is based on seasonal specialties, such as Cornish game hen in the fall. Seafood chowder is a thankful staple. End your meal with one of the extravagant desserts.

See map p. 246. 4 Sydney St. ☎ 902-894-6868. Reservations recommended. Main courses: C$16–C$28. AE, MC, V. Open: Tues–Fri 11:30 a.m.–1:30 p.m., Tues–Sat 6–8 p.m.

Mavor's
$$ **Downtown   CONTEMPORARY**

The bland-looking Confederation Centre of the Arts is hiding a surprise. Mavor's is an ultra-slick bistro where the lunchtime fare includes sweet-potato fries served with sides of sour cream and chipotle dip (a personal favorite), salmon burger topped with mango tartar sauce, and smoked salmon linguine. Dinner mains include grilled arctic char, a northern delicacy not found in many Island restaurants. This listing gives you the kitchen hours, but you can order Starbucks coffee daily 8 a.m. to 8 p.m., complete with the fancy names and wireless Internet.

See map p. 246. 145 Richmond St. ☎ 902-628-6107. Main courses: C$16–C$24. AE, MC, V. Open: Daily 11 a.m.–2 p.m. and 5–9 p.m.

Meeko's Mediterranean Cafe
$–$$ **Downtown   GREEK**

Meeko's has the best Greek food on Prince Edward Island, served in a nationalistic blue-and-white room with murals on the walls and mellow Greek music in the background. You can take a break from seafood by choosing a tzatziki-and-mousakka combo, which sets you back just C$20. The same menu is offered all day, with well-priced salad and sandwich choices at lunchtime.

See map p. 246. 146 Richmond St. ☎ 902-892-9800. Main courses: C$10–C$21. MC, V. Open: Daily 11 a.m.–10 p.m.

Merchantman Pub
$$ **Downtown** **PUB FARE**

In an 1850s building across from Confederation Landing Park, the Merchantman is a typical British-style pub — think dim lighting, exposed beams, and red-brick walls — with an ambitious selection of food that goes well beyond the traditional bangers and mash. You can order all sorts of fresh seafood, chicken, and steaks, some prepared with Cajun or Asian influences. While researching this edition I ordered pan-fried haddock smothered in zucchini relish followed by bourbon chocolate pecan pie, a delicious combination that came to around C$20.

See map p. 246. 23 Queen St. (at Water Street). ☎ *902-892-9150. Main courses: C$12–C$27. AE, MC, V. Open: Mon–Sat 11:30 a.m.–11:30 p.m.*

Peake's Quay
$–$$ **Downtown** **PUB FARE/SEAFOOD**

Peake's Quay offers a wonderful waterfront location and well-priced food, though the service is not exactly stellar. This restaurant-cum-bar takes full advantage of its upstairs location with garage-style doors opening to a 200-seat deck overlooking the marina. While waiting for their meals, many diners gravitate to the Marine Touch Tank, where you can get up close and personal with local sealife. The menu mixes regular pub food with Maritimes staples like seafood chowder served in a bread bowl, lobster rolls, and a boiled lobster that comes with all the usual trimmings. Desserts are all around C$6, or head to the COWS ice-cream shop directly below for a scoop to go.

See map p. 246. 1 Great George St. (at Water Street). ☎ *902-368-1330. Main courses: C$9–C$18. AE, DC, DISC, MC, V. Open: Daily 11 a.m.–10 p.m.*

Water Prince Corner Shop
$–$$$ **Downtown** **SEAFOOD**

Disguised as a little shop at the corner of Water and Prince streets, this local favorite dishes up the freshest seafood at very reasonable prices. While not particularly creative, the menu covers all the familiar choices, including boiled lobster dinners (different sizes for different appetites), Malpeque oysters, steamed mussels, and seafood chowder. The patio is a popular spot on warm evenings, but this friendly restaurant draws a crowd throughout its limited season.

See map p. 246. 141 Water St. ☎ *902-368-3212. Main courses: C$12–C$26. MC, V. Open: May–Oct daily 9:30 a.m.–8 p.m.*

Exploring Charlottetown

As the provincial capital, Charlottetown has a number of major attractions. Most notable among them are Founders' Hall and Province House, both of particular interest to Canadians. One thing that everyone must do in Charlottetown is stroll through the narrow streets between Province House and the waterfront, where the mix of residential and commercial architecture has remained unchanged for over a century.

Beaconsfield Historic House
Downtown

Built in 1877 for local shipbuilder James Peake Jr., this gracious home is one of the finest pre-1900 residences on the Island. From the street, the sharp yellow exterior and gingerbread trim catches your eye. Inside are an impressive 25 rooms and eight fireplaces. The first two of three floors are furnished, while a narrow stairway leads to the belvedere, a turret with water views. Special events include musical performances and a weekday children's program in the adjacent carriage house. The on-site bookstore has a solid collection of Island literature.

See map p. 246. 2 Kent St. (at West Street). ☎ *902-368-6603. Admission: C$4.25 adults. Open: July–Aug daily 10 a.m.–5 p.m.*

Confederation Centre of the Arts
Downtown

This large, boxy structure in the heart of downtown is at odds with surrounding historic buildings, but once inside, you'll find many redeeming features, including the largest art gallery east of Montreal. The Confederation Centre Art Gallery is highlighted by the luminaries of Canadian art through the last 200 years. Many of the names won't be familiar (even to most Canadians), but Gordon Smith sculptures, paintings by the husband-and-wife team of Christopher and Mary Pratt, and an extensive collection of Robert Harris paintings (his most famous work, the official portrait of the Fathers of Confederation, was destroyed by fire in 1916) are standouts. The center also has three theaters (see "Nightlife" later in this chapter), a large library with the original manuscript for *Anne of Green Gables,* a craft shop, a memorial hall, and a cafe. Through summer, it hosts the Charlottetown Festival, which includes daily lunchtime entertainment at an amphitheater by the main entrance.

See map p. 246. 145 Richmond St. ☎ *902-566-1267.* www.confederation centre.com. *Gallery admission: Donation. Gallery hours: June–Sept daily 9 a.m.– 5 p.m.; Oct–May Wed–Sat 11 a.m.–5 p.m., Sun 1–5 p.m.*

Founders' Hall
Downtown

Using innovative state-of-the-art displays, this attraction transports visitors back in time to the 1864 Charlottetown Conference. It's contained within a historic railway building just steps from where the Fathers of Confederation stepped ashore on the Charlottetown waterfront. You begin your journey by entering the Time Tunnel, stepping back to life in the 1860s. The tunnel opens to the octagonal Hall of the Fathers, which describes the men who met to discuss the formation of the country.

Walk the walk

Joining a walking tour with the **Confederation Players** (☎ 800-955-1864 or 902-368-1864), a group of eager young locals dressed in Confederation-era garb, is a great way to learn a little about Charlottetown while taking advantage of warm summer temperatures. Choose from three tours: a trip back in time along Great George Street; the Settlers Tour, which recounts locals of note; or Ghostly Realm, an evening stroll through cemeteries and back alleys. All depart Founders' Hall in July and August once or twice daily and cost C$10 adults, C$5 children. Historical reenactments on the steps of Province House (July–Aug daily at 2:30 p.m.; free) are part of the same program.

Beyond this exhibit is a string of rooms, each dedicated to a province or territory, linking up in the order they joined the Dominion of Canada. Along the way, televisions, computer terminals, headsets, trivia games, and dynamic audiovisual displays enhance the story. Note that the hours change depending on the time of year, so best to call ahead, especially outside of high season.

See map p. 246. 6 Prince St. ☎ 902-368-1864. www.foundershall.ca. *Admission: C$7 adults, C$6 seniors, C$3.75 children. Open: Mid-May to mid-Oct Mon–Sat 9 a.m.–5 p.m., Sun 9 a.m.–4 p.m.; July–Aug Mon–Sat until 7 p.m.*

Government House and Victoria Park
Downtown

Perched on a slight rise at the edge of downtown, the 1835 Government House is the official residence of the lieutenant governor. The grounds are not open to the public, but the grand mansion is clearly visible through stands of mature white birch.

Beyond Government House, Kent Street passes through Victoria Park, a pleasant green space that ends at the shoreline of Charlottetown Harbour. The best way to enjoy the park is on foot (although you'll be passed by a stream of jogging, skating, and biking locals). Near the entrance to the park, a row of six antique cannons points to the harbor entrance.

See map p. 246. Take Kent Street southwest through downtown.

Province House
Downtown

Still the seat of the provincial legislature, Province House is where the Fathers of Confederation met in 1864 to discuss the formation of the Dominion of Canada. This landmark meeting took place in the second-floor chamber, which has been restored to the way it looked back then, right down to the original furniture, and has an adjacent clerk's office and library. Also on the second floor is the current Legislative Chamber, a smallish room that looks to have changed little in well over a century.

Traditions are well entrenched here — the premier gets a small flag on his desk and the ruling party is always seated on the south side of the room, a throwback to the days before central heating when the afternoon sun warmed only this part of the chamber. You can walk through by yourself, but I highly recommend the guided tour.

See map p. 246. 165 Richmond St. (at St. George Street). ☎ *902-566-7626. Admission: Free. Open: June to early Oct daily 8:30 a.m.–5 p.m., early Oct to May Mon–Fri 8:30 a.m.–5 p.m.*

St. Dunstan's Basilica
Downtown

Distinctive for its twin Gothic spires, St. Dunstan's Basilica is one of Canada's largest churches. The interior is notable for its intricate vaulted ceiling, ornate Italian carvings, and polished marble columns.

See map p. 246. 45 Great George St. ☎ *902-894-3486. Admission: Free. Open: Daily 8 a.m.–5 p.m.*

Other cool things to see and do

When you've had your fill of downtown attractions, and are ready for other diversions or sights lying beyond city limits, here are a few possibilities:

- ✔ **Peake's Wharf Boat Cruises** (☎ 902-566-4458), departs from Peake's Wharf on Water Street June through September. Choose from harbor tours with full commentaries (1, 6:30, and 8 p.m.; C$18) or a seal-watching excursion (2:30 p.m.; C$25).

- ✔ **Charlottetown Farmers Market,** 100 Belvedere Ave. (☎ 902-626-3373), opposite the university. Vendors at this indoor market sell everything from fresh seafood to Island-made crafts. It operates year-round Saturday 9 a.m. to 2 p.m., as well as Wednesday 9 a.m. to 2 p.m. in summer.

- ✔ **Orwell Corner Historic Village,** 30km/19 miles east of Charlottetown (☎ 902-651-8510). Experience life in the 1850s at this restored farming community. The village is open late May through mid-October Monday to Friday 9 a.m. to 5 p.m., plus week-ends in July and August. Admission is C$7.50 adults, C$3 children.

- ✔ **Port-la-Joye–Fort Amherst National Historic Site,** a pleasant 35-minute drive west, and then south, from downtown (☎ 902-566-7626). Not much remains of the island's first European settlement, which was established in 1720, but a visitor center (mid-June through Aug daily 9 a.m.–5 p.m.) at the site tells its story. The surrounding grounds, overlooking the water, are a great place for a picnic.

Shopping

As the hub of Prince Edward Island, Charlottetown shops cater well to the needs of Islanders, with a nod to the tourists down on the waterfront along Water Street. For mall shopping, head north from downtown along University Avenue. Here are some of my favorite shops in Charlottetown (in no particular order):

- ✔ **Anne of Green Gables Chocolates** (102 Queen St.; ☎ 902-368-3131) is the place for sweet tooths to pick up edible souvenirs.

- ✔ **Island Crafts Shop** (156 Richmond St.; ☎ 902-892-5152) is crammed with arts and crafts, including woodwork and weaved items.

- ✔ **Details Past and Present** (166 Richmond St.; ☎ 902-892-2233) displays fine art in the front and an eclectic range of antiques out back.

- ✔ **Pilar Shephard Art Gallery** (82 Great George St.; ☎ 902-892-1953) is another fine-art gallery. It features Island landscapes and Inuit sculptures.

- ✔ **The Bookman** (177 Queen St.; ☎ 902-892-8872) holds an impressive collection of used books, including many related to island history.

- ✔ **Moonsnail Soapworks** (85 Water St.; ☎ 902-892-7627) specializes in handmade soaps and other body treats made with natural ingredients.

- ✔ **PEI Specialty Chip Co.** is based in Marshfield, northeast of Charlottetown (☎ 902-629-1818), but look for their lobster-flavored potato chips at retail outlets throughout the city.

- ✔ **Canada Eh?**, in Founders' Hall (6 Prince St.; ☎ 902-368-1864), is crammed with Canadian souvenirs — maple syrup, smoked salmon, wooden fishermen, Canadian flag kites, and more.

Nightlife

No one can ever describe Charlottetown as a hotbed of after-dark action, but still, something is usually going on somewhere.

The Buzz is a free publication with listings of what's happening throughout Charlottetown. It comes out monthly, or check the online version at www.isn.net/buzzon. The Web site www.walkandseacharlottetown.com lists festivals and events, including all performing arts.

Of course, you can also drop by the Visitor Information Centre in Founders' Hall (☎ 902-368-7795) to find out what's on when you're in town.

Pubs and clubs

Victoria Row, a short section of Richmond Street between Queen and Great George streets, is designated as pedestrian-only through summer. The local restaurants and bars set tables out across the sidewalk and some have live music.

Most pubs open at 11 a.m. and close at midnight through the week, and at 1 a.m. on weekends.

Around the corner from Victoria Row, the **Olde Dublin Pub,** 131 Sydney St. (☎ 902-892-6992) is a lively Celtic-styled bar, with live Maritimes music on weekends and always with pints of Guinness. In the same vicinity, **Gahan House,** 126 Sydney St. (☎ 902-626-2337) is PEI's only brewpub — and it's a good one. Six ales are brewed in-house, including Sydney Street Stout, which gets rave reviews. The food is also a cut above pub grub (the beer-battered haddock and thick-cut chips are delicious). Named for one of the delegates at the Charlottetown Conference, **D'Arcy McGee's** sits in the heart of the city at the corner Prince and Kent streets (☎ 902-894-3627). Inside is a fun and fittingly British atmosphere, with visitors and regulars mixing easily. Overlooking the harbor, **Peake's Quay,** 1 Great George St. at Water Street (☎ 902-368-1330) has a slightly more touristy feel than the other places.

The club scene in Charlottetown is dominated by **Myron's,** at 151 Kent St. (☎ 902-892-4375), a two-story complex that books bands ranging from rock to country Wednesday to Saturday for the downstairs stage. The upstairs crowd is equally diverse, dancing to everything from hip-hop to disco, Thursday through Saturday.

The arts

The **Confederation Centre of the Arts,** at 145 Richmond St. (☎ 800-565-0278 or 902-628-1864; www.confederationcentre.com) hosts the Charlottetown Festival June through September. This theatrical event combines outdoor performances, a children's theater, and two or three musical productions. The star of the show is *Anne of Green Gables — The Musical,* a family-oriented production that brings Lucy Maud Montgomery's most famous character to life. Showtime is Monday to Saturday at 8 p.m. with additional 2 p.m. matinees in July and August on Monday, Wednesday, and Saturday. Expect to pay C$21 to C$64 adults, half price for children.

Harness racing

Harness racing has been a tradition in the capital since 1889, when **Charlottetown Driving Park Entertainment Centre,** 46 Kensington Rd. (☎ 902-892-6823) hosted its first races. Most race-goers attend the facility to gamble, so the operators welcome them with open arms — letting everyone in for free. Races are held on Saturdays May through January as well as Thursdays in summer; race time is 7:30 p.m. (call to confirm the schedule or visit the Web site www.cdpec.ca).

Fast Facts: Charlottetown

ATMs
Look for ATMs at most banks, including the **CIBC** at Queen and Grafton streets. A growing number of grocery stores and gas stations also have ATMs, but beware of additional charges.

Emergencies
Dial ☎ **911** for all emergencies.

Hospital
Queen Elizabeth Hospital is at 60 Riverside Dr. (☎ 902-894-2095).

Pharmacy
Murphy's Pharmacy, at 24 St. Peters Rd. (☎ 902-894-4449), is open Monday to Friday 8 a.m. to 10 p.m., Saturday and Sunday 9 a.m. to 10 p.m.

Information
The **Visitor Information Centre** is in Founders' Hall at 6 Prince St. (☎ 800-955-1864 or 902-368-4444; www.walkandsea charlottetown.com). It's open July and August daily 8 a.m. to 10 p.m.; September to June Monday to Friday 9 a.m. to 4:30 p.m. Call for opening hours outside of high season.

Internet Access
Café Diem, at 128 Richmond St. (☎ 902-892-0494) has public computers with a high-speed Internet connection.

Police
For emergencies, dial ☎ **911;** for general **RCMP** matters call ☎ 902-368-9300.

Post Office
The main post office is at 135 Kent St.

Restrooms
Public restrooms can be found in Founders' Hall on Water Street.

Taxis
Recommended companies include **City Taxi** (☎ 902-892-6567), **Co-op Taxi Line** (☎ 902-628-8200), and **Yellow Cab** (☎ 902-566-6666).

Transit Info
Local bus service is provided by **Charlottetown Transit** (☎ 902-566-9962). See "Getting Around Charlottetown," earlier in this chapter, for details.

Weather
Environment Canada maintains a Web site at www.weatheroffice.gc.ca with links to the forecast in Charlottetown, as well as locations around Prince Edward Island.

Chapter 19

Cavendish

· ·

In This Chapter

▶ Finding your way to Cavendish
▶ Picking the best places to stay and eat
▶ Making the most of "Anne's Land"
▶ Exploring the coast

· ·

C avendish is known worldwide through the writing of Lucy Maud
Montgomery, who used her childhood on the idyllic Island setting
as inspiration for her timeless tale, *Anne of Green Gables*. The setting for
the book was Green Gables, a farmhouse now protected as a National
Historic Site, which, along with other spots related to the author and her
writing, keep fans of Anne occupied for at least a full day.

The tranquility of the "Avonlea" that Montgomery wrote about so
floridly has mostly gone, thanks somewhat ironically to the popularity of
the book. Cavendish's main thoroughfare is lined with theme parks,
accommodations, and other touristy offerings. The only thing stopping
commercial sprawl from spreading to the adjacent coastline is Prince
Edward Island National Park, which protects long stretches of red-sand
beach and provides prime habitat for over 100 species of birds.

Cavendish has served as a summer retreat for decades. You need only to
take a drive through the rolling rural landscape, spend time down on the
beach, or walk the wooded trails to see why families return year after
year. The off season, however, really does mean lights off. November
through April almost everything is closed, including most accommodations and all the attractions and restaurants.

Getting There

Cavendish is 40km (25 miles) northwest of Charlottetown. To get there
from the capital, take Route 15 to Brackley Beach, and then head west
on Route 6; or take Route 2 west to Hunter River, followed by Route 13
north through New Glasgow.

Cavendish and Prince Edward Island National Park

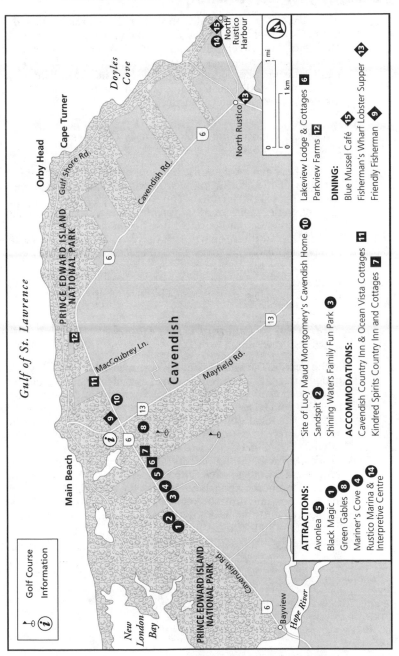

ATTRACTIONS:
Avonlea 5
Black Magic 1
Green Gables 8
Mariner's Cove 4
Rustico Marina & 14
Interpretive Centre

Site of Lucy Maud Montgomery's Cavendish Home 10
Sandspit 2
Shining Waters Family Fun Park 3

ACCOMMODATIONS:
Cavendish Country Inn & Ocean Vista Cottages 11
Kindred Spirits Country Inn and Cottages 7
Lakeview Lodge & Cottages 6
Parkview Farms 12

DINING:
Blue Mussel Café 15
Fisherman's Wharf Lobster Supper 13
Friendly Fisherman 9

Golf Course
Information

Staying in Cavendish

As well as being inundated with visitors from around the world, Cavendish is very popular with vacationing families from throughout the Maritimes. For travel in July and August, reserve your accommodations as far in advance as possible. Discounted rooms and a lack of crowds make June and September a fine time to visit Cavendish; in early September, it's still warm enough to swim in the ocean, yet some rooms are discounted up to 50 percent.

Cavendish Country Inn & Ocean Vista Cottages
$$–$$$ Cavendish

Choose between motel units, bed-and-breakfast rooms, or lovely wooden cottages at this sprawling resort within walking distance of both the national park and Cavendish. The cottages (from C$165) are the best value. Each has a deck with outdoor furniture and a barbecue, while inside, lots of polished wood and comfortable furnishings create an inviting atmosphere. Also on the property is a playground, two outdoor heated pools, and two hot tubs.

See map p. 261. Route 6, 1km (½ mile) east of Route 13, Cavendish. ☎ *800-454-4853 or 902-963-2181. Fax: 902-963-3213.* www.cavendishpei.com. *Rack rates: C$109–C$350 double. AE, MC, V. Open: May to mid-Oct.*

Kindred Spirits Country Inn and Cottages
$$$–$$$$ Cavendish

In the heart of Cavendish, but set well away from the busy main road, this delightful country estate is a world away from the rest of the bustling village. Green Gables Heritage Site is reached along Lover's Lane, a walking trail that remains exactly as described by Montgomery in *Anne of Green Gables*. The local golf course is even closer. Guest rooms in the inn are country cozy and loaded with local antiques. Three price levels are offered: The lower-priced rooms include all the basics, although more expensive rooms add a balcony and a fireplace. Surrounding the inn are 14 upscale cottages, each with kitchen, color TV, and a deck with a barbecue. The most expensive cottages have a king-size bed, air-conditioning, fireplace, and hot tub. Regardless of the type of accommodations they choose, all guests can enjoy the playground area, outdoor heated pool, bike rentals, and wireless Internet.

See map p. 261. Memory Lane, off Route 6, Cavendish. ☎ *800-461-1755 or 902-963-2434. Fax: 902-963-2619.* www.kindredspirits.ca. *Rack rates: Inn rooms C$160–C$265 double, C$210–C$450 cottages. MC, V. Open: Inn mid-May to mid-Oct, cottages year-round.*

Lakeview Lodge & Cottages
$$–$$$$ **Cavendish**

Close to everything, this large property with beautifully manicured grounds features a heated outdoor pool, a barbecue area, a playground, and a variety of room choices. Basic motel rooms cost under C$100. From June to September, the kitchen-equipped duplex cottages, with up to four bedrooms each, offer the best value for larger groups. Free-standing executive cottages, each with a kitchen and private deck, are a step up in quality (and price) while two modern suites in the main lodge are also well priced. In June and September, Lakeview has great off-season specials with rates reduced by up to 50 percent.

See map p. 261. 8715 Cavendish Rd. (Route 6), Cavendish. ☎ *800-565-7550 or 902-963-2436. Fax: 902-963-2493.* www.lakeviewlodge.cc. *Rack rates: C$94–C$365 double. MC, V. Open: Late May to early Oct.*

Parkview Farms
$$$–$$$$ **Cavendish**

Located 2km (1¼ miles) east of Cavendish, Parkview attracts the same vacationing families as the other cottage resorts along this stretch of the coast, but has the added attraction of being a working farm. Guests are invited to tour the property, and can even help out with milking cows if so inclined. Accommodations are in modern two- and three-bedroom cottages, each with a well-equipped kitchen and spacious living area. Take advantage of the barbecues supplied by purchasing fresh seafood at Doiron Fisheries (see the sidebar "Lovin' lobster" later on in this chapter).

See map p. 261. Route 6, Cavendish. ☎ *800-237-9890 or 902-963-2027. Fax: 902-963-2935.* www.parkviewfarms.com. *Rack rates: C$155–C$240 double. MC, V. Open: Late Apr to Oct.*

Dining in Cavendish

The Cavendish dining scene reflects many of the local accommodations — touristy, mostly overpriced, and always busy. Thankfully, a number of alternatives lie in surrounding villages.

Blue Mussel Café
$$–$$$ **North Rustico Harbour   SEAFOOD**

My favorite dining spot on all of Prince Edward Island is the Blue Mussel Café. The cafe is terribly small, but that's a good thing if you manage to get a table. Most of the seating is outside, on an old dock that catches the evening sun and has views extending back down the harbor. You can't go wrong with any of the seafood, like creamy chowder or lobster pâté to

Lovin' lobster

Believe it or not, it wasn't that long ago that the supply of lobster exceeded demand so much that Islanders used it as fertilizer. Things have changed, though; lobster is now promoted as a delicacy across the Maritimes. The trapping season for lobsters is short, but the lobsters are held live in holding tanks so they can be offered fresh year-round.

Lobsters served in restaurants and at lobster suppers usually weigh around one pound, which provides enough of the rich meat for most people. They are generally served whole, challenging diners to extract as much of the meat as they can using fingers, lobster crackers, and skewers. It can be a messy process, so most places — even upscale restaurants — supply a bib.

One of the best things about lobster is that it tastes best simply boiled, which means you can do the cooking yourself (many accommodations provide big pots especially for this purpose). **Doiron Fisheries**, on the dock at North Rustico (☎ 902-963-2442), is the best place around Cavendish to buy lobster. Expect to pay around C$12 per pound, live or precooked. This seafood market is also the place to pick up Malpeque Bay oysters, mussels, clams, and fresh fish. It's open May to early October, daily 8 a.m. to 8 p.m.

start, followed by a full lobster or poached fish, such as haddock or salmon. Best of all, the Blue Mussel must be one of the few seafood restaurants anywhere in the Maritimes without a deep fryer.

See map p. 261. 312 Harbourview Dr., North Rustico Harbour. ☎ *902-963-2152. Main courses: C$13–C$21. Open: Late June to Sept daily 11:30 a.m.–8 p.m.*

Fisherman's Wharf Lobster Supper
$$ **North Rustico**   SEAFOOD

A little more commercialized than the New Glasgow Lobster Suppers (see a bit later in this chapter), the North Rustico version is otherwise very similar. Up to 500 diners can be seated at once in the cavernous restaurant, which is lined on one side by a long buffet of hot and cold appetizers and desserts. Tables feature paper place mats that describe how lobsters are caught and, more importantly, the best way to eat them.

See map p. 261. Route 6, North Rustico. ☎ *877-289-1010 or 902-963-2669. Lobster supper from C$32. AE, MC, V. Open: Mid-May to mid-Oct daily noon to 9 p.m.*

Friendly Fisherman
$$ **Cavendish**   BUFFET

I wanted to include at least one restaurant in the town of Cavendish, so I joined the throngs of families and entered the fray to research the Friendly Fisherman, right at the town's main intersection. (It was friendly enough, but not a fisherman was in sight.) Because this buffet restaurant is perpetually busy, the turnover of food is fast, which keeps the salads fresh and the hot food hot. Seafood is limited to a lasagna and a couple of baked fish dishes, but you have plenty of other choices, including roast beef. Beer and wine are extra, but well priced. Pay for a ticket at the front door and wait your turn for a table. Children pay C$1 for every year of age. Breakfast and lunch are served cafeteria-style.

See map p. 261. 8258 Cavendish Rd. (Route 6), Cavendish. ☎ *866-963-2234 or 902-963-2234. Buffet dinner: C$15. AE, DC, MC, V. Open: Mid-June to mid-Oct daily 8 a.m.– 9 p.m. (buffet served from 4 p.m.)*

New Glasgow Lobster Suppers
$$ **New Glasgow SEAFOOD**

Held in community halls and restaurants throughout the province, lobster suppers are informal, fun, and good value. The one at New Glasgow is the oldest, having been in operation since 1958. Here, up to 500 diners can be seated at once in a two-level riverside building with its own lobster holding pond. Choose the size of lobster you want (1–4 pounds) and enjoy all-you-can-eat chowder, mussels, salad, breads, desserts, and non-alcoholic beverages for a set price. If you want to pass on the lobster as a main, breaded scallops, haddock, and roast beef are offered as alternatives. Children under 12 get their own menu, which includes a lobster supper for C$14, and kids under 3 eat for free. To get to New Glasgow, take Route 13 southeast from Cavendish. The big building is impossible to miss across the river in New Glasgow.

Route 258, New Glasgow. ☎ *902-964-2870. Lobster supper from C$30. AE, MC, V. Open: June to mid-Oct daily 4–8:30 p.m.*

Exploring Cavendish

The sites associated with *Anne of Green Gables* are somewhat overshadowed by amusement parks and tacky tourist traps (although you won't hear any complaints from children). I divide this section up accordingly, with some suggestions for touring beyond Cavendish sandwiched in between.

Anne attractions

Separating fact from fiction is somewhat difficult when it comes to visiting the childhood haunts of Lucy Maud Montgomery. Many of these places ended up in her famous novels and are now shrines visited by fans from around the world.

Anne of Green Gables Museum
Park Corner

Owned and operated by relatives of Montgomery, this museum is housed at Silver Bush, a name given to the home of the Campbell family who

Anne's land

Anne of Green Gables chronicles the life of Anne Shirley, a lovable character created by one of Canada's best-known authors, Lucy Maud Montgomery (1874–1942). Although the enduring tale of the red-haired orphan girl and her life at Avonlea is fictional, it draws on Montgomery's own experiences growing up in her grandparents' Cavendish home and spending her younger days exploring the rural surroundings.

On the Island, the tale has spawned an entire industry. *Anne of Green Gables* has been translated into dozens of languages and has been reprinted over 100 times. The character of Anne has been re-created in a musical and television drama. Half a world away, it's even part of the official curriculum in Japanese schools — and hence Cavendish receives large numbers of Japanese visitors.

If you're an Anne fan, plan your time in Cavendish to coincide with the **L.M. Montgomery Festival** (www.lmmontgomeryfestival.com), held annually on the second weekend of July. Festivities include readings, a coloring competition at the local schoolhouse, and afternoon high tea served outdoors at the site of Montgomery's childhood home.

appear in two of her novels. The residence is decked out in period furnishings and a selection of the author's personal belongings is on display. The parlor, where Montgomery was married in 1911, is now a popular spot for Japanese couples to say their vows. You can relax in the small tearoom, which serves hot drinks and homemade goodies, or enjoy a carriage ride (C$10 per family) along the nearby beach.

Route 20, 24km (15 miles) west of Cavendish in Park Corner. ☎ 902-886-2884. Admission: C$2.50 adults, C$1 children. Open: May–Oct daily 11 a.m.–4 p.m., extended hours July–Aug daily 9 a.m.–5 p.m.

Avonlea
Cavendish

Of the many amusement parks in Cavendish, only Avonlea, which reconstructs Montgomery's version of rural PEI, has any connection to the book *Anne of Green Gables.* The park comprises a general store, a church, farm animals, old-fashioned games, themed rides, and a chocolate factory (which wasn't in the book, but is a popular spot nevertheless). Throughout the day, costumed performers go about their business: milking cows, leading pony rides, giving dance lessons — and did I mention the chocolate factory?

See map p. 261. Route 6, Cavendish. ☎ 902-963-3050. Admission: C$19 adults, C$18 seniors, C$16 children 6–12. Open: June daily 10 a.m.–5 p.m., July–Aug daily 10 a.m.– 6 p.m.

Green Gables
Cavendish

Within easy walking distance of Montgomery's childhood home is Green Gables, which belonged to her grandfather's cousins. Anchoring Lucy Maud Montgomery Cavendish National Historic Site, this green-and-white farmhouse served as the setting for *Anne of Green Gables*. At the main entrance is an interpretive center; inside the picket fence, rooms in the main house have been restored and the barn re-creates early farm life. Two of the most loved connections between the property and the book are Haunted Wood and Balsam Hollow, reached by short trails from the house.

See map p. 261. Route 6 (just west of Route 13). ☎ *902-963-7874. Admission: C$7.15 adults, C$5.90 seniors, C$3.45 children. Open: May–Oct daily 9 a.m.–5 p.m., extended hours July–Aug daily 9 a.m.–6 p.m.*

Lucy Maud Montgomery Birthplace
New London

This unassuming home is where the writer was born in 1874. The interior is decorated in corresponding Victorian style. Among personal effects on display are a replica of Montgomery's wedding dress, as well as scrapbooks she put together as a child.

New London, southwest of Cavendish on Route 6. ☎ *902-886-2099. Admission: C$3 adults, C50¢ children. Open: Mid-May to mid-Oct daily 9 a.m.–5 p.m.*

Site of Lucy Maud Montgomery's Cavendish Home
Cavendish

This is where the writer lived with her grandparents after the premature death of her mother. All that remains of the home are the foundations, but the well-tended gardens and mature groves of apple trees provide a peaceful retreat from the rest of Cavendish. A small museum and bookstore at the site are operated by members of Montgomery's family.

See map p. 261. Route 6 (just east of Route 13). ☎ *902-963-2231. Admission: C$3 adults, C$1 children. Open: Mid-May to mid-Oct daily 9 a.m.–5 p.m., extended hours July–Aug daily 9 a.m.–6 p.m.*

Cool things for kids to do in Cavendish

Amusement park-style attractions open June through September are strung out along Route 6 between Cavendish and Stanley Bridge. They strongly contrast the idyllic Avonlea so loved by Anne fans — but children love them. Here's just a sampling:

- **Sandspit** (☎ 902-963-2626) has old-time fairground rides, including a roller coaster, carousel, and Ferris wheel, as well as bumper boats, a miniature railway, and go-carts.

✔ **Shining Waters Family Fun Park** (☎ 902-963-3939) features rides for younger children and is extremely popular on hotter days for its waterslides.

✔ **Mariner's Cove** (☎ 902-963-2242) is the most challenging of Cavendish's many minigolf courses.

✔ **Black Magic** (☎ 902-963-2889) is minigolf with a twist — indoors and in the dark.

Touring Beyond Cavendish

After you manage to pry the Anne fan in your family away from Cavendish, you'll discover that the surrounding area is well worth exploring. Take a walk from the village to the natural, rugged beauty of Cavendish's coast or drive east along the shoreline to Tracadie Bay and loop back on Route 6 to take in a mix of coastal and rural scenery.

Prince Edward Island National Park

This narrow park protects a sliver of coastline extending from London Bay in the west to Tracadie Bay in the east, as well as a separate chunk of coastline farther east near St. Peters. The park encompasses a varied landscape with wide beaches, attractive red sandstone cliffs, and rolling dunes. It can be accessed from seven different points along Route 6.

Swimming and sunbathing are the big summertime attractions for most visitors. The water is warm enough for swimming in July and August. Trained supervisors watch out for the well-being of those who take to the water at the busiest spots. The best — and busiest — beaches are those near Cavendish.

Gulf Shore Road, which begins as a northern extension of Route 13 through Cavendish, hugs the coastline, passing more park beaches, numerous lookouts (Orby Head is my fave), and a pretty picnic area at Cape Turner.

The section of park east of Rustico Bay is a lot quieter. Here you can enjoy a long beach walk, or take a morning stroll along the marshland behind the dunes in search of local birds, such as piping plovers and northern phalarope. **Brackley Beach,** at the north end of Route 15, has supervised swimming, change rooms, a concession, and an information center.

Rise early to experience Prince Edward Island National Park in its most picturesque and pristine state. Overnight, wind and water action creates textured herringbone patterns across the beaches and dunes, and the rising sun casts an intriguing red glow across the entire park.

A National Park Day Pass costs C$6.90 adults, C$5.90 seniors, C$3.45 children, to a maximum of C$17 per vehicle. **Cavendish Visitor Centre,** just north of the junction of routes 6 and 13 in Cavendish (☎ 902-963-2391),

Starving art lovers, tuck in!

If not the most notable Island gallery, then **The Dunes Studio Gallery & Cafe,** on Route 15 at Brackley Beach (☎ 902-672-1883), is certainly the most unique. Made up almost entirely of windows, this ultra-contemporary building is part gallery, part restaurant, and all tourist attraction. The Island's preeminent painters, woodcarvers, and sculptors have their work on display in a multi-level, spiral room, with a narrow stairway leading to a fourth-floor lookout. Hungry? The gallery restaurant outdoes itself with dishes such as crab cakes with wasabi mayonnaise (C$14) at lunch and a roasted pork tenderloin with rosemary apricot mustard in the evening (C$25). The gallery is open May through September daily 10 a.m. to 6 p.m. while the restaurant hours are June to September daily 11:30 a.m. to 10 p.m

has park maps, posted weather forecasts, and natural history displays. It's open June through September daily 9 a.m. to 5 p.m. (July and Aug until 8 p.m.).

North Rustico Harbour

At the entrance to Rustico Bay, the tiny hamlet of North Rustico Harbour comprises a lighthouse and a smattering of trim homes lodged between the beaches of Prince Edward Island National Park and a small harbor packed with fishing boats. The picturesque setting attracts hordes of visitors, but somehow the village maintains a peaceful demeanor.

Down on the dock is **Rustico Harbour Fisheries Museum (☎ 902-963-3799),** a small facility that catalogs local history. Native displays share space with exhibits on harvesting Irish moss, artifacts from local canneries, and a tank of live lobsters. The story of the Mi'Kmaq, who left middens of shells on nearby Robinsons Island as evidence of 1,500 years of habitation, is most intriguing. Admission is a worthwhile C$3 adults, C$2.50 seniors and children.

Court Brothers (☎ 902-963-2322) is one of many local operations that take visitors out to sea for mackerel fishing. Trips last around three hours and cost a reasonable C$25 adults and C$15 children, although the catch belongs to the boat. **Outside Expeditions (☎ 800-207-3899 or** 902-963-3366; www.getoutside.com) launches sea kayak tours from a beach right beside the dock. If you've never kayaked before, the 90-minute trip is a great introduction to the sport. The cost is just C$45 per person and includes instruction in basic paddling skills and the chance to view a wide range of seabirds while paddling along the calm waters of the bay. If you're feeling adventurous, consider a day trip to Robinsons Island, where a picnic lunch is included in the price of C$100.

To get to North Rustico Harbour, take Route 6 east from Cavendish and veer left at the main intersection in North Rustico.

Chapter 20

Prince County

• •

In This Chapter

▶ Soaking up Summerside
▶ Exploring Acadian culture
▶ Meandering around Malpeque Bay
▶ Reaching North Cape

• •

*M*any visitors only tour the central portion (Queens County) of
Prince Edward Island — they cross Confederation Bridge and
head straight for Charlottetown, and then venture north to Cavendish
and maybe loop through Kings County before leaving via the ferry. But,
to experience the Island's less touristy side, consider including Prince
County, the western third of the island, in your itinerary.

The low-lying landscape of Prince County is mostly rural. It's surrounded
by some of the Maritimes' best beaches, long sand dunes, and low, red
cliffs. To appreciate the best of the west, stick to the coast wherever
possible (Route 14 between West Point and Tignish is the highlight) and
give the main thoroughfare — Route 2, which runs through the middle of
Prince County — a miss.

Summerside

Summerside (population 15,000), 71km (44 miles) west of Charlottetown,
is the second-largest city on Prince Edward Island and is the gateway to
Prince County. Spread around a south-facing harbor, the waterfront is
the most appealing section of the city, although a recent rejuvenation
extends to commercial buildings adorned with colorful murals.

Getting there

From the Confederation Bridge, take Route 10, and then Route 1A, to
reach Summerside in less than 30 minutes. The most direct route from
Charlottetown is Route 2 through Kensington. Both these routes merge
east of Summerside, with a well-signposted exit leading right downtown.

Staying in Summerside

A strip of motels on the eastern approach to downtown (within walking distance of the waterfront) offers well-priced overnight accommodations — just don't expect valet parking and room service.

Baker's Lighthouse Motel
$ Summerside

Rooms at Baker's Lighthouse Motel are no better than similarly priced choices on the east side of downtown, but children will enjoy the playground while you cook up a storm (or a lobster — pots supplied) at the outdoor barbecue area.

802 Water St. E. ☎ 877-436-2996 or 902-436-2992. Rack rates: C$60–C$70 double. MC, V.

Quality Inn Garden of the Gulf
$$–$$$ Summerside

The 94 guest rooms at this chain motel are nothing exceptional, but the downtown location is perfect for an evening stroll along the waterfront, and kids love the choice of outdoor and indoor swimming pools.

618 Water St. E. ☎ 800-265-5551 or 902-436-2295. Fax: 902-432-2911. www.quality innpei.com. *Rack rates: C$139–C$189 double. AE, DC, MC, V.*

Silver Fox Inn
$$ Summerside

A distinctive 1890 Queen Anne Revival residence, this inn offers six comfortable guest rooms decorated in frilly Victorian style. Afternoon tea and cookies are served noon to 4 p.m. for a minimal extra charge. A tiered deck and well-stocked library provide alternate relaxation areas. Rates include a cooked breakfast. Dinner is available with advance reservations.

61 Granville St. ☎ 800-565-4033 or 902-436-1664. www.silverfoxinn.net. *Rack rates: C$100–C$150 double. AE, DC, MC, V.*

Dining in Summerside

Summerside has many restaurants, including a string of places along the waterfront, and none of them will break your bank account. If you plan on just one meal in town, sacrifice the water views and head for the nearby Brothers Two.

Brothers Two Restaurant
$$–$$$ Summerside CANADIAN

Locals love this casual, pine-paneled place for its wide selection of dishes that go well beyond seafood (I had the meatloaf and loved it). Naturally, you can't go wrong with local seafood either. Try scallops poached in white wine or a lobster club, or chose two favorites from a list (haddock, salmon, scallops, shrimp, and so on), accompanied by potato, vegetables, and bread for C$23. Seating choices are tables, booths, or out on a rooftop patio.

618 Water St. ☎ 902-436-9654. Main courses: C$12–C$24. AE, DC, MC, V. Open: Daily 11 a.m.–9:30 p.m.

Exploring Summerside

Start at the waterfront, where you find plenty of free parking, and **Spinnakers' Landing Boardwalk**, which has a small interpretive display telling the story of the once-thriving shipbuilding business. Also here is a pub with a waterfront deck, bike rentals, summertime weekend entertainment on an outdoor stage, the **Visitor Information Centre** (☎ 902-436-6692), and a lighthouse that you can climb for 360-degree views.

College of Piping
Summerside

This college, the only one of its type in North America, is for people who want to learn Highland and step-dancing, or how to play the bagpipes. Students from around the world live in residences during the year, but for the casual observer, the college is also worth a visit. The summer-long Celtic Festival is a great chance to learn about ancient Celtic culture and the skills involved in the various disciplines taught on campus. Mini-concerts are held Monday to Friday at 11:30 a.m., 1:30 p.m., and 3:30 p.m. Admission is C$5 per person. July through August, Tuesday, Wednesday, and Thursday, a ceilidh (pronounced "*kay*-lee") showcases lively Celtic music at 7 p.m. Admission is C$24 for adults, C$20 seniors, C$15 children.

619 Water St. E. ☎ 902-436-5377. www.collegeofpiping.com.

Région Évangéline

The Acadians comprised the first group of Europeans to settle on Prince Edward Island. When the British took control of the island in 1755, many of these French nationals escaped exile by hiding out in the remote western portion of the island. Over time, they resumed normal, mostly rural lives. Their descendants now make up over 15 percent of the island's population and are concentrated along the portion of the island covered in this next section — the southern coastline of Prince County, west of Summerside along Route 11.

Getting there

Route 2 west from Summerside flies right through the middle of Région Évangéline. You can take Route 11 south at Miscouche to follow the coast to Cap Egmont for more scenic views, and then rejoin Route 2 at Mount Pleasant. But plan on staying in Summerside or Charlottetown for the night, as decent accommodations and dining options are very limited here.

Exploring Région Évangéline

Trim homes, impressive churches, and flapping flags are signs that pride in Acadian culture is strong in Région Évangéline. Traditions are also showcased at Musée Acadien — and I include an eccentric non-Acadian sight as a bonus.

Bottle Houses
Cap Egmont

Think you know the world's most obsessive collector? Think again. Originally put together by the late Edouard Arsenault, over 25,000 bottles have been cemented together to form three buildings, including a church complete with altar and pews, at this unique attraction. The surrounding gardens alone are worth the price of admission.

Route 11, Cap Egmont. ☎ *902-854-2987. Admission: C$5 adults, C$4.50 seniors, C$2 children. Open: May to mid-Oct daily 10 a.m.–4 p.m., July–Aug daily 9 a.m.–8 p.m.*

Musée Acadien
Miscouche

Protected as a National Historic Site, this museum commemorates the trials and tribulations of the Island's early French settlers. It boasts a permanent display of Acadian history, as well a remarkable audiovisual presentation that tells the story of their mass expulsion from Prince Edward Island in moving detail. Acadians gathered in Miscouche in 1884 to officially adopt the Acadian flag and an anthem, which gives the museum extra appeal.

Miscouche, Route 2. ☎ *902-432-2880. Admission: C$4 adults, C$1.50 children. Open: Mon–Fri 9:30 a.m.–5 p.m., extended in July–Aug to daily 9 a.m.–7 p.m.*

Our Lady of Mont-Carmel
Mont-Carmel

Facing the highway, but sitting atop red cliffs that descend to Northumberland Strait, this magnificent church is the architectural highlight of Région Évangéline. The town's first inhabitants came from the Poitou region of France, and this is reflected in the cathedral's ornate interior. Most visitors are happy to do their admiring from the surrounding grounds, but Sunday Mass is open to the public.

Route 11, Mont-Carmel. ☎ *902-854-2260.*

Malpeque Bay

The calm waters of Malpeque Bay are famous for oysters, but the area's pleasant beaches, its human history, and its native culture make this massive tidal waterway a worthwhile detour from the drive north through Prince County.

Getting there

If you're coming from Cavendish, follow Route 6 through to Kensington, and then take Route 20 north to Cabot Beach or Route 2 around the head of the bay. Tyne Valley, on the western side of the bay, is reached by taking Route 132 from Route 2.

Staying around Malpeque Bay

Lodging around Malpeque Bay is limited, so reserve a room well ahead of time, especially for July and August.

Doctor's Inn Bed and Breakfast
$ Tyne Valley

On a rise above the village of Tyne Valley, this rambling 1860s home is more farm than bed-and-breakfast. It contains only two guest rooms and a single guest bathroom, but you'll remember hospitable hosts Jean and Paul Offer and their wonderful down-home cooking long after you've gotten over having to share a bathroom. A full cooked breakfast, prepared in the old-fashioned kitchen complete with wood stove, is included in the rates. If you choose to pay the C$55 per person extra for the four-course dinner, you'll enjoy appetizers and wine in the sitting room, followed by seafood complemented by wonderful salads in the dining room. Freshly baked desserts complete the cozy dining experience. Non-guests are also welcomed for dinner with 24 hours' notice.

Route 167, Tyne Valley. ☎ *902-831-3057. Rack rates: C$60 double. MC, V.*

Malpeque Cove Cottages
$$ Malpeque Harbour

If you're looking for an escape from touristy Cavendish, you can't do any better than these cottages perched right on the water beside Cabot Beach Provincial Park. Malpeque Harbour has delightful red-sand beaches and warm water for swimming, but is also close to Cavendish, while a ten-minute drive southeast is the Kensington Towers theme park. Each modern, woodsy cottage has two to three bedrooms, a full kitchen, color television, and deck. In July and August a three-night minimum stay is required, but in spring and as early as late August, this condition is dropped and cabins rent from just C$101 per night.

304 King St., Malpeque Harbour, north of Malpeque. ☎ *888-283-1927 or 902-836-1072.* malpeque.ca. *Rates: C$330–C$405 double for three nights. MC, V. Open: May–Dec.*

Exploring Malpeque Bay

Prince Edward Island itself is so small that the big foldout tourism map skews distances — you can drive from one end of Malpeque Bay to the other in just two hours.

Lennox Island
North Malpeque Bay

The Mi'Kmaq, the original inhabitants of Prince Edward Island, had their 10,000-year nomadic lifestyle wiped out after Europeans arrived and cleared the land for farming. Around 1800, some had been persuaded to resettle on Lennox Island, which was later purchased for their people. Now linked to PEI by a short causeway, descendants of the Mi'Kmaq still live on the island, living a mostly traditional lifestyle that includes fishing and harvesting peat moss. They share their culture with interested visitors at **Lennox Island Cultural Centre,** down by the main dock (☎ 902-831-2702). Official summer hours are daily 10 a.m. to 6 p.m., but call ahead to confirm. Across the road is **Indian Art & Craft of North America** (☎ 902-831-2653) where you can purchase Mi'Kmaq baskets, pottery, and jewelry.
Take Route 163 east from Route 12.

Green Park Shipbuilding Museum
Port Hill

If you want to revisit the 1860s, when shipbuilding was Prince Edward Island's main industry, plan on a visit to this sprawling property on the western shore of Malpeque Bay. The mansion of James Yeo, who owned the yards, sits in the heart of sweeping grounds. It's fully furnished in Victorian style, including the top-floor cupola from which Yeo was able to watch over his workers. If you walk down to the site of the actual shipyards, two wooden buildings and the slips are all that remain, although interpretive panels do a good job of describing the once bustling business.

To get to the museum, you pass through **Green Park Provincial Park,** protecting a low peninsula scattered with stunted birch and laced with trails leading along the waterfront.
Route 12, Port Hill. ☎ *902-831-7947. Admission: C$5 adults, C$2.50 children. Open: June–Sept daily 9 a.m.–5 p.m.*

Western Prince County

Western Prince County is an arrow-shaped chunk of land that comes to a point at North Cape. Potato farms dominate the landscape in the central portion of the region although small fishing villages and long stretches of uninhabited coastline lined by sea cliffs beckon to the south and west.

Getting there

Route 2 splits western Prince County neatly in two, but steer away from this highway and take the coastal route wherever possible.

Staying in western Prince County

The Prince Edward Island Visitors Guide lists dozens of cottage-style accommodations, but the following three spots stand out.

Heritage Inn & Gardens
$$ Tignish

Located in the village of Tignish, this lodging is a good choice if you want inexpensive accommodations close to the cape. Built with locally fired red brick in 1868, a thorough renovation and the creation of beautiful gardens has removed any clinical feel from this former convent. Seventeen simple guest rooms are available, all with private bathrooms. Rates include a light breakfast and use of a kitchen.

Maple St., Tignish. ☎ *877-882-2491 or 902-882-2491. Fax: 902-882-2500.* www.tignish.com/inn. *Rates: C$75–C$90 double. AE, MC, V. Open: Mid-June to mid-Oct.*

Rodd Mill River
$$–$$$$ Mill River Provincial Park

Families will love this modern resort, the largest in Prince County, for amenities that include a waterslide and pool, canoe rentals, and hiking trails. A bonus for golfers is one of Canada's top-rated golf courses. The 90 guest rooms are adequate, with the choice of park or golf course views and standard amenities that include wireless Internet and air-conditioning. Both the main dining room and a casual bistro-cafe overlook the golf course.

Route 2, Mill River Provincial Park. ☎ *800-565-7633 or 902-859-3555. Fax: 902-859-2486.* www.rodd-hotels.ca. *Rates: C$145–C$260 double. AE, DC, MC, V. Open: Jan–Oct.*

West Point Lighthouse
$$ West Point

Have you ever stayed in a lighthouse? Here's your chance. Built in 1875 as a navigational aid to vessels entering Northumberland Strait, West Point is one of the oldest and tallest lighthouses on the Island. It has since been converted to an inn with a coveted Tower Room, in the lighthouse itself, in addition to the Light Keeper's Quarters in the adjoining building. All nine guest rooms are furnished with handmade quilts and antiques; a restaurant supplies three meals daily. Book well in advance for the room of your choice.

Route 14, West Point. ☎ *800-764-6854 or 902-859-3605. Fax: 902-859-1510.* www.west pointlighthouse.com. *Rates: C$110–C$145 double. AE, MC, V. Open: Late May to Sept.*

Touring through western Prince County

A tour through western Prince County is more about soaking up the scenery than visiting specific sites. The following are highlights of a driving tour that follows Route 2 as far as Mill River Provincial Park, and then continues on Route 12 to North Cape, returning along the west coast on Route 14. This entire loop is around 400km (250 miles) and you can complete it easily in one day.

✔ **Prince Edward Island Potato Museum,** in O'Leary, along Route 142 west of Route 2 (☎ 902-859-2039; June to mid-Oct Mon–Sat 9 a.m.– 5 p.m., Sun 1–5 p.m.). Surrounded by potato farms, exhibits at this small museum catalog the local industry, which dates back to the 1830s when an Irish farmer planted the Island's first spuds. Admission is C$6 per person to a maximum of C$14 per family.

✔ **Mill River Provincial Park,** beside Route 2 at St. Anthony. This park is best known for its **golf course** (☎ 902-859-2486), where the river comes into play on many holes. Greens fees are a reasonable C$60.

✔ **North Cape,** 16km (10 miles) north of Tignish. Prince County narrows to a point of land at North Cape, with a lighthouse and long reef that becomes exposed at low tide. Nearby is the **Atlantic Wind Test Site,** where wind turbines generate 5 percent of the Island's electricity.

✔ **Elephant Rock,** 4km (2½ miles) north of Norway on Route 182. Detached from high cliffs by erosion, this geological oddity lost its "trunk" in 1998, but the pinnacle of rock and the surrounding barren landscape are well worth the effort to reach it.

✔ **Irish Moss Interpretive Centre,** Route 14, Miminegash (☎ 902-882-4313; June–Sept Mon–Sat 10 a.m.–7 p.m., Sun noon to 8 p.m.). A type of seaweed used in the production of ice cream, Irish moss is collected by hand and on horseback from local beaches. This small museum, operated by families involved in the process, tells their story. Admission is C$2. Attached to the museum is the Seaweed Pie Café. Its namesake (C$3.50 per slice) actually tastes better than you may think.

✔ **West Point Lighthouse,** off Route 14 (☎ 902-859-3605). Manned from 1875 through to 1963, this historic structure has been converted to an inn (see earlier) and restaurant, but is well worth just a casual stop. Part of the complex is a small museum describing the structure and its importance to shipping in Northumberland Strait. The lighthouse is within Cedar Dunes Provincial Park, where you can walk the wooded nature trails and try your hand at digging clams.

Chapter 21

Kings County

● ●

In This Chapter

▶ Searching out seals in southern Kings County

▶ Striding the fairways of Brudenell River Golf Course

▶ Wandering through the shifting, singing sand of northern Kings County

● ●

*L*ike the rest of Prince Edward Island, Kings County is dominated by green farmland crisscrossed by rural roads. The biggest difference in the landscape is along the east coast, where the shoreline is more rugged than elsewhere on the Island, as the red sea cliffs are replaced by a rocky, forested foreshore.

The region is encircled by a coastal highway that passes through all of the towns and parks that this chapter details. From Charlottetown, it follows the Trans-Canada Highway east to Wood Islands, the departure point for ferries to the mainland, and then jogs north along the convoluted east coast before returning to the capital as Route 2. The entire loop is 374km (232 miles), easily tackled in one day.

For the purposes of the this chapter, I break Kings County in two, with southern Kings County and northern Kings County divided by the Cardigan River, which runs roughly through the center of the county and drains into Cardigan Bay just north of Brudenell River Provincial Park.

Southern Kings County

Mostly rural, the southern portion of Kings County is dotted with picturesque villages, fishing ports, lighthouses, and a number of provincial parks.

Getting there

From Charlottetown, take the Trans-Canada Highway (Route 1) east. After 20km (12 miles), Route 3 branches east to Brudenell River while the main highway heads south toward Wood Islands.

Between May and mid-December, ferries ply Northumberland Strait, linking Caribou (Nova Scotia) with Wood Islands just across the county line from Kings County. In summer, there are eight departures daily in each direction. Service in spring and fall is less frequent, and ice prevents ferries from operating mid-December to April. No reservations are taken, so plan on catching a mid-week, early morning departure to avoid a long wait. The round-trip fare of C$59 per vehicle, including passengers, is collected upon leaving the Island. (If you drive back to the mainland via the Confederation Bridge, a toll is collected there.) The service is operated by **Northumberland Ferries** (☎ **888-249-7245** or 902-566-3838; www.peiferry.com).

Staying in southern Kings County

The lodging scene in southern Kings County is dominated by small bed-and-breakfasts and family-style cottage accommodations. The following are my faves.

Forest and Stream Cottages
$$ **Murray Harbour**

If you can go without room service and robes, and if you like the idea of cooking your own meals, then this is the spot for you. Set on a small lake, each of five standard cottages has an older but well-equipped kitchen, a separate bedroom, and a screened porch. The Deluxe Cottage has two bedrooms and upgraded everything. Bed-and-breakfast rooms are also available. Guests have use of rowboats (perfect for an early morning fishing expedition — trout for breakfast, anyone?), a hot tub, and bike rentals. Children will love the shaded playground. Breakfast (C$5 per person) is served on the veranda of the main house.

446 Fox River Rd., Murray Harbour. ☎ *800-227-9943 or 902-962-3537. Fax: 902-962-3537.* www.forestandstreamcottages.com. *Rack rates: C$85–C$125 double. MC, V. Open: May–Oct.*

Rodd Brudenell River
$$–$$$$ **Roseneath**

This sprawling destination resort takes prime advantage of its bayside setting within the boundaries of Brudenell River Provincial Park. The unequaled choice of activities is what makes this resort a standout — two 18-hole golf courses, indoor and outdoor pools, tennis courts, bike rentals, canoeing and kayaking, horseback riding, and a full spa facility. Kids are catered to with their own activity program and a children's center. The main lodge holds 99 spacious hotel-style guest rooms decorated in simple, contemporary way. Each has a balcony or patio with water or golf course vistas. Close to the main resort is a cluster of 50 Riverside Country Cabins, which look rather boxy from the outside, but are well suited to budget travelers. Finally, each of 32 Echelon Gold Cottages has one or two bedrooms outfitted with king-size beds, a jetted tub, a full-sized kitchen, and a private deck with barbecue. Resort dining and drinking choices include three restaurants (Stillwater has the most inviting ambience) and a poolside bar.

Route 3, Roseneath. ☎ *800-565-7633 or 902-652-2332. Fax: 902-652-2886.* www.rodd-hotels.ca. *Rack rates: C$135–C$345 double. AE, DC, MC, V. Open: Mid-May to mid-Oct.*

Thought's End
$$ **Panmure Island**

The three motel-like rooms at Thought's End are unspectacular, but the setting is unbeatable — a 5.6-hectare (14-acre) property on remote Panmure Island, which is east of Montague on Route 17 and linked to the rest of PEI by a causeway. The island is ringed by beaches, and those fronting St. Mary's Bay are the most protected. Ask the friendly hosts about local boat tours.

Route 347, Panmure Island. ☎ *866-838-4522 or 902-838-4522. Rack rates: C$79 double. MC, V. Open: Mid-June to mid-Sept.*

Dining in southern Kings County

If you've just docked at Wood Islands, no better introduction to the island is better than enjoying a seafood feast — chowder, boiled lobster, or steamed mussels — from **Crabby's Seafood,** right beside the ferry dock (☎ 902-962-3228; open June to September daily noon to 7 p.m.) at one of surrounding picnic tables. Farther afield, plan on taking a full meal at Rodd Brudenell River (see earlier), or Windows on the Water in Montague.

Windows on the Water Cafe
$–$$ **Montague   CAFE/SEAFOOD**

This old-fashioned eatery combines country charm with a prime waterfront location overlooking Montague Marina. You can dine inside where the ambience is warm and inviting, but if the sun is shining dine out on the large deck. I loved the chowder made with homemade fish stock and chockablock full of haddock, clams, and scallops. It was lunchtime, so I skipped the mains (whatever seafood is in season, cooked simply) and dived straight into a generous serving of perfectly cooked apple crisp to finish.

106 Sackville St. ☎ *902-838-2080. Main courses: C$8.50–C$16. AE, DC, MC, V. Open: Mid-May to Sept daily 11:30 a.m.–8 p.m., until 9:30 p.m. in July and Aug.*

Exploring southern Kings County

If you're approaching Kings County from the Trans-Canada Highway, take the coastal route from Charlottetown to Wood Islands, where the ferry from Nova Scotia docks. At the junction of the main highway and the ferry access road, **Wood Islands Visitor Information Centre** (☎ 902-962-7411; open mid-May to mid-Oct daily 9 a.m.–5 p.m.) is a good place to find out more about the region.

Fairways to heaven

Quietly, Prince Edward Island has become one of Canada's premier destinations for golfers. A solid collection of more than 20 courses makes the most of the rolling rural landscape and picture-perfect coastline, varying from rural nine-hole courses to world-class resort layouts. The best Island golf courses are equal in quality and challenge to any others in Canada, yet greens fees (all under C$100) are a fraction of what you pay elsewhere.

Golf PEI (☎ 866-465-3734; www.golfpei.ca) is a government-operated reservation service that also promotes accommodation packages that make Island golfing an even better deal.

Here are my favorite courses:

Belvedere (Charlottetown ☎ 902-368-7104) is an old-fashioned layout that nurtured LPGA star Lorie Kane.

Brudenell River (Brudenell River Provincial Park; ☎ 800-235-8909 or 902-859-8873) mixes tree-lined fairways with open riverfront terrain. Thinking golfers are well rewarded at this renowned course.

Countryview (Fairview; ☎ 902-675-2800) is a sporty nine-hole layout with water views. It is surrounded by farmland, yet lies just ten minutes by road from Charlottetown.

Links of Crowbush Cove (Morell; ☎ 800-235-8909 or 902-961-7300) is routed around natural waterways behind North Shore dunes. Crowbush Cove is one of Canada's top courses.

Eagles Glenn (Cavendish; ☎ 866-963-3600 or 902-963-3600), although not overwhelming in length, is a challenging 27-hole, links-style creation through rolling highlands.

Glasgow Hills (Hunter River; ☎ 866-621-2200 or 902-621-2201) is in the middle of the Island, but the ocean is in view from its lofty location. Be prepared for major elevation differences between tee and green.

East from Wood Islands

From Wood Islands, it's 9km (5½ miles) to the first worthwhile stop, **Rossignol Estate Winery** on Route 4 (☎ 902-962-4193), the island's only commercial vineyard. Its eye-pleasing location above Northumberland Strait plays second fiddle to the serious business of producing surprisingly good red and white table wines, as well as award-winning fruit-based wines and maple cider. You can try before you buy at the on-site wine shop, which is open May to October, Monday to Saturday from 10 a.m. to 5 p.m., Sunday 1 to 5 p.m.

Murray Harbour

This tiny fishing village 10km (6¼ miles) east of Murray River is a little off the beaten track, but is well worth the detour. The **Old General Store** (☎ 902-962-2459) and **Miss Elly's** (☎ 902-962-3555), both on Main Street, hold fine collections of antiques and gifts. Meanwhile, **Marine Adventures Seal Tours** (☎ 902-962-2494) departs the downtown dock up to three times daily mid-May through September for a short boat cruise to a large colony of seals via a mussel farm. The tour costs C$19 adults, C$17 seniors, C$12 children.

Northern Kings County

If the weather is good, your time in the northern section of Kings County will be a highlight of your visit to Prince Edward Island. The beaches lining the Gulf of St. Lawrence are as nice as you find anywhere around the Island, yet tourist crowds are minimal. The entire region is more lightly settled than elsewhere in the province; the largest town, Souris, holds a population of just 1,200.

Getting there

Route 4 is the most direct route between Pooles Corner and Souris, but the scenic countryside on alternate routes 311 and 310 is enjoyable. From Cavendish, Route 2 enters Kings County near St. Andrews and veers inland to join Route 4 at Fortune Bridge. On any of these approaches, distances are not as long as they may seem from glancing at a provincial map. Souris is 82km (51 miles) from Charlottetown and 70km (43 miles) from Wood Islands.

Staying in northern Kings County

Accommodations in the northern half of Kings County are more spread out than elsewhere on the Island, but the choices you do have run the gamut of prices — from one of PEI's best bargains to one of its most upscale (and expensive) inns.

A Place to Stay Inn
$ Souris

Once you get over the corny name, you discover that this inexpensive lodging has everything going for it — comfortable rooms, cooking facilities, television lounges, bike rentals, and a location within walking distance of the Souris waterfront. Beds are in downstairs dormitories or in upstairs bed-and-breakfast rooms that share bathrooms.

9 Longworth St., Souris. ☎ 800-655-7829 or 902-687-4626. Rack rates: C$22 dorm bed, C$70 double. MC, V. Open: Mar to mid-Oct.

Inn at Bay Fortune
$$$–$$$$ Bay Fortune

Built as a summer retreat for Broadway playwright Elmer Harris, Inn at Bay Fortune is now an upscale, 18-room inn on the calm shores of Bay Fortune. The lodge and its well-manicured grounds are rather aristocratic, and yet the ambience remains unpretentious. The elegant rooms are furnished with a pleasing mix of antiques and Island-made furniture; some have wood-burning fireplaces.

The restaurant here has a reputation as one of the finest in the Maritimes. The tables along the covered veranda provide the best views. Enjoy views of the bay in a refined setting while dining on local seafood, carefully prepared using ingredients harvested from the inn's own garden. A full breakfast is included in the rates, or choose a package that includes dinner and a picnic lunch.

Route 310, Bay Fortune. ☎ *888-687-3745 or 902-687-3745. Fax: 902-687-3540.* www.innatbayfortune.com. *Rack rates: C$200–C$335 double. MC, V. Open: Mid-May to mid-Oct.*

Rodd Crowbush Golf & Beach Resort
$$$$ Morell

Strolling the fairways of one of Canada's top-ranked golf courses is the main attraction at Rodd Crowbush. Guest rooms are spacious and decorated in a casual, contemporary style. All have a private patio or deck and come with niceties such as bathrobes, television and DVD combos, and evening turndown service. Cottages scattered around the property are a luxurious splurge. A long stretch of sandy beach, tennis courts, an indoor pool, and a restaurant specializing in modern Canadian cooking round out the resort. Although you pay top dollar to stay here, the atmosphere is refined-casual. The staff is service-oriented, friendly, and approachable. Always ask about packages that may include greens fees or meals in the price.

Route 350, Morell. ☎ *800-565-7633 or 902-961-5600. Fax: 902-961-5601.* www.rodd-hotels.ca. *Rack rates: C$230–C$520 double. AE, DC, MC, V. Open: Mid-May to mid-Oct.*

Dining in northern Kings County

Inn at Bay Fortune and Rodd Crowbush Golf & Beach Resort (refer to the previous section) both feature excellent restaurants that welcome non-guests. You can also dine at one of the following two choices.

Bluefin Restaurant
$–$$ Souris SEAFOOD

A great place to dig into a hearty seafood meal with the locals. The simple, wide-ranging menu has something to suit everyone at this casual eatery — think Caesar salad, roast beef and mashed potatoes, and deep-fried halibut and chips. If you're not lobstered out, head to the downstairs section, where the lobster supper comes with all-you-can-eat seafood chowder and mussels.

10 Federal Ave., Souris. ☎ *902-687-3271. Main Courses: C$10–C$24. Open: Daily 7 a.m.–8 p.m. MC, V.*

St. Margarets Lobster Supper
$$ St. Margarets SEAFOOD

Unlike the lobster suppers in neighboring Queens County, the St. Margarets version is put on for residents as much as for visitors. It's served up in the local church throughout summer, although because they have no holding pond, the lobster may be frozen. The fixed-price meal includes a full lobster, freshly baked breads, delicious fish chowder, and strawberry shortcake for dessert.

Route 16, St. Margarets. ☎ *902-687-3105. Lobster supper: C$28. Open: Mid-June to mid-Sept daily 4–9 p.m.*

Exploring northern Kings County

You can easily hit the hot spots of northern Kings County — Souris, East Point, and the eastern end of Prince Edward Island National Park — in a single day, including stops. The road around the peninsula is never more than a few minutes' drive from the water, while rural routes cut across the entire peninsula, opening up various options for exploring the interior.

Souris and area

Souris (pronounced "Surrey"), 39km (24 miles) north of Pooles Corner, has a population of just 1,100, yet is the biggest town in all of Kings County. **St. Mary's Catholic Church,** on Chapel Avenue, soars higher than any other building in town. It was built in 1901 using red-colored island sandstone. At the west entrance to town is a beach and a concession renting kayaks and bikes.

Around 10km (6¼ miles) up the coast from Souris is **Basin Head Fisheries Museum** (☎ 902-357-7233), at the oceanfront site of an abandoned fish cannery. The original wooden buildings, weathered by sun and salt, hold displays tracing the history of the industry as well as touch tanks and exhibits describing local sea life. The museum is open June to September daily 9 a.m. to 5 p.m., and admission is C$4 adults, free for children. Below the museum is **Singing Sand Beach,** so named for the squeaking sound when you walk on the sand.

North Shore

The octagonal **East Point Lighthouse** (☎ 902-357-2106) stands on a low knoll at the easternmost point of land on Prince Edward Island. Built in 1867, the timber structure is open for inspection mid-June to August daily 10 a.m. to 6 p.m. The attached light keeper's residence has been converted to a gift shop with a good selection of seafaring literature.

Take Route 313 west from St. Peters to reach the Greenwich unit of **Prince Edward Island National Park,** which is dominated by massive sand dunes. The unstable dunes are slowly moving inland, burying the coastal woods and leaving bleached tree trunks sticking up through the sand. The access road ends at **Greenwich Interpretation Centre** (☎ **902-963-2391;** open mid-May to mid-Oct daily 9 a.m.–5 p.m. and until 8 p.m. July–Aug) where the unique ecology of the protected peninsula is explained. To see for yourself, take the 4.5km (2.8-mile) **Greenwich Dunes Hiking Trail.** Allow 90 minutes to complete the loop. Admission to the park is C$6.90 adults, C$5.90 seniors, C$3.45 children.

Part VI
The Part of Tens

The 5th Wave   By Rich Tennant

"WHAT DO YOU MEAN YOU FORGOT THE WHITE WINE?! YOU
KNOW DARN WELL I CAN'T SERVE FISH WITHOUT WHITE WINE!"

In this part . . .

Presented in a top ten format, the following three chapters aren't required reading, but I recommend you give them a look. Find inspiration in Chapter 22, which condenses the best Maritime experiences. If you want a quick reference of the region's top restaurants (okay, not really — they're my favorite places to eat), check out Chapter 23. Finally, Chapter 24's rundown makes you the ace of trivia, with ten Maritimers of note.

Chapter 22

Ten Maritimes Experiences

● ●

In This Chapter

▶ Drinking up the local culture
▶ Casting a line
▶ Watching the whales

● ●

*I*n this chapter, I describe experiences that represent the best of the Maritimes — a combination of specific destinations and things to do throughout the three provinces.

A Day in Anne's Land

If you've read *Anne of Green Gables,* you'll want to spend at least a day exploring the area around Cavendish, on Prince Edward Island — the area Lucy Maud Montgomery waxed lyrical about in her famous novel. You can visit Montgomery's birthplace, stroll through the home in which she was married (or even tie the knot yourself), and walk — or skip for the full effect — along Lover's Lane through Balsam Hollow.

Drinking and Dancing

Maritimers love their beer (especially local brews such as Keith's) and they love traditional Celtic music. Combine the two in the surroundings of a local pub, and you're in for an energetic night of fun. Nearly every town throughout the region has at least one pub, each with its regular clientele, but welcoming of visitors. A ceilidh (*kay*-lee) is an organized gathering that combines the two pleasures, often in a community hall or outdoor venue.

Fishing the Miramichi

Serious anglers from around the world are drawn to the wildly remote Miramichi River for spring and summer runs of Atlantic salmon, weighing up to 13 kilograms (30 pounds) each. Fish populations have increased remarkably since a catch-and-release policy was implemented a decade ago. Lots of fish are up for grabs, but catching them is an art. Better your odds by hiring a local guide, many of whom are associated with riverside fishing lodges.

If the fish aren't biting, head to the Atlantic Salmon Museum in Doaktown and read about other anglers' successes.

Going Golfing

Imagine striding the fairways of one of Canada's finest golf courses, staying the night just a chip and a putt from the 18th green, and then teeing off again the next morning — all for less than you pay for a single round at a top city course elsewhere in North America. Golfing and golf packages are a relative bargain across the Maritimes, but Rodd Crowbush Golf & Beach Resort on Prince Edward Island offers the bonus of activities for everyone in the family — think tennis, horseback riding, hiking, canoeing, and more.

Having a Whale of a Time

Hundreds of whales spend the warmer months feasting in the nutrient-rich waters of the Bay of Fundy. Species such as finback, minke, and humpback are commonly sighted, while a lucky few spot the world's rarest whale — the North Atlantic right whale. Tour boats depart from Digby Neck (Nova Scotia) and St. Andrews (New Brunswick) throughout the summer, with trips lasting two to three hours. If the whales are playing hide-and-seek, strike up a conversation with your captain. Most are local fisherman making a little extra money in their downtime, and all are characters with a whale tale or two to tell.

Hiking the Highlands

Views along the Cabot Trail, which winds through Cape Breton Highlands National Park, are stupendous, but this "trail" is a paved road for vehicles (or cyclists who take their lives into their own hands by traversing the narrow road by pedal power). You'll best appreciate the park's scenery if you move away from the road and hike along one of the walking trails. The Skyline Trail is a classic. Easily traversed in a half-day, it ends at a magnificent lookout high above the ocean. And if you're lucky, you may spy whales frolicking far below.

Making the French Connection

Acadian culture, which has its roots in the region's early French settlers, can be experienced in many places and in many ways. Visiting a
museum — those in Caraquet and Miscouche are best — provides a
good introduction to the Acadians and their heroic history. But soaking
up the history of Grande Pré National Historic Site, taking in a concert
at Village Historique Acadien (Caraquet), or feasting on a rappie pie at
Rapure Acadienne (Meteghan) really brings the culture to life.

Sailing into the Sunset

No other boat is better known in Canada than the *Bluenose* (look on the
back of the Canadian dime for a scaled-down version), and nothing is
more romantic than spending an evening under sail on the *Bluenose II*,
an exact replica of the original. She has a packed summer schedule of
public cruises throughout the Maritimes, with regular departures from
her home port of Lunenburg as well as from nearby Halifax. Book well
ahead of time to be assured of a spot on board — otherwise you'll be left
waving from the dock.

Snapping the Perfect Picture

The combination of colorful subject matter and superlative scenery
makes taking good photos in the Maritimes a snap. South of Halifax, pic-
ture-taking opportunities line up along the coast — the world's most
photographed lighthouse at Peggy's Cove, the trio of bayside churches
in Mahone Bay, and the colorful clapboard buildings of Lunenburg. On
the rest of your travels, go beyond the obvious. In New Brunswick, have
your family stand at a tilt in front of Moncton's Magnetic Hill and snoop
around the narrow back streets of Saint John for a historical perspective. On Prince Edward Island, rise early to catch the first flush of light
along the red dunes of Prince Edward Island National Park and take to
the back roads for rural panoramas.

Walking on the Ocean Floor

Okay, maybe this description is a little overdramatic, but it's true in a lit-
eral sense. The action happens at Hopewell Rocks, on the New
Brunswick side of the Bay of Fundy. As the massive Fundy tide recedes,
it leaves the "ocean floor" bare around the entire bay. What makes this
place even more notable is the dozen or so rock towers separated from
the mainland by the forces of erosion.

Chapter 23

Ten Places to Eat Great Seafood

* *

In This Chapter

▶ Checking out the cream of the crop of seafood restaurants

▶ Discovering what makes each place special

* *

*F*ishophobes beware! Seafood dominates the Maritimes dining scene. Just about every restaurant offers seafood in some form or another, and many specialize in it. The food in major Maritimes cities is comparable in presentation and creativity to that in other North American cities, but it's offered at a fraction of the price. Beside the regular restaurants, many small-town cafes serve up seafood; you can count on the fish being battered, but lobster and mussels are usually boiled, and scallops sautéed. Finally, there are fish markets. Most coastal villages have one, usually down near the harbor, selling a range of fresh seafood — perfect for a home-cooked meal in your cabin.

And so, without further ado, here are the top ten places in the Maritimes to eat seafood.

Blue Mussel Café

Fresh ingredients, locally sourced whenever possible, are prepared at Prince Edward Island's renowned Blue Mussel Café with simple style. The highlight for many diners is what this restaurant *doesn't* have — a deep fryer. One local specialty is the soft-flavored Malpeque Bay oyster. Order them au naturel for the full effect. The restaurant setting is as memorable as the food — a cluster of outdoor tables over the water is protected from the wind by a renovated wharf building that serves as the kitchen.

Butland's Seafood

If you're visiting Fundy National Park in New Brunswick, drive through to the adjacent village of Alma, where Butland's holds a prime position above the small harbor. Inside this lively market is a bathtub-sized container overflowing with cooked lobsters. They are pre-weighed, with prices (around C$12 per pound) marked on the claws. If someone has beaten you to the single picnic table out back, head into the national park and enjoy lunch at any one of its numerous picnic spots.

Chowder House

How does a restaurant that hasn't seen a coat of paint for years and doesn't even offer table service make my top ten? Easy — by serving up huge portions of super-fresh mussels, crab, and lobster at ridiculously low prices. The location also helps, perched on a grassy bluff overlooking the Atlantic Ocean in the village of Neil's Harbour, on Cape Breton Island.

Five Fishermen

In Halifax, if you're looking to choose from a wide range of seafood in a stylish setting, make reservations at the Five Fishermen. Ensconced in an 1816 red-brick building that was originally a school — and, more infamously, a morgue for bodies of first-class passengers from the *Titanic* tragedy — tables are spread through numerous nautical-themed rooms. A massive wine rack holds pride of place in the center of the restaurant, and a century-old stained-glass window is the feature in the main dining room.

Muddy Rudder

The Muddy Rudder is nothing more than a ramshackle shed where orders are taken, a gas burner, and a bunch of plastic table settings on a grassy area beside the Cabot Trail. The seafood — crab, lobster, mussels, clams, and more — is dunked in a pot of boiling water to order. A truly unique Maritimes dining experience.

Murphy's

Murphy's, in Truro, Nova Scotia, gets my nod for "The Best Maritimes Seafood Restaurant That's Nowhere Near the Ocean." Not only is water out of sight, but the strip mall setting is unremarkable. Inside, the distinctly nautical setting includes model ships on the walls and fishnets hanging from the ceiling. Battered fish with a pile of perfectly cooked chips is the specialty, served up by no-nonsense waitstaff.

New Glasgow Lobster Suppers

Lobster suppers have been held throughout Prince Edward Island for over 50 years. They originated as gatherings in community halls and church basements, often as fundraisers for some local cause or another. New Glasgow Lobster Suppers is one of the best. It attracts quite a few locals, as well as visitors staying in nearby Cavendish. But it has plenty of room for everyone, with 500 seats on two levels. Don't come here for the view (although some tables overlook the River Clyde) or the atmosphere (which is fun and informal). Choose this lobster supper for the food: a fixed-price meal of lobster, complete with all-you-can-eat mussels, seafood chowder, potato salad, and coleslaw. Just make sure to save room for the strawberry shortcake.

O'Neil's Royal Fundy Market

Digby, on the Nova Scotia side of the Bay of Fundy, is renowned for its fleet of scallop boats that harvest the sweetest, plumpest scallops you can ever imagine. At Digby's dockside fish market, they're sold raw to go, or rolled in flour and fried up on the spot. The market also sells Digby chicks, a chewy, jerky-style snack of smoked herring, as well as mussels, oysters, lobsters, and a variety of Fundy fishes such as halibut.

Seaweed Pie Café

At Miminegash, in Prince County, Prince Edward Island, a group of local women have formed a co-operative to harvest and process Irish moss, a type of seaweed that washes up on local beaches in big storms. Irish moss has traditionally been used as a thickening ingredient in ice cream and toothpaste, but the ladies of Miminegash market its nutrient-rich values for health-related products. Not all of it is shipped to outside markets. Some ends up in seaweed pie, a surprisingly delicious dish served up in a small cafe that is part of a larger interpretive center.

Shediac Bay Cruises

Add a little spice to your seafood feast by helping haul in the catch aboard Shediac Bay Cruises. With Captain Eric LeBlanc at the helm, these trips leave daily from Shediac, north of Moncton, New Brunswick. The tour begins with an informative talk about the life cycle of the lobster and harvesting methods. The traps are then lifted onto the boat, the lobsters are extracted, and then they're boiled in preparation of an onboard seafood feast of the freshest proportions.

Chapter 24

Ten Famous People You Probably Didn't Realize Were Maritimers

• •

In This Chapter

▶ Inventing the telephone
▶ Cooking french fries
▶ Sailing around the world

• •

*W*hile the stunning landscape is the Maritimes' most obvious asset, the people (universally known as "Maritimers") themselves are notable. Frank, friendly, and always with a story to tell, they contribute to making the region a great place to visit. The following Maritimers have gone on to greatness beyond their own borders.

Alexander Graham Bell

Prolific inventor Alexander Graham Bell spent his latter years at Baddeck, on Cape Breton Island, where his waterfront home is still owned by the Bell family. At the large museum in town, you can learn about his most famous invention, the telephone, as well as quirky facts, such as why he could never call his mom (she was deaf).

Stompin' Tom Connors

If you're not from Canada, you're probably not familiar with the patriotic tunes written and sung by this legendary musician, who was born in Saint John, New Brunswick, and raised on Prince Edward Island. Stompin' Tom has sold three million albums without ever having a song on the Canadian country charts and without ever releasing a song outside of Canada (who says "Bud the Spud" isn't radio-friendly?).

Samuel Cunard

Born the son of a Halifax carpenter, Samuel Cunard was the man behind Cunard Steamship Limited, the most recognizable name in ocean travel. In 1840, a Cunard ship made the first trans-Atlantic passenger service, marking the start of the company's heyday. Today the company has just one boat in service, the *Queen Mary II*, the largest passenger ship ever built.

Sam Langford

Generally regarded as one of the ten greatest heavyweight boxers of all time, Nova Scotia–born Langford stepped into the ring over 600 times through the first two decades of the 1900s. During his career, he fought in five weight divisions — lightweight through to heavyweight — but makes this list for his final fight, which he fought after having been declared legally blind. The result? He won. By a knockout.

The McCain Family

Like thousands of others, the McCain family emigrated from Ireland to the Maritimes in the 1820s, farming hay on a small plot of land alongside the Saint John River. By the mid-1900s, hay had been replaced by potatoes. A half-century later and McCain Foods is the world's largest supplier of frozen french fries. They have 20,000 employees working in 50 factories to process 346,000 kilograms (760,000 pounds) of potatoes every *hour*. Probably the most amazing fact is that McCain world headquarters is in the family's hometown of Florenceville, New Brunswick (population 800).

Lucy Maud Montgomery

No other person in Canada has as well-preserved a childhood as this famous writer, who grew up at Cavendish on Prince Edward Island and used her early memories to create the character Anne of Green Gables, a lovable orphan girl. The paths Montgomery walked, the room in which she was married, and the unremarkable but much-visited farmhouse known as Green Gables make up Anne-fan favorites.

Anne Murray

With sales of 54 million albums and more awards than any other female singer, Anne Murray continues to entertain people worldwide with her sultry voice that blends pop and country. Murray was born in Springhill, Nova Scotia, and retains strong ties to the region through the town's Anne Murray Centre.

John Patch

Patch, a fisherman from Yarmouth, Nova Scotia, developed the screw propeller in 1832. It soon became the preferred method of propulsion in ships, more effective than either sails or paddlewheels. In 1845, a large steamship became the first to cross the Atlantic Ocean using his invention. In the later years of his life, Patch lost the rights to the propeller. He died penniless.

Harry Saltzman

Harry Saltzman had the movie mogul look: tubby, loud, and always brightly dressed. He also had the blockbusters to go with the look. Born in Saint John, New Brunswick, in 1915, Saltzman left home to join the circus at the age of 17, ending up in Paris during World War II. After producing *The Iron Petticoat,* which starred the unlikely duo of Bob Hope and Katharine Hepburn, he bought the screen rights to Ian Fleming's James Bond novels and then went on to produce the first nine Bond movies, the biggest espionage thrillers in movie history.

Joshua Slocum

Born in 1844 and raised around Digby, Joshua Slocum left Nova Scotia for a life on the high seas at a young age. He is remembered today for one particular feat: being the first person to sail solo around the world.

Appendix

Quick Concierge

• •

Fast Facts

AAA

The Canadian affiliate of AAA is the Canadian Automobile Association (www.caa. ca). Check the Web site for the location of regional offices or contact CAA Maritimes at ☎ 800-561-8807 or 506-634-1400.

American Express

American Express has no full-service International Service Centers in the Maritimes. Instead call ☎ 905-474-8700 for cardholder services. For lost or stolen traveler's checks, call ☎ 800-668-2639.

Area Codes

The telephone area code for Nova Scotia and Prince Edward Island is 902. The area code for New Brunswick is 506.

ATMs

The most common place to find bank machines is at the entrance to major banks. Check the back of your debit or credit card to see what network your bank belongs to, and then contact Plus (☎ 800-843-7587; www.visa.com) or Cirrus (☎ 800-424-7787; www.mastercard.com) to find the location nearest to you.

Business Hours

Business hours vary throughout the Maritimes. The following is only a guideline. Banks: Monday through Thursday 9:30 a.m. to 3:30 p.m., Friday 9 a.m. to 5 p.m. Retail stores: Monday through Saturday 9:30 a.m. to 5 p.m. Mall shops often stay open until 9 p.m. later in the week and open on Sunday from around noon until 5 or 6 p.m. In tourist areas, hours fluctuate greatly, and many shops close completely for the winter.

Credit Cards

For lost or stolen credit cards, contact the following: American Express (☎ 800-668-2639), Diners Club (☎ 800-363-3333), Discover (☎ 800-347-2683), MasterCard (☎ 800-307-7309), or Visa (☎ 800-847-2911).

Currency Exchanges

The best place to exchange money is a bank. Refer to the "Fast Facts" section at the end of each city chapter of this book for bank locations. Airports at Halifax, Moncton, Fredericton, and Charlottetown have currency exchange bureaus. Many Canadian businesses accept U.S. dollars, but at a lower rate than a bank would offer you. The Web site www.xe.com/ucc is a good tool for checking the latest exchange rates.

Customs

Representatives of Canada Border Services Agency (☎ 800-461-9999 or 204-983-3500; www.cbsa-asfc.gc.ca) are located at every major border crossing and at airports that receive international flights.

Electricity

Canada's electrical outlets put out 110 volts AC, the same as in the United States.

Emergencies

For ambulance, police, or fire department assistance, call ☎ **911.**

Hospitals

The location of local hospitals is listed in the "Fast Facts" sections of each city chapter.

Internet Access

Public libraries throughout the Maritimes allow visitors to use their computers for Internet access at no cost.

Most major hotels have in-room Internet access or provide access from a "business center." Bed-and-breakfast owners are often more than happy to let you send e-mail (especially if you say something nice about where you're staying).

Liquor Laws

You must be 19 years old to consume alcoholic beverages in the Maritimes.

A "licensed" restaurant or cafe is one that is licensed by the province to serve alcohol to those 19 years of age and older.

Mail

At the time of publication, stamps for mailing standard letters or postcards cost C52¢ (within Canada), C93¢ (to the United States), and C$1.55 (international).

You can receive mail on the road by having it addressed to your name and "General Delivery," care of the post office in the town of your choice.

Maps

Each of three provincial tourism offices (see "Where to Get More Information" later in the Appendix) offers free information packages, which include a map that is sufficient for general touring.

Map Art (☎ **905-436-2525;** www.mapart. com) publishes a number of excellent regional and city street guides for the Maritimes. Rand McNally produces a softcover Atlantic Canada atlas.

The region's only specialty map store is Maps and Ducks, at 1869 Upper Water St. in Halifax (☎ **902-422-7106**). Independent bookstores and chains such as Chapters (located in all major cities) also carry maps.

Police

Dial ☎ **911** for emergencies.

Safety

The Maritimes is no more or less safe than anywhere else in Canada. You need to take the usual common-sense precautions for your own safety and personal belongings, just like you would when traveling anywhere else.

Refer to Chapter 7 for details about driving in the Maritimes and Chapter 10 for tips on keeping healthy when you travel.

Smoking

Anti-smoking laws in all three provinces limit smoking in public places such as malls, museums, and sporting arenas. In New Brunswick, smoking is not allowed in restaurants and bars. In the other two provinces, many restaurants have set aside an enclosed area for smokers, or have put limits the hours patrons can light up. Hotels often have floors reserved for nonsmokers, while smoking at bed-and-breakfasts is nearly always limited to outdoor areas. Because ordinances vary from province to province and even town to town, you should check before lighting up anywhere.

Taxes

The federal Goods and Services Tax is 5 percent. Each Maritimes province tacks an additional tax on all purchases except food. The Provincial Sales Tax on Prince Edward Island is 10 percent, for a total of 15 percent in taxes. In Nova Scotia and New Brunswick, a provincial tax of 8 percent is blended with the GST to make a Harmonized Sales Tax of 13 percent.

Time Zones

All three provinces are located in the Atlantic standard time zone (AST), one hour ahead of New York and four hours ahead of Los Angeles. From the second Sunday in March through to the first Sunday in November, daylight saving time

is observed throughout the region, along with the rest of Canada (except Saskatchewan).

Tipping

Tipping in the Maritimes is no different to anywhere else in Canada or in the United States. Refer to Chapter 5 for details.

Weather Updates

The best online source of weather reports, complete with long-range forecasts, satellite pictures, and historical tidbits of meteorological data, is the Environment Canada Web site at www.weatheroffice.gc.ca. If your hotel room has cable television, it will probably be tuned in to Canada's Weather Channel.

Toll-Free Numbers and Web Sites

Major airlines serving the Maritimes

Air Canada
☎ 888-247-2262
www.aircanada.com

Continental
☎ 800-231-0856
www.continental.com

Delta
☎ 800-221-1212
www.delta.com

Northwest
☎ 800-225-2525
www.nwa.com

WestJet
☎ 800-538-5696
www.westjet.com

Major car rental agencies in the Maritimes

Avis
☎ 800-331-1212
www.avis.com

Budget
☎ 800-268-8900
www.budget.ca

Discount
☎ 800-263-2355
www.discountcar.com

Dollar
☎ 800-800-3665
www.dollar.com

Enterprise
☎ 800-261-7331
www.enterprise.com

Hertz
☎ 800-654-3131
www.hertz.com

National
☎ 800-227-7368
www.nationalcar.com

Rent-A-Wreck
☎ 800-327-0116
www.rentawreck.ca

Thrifty
☎ 800-847-4389
www.thrifty.com

Major hotel and motel chains in the Maritimes

Best Western
☎ 800-780-7234
www.bestwestern.com

Cape Breton Island Resorts
☎ 800-565-5660
www.capebretonresorts.com

Coastal Inns
☎ 800-665-7829
www.coastalinns.com

Comfort Inns
☎ 800-424-6423
www.choicehotels.ca

Country Inns and Suites
☎ 800-456-4000
www.countryinns.com

Days Inn
☎ 800-329-7466
www.daysinn.com

Delta Hotels
☎ 888-890-3222
www.deltahotels.com

Fairmont Hotels and Resorts
☎ 800-257-7544
www.fairmont.com

Holiday Inn
☎ 888-465-4329
www.ichotelsgroup.com

Hostelling International–Canada
www.hihostels.ca

Maritime Inns & Resorts
☎ 877-768-3969
www.maritimeinns.com

Ramada
☎ 800-272-6232
www.ramada.com

Rodd Hotels & Resorts
☎ 800-565-7633
www.rodd-hotels.ca

Signature Resorts
www.signatureresorts.com

Super 8
☎ 800-800-8000
www.super8.com

Wandlyn Inns
☎ 800-561-0000
www.wandlyninns.com

Where to Get More Information

You'll find most of what you need to know for your Maritimes trip in this book, but if you're thirsting for more, try the following resources.

Tourist information

Each of the three provincial tourism offices operates visitor information centers at the major gateways to their respective provinces.

Provincial tourism bureaus offer free information packages and maps to boost your pre-trip planning. To get the goods, contact the following:

- ✔ **Tourism Nova Scotia** (☎ **800-565-0000** or 902-425-5781; www.novascotia.com)
- ✔ **New Brunswick Tourism** (☎ **800-561-0123;** www.tourismnewbrunswick.ca)
- ✔ **Prince Edward Island Tourism** (☎ **800-463-4734** or 902-368-4444; www.gov.pe.ca/visitorsguide)

These Web sites dish out information on specific cities, parks, and traveling in Canada beyond the Maritimes:

- ✔ **Canadian Tourism Commission:** www.canada.travel
- ✔ **Fredericton Tourism:** www.tourismfredericton.ca
- ✔ **Parks Canada:** www.pc.gc.ca
- ✔ **Tourism Charlottetown:** www.walkandseacharlottetown.com
- ✔ **Tourism Halifax:** www.halifaxinfo.com
- ✔ **Tourism Moncton:** www.gomoncton.com
- ✔ **Tourism Saint John:** www.tourismsaintjohn.com

Other guidebooks

Frommer's Nova Scotia, New Brunswick & Prince Edward Island complements this book perfectly. It covers destinations not included in these pages and offers a different perspective on those that are. *Frommer's Canada* is the preferred option for travelers planning on exploring the rest of the country. Another excellent resource is www.frommers.com, which offers travel tips, online booking options, and a daily e-mail newsletter filled with travel specials.

Index

• *G* •